A Brief Apocalyptic History
of Psychoanalysis

A Brief Apocalyptic History of Psychoanalysis returns us to the birth of psychoanalysis and the trauma of castration that is its umbilicus.

The story told in this book centers on the genital mutilation endured in her childhood by Emma Eckstein, Freud's most important patient in his abandonment of the "seduction theory." For both cultural and personal reasons, Freud could not recognize the traumatic nature of this *"Beschneidung"* (circumcision), which nevertheless aroused in him deep anguish, conflating his own circumcision, the echoes of a violently anti-Semitic environment, and conflicts with his father. Taking Freud's countertransference to Eckstein's trauma into account leads to a radically different understanding of the origins of psychoanalysis from the one based on the solipsistic perspective of his self-analysis. Carlo Bonomi argues that the unacknowledged trauma of circumcision was inscribed in Freud's system of thinking as an amputated legacy from which the dreams and fantasies of his closest disciples would germinate and bloom. In particular, Sándor Ferenczi, Freud's pupil and confidant, would help to restore this wounded body, thereby laying a new foundation for psychoanalytic theory and practice.

Bonomi's "apocalyptic" narrative will expand the conceptual horizons of psychoanalysts and psychoanalytic psychotherapists, historians of psychoanalysis, and scholars of both gender studies and Jewish studies.

Carlo Bonomi, Ph.D., is a training and supervising analyst of the Società Italiana di Psicoanalisi Sándor Ferenczi, president of the International Sándor Ferenczi Network (ISFN), co-editor-in-chief of *The Wise Baby/Il poppante saggio*, and associate editor of the *International Forum of Psychoanalysis*.

History of Psychoanalysis
Series Editor
Peter L. Rudnytsky

This series seeks to present outstanding new books that illuminate any aspect of the history of psychoanalysis from its earliest days to the present, and to reintroduce classic texts to contemporary readers.

Other titles in the series:

Karl Abraham
Life and Work, a Biography
Anna Bentinck van Schoonheten

The Freudian Orient
Early Psychoanalysis, Anti-Semitic Challenge, and the Vicissitudes of Orientalist Discourse
Frank F. Scherer

Occultism and the Origins of Psychoanalysis
Freud, Ferenczi and the Challenge of Thought Transference
Maria Pierri, Translated by Adam Elgar

Sigmund Freud and the Forsyth Case
Coincidences and Thought-Transmission in Psychoanalysis
Maria Pierri, Translated by Adam Elgar

A Brief Apocalyptic History of Psychoanalysis
Erasing Trauma
Carlo Bonomi

For further information about this series please visit https://www.routledge.com/The-History-of-Psychoanalysis-Series/book-series/KARNHIPSY

A Brief Apocalyptic History of Psychoanalysis

Erasing Trauma

Carlo Bonomi

Routledge
Taylor & Francis Group

LONDON AND NEW YORK

Designed cover image: Cover image © Carlo Bonomi, Exodus, 2009 (oil, 100x100, detail)

First published 2023
by Routledge
4 Park Square, Milton Park, Abingdon, Oxon OX14 4RN

and by Routledge
605 Third Avenue, New York, NY 10158

Routledge is an imprint of the Taylor & Francis Group, an informa business

British Library Cataloguing-in-Publication Data
A catalogue record for this book is available from the British Library

ISBN: 978-1-032-40434-9 (hbk)
ISBN: 978-1-032-40433-2 (pbk)
ISBN: 978-1-003-35305-8 (ebk)

DOI: 10.4324/9781003353058

Typeset in Times New Roman
by codeMantra

Dedicated to the many fellow travelers of the Ferenczi Renaissance as well as old and new friends of the International Sándor Ferenczi Network

Contents

Figure

Preface by Philippe Réfabert

Translated by Agnès Jacob

What happened did not take place

Carlo Bonomi invites Freud to join a whole host of analysts, including myself, who at one time or another were summoned by a patient to the site of their undoing. Until then, they had succeeded in turning away from the shores to which their sirens were beckoning them, they had "successfully" gone beyond them, pretending not to see them or hear them, so that they found themselves cut off from the sensations and feelings they had had on those shores where something "happened," but was not experienced. The event only left behind hollow representations, and few signs other than this inability to feel. But one day, an analysand may impel the analyst to experience what happened but was not felt because of the lack of a *Nebenmensh* (someone standing close), an attentive and well-meaning other who can feel and echo it. I myself had to go through such an experience, and I had to write a book, *From Freud to Kafka*, and make a certain encounter to learn that what I was discovering in someone else's story had happened to me. It took the writing of a book for it to happen to me, for experiencing what did happen.

In Bonomi's *Erasing Trauma*, Freud stands alongside all those—analysts and non-analysts—who, left stranded in their childhood on the verge of the void, keep trying to be born, as Serge Leclaire described in a passage pointed out to me by Françoise Bessis: "Present at the door of death as only those who strive to be born are able to be." Although Freud declined to benefit from the analytical listening Jung offered him in his own way, and Ferenczi proposed repeatedly, he kept going back, until the end of his life, to what had happened in 1895 and 1897.

The history of the origins of psychoanalysis takes a major step forward when Carlo Bonomi exposes what "happened" to Freud, a young, ambitious physician, a daring researcher endowed with exceptional intelligence and great working capacity, when he suddenly found himself compelled to go back to the site of his undoing, by his only female patient in long-term therapy, Emma Eckstein.

A constellation of signifiers and feelings of terror in the patient suddenly entered into resonance with her therapist's universe so violently that the trauma theory he elaborated with Breuer was swept away instantly. The unexpected encounter of these two universes triggered intense dream activity in Freud and forced him to conduct self-analysis. Emma Eckstein came to see him again in 1905, then in 1909, when she suffered a relapse. This time, Freud withdrew from the case abruptly. The painful ending of this patient's therapy haunted him to the end of his life, as evidenced by the dispersion of the pieces of the puzzle representing the initial catastrophe. Carlo Bonomi demonstrates to us how these pieces are disseminated throughout Freud's work.

I myself had taken up the study of the origins of psychoanalysis. Barbro Sylwan and I were both convinced that the edifying narrative about Freud's abandonment of trauma theory hid a catastrophe. I was in agreement with Maria Torok and Barbro Sylwan's research perspective, claiming that the dramatic events surrounding Uncle Joseph's arrest and conviction for passing counterfeit rubles were at the root of Freud's repression. But this path turned soon into a blind alley. Meanwhile, I was looking for the traces and sequestrations left by Freud's passionate relation with Fliess in the Freudian oeuvre. An important first step in this direction was taken when Max Schur, Freud's physician, lifted the censorship of the dramatic effects of the surgery performed by Fliess on Emma Eckstein. Until then, the circumstances and consequences of the surgical error committed by Fliess had been shrouded in silence. I saw this professional error as an event which, if properly understood, revealed the thinking behind the dream known as "Irma's injection," and made it possible to decipher this seminal dream quite clearly. The exchange of letters which followed this tragic event also helps to explain that Fliess' refusal to take responsibility for placing his patient's life in danger contributed to the break between Freud and the man he had emphatically called as the Kepler of biology. I saw Fliess' failing as illustrative of the refusal to bear witness.

This was as far as I went before abandoning my research on the foundation of psychoanalysis. There were several reasons for this. First, I was discouraged by the criticisms leveled at me from all quarters for presuming to analyze Freud, although I considered this argument fallacious, given that self-analysis was the origin of psychoanalysis. Moreover, I had not been able to dispel the discredit in which American psychoanalytic literature was held in France. Finally, the publication of Ferenczi's *Clinical Diary* in 1985 convinced me of the need to wait on the sidelines of the analytic world until the accuracy of the ideas contained in it could effect a change in attitudes. I opted for patience and, in the meantime, I pondered Kafka's teaching.

Some 30 years later, I discovered *The Cut*, the work in two volumes in which Carlo Bonomi presented his original research that, in a more structured form, became *Erasing Trauma*. Starting with the intuition that castration anxiety is not symbolic, but based on an actual traumatic event, Bonomi embarked on a long-term enquiry involving historians of psychoanalysis as well as fellow analysts or Jewish thinkers, especially American colleagues who were interested in the foundation of psychoanalysis. Reading Bonomi gave me a feeling of jubilation and liberation. The scene of the foundation took on life and color, like the world in which Sleeping Beauty awakened. In my enthusiasm for this work, I wrote a review of the book. This is how I met Carlo Bonomi.

When I read *The Cut*, I discovered that I had missed a detail, recorded by Freud on January 24, 1897, when he wrote to his friend Fliess, in order to reassure him, that he had "obtained a scene about the circumcision of a girl," specifically "the cutting off of a piece of the labium minor (which is even shorter today)."

This detail could only concern Emma Eckstein, and seizing its importance meant acquiring the Archimedean point needed to pursue the research undertaken based on Bonomi's initial intuition. Clearly, a real act of castration had taken place.

Not only had I missed this detail, I had also neglected to take into account the non-negligible fact that Freud himself prescribed the operation on Emma's nose, a procedure Fliess, the "otolaryngynecologist" as Didier Anzieu calls him in jest, recommended. Fliess, who was convinced he had discovered a "connection between the nose and the female genitalia," cut or cauterized a portion of the "*Nasalemuscheln*," which in German slang means the mold of the nose which is literary, but in slang, the nose mussels. It was a "distal procedure," like a displacement on the nose of the "circumcision-castration" Baginsky thought it advisable to perform on the genital organs of little girls who masturbated. Freud, as Carlo Bonomi also discovered, had been in training with Adolf Baginsky in Berlin, when he returned from Paris. The eminent professor recommended either the cutting of the labium minor, the excision of the clitoris, or the cauterization of the entrance to the vagina. Another important detail: a few days before operating on Emma, Fliess had cauterized Freud's nose once again, as he had done repeatedly.

Without a doubt, Carlo Bonomi's most decisive discovery, which can explain the guilt evident in Freud's original dream of Irma's injection, is reflected in the cryptonyms *Amyl* and *Trimethylamine*. Adrian de Klerk, a Dutch analyst since deceased, was the one who suggested to Bonomi that this word should be seen as an anagram of the Hebrew words meaning circumcision, *Brit milah*: the sign of the alliance of the Jewish people with their God. Indeed, circumcision proves to be the cornerstone, *Eck-Stein*, the intersection of the destinies of the one who inflicted it, even in a lesser form, as Freud did—, of those who were subjected to it, like Emma and Freud—, as well as the one who inflicted a wound on his father by deciding not to have any of his sons circumcised, as tradition demands, like Freud, again.

I speak of a "decisive" discovery to point out that, for the first time as far as I know, research work reveals, in a simple expression, the incandescent core of Freud's anxieties. Indeed, *"Brit milah"* is the point of convergence of everything that terrorized the child Sigismund, and the echo of the threats that, in a hostile environment, cast a shadow on the existence of a Jewish researcher, and discredit on his discoveries. At the same time, the researcher is seduced by the advantages and shelter offered by Greek culture and by assimilation.

Today, we can easily draw a parallel between the surgical act that a "therapeutic" circumcision constitutes and the equivalent of sexual aggression because social consensus takes this for granted. But at the end of the nineteenth century in Vienna, Berlin, or the United States, the conventional eye cannot see a "seductive father" in the person of a respectable surgeon. Like Carlo Bonomi, I am convinced that reality exists only if it is shared; it would be more accurate to say that what is obvious today was, at that time, not unlikely, as Freud says in "The History of the Psychoanalytic Movement," but unthinkable. Neither Freud nor Emma Eckstein could have seen "sexual aggression" in such a "benign" surgical procedure, nor identify a seducer when he wears the surgeon's coat, or when he is a well-respected otorhinolaryngologist. This is what Gaston Bachelard calls an "epistemological obstacle," at the start of *The Formation of the Scientific Mind*. It's not that the seducer is improbable, he is impossible to find. It's not that he was cut out, like Trotsky from the famous photograph taken with Stalin; rather, the figure of such a seducer is yet to be created. It is not repressed, rejected, or cut out. It simply does not exist yet. Circumcision, *Beschneidung*, before being described as a traumatic sexual scene, has to be scanned by the radar of thinking that would reveal it to be sexual aggression. Before this, Freud could not see Baginsky, Fliess, or himself as seductors. The same incapacity applies to Emma Eckstein: she merely plays the role of the patient, offering Freud an abundance of fantasies rich in material pointing to something "that happened," to a genital amputation and to its more recent "displaced" repetition on the nose.

Here, Carlo Bonomi's work discloses that faced with this revelation, namely that a circumcision-castration took place, Freud loses his hold on the ground of reality and finds himself instantly propelled to the site and the time of a "this will be the end of me," on the edge of the chasm. Caught in a web of circumstances that make him a criminal, for he "repeated the crime," to use Ferenczi's expression, and prescribed circumcision, an operation he abhors and which, at the same time, is at the center of his opposition to his father—, Freud panics.

Therefore, like the man Ferenczi described, who falls from the fourth floor, flips over in the air, and lands on the third floor balcony, Freud seizes upon Emma Eckstein's fantasy of a "great Lord Penis," and transforms it into a universal idea. Out of the blue, Freud reverses his position, advancing a hypothesis contrary to his earlier discovery and assertion that behind a "*Szene*," behind a fantasy, an actual event is hidden, waiting to be translated into words, to be interpreted.

Thanks to his acrobatic feat, Freud places himself on new ground (*Grund*) on which he can find the representation of a new construction, sketching the outline of a new theoretical puzzle on the panels of the polyptych altarpiece. On the edge of the chasm, *Abgrund*, glimpsed as he sees the irrevocable end, *Untergang*, at the instant when he is seized with panic, *Panik*,— these are the words he uses in his 1927 essay "Fetishism"—, Freud fixates on Emma Eckstein's of the "great lord Penis," just as the fetishist seizes upon the last image glimpsed before being exposed to the "absence of the mother's penis."

Carlo Bonomi shows that the worship of the phallus emerged from this amputation and its repetition, masking them both. Faced with Emma Eckstein's genitals, which bear such a sign, and in the absence of a seducer, the ground, *Boden*, crumbles under his feet. He did not find his footing again until he posited that the seduction is an internal creation of the child. In his letter dated January 3, 1899, he wrote to Fliess: "What happened in earliest childhood? Nothing, but the germ of a sexual impulse existed." In place of the untraceable seducer, there emerges the fundamental concept that saves Freud's undertaking from sinking. In place, not of the maternal penis, but of the seducer in whom no one is there to tell Freud to recognize himself, the researcher, panic-stricken, takes hold of a fetish: the universal notion of castration anxiety, and penis envy in women, to which the concept of "drive" would later be added.

The reading of this book leads me to see the fundamental concept, *Grundbegriff*, as the reconstituted ground on which Freud finds his footing. The word "drive," *Trieb*, —we might note in passing—, is in consonance with *Brit*, revealing it to bear the trace of its hidden origin; thus, "drive" becomes the pillar of the new edifice. "Drive" is the concept that compensates, not for the repression of the scene of a "crime," but for the fact that something that happened did not "take place" and the seducer is nowhere to be found. Not surprisingly, the seducer remains untraceable when he is also the researcher. This is one of the aspects of the tragic situation in which a criminal insists on conducting the investigation of his crimes himself. Like Oedipus who rejected Tiresias' advice, Freud refused Jung and Ferenczi's repeated offers of psychoanalytic listening. Contrary to Oedipus, who pursued his investigation, Freud put an end to it and constructed a new metapsychology.

I can add here that the association between *Brit* and *Trieb* gives me the opportunity to mention an intuition Maria Torok only discussed in private. The signifier *Trieb* made one think of "Brit(ish)," that is, of Freud's older brothers living in Manchester, who had ensured the family's survival in Vienna in the early years by sending them money. Maria Torok considered, as we do, that at that time English was still very important to take into account for those who remembered the Wolf Man's hallucination: "*Ein*

Glanz auf der Nase," a sentence which the English-speaking patient also hears as "a glance at the nose." This glance takes us back to Emma Eckstein and Freud's noses, that is, to the nasal version of circumcision. This comment has special interest for those who know that the Wolf Man was close enough to Freud to become a ventriloquistic magnifier of his analyst's unconscious messages. Carlo Bonomi reminds us here that Rank saw the wolves in the Wolf Man's famous dream as Freud's disciples sitting on the branches of the tree outside the window.

In this scene depicted on the panels of the altarpiece which screen the original setting bringing together Breuer, Freud, Fliess, and Emma Eckstein, the seducers and victims have disappeared, and with them, the emotional ties existing between them. The truly "love relationship" referred to in the essay "The Aetiology of Hysteria" disappears in Freud's theoretical overturn. The neurologist, who does not yet designate his activity by the name of the new field he is elaborating—psychoanalysis—, is deflected from the scene and places on the throne of the new kingdom, or on the stone, "*Stein*" of the new Church, a word taken from the vocabulary of mechanics: "drive."

Thanks to this work, the drama in which Emma Eckstein plays the lead role is given its foundational place. Bonomi helps us to better understand why this patient is mentioned, along with Ferenczi, in the essay "Analysis Terminable and Interminable," written in 1937. Emma Eckstein and Sandor Ferenczi are Freud's two paradigmatic analysands who crashed against the *gewachsene Fels*—the strange expression used by Freud, usually translated as "bedrock." German artist Domenika Kaesdorf suggested that I should read Freud's expression as "*Erwachsener Fels*," an adult-rock; thus, one who in a terrifying situation becomes "an adult [standing rigid like a rock]" and projects this figure on those who oppose him. Emma Eckstein and Ferenczi, each in their own way, tried to convey to Freud that something "happened" but was not experienced by him.

Thanks to the acrobatic recovery of the therapist, the seducer has been made to disappear. And with him, the *Nebenmensch*, the attentive and sensitive witness, the one whose practice is guided by Goethe's phrase, taken up again by Freud: "What have they done to you, you poor child?" Thus, in the new edifice, this witness has been silenced. More precisely, the pages on which these terms, seducer and *Nebenmensch*, were written have disappeared, replaced by those on which *Trieb*, drive, is inscribed. The "concept," a word that comes from *capere*, meaning to take, to seize (just a *Begriff* comes from the German *greifen*, meaning to seize, to take hold of)—this fundamental concept then—, has taken hold of *Nebenmensch* and made it disappear. Carlo Bonomi applies this dissociative process to the catastrophe which "occurred" to Freud in his second year, when he was suddenly abandoned by both his mother, who left to give birth to another child, and his Nania, sent away for stealing, and found himself in a state of endless despair. Carlo Bonomi describes what "happened then" as an event which left the youngster divided between a dying child and a prodigiously intelligent child who did not feel anything—the figure of the "guardian angel" Ferenczi would allude to. This child who didn't feel anything is still alive in Freud the adult, who asks his son, whose finger was caught in a swing: "Why did you do this to yourself?" He is also the one whom Ferenczi glimpses as the therapist who no longer likes patients, and who "is still attached to analysis intellectually, but not emotionally," as we can read in *The Clinical Diary*. As for the child still alive in Freud who experienced a sensation of imminent death, Carlo Bonomi points out the occasions on which he showed his presence through a fainting episode in front of Jung or Ferenczi, who each offered to take him into analysis—an offer repeatedly declined.

As Bonomi recreates these tragic events, it becomes clear that analysts who support their master's self-analytic spin—"spin" which is another image to describe Freud's about-face, is a nautical term referring to a vessel forced by a violent wind or current to rotate around itself—, those analysts seduced by him will apply, in their practice, a psychoanalytic theory in which metapsychology and transference are discordant. The analysis of the relation created between two protagonists, the analyst and the analysand—the transference—and the metapsychology based on the exclusion of the seductor *and* of the *Nebenmensch* are incompatible. Associating them within the same theoretical discourse is dissonant. Indeed, when Freud, Emma's psychotherapist, does not admit that he himself is, in this circumcision scene, in the same place as his patient is when placed in Fliess' care, he excludes himself from the scene on two levels: as the one who repeats the crime, and as someone like her, on whom the crime was perpetrated. In other words, after Freud's "spin," metapsychology and transference could not coexist in the same universe before Ferenczi's intervention. In fact, the "psychoanalysis" which emerged from Freud's self-analytical spin resembled a religion, with its doctrines and dogmas.

This said, Carlo Bonomi also shows that Freud had the great merit of leaving the traces of his undoing, and of creating ties with someone like Ferenczi, an analyst who could continue the inquiry, to question the doctrine and the dogma over which hung the threat of death, as Freud feared. Bonomi also describes how Ferenczi adopted Freud's ideas, but pushed them to extremes, to the point of subverting them. And he reveals what subtlety, what treasures of unconscious stratagems Ferenczi employed to make his own the circumvolutions Freud performed around the core of his terrors: circumcision-castration.

Thanks to this accommodating attitude, the collaboration between the two men lasted many years and allowed Ferenczi—who was, in sequence and even at the same time, analysand, disciple, son, helpful friend, analyst—to modify from top to bottom and, even more remarkably, from the inside, Freud's doctrinal edifice founded on worship of the phallus. Ferenczi vigorously contested this system in his last articles, but it was in *The Clinical Diary*, written in the last two years of his life, that he addressed to posterity what he had been unable to make Freud hear. From the start of his *Brief History*, Bonomi shows how Ferenczi, hurt, and having regretfully left Freud to his indifference, became even more attentive to what his patients had to teach him (especially Elisabeth Severn), and so rediscovered his master's early intuitions, those that preceded the catastrophe. He connected these intuitions with the discoveries they had made together in their research over 25 years. And so it came to be that psychoanalysis survived self-analysis.

Happily, this *Brief Apocalyptic History of Psychoanalysis*, this *Erasing Trauma*, lets us recover from Freud's "tough healing" as we would from an illness, this long childhood illness afflicting psychoanalysis, embodied by the doctrine emerging from self-analysis, in which drive-based metapsychology and transference are dissonant. We now see this dissonance as the transposition into analytic discourse of Freud's "split in the ego," a split created in the urgency of ensuring psychic survival.

Introduction

In his memorable book on the psychoanalytic meaning of history, Norman O. Brown said that "The aim of psychoanalysis—still unfulfilled, and still only half-conscious—is to return our souls to our bodies" (Brown, 1959, p. 158). This simple sentence neatly captures what this book means to me.

The story told in this book is based on an event that has remained hidden until now. Taking it into account leads to a completely different narration of the foundation of psychoanalysis than Freud's and, above all, a different paradigm from the one inherited from self-analysis.

This event is nothing less than a circumcision, *"Beschneidung,"* endured in her childhood by a patient who, during the dawning of psychoanalysis, inspired Freud's ideas, inhabited his dreams, elicited his sudden turns, and eventually inspired the self-analysis from which Freud's masterwork, *The Interpretation of Dreams*, unfolds.

For cultural reasons, Freud could not recognize the traumatic nature of this circumcision. But it reignited his own experiences of circumcision, those he had seen performed on children as part of the medical crusade against masturbation and, above all, pointed to the one he had refused to practice on his own children. In fact, it was at the center of all his contradictions and aroused deep anguish because of the echoes of a violently anti-Semitic environment on the one hand, and the conflict with his father, with his fathers, precisely about circumcision on the other hand. Ultimately, this unbearable situation resulted in Freud's dreaming up a "scientific religion" and new system of thinking, that of psychoanalysis, in which "symbolic castration" will take the place of actual, lived circumcision.

The thesis of this book is that this unacknowledged trauma was inscribed in this system of thinking as an amputated legacy from which the dreams and fantasies of Freud's closest disciples would germinate and bloom. In particular, Sándor Ferenczi, Freud's pupil and confidant, would help to restore this amputated legacy, thus laying the groundwork for a new foundation.

*

DOI: 10.4324/9781003353058-1

Many conferences and publications have marked the steps of my itinerary as researcher. I will try to summarize these steps in the most synthetic way.

The starting point of my investigation was a strange dream that Sándor Ferenczi had the day before he asked the master to begin an analysis with him. This dream, in which a small penis, cut off and horribly flayed appears, elicited in me the idea of some real catastrophe. Could young Freud have come across a case of real castration in the early years of his medical practice? To test my hypothesis, I visited Professor Gerhard Fichtner, Director of the Institute of the History of Medicine at the University of Tübingen, in Germany, who, to my amazement, handed me various books and medical articles, all in German and all on the *castration* of women and the *circumcision* of girls during the second half of the nineteenth century. At that point, a totally new medical scenario and hypothesis took shape, one that had been surprisingly overlooked by prior historians of psychoanalysis.

In July of 1993, I presented some of my thoughts at the Ferenczi International Conference in Budapest, which piqued the interest of Professor André Haynal, the father of the Ferenczi Renaissance. He then invited me to present at the upcoming *Symposium "100 Year of Psychoanalysis,"* scheduled for September 1993 in Geneva. During the summer, I continued my research in Berlin, where Freud had undergone his pediatric training, which led me to write the article: "Why did we ignore Freud the 'pediatrician'? The relevance of Freud's pediatric training for the origins of psychoanalysis."

The discovery of the extensive use of real castration against women and girls in the medical practices prevailing in the years when psychoanalysis was built around the nuclear idea of symbolic castration, opened a series of questions. Why is this world of atrocities represented neither in Freud's writings, nor in those of his followers, nor finally by the historians of psychoanalysis? How was this world of unspeakable atrocities translated into "symbolic castration" by Freud? What was lost in translation?

Freud did not merely erase this world of real atrocities but, at the same time, elevated castration to the a priori form of the representability of trauma and turned the threat of castration into "the severest trauma" [das stärkste Trauma] in a child's life (Freud, 1938b, p. 190). In other words, he constructed a system of thought in which castration in the psychoanalytic sense, that is, the imaginary ablation of the penis, is the symbol of every possible trauma. This system relies on metapsychology. One of its pillars is the idea that the father of the primeval human family castrated his male children to enslave them to himself, and that this phylogenetically transmitted memory reinforces in the boy the fear of castration regardless of the actual threats. The other is that the woman is a "castrated man" who lost his (her) penis in the course of biological evolution. In this narrative, the concrete historical circumstances in which this or that woman or girl is castrated, excised, or circumcised by this or that doctor are lost and replaced with an impersonal tragedy projected into a biological past. In turn, this universal "bio-trauma" or "bio-drama" is instrumental in defining the alternative reality created by Freud's theory. The castration of the female proves in fact to the little boy that the threat he had never believed (the cutting off of the penis) is real, "henceforth he will tremble for his masculinity, but at the same time he will despise the unhappy creatures on whom the cruel punishment has, as he supposes, already fallen" (Freud, 1910b, p. 95). The circle is then closed in a self-supporting system in which the traumatic character of the excision of the clitoris is nullified, this "vestige of masculinity" that for Freud prevented the woman from becoming woman. In this alternative world, what is lost in translation is precisely female circumcision.

The problem that now arose was: when and how did the divorce between history and psychoanalysis occur? I soon became convinced that the broken thread must be found in Freud's dream from which *The Interpretation of Dreams* originated, the famous dream of Irma's injection.

This initiatory dream, dated July 1895, was the subject of a great deal and variety of studies, before and after the publication of the complete edition of Freud's letters to Fliess, in 1985. In addition to providing a vivid picture of Freud's life and work during the years of the gestation and birth of psychoanalysis, these letters shed light on the great influence of one of Freud's patients, Emma Eckstein, both on the genesis of the so-called "theory of seduction" in 1895 and on its abandonment in 1897. The Eckstein case, all traces of which had hitherto been censored, was intensely debated because prior to analysis, Freud had tried to cure her neurosis (hysteria) by letting his dear friend Dr. Fliess perform surgery on her nose only to witness her nearly bleeding to death afterward. According to many commentators, Freud's shock is evoked in the main scene of Irma's dream, where the dreamer recoils from the horrible vision that is presented to him when the patient opens her mouth. Privately, Freud had indicated that this was the precise moment in which the "secret of the dream" was unveiled. Understandably, Freud experienced a shock. However, we must admit that his dismay does not explain the fundamental reversal that followed, until we learn another detail. During her first analysis (years later she would have a second analysis) Emma Eckstein evoked "a scene about the circumcision of a girl" [*Eine Szene von Mädschenbeschneidung*]. In the new perspective opened by the study on Freud's pediatric training, it became easy for me to wonder if Emma Eckstein had not been a victim, as a child, of the medical folly that raged in Vienna not less than in Berlin. Had she actually undergone a circumcision as a "cure or punishment" for masturbation?[1]

The scene is reported in a letter to Fliess (January 24, 1897) which also contains Freud's remark on the still visible stigma in the body of his female patient: one *labium minor* was "even shorter today." The German word "*Beschneidung*," circumcision, when referring to girls, consisted of the "excision of the clitoris and labia minora," as Freud pointed out in the essay *The Taboo of Virginity* (Freud, 1918b, p. 197), the only one in which he refers to this practice. In the medical literature of the nineteenth century, the cutting of the labia is never presented as an operation independent from the cutting of the clitoris, and in younger girls both results were often obtained with a cauterization of the entrance to the vagina. Likely, the genital operation endured by Emma Eckstein was of this kind.

If so, the senseless operation on the nose was just one piece of a larger picture, and the horror that Freud felt in his dreams when confronted with Irma's mouth/vulva would begin to make sense. Had the operation on the nose, with its actual dramatic outcome, been a repetition of the circumcision undergone by the patient in her childhood?

Unlike all other psychotherapies, analysis requires a lasting closeness between doctor and patient, nearly an intimacy, and its most peculiar characteristic is the communication between the unconscious, and the mutual echoing of the deepest traumas, as well as, *last but not least,* in the psychoanalyst's capacity to take this echo into account, to explore it and to make it the object of his reflection. Embracing this perspective, I wondered about the way in which Freud dealt with circumcision and what was his attitude toward not only the circumcision of girls but also the ritual prescribed by the Jewish tradition. To my surprise, I again found that ritual circumcision was the center of his opposition to his father to the point that he had not practiced it on his children. New perspectives then opened up.

Piecing this complex puzzle together was an extremely slow process. In 2006, at the invitation of Elisabeth Roudinesco, I presented in Paris a paper on my ongoing research entitled *"Du sexe mutilé au culte du phallus"* [From the mutilated genital to the cult of the phallus]. My thesis was based on two interconnected points: the first was that after enduring castration in her childhood, Emma Eckstein developed various hysterical symptoms including the hallucination of having a penis. The second was that Freud had incorporated her hallucination into the pillar of his phallocentric doctrine.

As fanciful as this idea may seem, I merely applied to Emma Eckstein what Hermann Nunberg (1947) had elaborated for men: "that the trauma of circumcision released forces aimed at overcoming its effects" and that "all of the phantasies, thoughts and habits, served a single purpose: preservation of the phallus" (p. 154).

Ferenczi himself, in the *Clinical Diary*, criticized Freud's idea that the feeling of having a penis is innate in females, suggesting that it could also be a "hysterical symptom that set in for traumatic causes" (August 4, 1932). Since Freud evoked a vision of "the great Lord Penis" of the witches in the very same letter in which he reported Emma Eckstein's "scene about the circumcision of a girl," it seemed inevitable to conclude that although Freud had not intellectually recognized his patient's castration as a trauma, he had nonetheless felt it on his flesh, as attested by his identification with his castrated patient, a reaction culminating in his taking possession of her magical penis, the Phallus that conceals the trauma and exorcises impotence.

Repeatedly criticized, Freud's phallocentric system no longer plays a substantial role in contemporary psychoanalysis. However, it marks a fundamental moment in its birth and history. Beyond easy sociological analyses, what can it tell us today that we don't yet know? Can we consider it a symptom, a "monument to memory" from which to draw undreamed-of knowledge, just as Freud suggests at the beginning of *The aetiology of hysteria*? Comparing the hysterical symptom to the ruins of an archaeological site, he writes:

> the numerous inscriptions, which, by good luck, may be bilingual, reveal an alphabet and a language, and, when they have been deciphered and translated, yield undreamed-of information about the events of the remote past, to commemorate which the monuments were built. *Saxa loquuntur*! [Stones talk!]
>
> (Freud, 1896c, p. 192)

In 2009, I published in the *International Journal of Psychoanalysis* an article entitled "The relevance of castration and circumcision to the origins of psychoanalysis. 1. The medical context." A few weeks later I received a long email from a Dutch psychoanalyst, Adrian de Klerk, who confided in me his belief that the keyword in Irma's injection dream, *trimethylamin*, was a transcription of the phonemes that make up the word *(b)rith milah*, circumcision in Hebrew, literally "Covenant of the Cut." It was the missing key. It allowed the second part of the article to come into focus, which appeared in 2013 in *The Psychoanalytic Quarterly*, under the title "Withstanding trauma: The significance of Emma Eckstein's circumcision for Freud's Irma dream."

As the various pieces of the puzzle were slowly coming together, I began to reorganize material I had accumulated over time into a large study entitled *The Cut and the Building of Psychoanalysis*. Volume I was published in 2015 and volume II in 2018. Freud often compared psychoanalysis to a building under perpetual construction whose foundation rested on a solid cornerstone, namely, the Oedipus complex. In my deconstructive reading, however, Emma Eckstein's circumcision was the "stone that the builders rejected" (Psalm 118, p. 22). As an interesting aside, *"Eckstein"* was in fact the word chosen by Martin Luther, in his German translation of the Bible, to refer to the fundamental concept of cornerstone [*akrogoniaios lithos*] in the *Septuagint*. What had been petrified could be restored to speach.

This last book is the culmination of research that began almost 30 years ago with the question "Why did we ignore Freud 'pediatrician'?" From this research, a story of the origin of psychoanalysis takes shape that differs from consolidated narratives, on many points, and three in particular.

I will dwell on the first one at length here; it concerns the meaning of Freud's famous "self-analysis." The other two are closely related and can be dealt with more quickly. Although it may seem strange today, self-analysis remained for a long time the method recommended by Freud for those who were engaging in psychoanalysis. Not until his break with Jung did analysis by another analyst began to hold sway over self-analysis. This was not so with Freud but it was with the circle of his closest followers. Freud accepted this idea, which was to become an institutionalized rule from 1920 onward, but it is not easy to establish with what conviction. After all, it was through his own self-analysis that he had given life to the fundamental work of psychoanalysis: how could he question its validity?

Later, when the official history of psychoanalysis was established, all of Freud's great discoveries, whether it be child sexuality, the Oedipus complex, or the role of the unconscious in the formation of neurotic symptoms and in dreams, were presented as the fruit of his self-analysis, the unique and unrepeatable character of which was not missed.

The foundations of this "heroic" narrative were laid by Ernst Kris at the time of the first publication of Freud's letters to Fliess, in 1950. For Kris, Freud had succeeded in overcoming the erroneous "seduction theory" through the maturity and independence of thought gained through self-analysis. Specifically, it was Freud's personal conflicts with his father that led him to the faulty assumption that neuroses were caused by "seduction on the part of adults," typically the father, but then self-analysis imposed itself on the struggling man, serving "the function of liberation from suffering as well as from fatal error" (Kris, 1954, p. 181). Kris explained that by interpreting his own dreams, Freud had gone far beyond the traditional exercise of "self-observation" because, thanks to the psychoanalytic method, his ego functions emerged "from involvement in intense conflict to full and supreme autonomy" (p. 181). This gave godlike powers to autonomy—in ego functions and in life—as a goal of mental health, an idea which coincidentally reinforced the glorified solo, non-relational process of self-analysis.

Kris formulated this thesis in the years dominated by "Ego-psychology," when the autonomy of the ego had become the flagship of psychoanalysis and it was believed that the ideal analytic situation consisted of "one-person," namely the patient, while the analyst was just an external observer who remained outside the field of study like an objective scientist. At that time, the "two-person relationship" was not valued as it is now; analysis was not viewed as the unfolding of a "process"; and "countertransference" was considered to be obstacle. In short, the idea of psychoanalysis was filtered by what, later, has been called "the myth of the isolated mind" (Stolorow & Atwood, 1994), an "asocial paradigm" (Hoffman, 1998) in which there is no substantial difference between analysis and self-analysis. Thus, the birth of psychoanalysis became known as a solipsistic enterprise, and this attitude was adopted by Ernest Jones in his three-volume biography on Freud (1953, 1955, 1957), despite Jones' snide remarks and grotesque details about his persistent neurosis.

Years later, origin story that psychoanalysis was the quest of a solitary hero became the target of endless criticism, sometimes well-motivated, sometimes less so. Nevertheless, and this is the point I want to emphasize, even this very shaky narrative was never unseated from its central place. Perhaps this is because of the widespread need for a hero/godhead to worship, admire, and follow, or even an unconscious need to protect the master. Yet, I believe that a lack of alternatives played a major role in keeping this narrative alive. No other narrative of Freud's self-analysis, crediting its founding role in the birth of psychoanalysis, yet rejecting the solipsistic paradigm, has ever taken hold. Freud's self-analysis has been the subject of accurate and far-reaching studies such as those by Schur (1972), Grinstein (1980), and Anzieu (1975, 1986), and of an infinite number of micro-analyses of this or that dream, but from this tremendous body of research, a new paradigm has never been proposed. Consequently, in the latest great works on the birth of psychoanalysis (such as Makari, 2008; Roudinesco, 2014), self-analysis no longer plays any relevant role. But in this way, we lose the most peculiar feature of psychoanalysis, the fact that it was born from a dream.

Over the years, it has become increasingly clear that we are faced with a narrative hole. Filling this gap is the aim of this book, in which I adopt a perspective sketched by Sándor Ferenczi in his *Clinical Diary* (1932). He portrays Freud as recoiling when "the problem of countertransference opened [up] before him like an abyss." I will contextualize and develop Ferenczi's lapidary intuition through the first analysis of Emma Eckstein, and look at Freud's long self-analysis as an *après coup* of his countertransference toward her. Put simply: what is outlined here is a story of the origin of psychoanalysis resolutely thought from a bi-personal and not a solipsist point of view, in short, within the framework traced by the new paradigm.

We will be looking at the thorny question of Freud's great turning point as well—his abandonment of the seduction theory in favor of Oedipal fantasies—from an unprecedented perspective. This turning point, which has long been the backbone of psychoanalysis's self-narration, is now being shaken up due to a greater understanding of and sensitivity to traumatic factors in the wake of cultural shifts during the 1980s and a growing emphasis on the relational nature of human mind. However, on the historical level, the topic essentially remained prisoner of a polarization between facts and fantasies. If Freud's turn is brought back to the "scene about the circumcision of a girl," where facts and fantasies are inextricably mixed up, what "collapsed" was not the solid ground of reality, as Freud would later say. Rather, this reality remained unthought-of, while, at the same time, triggering in Freud powerful fantasies that fed his work in the years to come, as is attested by the speculations on "castration" that, in Freud's mature work, are found crystallized in the great apocalyptic scenarios of the beginnings of the human family. These scenarios, which no longer serve any function in contemporary psychoanalysis, have been the repository of the unthought-of real.

Here we encounter my third departure from the canons: my emphasis on the unconscious transmission of this erased traumatic reality. My thesis is that the gap left by Freud will be filled by the fantasies and dreams of his followers. When Freud was contemplating the primordial scenarios of the great catastrophe, his closest student was Sándor Ferenczi. He will ultimately develop an understanding of psychoanalysis significantly different from that of his master, emphasizing trauma and dislodging the analyst from his passive and an affective position, to see him act and react. Such a vision, which turned the games upside down, cost him dearly and, in fact, his final contributions were banned for over half a century by most psychoanalytic institutes. However, in the last few decades, his theories have been rediscovered and have gained both credibility and acclaim from progressive analysts who now acknowledge Ferenczi's work as the foundation of most contemporary trends in psychoanalysis.

As it is based on Ferenczi's latest contributions, this new narrative will risk resurfacing the same polarizations that have always plagued psychoanalysis. Here again, we come across a missing piece, that of the deep continuity between Freud and Ferenczi. Such a continuity can be restored by choosing to focus on the early Ferenczi, a Ferenczi who was deeply identified with Freud, adopted his language, and dreamed his dreams to the point of entering Freud's nightmares. My thesis here is that the dream is not only the place from which psychoanalysis sprang, but also the exquisite place of its unconscious transmission. From this perspective, it will be possible to show how the new paradigm proposed by the later Ferenczi sprouts exactly from what was transmitted by Freud, albeit in a dissociated form.

Bollas once wrote that Ferenczi "worked through for Freud, what Freud could not consider in his own mind" (Bollas, 2011, p. xvi). My thesis is similar but more specific, because it puts the emphasis on something that, having overwhelmed Freud, was not inscribed in his psyche, but has been felt and known by his body in the sense suggested by Ferenczi in the *Clinical Diary,* where he writes "In moments when the psychic system fails, the organism begins to think."[2] Thus, the story I tell in this book is the acephalous story of an amputated legacy that passes from generation to generation like a ghost that keeps returning until its story is told and listened to.

This book is divided into four parts. The first presents the image of the female as a "castrated male," a cornerstone of Freudian metapsychology, as the ground for both the encounter and the final disagreement between Freud and Ferenczi, illustrating it through the "paleontological fantasy" that Ferenczi created while in analysis with Freud. This analysis, we must say, did not help Ferenczi to recognize the traumatic origin of his "hatred of women," which will later be the focus of his mutual analysis with Elisabeth Severn. It was through this experience, from which the *Clinical Diary* takes shape, that Ferenczi succeeded in getting rid of the idea that the woman is a castrated man. A historical re-examination of the practice of female castration in nineteenth-century gynecological psychiatry and pediatrics, and the questions this raises, completes this introductory section.

The second part is the heart of the book. The reader is guided into the Freudian universe by a novel and surprising entry: the Hebrew word for circumcision (brit milah). It allows us to decipher the dream from which psychoanalysis sprung, to explore Freud's reaction to the scenes produced in analysis by Emma Eckstein, and to reconstruct the self-analytic "journey" that unfolds along *The Interpretation of Dreams*. The journey ends with the dream of the self-dissection of the pelvis, in which the father of psychoanalysis is split in two and observes the hole in his own genital area as an external spectator. It is the dream that will be repeatedly dreamt by Ferenczi and from which derived his theory of trauma as a split of the Self in a "brutally destroyed" part and a self-observing part that "knows everything" but "feels nothing."

Psychoanalysis had been the product of this pure Intelligence. Ferenczi's contribution to the history of psychoanalysis was to take care of this laceration between a brilliant part and a dead part, as we will see in the third part, dedicated to transmission. In particular, we will see in what ways Ferenczi absorbs an unconscious knowledge of what torments Freud, until he elaborates the reparative fantasy that underlies his genital theory known as *Thalassa*.

After the troubled publication of this work, Ferenczi will slowly begin to detach himself from Freud, until formulating a new metapsychology based on the fragmentation of psychic life. Some years after Ferenczi's premature death, Freud began to revise his ideas and to assimilate, as far as he could, the idea of traumatic fragmentation. This allows us to revisit, in part four, his final piece of self-analysis and to see how Freud recognized in Ferenczi's "scientific fantasy" an attempt to fill a gap inscribed in his dreams. Finally, we will turn to Freud's most famous clinical case, the Wolf Man, on which all of Freud's interest in "castration" had been poured, just after the catastrophic end of Emma Eckstein's second analysis. We will then see how this paradigmatic patient brings to the surface all the unresolved knots at the time of the foundation, to the point of filling a void for Freud, in ways that bring us back to the "primal scene" from which psychoanalysis was born.

Acknowledgments

Many friends from different languages and countries contributed to the construction of this book. The first Italian version of the manuscript was read by Adele di Florio, Francesco Migliorino, Franco Borgogno, Marco Conci, Gianni Guasto, Daniela Toschi e Clara Mucci, whom I thank for their helpful comments. The manuscript was then translated first into French and then into English, which contributed to a progressive definition of the text. For the translation into French, I thank Patrick Faugeras and especially Philippe Réfabert for his constant encouragement and the fundamental exchanges of ideas, which have given this book its final form. As for the English translation, it gave further rigors to the passages that were still vague or ambiguous. Here I have to thank Giselle Galdi, John Bliss, and especially Leslie Hendelman and Fergal Brady, both for their careful editing work, which turned my English version into a readable text, and for their observations that further enriched the book. The three versions, Italian, French, and English, have naturally been harmonized with each other with a continuous work of revision, which in any case left justified margins of freedom to each language.

But there is one person and one friend to whom I owe a special debt of gratitude, Philippe Réfabert, with whom I have collaborated almost daily for a year. Over time, he has become an increasingly indispensable interlocutor and co-author of the most difficult passages. In fact, the final version of the book is the product of a joint effort, born of a rare and precious community of visions and intentions.

*

Notes

1 Here, I am using the expression that Freud will use, several decades later, when referring to the circumcision endured by one of his American patients as a boy.
2 Dupont (1988, p. 52) (January 10). The original text says: "*In momenten, in dennen das psychische versagt, beginnt der Organismus zu denken.*" The verb *Versagen* has many meanings here ranging from collapse to rejection and denial.

Part I

The woman,
a castrated man

Chapter 1

The voice of Ferenczi

Freud once told Max Eitingon that "the secret of therapy is to cure through love, and ... with greatest personal effort one could perhaps overcome more difficulties in treatment, but one would 'lose his skin by doing so'". Freud, however, instead of "losing his skin," finally preferred *"to develop the thick skin we need"* in order to "dominate 'countertransference,' which is after all a permanent problem for us."

(Ernst Falzeder, 1994, p. 310)

The clash with the "indifferent power"

On September 2, 1932, Sándor Ferenczi stopped in Vienna to read to Freud the paper he intended to deliver to the Wiesbaden congress. It was called "The passions of adults and their influence on the sexual and character development of children"; it would subsequently be renamed *Confusion of Tongues between the Adults and the Child. The Language of Tenderness and of Passion.* It was the culmination of a life's work and a lucid meditation articulated on several levels. Childhood sexual abuse, the trauma around which psychoanalysis was born, was described by Ferenczi as a relational event. Ferenczi explored the intrapsychic consequences of the trauma, identified how it affects the analytic relationship, and indicated how the analyst could avoid re-traumatizing the patient. Nowadays this paper is considered the beginning of a new paradigm. Freud, conversely thought Ferenczi had "totally regressed" to the old etiological views on childhood sexual trauma he had held 36 years earlier and soon abandoned. Freud wrote to his daughter Anna the next day that the only difference that Ferenczi had added were observations on the necessity of psychoanalysts accepting the criticism of patients and "admitting one's error to them." The clash between the two men was terrible and the consequences were dramatic. Freud asked Ferenczi to withdraw the paper from the congress and, since he did not receive the expected answer, he turned his back and left the room without saying goodbye. At the moment of leaving the house of the professor, Ferenczi developed

DOI: 10.4324/9781003353058-3

a walking paralysis, perhaps a first symptom of the disease, severe anemia that would be diagnosed a few weeks later.

On October 2, Ferenczi penned his last entry to the *Clinical Diary* that he had begun in January 1932. He noted that the blood crisis had occurred when he realized that he could not rely on the protection of a "higher power." *"On the contrary,"* he added, "I shall be trampled underfoot by this indifferent power as soon as I go my own way and not his."

Ferenczi died nine months later, on May 22, 1933. The clash with Freud, the "indifferent power," had shaken him to his organic depths. But Ferenczi could not imagine a different life for himself. He had met Freud in 1908 and immediately became his friend, confidant, and collaborator. He was then 35 years old, 17 years younger than Freud. He was born in Hungary in 1873, the eighth of Baruch and Rosa's 12 children. His father died in 1888, when Sándor was 15. In Freud, he had found his "idolized and adored" father. In one of his writings, he recounted in the third person the extreme pain felt at the death of his father:

> the next day... he could not resist the temptation to take hold of a little flask of ether used as a drug to reanimate the dying father. He locked himself in a secluded place, and lit the ether, by which he could easily have caused a great fire.

At that precise moment, where the heartbeat had become "so loud you can hear it," he made the vow to think of the father "every day, at least once, for the rest of his life" (Ferenczi, 1928b).[1]

His attachment to Freud followed the same pattern. Not a day went by without his reading one of Freud's writings. Freud, for his part, had adopted Ferenczi as a son and named him his "secret Grand Vizier," as Ferenczi explained in the *Clinical Diary*. Thinking back to his relationship with this teacher and father, Ferenczi remembers his own "burning desire" to understand him "completely" to "win his approval" and his immediately making further progress "in the direction he recommended," all of which now, in 1932, made him feel like "a blindly dependent son" (August 4, 1932).

In fact, their relationship had been accompanied by a subtle and constant ambivalence for both of them, strengthened by the fact that neither Freud nor Ferenczi could do without each other. Somehow, they were complementary. They were the "Professor" and the "Doctor," as Judith Dupont reminds us:

> Freud ... wanted to understand and penetrate the depths of things and beings, without however jeopardizing his own inner equilibrium. Ferenczi instead wanted to feel, "feel with" (*mitfühlen*), "feel inside" (*einfühlen*), as he said, putting this inner balance into play every time without too many precautions. ... Freud wanted to understand, Ferenczi

wanted to cure. In their living environment this difference was perfectly perceived: when it came to the "Professor", everyone knew that it was Freud. When they said the "Doctor", it was useless to add Ferenczi's name to know who they were talking about.

(Dupont, 2015, p. 202)

Ferenczi, reader of Freud

In his effort to understand Freud perfectly, Ferenczi never replicated the Professor's thought, but always introduced a slight decentralization, in order to open up a new perspective. Freud was sometimes irritated by these original ideas of Ferenczi. Not infrequently, in their correspondence, he complains of the "disturbance" that this "understanding things differently" caused to his methodical and orderly work.

A good example of this decentralized way of reading Freud is the concept of "introjection" that Ferenczi coined in 1909 as opposed to that of "projection," presenting it as the translation in terms of object relations of the Freudian concept of "transference." It was therefore the same concept used by Freud, but passing through Ferenczi it had become another. It was the expression of a new perspective on the same process. Not only that, but it reflected Ferenczi's transference to Freud, as well as his "introjective" style.[2] In fact, he had "introjected" Freud, who had then become a part of himself.

We find such a reworking with respect to many crucial notions of psychoanalysis, such as the concepts of repetition compulsion, the death instinct, and countertransference. In all these cases, Ferenczi assimilates Freud's thought and makes it his own, opening up a different perspective, which Ferenczi constantly tries to minimize.

The impulse to repeat emerged as a central pressing question early in Freud's practice and development of the cathartic theory and therapy that, relying on Breuer's experience, Freud developed in 1892. The cathartic model was based on the assumption that when the emotions aroused by a painful event cannot be discharged with some kind of physical or verbal reaction, they remain imprisoned in a separate area of the psyche, splitting the mind and re-emerging in the form of symptoms. Therapy promoted an "abreaction" of the encapsulated affect by enabling the repetition of an experience to which the patient had failed to react originally and by compelling him "to complete his reaction" in a sort of private theater.[3]

Freud soon ran into the theoretical dilemma as to why the patient failed to react to the painful event, letting himself be guided now by hysteria, in which shock prevents the ego from defending itself, now by obsessive neurosis, in which the defense becomes an internal struggle without end. Precisely this struggle had allowed Freud to focus in 1894 on the model of repression and return of the repressed, which was destined to replace the model of psychic dissociation (called by Freud "Spaltung des Bewußtseins"). But, for a while, the fluctuations would continue. By the end of 1895, with the discovery of the deferred effects of infantile sexual shock, hysteria returned to guide his reflection. Freud found that when the ego fails to defend itself, a "psychic gap" takes place.[4] Then, in *The Etiology of Hysteria*, of 1896, he explained how, starting from the reproduction in analysis of "violent sensations" and "scenes," it was possible to find the erased traumatic memory which fills out the "empty gap [*freigelassene Lücke*]" like the missing piece of a picture-puzzle (Freud, 1896c, p. 205).

Then there was the turning point. In the course of 1897, the "objective" frame in which Freud believed he was moving, broke off. He had to acknowledge that the scenes that were emerging in analysis were so imbued with fantasies, as to undermine the assumption that psychic trauma was based on real and objective memories. As is known, this led to a radical shift toward a new paradigm, that of pathogenic fantasies. Certain painful events of life had lost the character of shock and were now viewed as mere precipitating factors that brought to light the patient's predisposition, in the form of sexual constitution. Freud's interest in trauma, however, did not fade away; rather it was displaced from the individual to the species and its distant animal past, following a scientific interest that had already formed in the course of his medical studies.

As a student, Freud was deeply impressed by Haeckel's theory, according to which the development of the individual proceeds by recapitulating the development of the species. When, in 1897, his belief that repressed traumatic memories were the specific cause of hysteria was shattered, the phylogenetic framework came to his aid. In this broader perspective, it mattered little whether the traumatic scenes that re-emerge in analysis were reality or fantasy, because, as Freud explained in the preface to the third edition of the *Three Essays on Sexual Theory* of 1905, in any case, "the phylogenetic disposition can be seen at work behind the ontogenetic process." The objectivity that Freud sought as a scientist had been restored. Behind fantasies, there were instincts, which, in turn, compelled the individual to repeat the traumas that were etched in memory in the course of phylogenetic development.

His research now encompassed the entire history of humanity, recalling a kind of totalizing knowledge more and more similar to the great myths about the beginning and end of the world. *Totem and Taboo* (1913a), a new version of the myth of the "original sin," will be a key step in this new direction that drove Freud to always search for historically earlier phases, even shifting into "bio-analysis." Freud worked on this in a metapsychological essay composed in 1915 which he discussed with Ferenczi, but then left in the drawer.[5] Freud revisited this field of "The last things" in 1920, in *Beyond the Pleasure Principle*, where he introduced the idea of a death instinct that seeks to restore an earlier inanimate state that preceded life. But it is Ferenczi who takes on the task of researching the ultimate symbolic meaning of biological phenomena. He did so with *Thalassa*, a work conceived in the years in which he was in analysis with Freud, but wasn't published until 1924.

In this visionary work, Ferenczi imagines the cosmic shock that started phylogenetic development, and which is repeated from generation to generation. It was Ferenczi's version of the death instinct. The object of his meditation is the same as that of Freud: the powerful regressive drive that runs across the entire universe. But the perspective was once again decentralized and the final result was something different, something which returns a vibrant voice to the "silent" death instinct postulated by Freud.

Freud considered *Thalassa* a great work and the highest point of their understanding, a "summit of achievement" after which Ferenczi "slowly drifted away from us," as Freud wrote in his obituary (Freud, 1933b, p. 229).

Remember/repeat

Thalassa was published in the most difficult year in the history of the psychoanalytic movement, 1924. Cancer had recently been discovered in Freud's mouth and the future had become uncertain.

In that year, *The Trauma of Birth* was also published, a book written by Otto Rank with the declared intent to free trauma from the phylogenetic past in which Freud had imprisoned it and bring it back to the ground of experience. The same aim had also informed a short work on the widening gap between theory and technique that Ferenczi and Rank wrote together, and that was also published in 1924 under the title *Entwicklungsziele der Psychoanalyse* (Perspectives on the development of psychoanalysis): Freud had read the manuscript and imposed some restrictions, but had no substantial objections. Even when Freud received the manuscript of *The Birth Trauma* from Rank, he saw a "grand discovery" in it.[6] Both works, however, were so harshly attacked within the Secret Committee,[7] that, on February 15, 1924, Freud felt compelled to write a circular letter in their defense. But Abraham had immediately retorted (February 21) that the two books marked a "scientific regression" similar to Jung's and that he saw in them "the omens of a fatal development." Also, Freud began then to see in these contributions a personal attack and a profound crisis followed which was resolved only with the removal of Rank.[8]

A thin thread unites all these works. It is the question of how to conceive of repetition for the purposes of therapy. It was an ancient problem, present from the very beginning. In the view of Ferenczi and Rank, psychoanalysis started from a purely practical basis but soon developed powerfully on the cognitive-theoretical side. However, the richer the knowledge, the more impoverished it was with therapeutic successes. It was therefore time to change direction starting a new phase that they (Ferenczi and Rank) suggested naming the *phase of emotional experience*.

In his last technical essay, *Remembering, Repeating and Working Through*, written in 1914, Freud had assigned to the analytic work the specific purpose of *remembering*, whereas *repetition* was considered a resistance. However, the renewed interest in the repetition compulsion at the center of *Beyond the Pleasure Principle* had encouraged Ferenczi and Rank to update the question on the side of treatment as well. In their joint work they wrote that, since it is unavoidable "that the patient should, during the cure, repeat a large part of his process of development" and the repetition concerns "those portions which cannot be really experienced from memory," the resulting practical necessity was "not to suppress the tendency to repetition in the analysis... Thus, we finally come to the point of attributing *the chief role in analytic technique to repetition instead of remembering*" (Ferenczi & Rank, 1924, pp. 3–4).

According to Ferenczi and Rank, the divorce between theory and therapy had occurred with the passage from the cathartic method to the one of free associations, which had entailed a notable "cooling" of the role of emotions. The discovery of the patient's transference to the doctor had indeed brought emotions back to the center of the scene, but with many limitations that will be Ferenczi's constant concern and the focus of his many technical experiments, starting with the "active technique." Ferenczi had been thinking of it since 1916, but only proposed it when Freud gave him the green light. The basic idea can be summarized as follows: as long as everything works, the analyst can and must limit himself to listening and interpreting, but when the work stops, he is forced to abandon the passive-receptive position and try to reactivate the conflict to advance the blocked analytic work.

Ferenczi dedicated six articles to the active technique, from 1919 to 1925, when he made public his "contra-indications" to this technique. This phase, which has light and shadow, helped him to clear up various problems. In particular, the importance of making certain pathogenic contents of early childhood accessible to analysis which, deriving from an age prior to the development of language, cannot be remembered but only relived. It was one of the problems, perhaps the most important, that Freud himself had to struggle with, alone, in the years of the foundation.

Indifference/empathy

Ferenczi and Rank's attempt to put experience back at the center of the cure triggered strong opposition and a fatal bifurcation in the history of psychoanalysis. Their claim was not only discarded as a theoretical regression, but the view prevailed that the control of emotions was more desirable than their release. The latter was now perceived as a sort of "insurrection." This political language was not accidental. It signals indeed that psychoanalysis had taken the road that would recognize in the super-ego the "fulcrum of psychotherapy," as later put by Strachey (1934). Through sophisticated structural theory (id, ego, and superego), identification and adaptation were becoming the royal road of psychoanalysis as therapy. Of course, it was a very different psychoanalysis from that of the beginning.[9]

In his later writings, Ferenczi took a stand against this emerging trend. "With the analysis of the ego," he wrote in 1929,

> Converted analytical treatment largely into a process designed to afford us the fullest possible insight into the topography, dynamics, and economy of symptom-formation, the distribution of energy between the patient's id, ego and super-ego being exactly traced out. But when I worked from this standpoint, I could not escape the impression that the relation between physician and patient was becoming too far much like that between teacher and pupil.
>
> (Ferenczi, 1929b, pp. 112–113)

For Ferenczi, the analysis could not advance a step further along this path. Already in *The Elasticity of Psycho-Analytic Technique* (1928a) he objected that basing treatment on the "substitution of one super-ego for another," could be a phase, but certainly not "the final aim of therapy" (p. 98). In this article, in which analysis is described as a "process of fluid development unfolding itself before our eyes, rather than as a structure with a design pre-imposed by an architect" (p. 90), Ferenczi suggested that the analyst should be guided in his clinical work not by a theoretical system, but rather by the *ability to put himself in another's shoes* which, with a sensorial metaphor taken from Freud himself, he calls tact to be utilized by the analyst. He thus formulates that principle of empathy which, despite being widely shared today, encountered firm opposition from Freud. For Freud, in fact, the use of empathy re-opened the door to the "subjective element" that he had strenuously fought since the beginning.[10]

By upholding the principle of empathy, Ferenczi had for the first time publicly expressed an idea that had not received Freud's approval. He had been strengthened in his convictions by an American patient, herself a psychoanalyst, who exerted a profound influence on him: Elizabeth Severn. Freud would blame her for taking Ferenczi away from him.

At that time the notion of empathy was not part of the psychoanalytic vocabulary as it captured a "subjective" dimension that did not accord with the "objectivity" of the scientist who inspired Freud. We find it, however, in *The Discovery of the Self*, the book that Elizabeth Severn published immediately after Ferenczi's death, in which the limit of Freudian psychoanalysis is identified precisely in the precept that the psychoanalyst must behave like a "scientist" rather than feel the patient "as a human palpitating being needing endless understanding and *Einfühlung*" (Severn, 1933, p. 53), i.e. *empathy*. For Severn, mere *analysis*—the intellectual "splitting the mental constituents into their component parts, and then leaving them to their fate" (p. 57)—was not sufficient to cure, that is, to reintegrate the dissociated parts of the self. To this end, sympathetic and soothing participation of the analyst was necessary to enable "the patient to relive, as though it were *now*, the traumatic events of his past aided by the dramatic participation of the analyst" (p. 72). For Severn, the main conceptual tool of this work was "emotional recollection" ("the *sine qua non* of successful analysis," p. 71), a phenomenon that Freud had neglected or reduced to mere "fantasies," but that could be brought back to life in a caring and warm atmosphere in which the patient regresses until he/she falls "into a kind of *trance*, in which *another* reality emerged." For this to happen, Severn specifies, the analyst must be "not only an onlooker but a participant in it" (p. 73). These ideas were shared by Ferenczi to such an extent that it is difficult to distinguish where the contribution of one or the other lies.[11]

Repression/dissociation

In the summer of 1929, Ferenczi presented his new ideas at the Oxford congress in a paper entitled "Progresses in Psycho-Analytic Technique" (later renamed *The Principles of Relaxation and Neocatharsis*). It was a provocative title, because Ferenczi returns to the technique that preceded the birth of psychoanalysis: the cathartic therapy of hysteria that Freud had inherited from Breuer. Ferenczi describes it as the "shared discovery" by "a genial patient and her understanding physician" (Ferenczi, 1929b, p. 109).

This image of a creative dyad, in which the "genial" part is recognized within the patient, not only serves to tell how everything was born from the coupling of two embodied minds but also pays homage to Ferenczi's own "genial patient," Elisabeth Severn. It was with her that Ferenczi rediscovered the hystero-traumatic basis of every neurosis, a material linked to visceral sensations encapsulated more in the body than in the mind. Above all, Elizabeth Severn had helped him to understand that amnesia and gaps in the psyche were the product of traumatic dissociation, causing part of the personality to live "on hidden, ceaselessly endeavoring to make itself felt, without finding any outlet except in neurotic symptoms" (Ferenczi, 1929b, p. 121). These were the same problems encountered by Freud at the beginning of his career as a psychotherapist, but the solution was different.

While rediscovering the hystero-traumatic basis of every neurosis, Ferenczi also rehabilitated the model of psychic dissociation that Freud had initially borrowed from Janet. Although he does not use this word, nor does he explicitly refer to Janet, there is a profound continuity that is reflected in the term Ferenczi begins to use, "fragmentation," which is closer to the French term initially used by Janet ("désagrégation") than its English translation ("dissociation").[12] Along with the theoretical framework, the technique also changed.

Ferenczi presented the dramatic technique in *Child Analysis in the Analysis of Adults* (1931). In the *Clinical Diary*, he tells that when he exposed it to Freud, the latter closed the question by saying that it was not permissible; he considered it a return to hypnosis.[13] Although the question remains controversial, it is nevertheless possible to recognize the idea that only after having consolidated the therapeutic alliance thanks to a long, attuned participation, can the analyst facilitate the emergence of "emotional memories" in patients, making then possible the process of reintegration of the dissociated parts. Put in another way, the analyst must not be just an onlooker but also an empathic *witness*.[14] "It appears that patients," Ferenczi writes on the page of January 31, 1932 of the *Clinical Diary*,

> cannot believe that an event really took place, or cannot fully believe it, if the analyst, as the sole witness of the events, persists in his cool, unemotional and, as patients are fond of stating, purely intellectual attitude, while the events are of a kind that must evoke, in anyone present, emotions of revulsion, anxiety, terror, vengeance, grief, and the urge to render immediate help…

That coldness of feelings, which for Freud was a guarantee of "objectivity," for Ferenczi blocked the patient in the "intellectual sphere." Not only that, but it led the analyst to repeat the disavowal that the patient experienced in the past:

> It appears that at this point in the analysis something of the patient's past history repeats itself. In most cases of infantile trauma, the parents have no interest in impressing the events on the mind of the child; on the contrary, the usual cure is repression: "It's nothing at all", "nothing has happened"…. [the events] are simply hidden in a deadly silence; the child's faint references are ignored or even rejected as incongruous, with the unanimous concurrence of those around him, and with such consistency that the child has to give up and cannot maintain its own judgement.

Ferenczi came to see in the compulsion to repeat a desire for a better solution, the outcome of which, in the therapeutic situation, depends to a large extent on the analyst's emotional response. The latter, in order to be reparative, must be different from the one that caused the patient the original trauma and splitting.[15] And given that the patient continues to harbor thoughts such as "It cannot be true that this has happened to me, or someone would come to my aid," he "prefers to doubt his own judgment rather than believe in our coldness, our feelings… " In other words, the patient's conscious and unconscious perception of how the analyst responds to his verbal and non-verbal communications is itself a very important part of the process. This was a fundamental correction of the solipsistic model of catharsis introduced by Freud and Breuer four decades earlier.

At the end of a long journey, Ferenczi returns to tackle the same basic problems that Freud had encountered at the beginning of his journey, but offers different answers. Thus, in the *Clinical Diary*, he writes "What is the content of the split off ego? Above all a tendency, probably *the* tendency, to complete the action interrupted by shock. … The content of the split-off ego is always as follows: natural development and spontaneity …" (January 24, II). Just then, the doctrine of the ego's "primary hostility" toward instincts, which would result in turning the focus of analysis on "defenses," was becoming mainstream. The theoretical and practical distance between Ferenczi and so-called classical psychoanalysis could not be greater.[16]

The differences we have sketched mark the general contours of Ferenczi's conflict with Freud and can be reduced to a single point. Freud gave few technical recommendations, but among these the recommendation to maintain a detached attitude was binding. He believed that a certain degree of coolness and indifference in the analytic situation could neutralize the subjective dimension. To retrieve a metaphor often used by Freud, the analyst had to keep the lucidity of a "surgeon," who, obviously cannot be distracted by emotions while operating. In particular, in his *Observations on Transference-Love*, Freud (1915) had explicitly recommended to "suppress the countertransference." Recalling how dangerous it is to indulge in feelings of tenderness toward the patient, he wrote that "One must not put aside the indifference acquired through the suppression of the countertransference."[17] As well summarized by Ernst Falzeder, "*Each* time Freud used the word 'countertransference' he emphasized that it must be kept in check. The analyst should 'dominate' it, 'surmount' it, 'overcome it', even 'overcome' it 'completely', and 'conquer' it to become 'free'" (Falzeder, 1994, p. 323).

The abyss of countertransference

Ferenczi's disagreement with Freud essentially concerned how to conceive of and treat the countertransference, a concept that, from the time it was coined by Freud in 1909/1910, until about 1970, was considered, with a few exceptions, an obstacle to treatment that had to be mastered and suppressed. Now, it was precisely this *indifference acquired with the suppression of countertransference* that for Ferenczi signaled the presence of an unresolved trauma planted like a nail in the heart of psychoanalysis.

Already in the work of 1924, written together with Rank, Ferenczi had traced the inharmonious development of psychoanalysis to Freud's recoiling from his initial intense emotional participation. The topic was then resumed by him in the 1929 article *The Principle of Relaxation and Neocatarsis*[18] but it is only in the *Clinical Diary* that Ferenczi fully tackled the question. He does so in the May 1, 1932 entry, in which he says that Freud had originally followed Breuer "with enthusiasm," working "passionately, devotedly, on the curing of neurotics," yet he "must have been first shaken and then disenchanted" when "the problem of countertransference opened up before him like an abyss."

This is how Ferenczi arrived at imagining the famous turn of Freud, the abandonment of the seduction theory that in the orthodox narrative is celebrated as the true birth of psychoanalysis. In Ferenczi's version, this moment corresponded

> to the discovery that hysterics lie. Since making this discovery Freud no longer loves his patient. He has returned to the love of his well-ordered and cultivated superego... Since this shock, this disillusionment, there is much less talk of trauma, the constitution now begins to play the principal role.
>
> (Dupont, 1988, p. 93)

In Ferenczi's final vision, Freud found refuge in the materialism of the natural scientist who "sees almost nothing in the subjective, except the superstructure of physical." Since then, Ferenczi writes, Freud had remained attached to analysis "intellectually but not emotionally" (ibid.).

As an example of this split, Ferenczi recalls how Freud once let slip in his presence the remark that patients were just "rabble," who served "to provide us with a livelihood and material to learn from." To Ferenczi this was not an outburst under stress, but rather the result of a painful emotional experience that, crystallizing in a skeptical attitude, had caused a mutation in the method, which, from passionate and involved, had become "impersonal" (ibid.)

"Method" means "way to"; it is the road that one must take to get to the place where certain phenomena can be disclosed and manifested. The choice between participating and not participating is a crossroads from which the roads diverge, leading to very different places. The road taken by Ferenczi had led him to see that the legacy of a trauma is not the repressed memory of a painful event, its memory trace, but *the change produced in the subject, the splitting of the psyche,* which is a primary phenomenon with respect to the ideative contents, memories included.[19] To Ferenczi the divorce between emotion and intellect, and more radically, between a frozen, dead, or dying emotional part and a lucid and paranoid intelligence, was the paradigmatic imprint of trauma. Now, this kind of split went through both Freud's work and personality, to the point that some of his disciples, Jung and Ferenczi in particular, tried to convince him to undergo an analysis. But Freud didn't want to know anything about it.

Who is crazy?

This page of the *Clinical Diary* of May 1, 1932, entitled *Who Is Crazy, We or the Patients? (the Children or the Adults?),* begins with a question that returns insistently: why did Freud, the inventor of psychoanalysis, never allow himself to be analyzed?

Freud's withdrawal into himself coincided in fact with his self-analysis. We are used to seeing it as the glorious moment when Freud discovers the mechanisms of dreams and the structure of the unconscious, and it certainly is. But beyond the undisputed genius, Ferenczi also saw the doubts that his self-analysis had left unresolved and from which Freud defended himself either by clinging "too strongly to theory" or by projecting them onto his patients: "he only analyzes others but not himself. Projection." Ferenczi will return to this on August 4, in a page where Freud's resistance to analysis is associated with his siding with the "Anti-traumatic" by creating theories that, like the one of the parricidal Oedipus, "applied only to others, not to himself. Hence the fear of allowing himself to be analyzed."

These doubts were present since the beginning, and if Ferenczi now was giving them a full voice it was because he had overcome his fear of being analyzed by placing himself in the hands of his patient, Elizabeth Severn, whose analysis resulted in "mutual analysis," the experiment around which the *Clinical Diary* revolves.

Returning to Freud's "impersonal" method, Ferenczi remarks how the elimination of subjectivity led the analyst to levitate above the poor patient "like some kind of divinity," creating a situation "comfortable for him," being allowed to revive his "infantile grandeur." Yet, while the analyst is spared from the "unpleasure of self-criticism," the patient is plunged into an "endless dependence on a parent... who appears to promise everything but inwardly withholds everything" (1 May).

In these harsh judgments, one feels the full weight of Ferenczi's disappointment in the man he had for so long idealized. But there is not only disappointment. Racker's (1968, p. 132) criticism of the "myth" that "analysis is an interaction between a sick person and a healthy one" is in fact here anticipated several decades earlier by Ferenczi, who also identifies the traumatic origin of this distortion, describes its implications, and suggests the only possible antidote: the analyst must be ready to listen to the complaints of patients and to admit his mistakes in front of them. For Ferenczi, in fact, the objective and indifferent analyst, who uses his knowledge and his authority to keep himself unapproachable, divides the patient's mind in two and seizes his/her feelings. Giving up this comfortable position frees the patient, instills courage in him/her, and loosens his/her tongue.

Not only that. In the entry of the *Clinical Diary* titled *Who Is Crazy, We or the Patients?* Ferenczi refers several times to the doctor's "scientific delusion."[20] Did he come to the conclusion that the Freudian system was built around a delusion?

What is certain is that in the whirling pace of the *Clinical Diary* we are witnessing a progressive dismantling of the cornerstones of this system, starting with the solution based on the "constitution" embraced by Freud when the seduction theory collapsed. We find in Ferenczi the acknowledgment that perversions are not "fixations" but "products of fear," and the idea that the theory of the child's "perverse" sexual disposition is a "projection of the psychology of adults onto children" (June 30) that implies the disavowal of the child's vulnerability and of the "difference between infantile fantasy and the realization of the same" (August 17). But if the incestuous fixation was not a "natural product of development but rather is implanted in the psyche from the outside," then a "revision of the Oedipus complex" (July 26), the theory that Freud had placed at the center of his system, had become necessary.

Resuming then his ongoing meditation on the father of psychoanalysis and on his contradictions, on August 4, Ferenczi recalls Freud's pessimistic view, shared with only a few trusted few, that "psychoanalysis as a therapy may be worthless." "This was the point where I refused to follow him," Ferenczi writes, revealing how this was the reason that prompted him to deal openly with questions of technique:

> I refused to abuse the patient's trust in this way ... I believed rather that therapy was good, but perhaps we were still deficient, and I began to look for our errors.
>
> (August 4, 1932, Dupont, 1988, p. 186)

Flight into sanity

In the summer of 1932, the play of mirrors between Freud and Ferenczi had reached the apex: Freud, conversely, came to see Ferenczi's new ideas as the product of a delusion. The reading of *The Confusion of Tongues* confirmed this belief. Freud turned his back on him, and the loss of his protection acted as a trigger for a collective reaction of expulsion that began to manifest itself within a month at the Wiesbaden congress. For Ernest Jones, Ferenczi's paper had exposed his "paranoia."[21] In Ferenczi's obituary, Jones (1933) wrote that in his last writings "Ferenczi showed unmistakable signs of mental regression in his attitude toward the fundamental problems of psycho-analysis" (p. 466).

Jones' judgment, which in September 1932 was privately shared by Freud too, led to the prohibition to publish in English the paper presented by Ferenczi in Wiesbaden. However, it was not substantiated by arguments and evaporated to nothing, while the progressive publication of the collected works of Ferenczi, first in German and then in English, gave hope to his students that the rehabilitation process would be quick and complete. A significant milestone was the so-called "Ferenczi number" of the *International Journal of Psychoanalysis*, in 1949. In the introduction, Michael Balint pointed out that "Psycho-analytical thinking is now beginning to re-examine Ferenczi's ideas" (Balint, 1949, p. 219). This time *The Confusion of Tongues* was also published, without meeting Jones' veto.

The works of Ferenczi's students on his technique followed—in addition to the numerous works by Michael and Alice Balint, those of Izette de Forest (1942, 1954) and Clara Thompson (1943)—and the gradual publication in German of the remaining volumes in which his works were collected (the "Bausteines"). Ferenczi's literary heir,[22] Michael Balint, expected these to have been followed by the publication of the Clinical Diary and of the correspondence with Freud, or at least part of it. A positive sign came from Margaret Little's review of the English translation of the last volume of Ferenczi's works, *Final Contributions*, published in 1955. Remarking that Ferenczi's final work was illuminated by Winnicott's latest development, she pointed out that Ferenczi "went further than his colleagues in ways they found unacceptable for unconscious reasons" (Little, 1957, p. 123).

This recognition, however, clashed with the new spirit that was spreading in the psychoanalytic community. Thus, reviewing the same volume in the same year, Alexander Bromley wrote that Ferenczi had abandoned "psychoanalytic technique in favor of what might be described as rapport therapy" (Bromley, 1957, p. 113). This way of presenting Ferenczi was new, since it made retrospective use of the distinction between psychoanalysis and psychotherapy that was emerging in those years. The astonishing result was that Ferenczi was thus placed outside the boundaries of psychoanalysis— which would have been absurd even for Freud, who, shortly after the death of Ferenczi, began to assimilate his ideas, as evinced by the importance in his last writings of the traumatic splitting and fragmentation of the psyche.

In 1957, the third volume of Freud's official biography appeared, in which Jones recounts the crisis of 1924, presenting it as the third wave of dissent after those of Adler and Jung, and attributing it to the mental insanity of two members of the committee that governed the psychoanalytic movement (the Secret Committee):

> Two of the members, Rank and Ferenczi, were not able to hold out to the end. Rank in a dramatic fashion presently to be described, and Ferenczi more gradually towards the end of his life, developed psychotic manifestations that revealed themselves in, among other ways, a turning away from Freud and his doctrines. The seed of a destructive psychosis, invisible for so long, at last germinated.
>
> (Jones, 1957, p. 47)

The alleged "heresy" of Ferenczi and Rank consisted in the emphasis put on "Erlebnis" (experience) in the psychoanalytic situation or, as put by Jones, in "the theory that study of repeating experience could supersede the need for a deeper genetic analysis: that Erlebnis therapy could replace psychoanalysis" (p. 77). According to Jones' historical reconstruction, the crisis of 1924 ended two years later with Rank's mental troubles and defection

(p. 81), while Ferenczi's mental troubles became apparent later, when he "began to develop lines of his own which seriously diverged from those generally accepted in psycho-analytical circles" (p. 156). In short, in Jones' judgment, Ferenczi's revision of psychoanalysis was nothing more than the product of serious mental pathology incubated for years, culminating in mental illness and death.[23] This judgment, immediately taken up and amplified by reviewers, quickly spread in the psychoanalytic community, leading to the ostracization of Ferenczi. Jones' allegation had blocked Ferenczi's rehabilitation process and frozen Balint's plan to publish the *Clinical Diary*, further resulting in the cancellation of teaching Ferenczi's work from most training programs. Ferenczi's voice had been silenced.[24]

Upon the death of Michael Balint in 1969, Ferenczi's literary legacy passed into the young hands of Judith Dupont, who, defying many negative opinions, managed to publish in 1985 the French translation of the *Clinical Diary*.[25] It was the beginning of a lively movement of opinion among psychoanalysts and training institutions of diverse traditions, which would later be called the "Ferenczi Renaissance" (Bonomi & Borgogno, 2014).

A second substantial contribution came from the progressive publication, in complete form, of the letters between Freud and Ferenczi, a project long cherished by Balint which only became possible after the death of Anna Freud. Under the direction of André Haynal and thanks to the editorial work of Ernst Falzeder, Eva Brabant, and Patrizia Giampieri-Deutsch, the first of the three volumes of the correspondence came out (in French) in 1992, followed over the years by subsequent volumes and editions in various languages. Thanks to these and other documents, the voice of Ferenczi is again audible. In the following chapters, we will try to understand what it can tell us that we do not yet know.

Notes

1 This paper, Psychoanalyse und Kriminologie, was not included in the English translation of Ferenczi's works.

2 On Ferenczi's introjective style, see Borgogno (2011).

3 Freud (1893, p. 39). In the Standard Edition, the text reads "causing an unaccomplished reaction to be completed." This lecture by Freud (of January 11, 1893) summarizes the "Preliminary Communication" (first chapter of Breuer & Freud, 1895), but it is not included in the Gesammelte Werke and therefore I could not check the original German text.

4 Describing the effect of an early sexual shock in the days of Christmas 1895, Freud wrote:"The raising of tension at the primary experience of unpleasure is so great that the ego does not resist it and forms no psychic symptoms... The first stage of hysteria may be described as 'fright hysteria'; its primary symptom is the *manifestation of fright* accompanied by a *gap* in the psyche [*psychischer Lücke*]" (Draft K "A Christmas Fairy Tale", Masson, 1985, p. 169).

5 See Freud (1985), the introduction by the editor, Ilse Grubrich-Simitis, and her further commentary in Grubrich-Simitis, I. (1988).

6 Freud at that time had named Rank as his "successor" (Lieberman & Kramer, 2012, p. 225); he had in fact been diagnosed with mouth cancer and doctors had given him a few years to live.

7 Freud's closest circle of collaborators consisted of Karl Abraham, Ferenczi, Otto Rank, Ernest Jones, Max Eitingon, and Hanns Sachs at that time. The Secret Committee was established at the time of Jung's retreat as the core group leading the psychoanalytic movement.

8 On these developments, see Lieberman's classic work (1985), the careful study by Rudnytsky (1991), and Marina Leitner's lashing reconstruction (1998). The crisis was also institutional: at a certain point, the Secret Committee ceased and was later reconstituted as titular governing body of the International Psychoanalytic Association.

9 A detailed overview of the relationship between Ferenczi and the nascent "Ego psychology" is outlined in Bonomi (2010).

10 Freud's opinion is reported in the article anonymously. Freud believed that the notion of tact could be used to justify any "arbitrary action" by analysts, that is, "the intervention of the subjective element (i.e., the influence of their unmastered complexes)" (Ferenczi, 1928a, p. 99). A reference to the "process that psychology calls 'Einfühlung'" (empathy) can be found in Freud (1921, p. 296). There were various occasional attempts to introduce this concept into psychoanalysis, but all failed because its phenomenological and subjective nature made it inferior to the abstract and objective concepts of Freudian metapsychology. As is well known, the importance of empathy will be rediscovered above all by Kohut and his school, the psychology of the Self.

11 Today these ideas seem to be substantiated by neuroscience, and by Allan Schore in particular, as Clara Mucci shows well in her latest book, *Borderline Bodies* (2018b), in which she illustrates all the importance of the intense exchange between the right hemispheres of the therapeutic dyad.

12 Rudnytsky (2022, p. 14) rightly underlines here too the influence of Severn, who had been formed within a tradition in which dissociation had remained the dominant concept. It must be said, however, that Ferenczi draws a psychodynamics of fragmentation that is lacking in Janet.

13 Dupont (1988, p. 24). Freud's opposition to this specific technique explains why, in *Analysis Terminable and Interminable*, he accused Ferenczi of wanting to undermine the analysis by replacing it with hypnotic influence (Freud, 1937a, p. 230). The technique of dramatic participation was later presented by Izette de Forest (1942, p. 136, 1954) as one of the innovations introduced by Ferenczi, alongside the use of countertransference, while another ex-patient of Ferenczi, much more influential, Clara Thompson (1943) rejected it as non-analytic. Certainly, his way of working, often referred to as "cold," was different, but in her rejection of this technique, the fact that Severn had been the inspiration could also have weighed. Thompson's incurable resentment for being excluded from the mutual analysis with Ferenczi and her jealousy and animosity toward Severn has been well outlined by Peter Rudnytsky (2015, 2022) in his reconstruction of the complex relationships between Ferenczi, Severn, and Thompson.

14 On the relationship between psychoanalysis and bearing witness, see the important works of Mucci (2018a) and Réfabert (2018).

15 This view will be taken up in the concept of "corrective emotional experience" developed by Franz Alexander (1950) and strongly attacked by the mainstream in the 1950s. For a reassessment see Haynal (2011).

16 See on this point, my article on *Ferenczi and ego-psychology* (Bonomi, 2010).

17 Freud (1915, p. 164). The original passage, which reads "... man darf die Indifferenz die man sich durch die Niederhaltung der Gegen übertragung erworben hat, nicht verleugnen," in the Standard Edition was translated as "We ought not to give up the neutrality towards the patient, which we have acquired through keeping the counter-transference in check." On the question, see Hoffer (1985). As is well known, this translation gave way to the concept of "neutrality" which over time has been enriched with new meanings. But Freud never used the term "Neutralität" either here or elsewhere. The misunderstanding arises from Strachey's English translation of the German term "Indifferenz" with "neutrality" in the Standard Edition of Freud's works.

18 Ferenczi (1929b) described the "cool aloofness on the analyst's part" (p. 118) as an attitude that made its appearance when the cathartic relationship "gradually cooled down to a kind of unending association-experiment" becoming a "mainly intellectual" process (p. 110).

19 In *Analysis Terminable and Interminable*, Freud will assert exactly the opposite, namely, that where trauma prevails, the ego does not undergo alteration, resulting in a favorable condition for analysis, in contrast to situations where the constitutional force of instincts results in an alteration of the ego that is unfavorable to analysis (see Rudnytsky, 2022, p. 258). The distinction between primary or stigmata (among which disaggregation) and secondary, or ideogenic, symptoms is made by Janet, 1893/1894, who however believed that disaggregation could not be explained psychologically.

20 "Certain theories of the doctor (delusional ideas) may not be challenged; if one does so nevertheless, then one is a bad pupil, one get a bad grade, one is in a state of resistance" (May 1, 1932, Dupont, 1988, p. 94; see Réfabert, 2001).

21 See Jones' letters to Freud of September 9, 1932 and June 3, 1933.

22 After Michael Balint's death, Ferenczi's writings were managed in part by Balint's niece, Judith Dupont, who eventually donated her archive to the Freud Museum in London, and in part by Enid Balint, who commissioned the publication of the correspondence with Freud to André Haynal (Dupont, 2015; Haynal, 2016).

23 Jones (1957) stated that Ferenczi had "delusions about Freud's supposed hostility" (p. 190), that his illness "exacerbated his latent psychotic trends" (p. 188), that "the mental disturbances had been making rapid progress in the last few months" (p. 190), finally culminating in "violent paranoic and even homicidal outbursts, which were followed by a sudden death" (p. 190).

24 For a detailed reconstruction of the origins and consequences of Jones' allegation, see my essay "Flight into sanity" (Bonomi, 1999) or its abridged version (Bonomi, 1998).

25 Judit Dupont has recounted this adventure in various writings, including Dupont (2006). I recommend her latest book, *Au fil du temps … Un itinéraire analytique* (Dupont, 2015) in which the story of one of the most important dynasties of psychoanalysis is told.

Chapter 2

Hatred of the woman and veneration of man

> We call everything that is strong and active male, and everything that is weak and passive female.
>
> (Sigmund Freud, 1938b, p. 188)

> Here is a classic example of definition by opposition, in which one pole of the binary – in this case, masculinity – is defined by excluding the other – the femininity, vulnerability, penetrability – from its definition.
>
> (Aron & Starr, 2013, p. 284)

The breaking point between Ferenczi and Freud

In the previous chapter, we outlined the growing divergences between Ferenczi and Freud, but is there a real breaking point? At different times it was argued that the break was determined by Ferenczi's ideas on trauma, or by his innovative approaches to technique. However, these explanations collide with a simple fact: these differences were well known to Freud when, in an attempt to strengthen their relationship, he offered Ferenczi the presidency of the International Psychoanalytic Association (IPA), as a sort of "shock therapy." In May 1932, after a long hesitation, Ferenczi had finally decided to embrace the hand extended by Freud and accept the presidency of the IPA. But, immediately after, on May 22, he sent him a postcard from the Café Florián in Venice, with these words:

> P.S. to the last letter. It will interest you to know that in our group lively debates are going on about the female castration complex and penis envy. I must admit that in my practice these don't play the great role that one had expected theoretically. What has been your experience?

This question will be fatal to the attempt to reach an agreement; they will both take a step back. A few days before their last meeting, Ferenczi

DOI: 10.4324/9781003353058-4

informed Freud that he could not accept a role whose "main concern should be conserving and consolidating what already exists" (August 21). But in the meantime, Freud too had changed his mind, as attested to by the letters he sent to trusted collaborators. In short, with his question, Ferenczi had dug an insurmountable ditch.

This stiffening of positions around a problem that today does not even figure in the agenda of contemporary psychoanalysis leaves us perplexed also because Ferenczi had made his own the equation woman=castrated man at the basis of Freud's theory, to the point of becoming its spokesperson. Consider the following passage, in which the anthropologist and psychoanalyst Geza Róheim invokes the authority of Ferenczi in support of the idea that the deliberate elimination of the clitoris was a dramatically shortened repetition of biogenetic and ontogenetic development. The passage is part of the long report published in the 1932 edition of the *International Journal of Psychoanalysis* on the ethnological expedition of 1929–1930 sponsored by Princess Marie Bonaparte to evaluate the validity of Freud's theories. Referring to the practice of female genital mutilation in Somalian tribes, Róheim wrote:

> This story shows that infibulation in this form really signifies to the man the destruction of the sexual object. After it is sewn up, the vagina disappears; after the clitoris is cut, the woman's penis is gone. Hence the strong traumatic element in the whole operation. The man forces coitus on the woman in an extremely painful form; he uses the penis and a knife. Before we ask, however, why he needs thus to destroy the sexual object, we must try to understand what the operation means to the woman. *First of all, however, we must note that it is really a dramatically abridged repetition of biogenetic and ontogenetic development.* For women have to give up their original erotogenicity based on the clitoris and advance to the vaginal type. They must also accept their 'defeat' (Ferenczi) and preserve the feminine-masochistic attitude. All this and the biological 'innovation' of the hymen is represented in the operation. *We might therefore suppose that it fosters the right attitude of women in sexual life.*
>
> (Róheim, 1932, p. 202; emphasis added)

Today it is rather unbelievable that psychoanalysis supported these ideas. But that's what the files say.

In this chapter, we will try to understand how Ferenczi became the spokesperson for this view; we will describe the vicissitudes that led him to change perspective, and then outline the edges of his conflict with Freud. Along the way we will talk about many different things that converge in one place: "hatred of the woman, veneration for man," to quote a passage from Ferenczi's *Clinical Diary* (July 19, 1932).

Penises in the process of extinction

Freud's ideas of the woman as "a castrated man" were reorganized in the years 1910–1912 and again in the 1920s, but came from far away, since they played a decisive role in the great turning point of 1897, when sexual constitution replaced traumatic experience in his theory of the etiology of neurosis. In the *Three Essays on the Theory of Sexuality*, he would then posit "an originally bisexual physical disposition" which, in the course of evolution, had "become modified into a unisexual one, leaving behind only a few traces of the sex that has become atrophied" (Freud, 1905, p. 114).

According to Freud, the clitoris was an atrophied penis. In this he adhered to ideas of his time, which are very distant from ours.[1] Freud, after all, never presented this thesis as his original idea, but rather as a scientific fact that curiously coincided with what he called the "infantile theories" on sexuality. Thus, in the chapter on "Femininity" composed in the summer of 1932, on the eve of the last meeting with Ferenczi, Freud repeats that "science" teaches that "portions of the male sexual apparatus also appear in women's bodies, though in an atrophied state" (Freud, 1933a, p. 114).

The idea that the clitoris was the remnant of an archaic past circulated at the end of the nineteenth century, when it was thought that its length varied according to the degree of civilization and latitude: it would be larger in African women and smaller in women who lived in the cold climates of the north. In those years anthropologists measured everything, in the manner of Lombroso. The clitoris did not escape the rule, indeed it was the subject of a special "scientific" attention, because it was believed that Nature, in its evolution, wanted to abolish it, as championed in popular essays such as "Is evolution trying to do away with the clitoris?" by Robert Morris (1892). Although the hypothesis was not confirmed by the data[2], a large clitoris was seen as a sign of *primitivism* and, within the framework of the ideas of the time, of an atavism. In short, the prejudices of the time weighed on this issue, as well as on other ideas Freud held of women, for example his belief that civilization was a male product, to which the woman was not only foreign but also hostile (Freud, 1930), or the belief that women were ethically deficient given the inconsistencies of their super-ego (see Schafer, 1974).

Freud's view of the clitoris had a special connection with the theory of congenital bisexuality advanced by his friend Wilhelm Fliess on Easter 1897, in a meeting that had profound repercussions, and to which we will return in the last part of this book. Fliess had introduced his theory almost casually, commenting on the recurring dream of giant snakes of a female patient of Freud, who was then extremely impressed by his friend's remark. At that time Freud's theory of real trauma was seriously jeopardized and the idea of a congenital bisexuality helped him to reorganize his whole theory along biological lines. In particular, it helped him to better define the psycho-biological theory of the abandonment of erogenous zones in the course of phylogenetic evolution.[3] The abandoned erogenous zone in question was the "male zone" in the female, the clitoris.[4] The peculiarity of Freud's theory, with respect to the beliefs of the time, consisted in his idea that what had been abolished in the body was still surviving in the mind.

For Freud, girls were in fact born with the *feeling* of having a penis, and only when their expectation that the clitoris will grow as much as the male penis is finally disappointed, are they forced to give up such an atavistic illusion, abandon male orientation, discover the vagina, accept passivity, and become female. Freud was convinced that females become females only by accepting their "castration." Explaining this to Karl Abraham, he wrote that women are "made" (February 24, 1910). As he would succinctly say in *Some psychical consequences of the anatomical distinction between the sexes,* "the elimination [Wegschaffung] of clitoridal sexuality is a necessary precondition for the development of femininity" (Freud, 1925a, p. 255). With this "Wegschaffung" which means to *take away, clear away,* the biological castration is repeated at the ontogenetic level, leaving a wound neither curable nor further analyzable, as Freud would state at the end of *Analysis Terminable and Interminable,* where all this is synthesized in the famous statement: "The repudiation of femininity can be nothing else than a biological fact" (Freud, 1937a, p. 252).

But what was the meaning of this "taking away"? Did it have a metaphorical or literal sense? The boundaries are blurred. Freud described it as a psychical process, yet its template was very "physical," as it becomes apparent from what Marie Bonaparte says in her article "Notes on excision," which was written shortly after the death of Freud, but published later, in 1948, together with the article "Female mutilation among primitive peoples and their psychical parallels in civilization." In the latter, Bonaparte wrote that excision

> seemed to Freud a way of seeking to further "feminize" the female by removing this cardinal vestige of her masculinity. Such operations, as he once said to me, must be intended to complete the "biological castration" of the female which Nature, in the eyes of these tribes, has not sufficiently effected.
>
> (1948a, p. 153)

The clitoris was often at the center of the Princess's conversations with the Professor. In 1927, six months after the beginning of her analysis with Freud, Marie Bonaparte underwent an operation to bring the clitoris closer to the vagina, hoping to reach orgasm.[5] This did not happen and soon after Freud presented her a new book on the tribal rites of excision of Nandi (cauterization of the vagina with a hot stone), explaining to her that the males of this tribe would "never have allowed a custom which deprived them of mutual participation in voluptuous pleasure, which all men prize in all climes" (1948b, pp. 191–192).[6]

These were the years when Bonaparte financed Róheim's ethnological expedition to test Freud's hypotheses in the field. Bonaparte, a "masculine" or "clitoral" woman, was interested in the practice of cutting the clitoris not only in tribal rites but also in contemporary treatments for masturbation. In 1929 she made an inquiry in a German hospital where various types of female genital interventions were performed as a cure for masturbation[7], coming to the conclusion that the removal of the clitoris neither inhibited masturbation nor facilitated the transfer of sensitivity from the clitoris to the vagina. Her research thus failed to confirm Freud's opinion that "excising the clitoris might help to internalize the erotogenic zone, and in some degree intensify internal vaginal sensitivity" (1948b, p. 204). Referring again to excision, Bonaparte writes: "We know that for fifty years, European surgeons did not hesitate to resort to it at times. Yet the children and adolescents who underwent this operation, continued to masturbate as much as before" (1948a, pp. 156–157). "The more or less unconscious motives for excision," she added, suggested "a factor" present which tended to "repress the feminine sexuality" (pp. 157–158).

For Freud female circumcision (excision) was undoubtedly "cruel," as he writes in his essay on the taboo of virginity (Freud, 1918b, p. 197). Nevertheless, he considered it a natural fatality, a *bio-trauma*, and if it was "cruel" it was because Nature was cruel.[8] If we consider that all his life he fought against male circumcision, one is struck by the abysmal difference which divided, in his eyes, male from female circumcision.

For Freud, the circumcision of the male turned the body into a book that had to be read and deciphered. It contained in fact the memory of mankind's history, in particular the memory of the "Castration" that the father of the primordial family practiced on his sons to enslave them. It was a product of cultural repression. Female circumcision was instead a product of biological repression. There was no book to browse and nothing to tell. In fact, on this subject, for about a century psychoanalysis has been silent like a fish.

A strange paleontological fantasy

Ferenczi did more than share Freud's ideas. While in analysis with Freud, Ferenczi tried to make this mute biological fact "legible," formulating a paleo-biological speculation adored by his analyst: at the beginning of time, in an unspecified remote past, the female as well had a fully developed penis, like the male, but then, during a violent battle to decide who should bear the burden of motherhood, she had been "defeated" and then she lost her penis.

Freud was so enthusiastic about this bold hypothesis that he cited it in his essay *The Taboo of Virginity*, the only time in his entire body of work in which the "cruel" tribal practice of cutting the clitoris is mentioned. Ferenczi's speculation was in fact a perfect complement to the essay's central thesis, the idea that defloration revives a woman's desire to castrate the man and keep his penis for herself. Above all, it explained the origin of what Freud called the "woman's hostile bitterness against the man, which never completely disappears in the relations between the sexes, and which is clearly indicated in the strivings and in the literary productions of 'emancipated' women" (Freud, 1918b, p. 205). In short, it explained their *penis envy*.

It is not clear why Ferenczi developed this fantasy. His pre-analytical writings show him as an author committed to the social good, open to transsexualism, sensitive to the issue of prostitution, in short, a politically oriented author and proto-feminist, in a period when women were denied the same rights of men and were viewed as "inferiors" by educated men and scientists. Sensitivity to the female question also characterized his debut in psychoanalysis (Borgogno, 1999). It is no coincidence that he had bonded with Rank, the only one of the pioneers to protest against the "curse" hanging over the woman's genitals (*The Trauma of Birth* contained a political agenda: rehabilitating the female genital, freeing it from the ancient curse and contemporary contempt), and with Groddeck, who had reversed the envy of the penis to envy of the uterus, and whose feminism was even more radical. And so, why did he say these things? Was it not his voice that was speaking? Was it an act of love for his analyst or an unconscious attack on the absurdity of his theories?

As noticed by Clara Thomson (1988), Ferenczi would often develop an idea of Freud's to such a fantastic degree, that, in the end, it became "absurd" (p. 185). This is exactly what happened with his paleo-biological fantasy. In the *Clinical Diary,* Ferenczi would attribute to children who were crushed by authority a tendency to mimicry in their faces, exaggerating their features to the point of the grotesque. Similarly, his paleo-biological speculation seems an unconscious attack on the revered professor, who saw the lack of a penis in women reason for the unavoidable contempt men feel for these "unhappy creatures" (as Freud writes in the essay on Leonardo). On the other hand, Ferenczi's adherence to Freud's misogynistic vein was a powerful way of consolidating his bond with him.

Despite the honor and privilege of being mentioned by the master, Ferenczi was unable to put his paleo-biological fantasy in writing. It was part of the same strain of ideas and fantasies from which his genital theory arose, but Ferenczi failed to include it in *Thalassa*, or at least in the original text published in 1924. The history of this text is also complicated: in 1915, when Ferenczi was in analysis with Freud, his genital theory was already fully formed in his head. But every time he tried to put it in writing, he was seized with blocks, anxiety attacks, and psychosomatic disturbances. He would succeed only eight years later, but even then, he failed to include the paleo-biological fantasy cited by Freud in *The Taboo of Virginity*. Only in 1929, when his detachment from the master Freud had become sharper, did Ferenczi decide to publish the essay *Male and Female*, centered on the "tale" (as he now calls it) born from his imagination years earlier. Published separately in 1929, it will be included in *Thalassa* as the final chapter of the genital theory. But we find in it a surprise.

Ferenczi took up again the idea that originally both sexes "developed the male sexual organ," as recapitulated in embryological development, in which the clitoris is identified as a real penis. Yet, in contrast with the progressive growth of the male's phallus, the clitoris fails conspicuously to keep pace with the subsequent development of the body. This embryological identity and anatomical diversity was the solid rock on which Freud based his belief that the "repudiation of femininity" was a biological, not cultural, fact. However, Ferenczi overturns Freud's argument and conclusion. He resumes the idea that the anatomical diversity between sexes was the result of a "tremendous struggle" which ended with the capitulation of the female before the brutality of the male, so that the "defeated" one had to take upon herself the pains and duties of motherhood and of the passive endurance of genitality. But Ferenczi adds that it was precisely through her surrender that the female gained in sensitivity and an ability to tolerate suffering. Psychically, she had become wiser and organically "a more *finely differentiated being*" and therefore adaptable to more complex situations, in contrast to the male, who has not been able to evolve, remaining, therefore, "the more primitive" (Ferenczi, 1929c, pp. 103–104). In short, Ferenczi made use of Freud's scheme to overturn the image of the woman as an "inferior" being, who is "worthless" because "castrated" and therefore "hostile" and always ready to take revenge.[9] As a matter of fact, with this reflection Ferenczi attributes to the "defeated" woman all those qualities that, at the end of his long journey, he had come to consider essential qualities of the analyst: sensitivity, elasticity, ability to endure pain and of containing within himself the trauma of the patient. Freud did not know what surrender meant. He was a formidable fighter who had built not only his theory but also his personality upon a "masculine protest." Freud taught us to fight, Ferenczi, on the other hand, to surrender.

The next step will be taken in the *Clinical Diary*. Among the principles of Freudian theory crumbled by Ferenczi, we find also the significance of the clitoris. Ferenczi returns to this issue several times and then, after noting that "it was too hasty to represent female sexuality as beginning with the clitoris…" (July 26, 1932), on August 4 he wrote:

> The ease with which Freud sacrifices the interests of women in favor of those of male patients is striking. This is consistent with the unilaterally androphile orientation of his theory of sexuality. In this he was followed by almost all his pupils, me included.
>
> (Dupont, 1988, p. 287)

Even his genital theory (*Thalassa*), he adds, was clinging "too closely to the words of the master," indeed to the point that "a new edition would mean complete rewriting." What Ferenczi found especially unacceptable was Freud's theory of the woman as a castrated man, which now appeared to him as the expression of "a personal aversion to the spontaneous female-oriented sexuality in women." According to Ferenczi, Freud had perhaps endured a humiliation by "his mother's passionate nature," from which he defended himself by displacing it to the father and by burying it in a theory

> in which the father castrates the son and, moreover, is then revered by the son as a god. In his conduct Freud plays only the role of the castrating god, he wants to ignore the traumatic moment of his own castration in childhood; he is the only one who does not have to be analyzed.
>
> (p. 287)

As can be seen from this conclusion, a whole series of threads were knotted around the theory of female castration, including what had always been a puzzle to Ferenczi. Why would the man who created psychoanalysis not be analyzed?

Hatred of the woman in Ferenczi's analysis with Freud

This dilemma brings us to a long letter that Ferenczi wrote to Freud on December 26, 1912, reacting to a criticism by Jung. In November, Freud experienced a particularly spectacular fainting spell, and, in the aftermath, he tried to reassure his closest followers informing them by letter that he had already begun to analyze the "bit of neurosis" behind this incident. Jung was, however, skeptical for three reasons which he brought together in a single argument: the neurosis of Freud was not just a "bit"; it stood in plain sight already in his identification with the female patient of his dream of Irma's injection (the starting point of Freud's self-analysis); and when Freud had the chance to be analyzed, he stepped back saying that he could not "risk his authority."[10]

In the following weeks, the already frayed relationship between Freud and Jung broke completely. In this difficult situation, Ferenczi sided with Freud. Until then, he had desired to have a relationship with Freud marked by equality, transparency, and reciprocity, but now he repressed such a desire, underlining in a reassuring letter, that Freud's special position of founding father put him above the others, exempting him from the passive role of the patient. Yet, also in this situation, Ferenczi went over the top: he asked Freud to take him in analysis, thus offering himself in the role rejected by Freud!

Ferenczi's analysis would be postponed for years, until October 1914, but in the long letter of December 26, 1912, Ferenczi describes and analyzes two dreams which he presented as material to start with. Here I just mention them, but we will return to them with more details in a later chapter. Both have to do with the hatred of women. The first one was the dream of the Dangerous Coitus, in which Ferenczi is repeatedly attacked by a small cat (as the female genital is also called), the second was the dream of the Penis on the tray, in which a small erect penis is served on a plate as a lunch. Many years ago, these dreams were the starting point of my research.

These dreams are intimately connected. In both a self-castration is staged, as would be repeated again almost two years later, with the famous dream of the Obstructive pessary that Ferenczi dreamt when he finally decided to begin his analysis with Freud. In all these dreams one finds an echo of the dream which stood as a symbol of Freud's self-analysis, Freud's dream of self-dissection of the pelvis.

Of course, in these three dreams, Ferenczi also spoke of the impasse in which his sentimental life was stuck. Ferenczi was soon convinced that at the origin of his neurosis there was a lack of tenderness and love from his strict and controlling mother, but it was only in the last year of his life that he was able to understand how deeply his life had been jeopardized. In the *Clinical Diary*, he tells how his mother had generated in him a hatred which was repressed and replaced by a "compulsive desire to help anyone who is suffering, especially women" and by a tendency to flee "from situations in which [he] would have to be aggressive" (March 17, 1932). Over and above repressing his "infantile aggressiveness" he had developed an artificial "super kindness" and a split between "heart" and "head." The outcome was a "castration hysteria" (April 12) which, besides sometimes affecting his work as an analyst, had ruined his unfortunate sentimental life.

In 1900, at the age of 27, Ferenczi had started a relationship with a 35-year-old woman, Gizella Altschul, then married to Geza Palos, who will eventually become his wife in 1918. It is a complex story that cannot be summed up in a few lines; I therefore refer the reader to the excellent essay by Emanuel Berman (2004).

Ferenczi esteemed her intellectually and was fond of her, but felt no passion, and, above all, she could not give him the children and family he wanted. Gizella had two daughters, Elma and Magda (born in 1887 and 1889). When, in 1909, the younger brother of Ferenczi, Lajos, married Magda, Sándor was very upset. Unable to end the relationship with Gizella to pursue his desires, Ferenczi sought comfort and help from Freud to get rid of his "mother fixation." Things then got complicated when Ferenczi fell in love with Elma, Gizella's "difficult child," while helping her overcome depression through psychoanalysis.

In November 1911, Ferenczi went to Vienna to announce his marriage with Elma to Freud, who stymied him. Ferenczi was still young and hoped to have with Elma the children that Gizella couldn't give him. But Freud had come to appreciate Gizella's qualities and viewed unfavorably Ferenczi's efforts to break away from her. Nevertheless, Freud made himself available as analyst of Elma, presenting the analysis as "a test as to whether she shows herself to be improved," as he wrote to Gizella on December 17. Ferenczi, who was constantly updated by Freud on the progress of this short analysis (January–April 1912), waited with trepidation for the letters on which his happiness depended: he would marry Elma only if she would pass the test. Freud was not very reassuring. On February 13, he wrote to him:

> With regard to your indecision, I would like to note that masochistic impulses very frequently take their course in an unfavorable marital choice. One then gets one's misfortune, is punished by God, and doesn't have to worry anymore.

Here we find a theme dear to Freud, that of the woman as the incarnation of Fate. In the Freudian version of the figure of the "femme fatale" that took shape in the collective imagination of the late nineteenth century (Klerk, 2003c), the fate embodied by the woman was castration or its equivalent, Death. On March 3, Freud writes of the "great leap forward" in Elma's analysis: her "desire of revenge" was traced back to her compulsively repeating "being disappointed by her father."

Once Elma's short analysis with Freud was terminated with none of the problems solved, for a brief time she resumed her analysis with Ferenczi. Elma became more and more taciturn, as he grew more and more confused about his ability to choose the partner of his life. The coup de grace came in June, in the wake of a new idea by Freud that will be developed in the essay *The theme of the three caskets*. Published the ensuing year, the essay takes up a central theme of his self-analysis, well summarized in the dream of the Three Fates—the Three Sisters of Destiny of the Greek myth. In it, Atropos the Terrible cuts the thread of life. It is again the theme of the fatal woman now intertwined with heterogeneous material drawn from myths, folklore, and literature, turning around the idea that the one who is chosen, despite having the appearance of the Goddess of Love, reveals herself to be the Goddess of Death (Freud, 1913b, p. 230). This meditation revolves around an image of the woman that Freud repeatedly evoked and exorcised in the course of his life. Today we would say that it was a meditation on the compulsion to repeat a traumatic attachment in the choice of a new love object.

On June 23, 1912 Freud shared his new idea with Ferenczi, who was an extremely attentive reader and correspondent of Freud. This time, however, he said nothing. Yet, this meditation had a profound impact on him. At first, he experienced an "almost disagreeable increase in sexual libido," as he wrote on July 12. Soon after he then recognized Elma as "the one who brings death." On July 18 he wrote to Freud that he understood that Elma had in his fantasy

> played the role of the one who brings death, who spoils. In puberty, the thought of death, which I had evidently strongly invested with libido, was on my mind night after night.

In the following days, he announced that his "(almost realized) fantasy with Elma" was put "to death" (July 26). A few days later he gave up the analysis of Elma, thus "severing of the last thread of the connection between us" (August 8). But the real troubles had just begun.

In September, just before or after his trip with Freud to Rome, Ferenczi had a "dangerous coitus" with a "whore" which marks the beginning of a real Calvary. A severe pelvic disorder set in: a "hysterical materialization"[11] located at the base of the penis so intense that the physician consulted by Ferenczi made the diagnosis of syphilis. But it was not only the body that would be attacked. Every night he had fantasies of bleeding to death and breathing difficulties became so severe that he planned to undergo nose surgery in Vienna during the Christmas holidays. But he postponed the operation and, in its place, he had two dreams that brought into representation the "thing" that was attacking his body and tormenting his mind. Ferenczi recounts them in the letter to Freud of December 26, 1912, in which he asks to begin the analysis with him.

In the dream of the Dangerous Coitus, Ferenczi is repeatedly attacked by a little black cat. To defend himself he grabs it and throws it onto the floor, but it jumps back again and again, and, despite his remorse for mistreating the little animal, he throws it forcefully until it smashes to bits and a poisonous snake raises its head from the cat's blood.

In this brutal action, Ferenczi recognizes his fear and his hatred of women, his small acts of sadism toward his sister, and the mistreatment of Gizella during the story with Elma. Above all, the dream reminds him of the violent and explosive anger toward his mother who treated him too harshly, like when, at the age of three, he was caught by her mutually touching with his sister and threatened to cut off his penis with a knife. And then the vague sensation of a murderous fantasy which was immediately turned toward himself. At the center of the dream, there was his "impotent rage toward his mother" reactivated by the obstacles placed on his desire to love Elma and dramatized in the "dangerous coitus" with which he simultaneously wanted to do what is "forbidden" and "to be punished." This "dangerous coitus" had cast him in anxiety without end.

If we consider that the "snake" was immediately recognized by Ferenczi as the male genital, the torn kitten may well represent the destroyed female genital. The snake rises from this destruction of Ferenczi's longing for Elma as a *poisonous phallus*. Besides expressing his infantile and current anxieties, Ferenczi's dream stages his *toxic* identification with Freud, as we will clarify in another chapter, when we reveal with whom Ferenczi actually enacted his "dangerous coitus."[12]

The dream was told in connection to Ferenczi's request to begin an analysis with Freud. In reality, neither of them wanted to take this step. Freud did not want to spoil their friendship, while Ferenczi felt paralyzed before the Professor.[13] Only the outbreak of the First World War put an end to procrastination, but even then Ferenczi continued to postpone the first session, showing all his "ambivalence toward the one whom he has chosen as his analyst" (Dupont, 1994, p. 304). And when the date was finally set, he arrived late at the station and missed the train and the first session. Ferenczi loved Freud but was also frightened by him.

Then, as expected, Ferenczi was mobilized for the war and the analysis was concentrated in three short periods of eight and a half weeks (for a total of 131 hours) between October 1914 and October 1916, when Freud decided that the analysis was finished, but not terminated (October 24, 1916), "broken off because of unfavorable circumstances" (November 16, 1916), throwing Ferenczi into a state of despair because he had not yet found the courage to really open up to Freud. In an extreme attempt to make him change his mind, on November 18, 1916, Ferenczi told Freud what he had hitherto kept silent about the dream of the Dangerous Coitus. And then, as if resuming the self-analysis of that dream, he writes: "I am taking out on my mother what I am sparing Gizella and am thereby returning to the original source of my hatred of women." And again: "But what is my fate? Must, I dissociate myself from every woman—like the Flying Dutchman (or, like him, kill the woman and myself)?"

Under "Freud's unrelenting pressure" (Berman, 2004, p. 517), Ferenczi finally married Gizella in 1919. Soon after, on May 23, he wrote to Freud that he had felt a "resistance" toward him from the moment in which he advised him against marrying Elma.

Summarizing the analysis of Ferenczi in *Analysis Terminable and Interminable*, Freud will say that it had ended successfully: his patient had overcome the rivalry with brothers and married the woman he loved... (Freud, 1937a, pp. 220–221).

Hatred of women in Ferenczi's analysis with Severn

Obviously, the "hatred of women" remained completely unresolved in Ferenczi's analysis with Freud. It resurfaced, however, in his third analysis (Ferenczi had a second analysis with Groddeck). In 1932, the long analysis of Elisabeth Severn turned, in fact, into the experience of "mutual analysis" at the center of his *Clinical Diary.* It was only during this experience that Ferenczi was able to relive and understand the traumatic impotence at the origin of his "hatred of women."[14]

When she landed on Ferenczi's couch, Severn was 45 years old, she suffered from chronic fatigue, depression, suicidal impulses, and had a complete amnesia about her first 12 years of life. Analysis will bring to light a fragmentation of the self, which is described in the initial pages of the *Clinical Diary* (where Severn appears under the acronym RN) as the product of a series of extreme violent assaults and abuses.

Initially, Ferenczi had been unpleasantly struck by some traits of Severn, but instead of heeding these impressions, he had shielded himself with the typical superior attitude of the doctor. Shortly after, he began to yield more and more to the patient's requests until the sessions multiplied in an almost unlimited way. In the years 1928–1930, childhood traumas began to resurface in states of deep regression. As he wrote to Groddeck on December 21, 1930, Severn had become his "main patient," the "queen" to whom he devoted up to "four, sometimes five hours a day." However, when the trance dissolved, these reenactments left a sense of uncertainty regarding the veracity of the memories; in other words, the dissociation persisted despite all efforts. Exhausted, at a certain point he was scared by the intensity of the transference: the patient had developed the delusional belief that he was "the perfect lover." Ferenczi then began to step back, limiting the number of sessions, but this increased Severn's demands and imperiousness. They had entered a vicious circle. At this point, she began to say that the analysis would not make any progress if Ferenczi would not allow her to analyze the feelings of hatred she felt in him. Ferenczi resisted for about one year before giving his consent. At the end, with his "huge surprise," he had to admit that "the patient was right in many things" (Dupont, 1988, May 5, 1932).

Mutual analysis had begun. Ferenczi allowed himself to be analyzed by Severn to dissolve those elements of negative countertransference which prevented him from completing her analysis. Thus, Severn was the true architect of the mutual analysis, Ferenczi's last technical experiment, amply documented in the *Clinical Diary*.[15]

Ferenczi and Severn had planned to write a book together about their experience, but Ferenczi's illness and premature death prevented this. Partial heir to this project is Severn's *Discovery of the Self*, the manuscript of which seems to have been read and approved by Ferenczi before his death. Published in 1933, only recently has it been rediscovered and republished. Besides illuminating Severn's contribution to the new vision of the fragmentation of psychic life that we find in the last works of Ferenczi (Bonomi, 2018b), it contains, in anonymous form, the case histories of both Ferenczi that the Severn, something which "immediately transforms the book into one of the essential texts in the history of psychoanalysis" and an indispensable complement to the *Clinical Diary,* as pointed out by Peter Rudnytsky (2015, 2022).

Ferenczi realized that the anxiety he felt about Severn had been coming from his childhood years. In the *Clinical Diary*, he writes:

> Women of her type ... fill me with terror, and provoke in me the obstinacy and hatred of my childhood years. The emotional superperformance, particularly the exaggerated friendliness, is identical to feelings of the same kind I had for my mother. When my mother asserted that I was bad, it used to make me, in those days, even worse. She wounded me most by claiming that I was killing her; that was the turning point at

which, against my own inner conviction, I forced myself to be good, and obedient.

The patient's demands to be loved corresponded to analogous demands on me by my mother. In actual fact and inwardly, I hate the patient, despite all the friendliness I displayed.

(May 5, 1932)

The vicious cycle began to turn into a virtuous one only when Ferenczi felt free to vent his antipathy. This had a "tranquilizing effect" on Severn, who began to reduce her demands. In turn, Ferenczi began to find Severn "less disagreeable" and this allowed him to put himself in the hands of a "very dangerous" patient, trusting her and letting go despite his fear. At this point, Ferenczi's "proud virility" crumbled when—now it is Severn who tells in *The Discovery of the Self*—his infantile psychosis burst onto the scene:

He spoke to me suddenly one day of Strindberg's play *The Father* and became almost immediately the insane son. He broke down and asked with tears in his eyes if I would sometimes think of him kindly after he had been put away in the asylum.

(pp. 96–97)

Severn notes that her patient "evidently expected to be thus sent away." With "terrible pathos," then Ferenczi said: "And we like, when the strait-jacket must be put on us, that it shall be done by our mother."

Severn (1933) writes:

I immediately saw by this that the patient was reexperiencing a severe trauma in which he expected his mother to send him away as insane. ... We already knew something of this story, of his mother as an angry, hysterical woman, often scolding and threatening her child, and especially for a certain event that she had treated with such harshness and vituperation as to make him feel completely crazy and branded as a felon.

(p. 97)

This was the episode that Ferenczi recalled in his letter to Freud dated December 26, 1912, when at the age of three he was "threatened with a kitchen knife" for "mutual touching" with his sister. For Severn, "the unexpected reproduction in the analysis of a part of this painful scene enabled him to acknowledge this traumatically-caused insanity for the first time, as living fact in himself, which was the beginning of its dissolution" (p. 97).

Severn then proceeds to narrate "still another serious trauma, allied to that caused by the mother," an "unscrupulous attack by an adult person on the child's sensibilities, which was ruinous to Ferenczi's mental integrity and subsequent health" (p. 97). When he was a boy of six, he was sexually assaulted by a servant girl, "a comely young woman of voluptuous type who, for the satisfaction of her own urgencies, seduced the child, i.e., used him forcibly as best she could in lieu of an adult partner" (p. 98). The child had been "emotionally shocked" but also "really seduced," that is, made "unduly precocious," arousing in him a desire "that was beyond his years and his capacity, but which remained, nevertheless, to act as a constant excitation, with an inclination to a repetition of the experience" (p. 98).

We find the same episode in the *Clinical Diary*, where Ferenczi in turn recounts, on the page of March 17, how he had gone into "the reproduction of childhood events":

> ... The most evocative image was the vague appearance of female fig-ures, probably servant girls, from earliest childhood; then the image of a corpse, whose abdomen I was opening up, presumably in the dis-section room; linked to this, the mad fantasy that I was being pressed into this wound in the corpse. Interpretation: the after-effect of pas-sionate scenes, which presumably did take place, in the course of which a housemaid probably allowed me to play with her breasts, but then pressed my head between her legs, so that I became frightened and felt I was suffocating. This is the source of my hatred of females: I want to dissect them for it, that is, to kill them.
>
> (Dupont, 1988, p. 123, March 17, 1932)

The question that Ferenczi had repeatedly asked himself was why he was so compliant, why in situations where he had every right to defend himself, he could not be aggressive, and why his clumsy attempts to "be bad" made him feel even more guilty, to the point that he had become a "good guy." All these elements were already contained in the dreams that had accompanied his request for analysis with Freud, but they didn't receive the due attention. The experience with Severn had shaken him deeply, but also changed him.[16]

The fact of reliving the traumatic impotence at the root of his psychotic fault helped him to get insight into his "emotional emptiness," which had been shrouded by overcompensation, fueling his "hatred of women" and his "veneration for man," as he writes on the page of July 19 of the diary, where he recognizes that a residue of "blindness (cowardice) in the face of male authority" was still persisting in him. Ferenczi hoped to be able to work it through, confronting Freud, speaking openly and detaching himself from him calmly, and then perhaps "cure" him.

In short, his experience with Severn had resulted in a new perception of his misogynist alliance with Freud and more generally of his relationship with the Professor. On July 19, he writes

> ... In the end: *insight* into the paranoia of authority.... Realization: my paranoia was only the *imitation* of his, that is, of the powerful adult's.
>
> (p. 252)

A few days later, on August 4, he rethinks his relationship with Freud and his "burning desire" to win his approval by showing him that he had understood him "completely," that now made him feel like "a blindly dependent son." He is amazed at the "ease with which Freud sacrifices the interests of women in favor of male patients," and how everyone, including himself, has followed him in this. And finally, he questions the foundation of the Freudian phallocentric system, the "castration theory in femininity."

Women "cannot have any fear of castration"

In *Analysis Terminable and Interminable*, while questioning what can and cannot be achieved by analysis, Freud anonymously reports two cases histories, one after the other. The first is Ferenczi's, the second is of a woman that has been identified as Emma Eckstein.[17] She had been in analysis with Freud from 1894 to 1897 and again, after a relapse, between 1909 and 1910.

Freud introduced her case history by saying that it posed "the same problem" as the earlier one (Freud, 1937a, p. 222). But his exposition offers no clarifications in this regard. So why does Freud juxtapose Emma Eckstein with Sándor Ferenczi? Perhaps because she endured a castration as a child?[18]

For Freud, the threat of castration was "the severest trauma" [das stärkste Trauma] in a child's life (Freud, 1938b, p. 190). This argument is perplexing because of the underestimation of the impact of abandonment and of the traumas that undermine the sense of cohesion and continuity in a forming Ego. But the point I want to highlight here is another and concerns the disparity in his views between males and females. In fact, according to Freud the traumatic quality of "castration" was true for males but not for females, as he wrote in the summer of 1932, on the eve of his last meeting with Ferenczi, perhaps precisely in response to Ferenczi's provocative question.

That summer, while Ferenczi was noting in his *Clinical Diary* how striking was "The ease with which Freud sacrifices the interests of women in favor of those of male patients" (August 4, 1932), Freud was composing his lecture 32, "Anxiety and instinctual life" of the *New Introductory Lectures on Psycho-Analysis*, where we find the only passage in his entire work on circumcision as a treatment for masturbation—in boys.

Trying to clarify why, in the Oedipal age, the male fears the punishment of castration, Freud explains how the real threats that the child can receive are reinforced by the phylogenetic inheritance. "It is our suspicion," he writes,

> that during the human family's primaeval period castration used actually to be carried out by a jealous and cruel father upon growing boys, and that circumcision, which so frequently plays a part in puberty rites among primitive peoples, is a clearly recognizable relic of it.
>
> (Freud, 1933a, pp. 86–87)

And here, after recalling that the fear of castration is one of the strongest motives of repression and therefore of the formation of neuroses, he adds:

> The analysis of cases in which circumcision, though not, it is true, castration, has been carried out on boys as a cure or punishment for masturbation (a far from rare occurrence in Anglo-American society) has given our conviction a last degree of certainty.
>
> (p. 87)

This passage, unique of its kind, shows all the importance that circumcision—which here, as elsewhere, is interchangeable with castration—had for Freud also on a clinical level. However, it raises some questions. Why Freud displaces this "cure or punishment" only to the far and disliked America, when it was widely practiced in Vienna in the years when he initiated his profession? And why does he refer only to boys? And again, did the case of the American patient who endured a circumcision as "cure or punishment" for masturbation, awake in him the memory of Emma Eckstein's circumcision? Such a memory seems indeed to resurface in his mind, but only as an occasion to deny once again that circumcision can be experienced as a trauma by girls or women. Indeed, his conclusion is that all this is true only for males, since women "cannot have a fear of being castrated [keine Kastrations angst haben können]" (p. 87), as they are castrated by default.

This statement has met various types of objections over time. I want to mention here only the one that goes directly to the point that interests us. In his 1950 article "The Psycho-Biological Origins of Circumcision," Dangar Daly protested against Freud's claim because "In female circumcision (the extirpation of the clitoris) the castration of the homologous penis in girls *actually takes place*" (p. 220, emphasis by Daly).

Confusion between genital mutilation and the loss of an imaginary phallus

In the rich psychoanalytic literature of the first half of the twentieth century, circumcision of men is often discussed, but never circumcision of women. Even in the basic texts where Theodor Reik (1931) develops Freud's thesis on puberty rites in savages, female circumcision is never mentioned. Captain Daly, who had lived for a long time in India, where female circumcision was widespread, could not understand the reason for this silence.

Daly was in analysis first with Freud in 1924 and soon after with Ferenczi, and one can well imagine that he had thoroughly discussed the question with both. He had also had a long correspondence with Freud, which unfortunately was lost in the burning of the hotel in which he lived. It would have helped to make Freud's position clear and explicit.

Eventually, Daly had embraced the vaginal theory of the foreskin that Ferenczi expounds in *Thalassa*, developing it in his own way. He believed that circumcision appeared in the course of human evolution to promote heterosexuality by removing the female element in the boy (the foreskin) and the male element in the girl (the clitoris), thus leaving both with the unconscious desire to re-establish their original bisexual unity. A similar thesis was proposed by Nunberg in his pivotal 1947 study "Circumcision and the Problems of Bisexuality," which however was limited to male circumcision alone. In the pioneering psychoanalytic literature, which is full of references to the Jewish rite of circumcision, there is total silence on female circumcision, the actual "dark continent" of Freud's thinking on women, as was rightly pointed out by Elisabeth Roudinesco (2014, p. 391). Thus, trying to fill this gap, Daly (1950) associated the custom of eradicating the clitoris with the idea that "the women can give up their aggression, become more docile and be good wives," concluding that "this primitive custom is based on sound psychological premises" (p. 221). Reviewing this article, Jacob Arlow, a prominent and prolific analyst, found nothing to complain about and summed up the matter by simply saying that "Circumcision tended to counteract the pathological tendency to inversion in males by removing the female element (prepuce equals vagina). Clitoridectomy accomplished the corresponding object in the female" (Arlow, 1952, p. 437).

This acquiescent and adaptive view will prevail in the following decades, but it was not that of its origins. Freud and his first followers had in fact powerfully rebelled against not only religion in the abstract but also against its rituals, in particular the Jewish ritual of circumcision.[19] This spirit of rebellion against the patriarchal order, shared by his first followers, was valuable, but only for males.

A dissent toward female circumcision did not surface in the vast psychoanalytic literature before circa 1985, except for Marie Bonaparte's articles of 1948, Spitz's powerful overview bibliographic of 1952, and a short but significant remark found in Abram Kardiner's memoirs of his analysis with Freud.[20] Kardiner (1977) wrote:

> The method used to control children ranged from all kinds of dire threats to actual physical means, such as *the removal of the clitoris in the females*. This attitude toward masturbation, and the general puritanical attitude to sex, was responsible for many of the neuroses of the patients that Freud saw. It was largely around this constellation that Freud constructed his libido theory.
>
> (p. 126, emphasis added)

Though one is inclined to believe that female circumcision aroused, in private, a strong opposition from most analysts, the point is that it was not voiced and certainly not represented in the theory. Indeed, Freud's theory of the female castration complex and penis envy had managed to cancel it, just as real incest was canceled by the Oedipus complex theory.

It is rather baffling that Ernest Jones, the man who for over 30 years was the highest authority in psychoanalysis, in the first volume of Freud's official biography justified the turning point of 1897 by saying:

> Freud had discovered the truth of the matter: that irrespective of incest wishes of parents towards their children, and even of occasional acts of the kind, what he had to concern himself with was the general occurrence of incest wishes of children towards their parents, characteristically towards the parent of the opposite sex.
>
> (Jones, 1953, p. 354)

Bennett Simon (1992) has clearly shown that this led to a systematic neglect of the treatment of actual incest, to the point that when the entry "incest" was listed in the index of classic psychoanalytic text, it was sent to the entry "Oedipus complex." The same confusion between fantasy and reality is found in the assimilation of the actual excision of the clitoris into the idea of loss of an imaginary phallus. But one must say that the case of female circumcision is even worse because, the fact that the traumatic impact of infantile sexual abuse had been first exposed and then retracted by Freud, at least served to keep the question open. The same did not occur with female circumcision, which was neither categorized as trauma nor listed among the questionable points of the still widely questioned psychology of woman proposed by Freud.

A different mentality will begin to emerge only in the 1990s when together with other millennial practices of domination over the woman's body—suppression of females at birth, death sentences for female infidelity, forced suicide at the funeral of the groom, and so on—genital mutilation also began to call for attention and to be distinguished from the loss of an imaginary phallus. But even then, the discussion of Emma Eckstein's circumcision would remain taboo. No one wondered if the final scene of her analysis, the scene of the "circumcision of a girl," had a nucleus of historic truth, and, if so, what were the implications.

Asking this question will allow us to access the foreclosed part of the foundation of psychoanalysis.

Notes

1 An updated overview of the anatomy and physiology of the clitoris and its implications for psychoanalytic theory can be found in the article "The Clitoris: Anatomical and Psychological Issues" by Mark Blechner (2017).
2 A review is contained in the 1897 edition of the famous book by Heinrich Ploss and Max Bartel, Das *Weib in der Natur und Völkerkunde* [Woman in nature and in folklore] in which the authors conclude that there was great variability in the extent of the clitoris even among European women.

3 On Freud's psychobiological turn see the partial but remarkable study by Sulloway (1979). The idea of abandoned erogenous zones, around which this turn was built, was present as a collateral line of thought from the end of 1896 (see Freud's letter to Fliess of December 6, 1896).

4 See Freud's letter to Fliess of November 14, 1897.

5 Marie Bonaparte repeatedly underwent genital surgery in the years she was in analysis with Freud (1927) resection and repositioning of the clitoris to bring it closer to the vagina (Dr. J. Halban); 1930 resection of the innervation of the external genitalia and complete hysterectomy (this time she was accompanied by Max Schur, who had been her private physician before becoming Freud's physician, who in turn was forced to undergo a surgical operation after the other in the mouth, due to tumor proliferation in the mouth and to adjust the prosthesis); 1931 new operation by Dr. Halban (no specific information). See Bertin (1982); Amouroux and Stouten (2014). Elisabeth Roudinesco (2014) writes on the subject that Freud was "fascinated by the stories of women whose clitoris was cut must have found the 'biological echo' of his theses in Maria's surgical obstinacy" (p. 390). Underlining the ambivalence of Freud and the failure of the analysis of the princess, E. Roudinesco rightly points out the *impossibility* for Freud to "escape the infernal spiral of the 'cut clitoris', the true *dark continent* of his thought on the feminine" (p. 391).

6 The book in question was *Eros Negro* by Felix Bryk (1928).

7 Bonaparte (1948b) mentions procedures such as resection of the nerves of the genital region, cutting of the labia minora, excision of the clitoris, and removal of the fallopian tubes and ovaries. This report should be read because it describes the cruel practices still in vogue at the time in Central Europe.

8 On Freud's image of Nature as cruel and terrifying, see Trosman (1973).

9 As noted by Rudolf Pfitzner (2006), having taken Freud's theoretical implant as a model, Ferenczi did not come to formulate his own theory of female sexuality; however, he overturned Freud's dogmatic theory in many places, until he opposed Freud himself.

10 The event in question occurred during the famous trip to America in 1909, in which Freud and Jung mutually analyzed their dreams. We will return to the circumstances and modalities of the fainting spell in a later chapter.

11 This painful experience would inspire Ferenczi's article *Phenomena of Hysterical Materialization* (1919).

12 It is worth noting that Ferenczi immediately after published a very short note entitled "Who do you tell your dreams to?" The answer was: "to the person to whom the latent contents of the dream refer" (Ferenczi, 1913a). It should be added that Ferenczi borrowed this idea from Freud himself, who had expressed it in the letter to Ferenczi of 10 January 1910, which was about a dream that Ferenczi had told him.

13 For instance, on April 18, 1914, Ferenczi wrote to him: "my position with respect to you ... is still not completely natural, ... your presence arouses inhibitions of various kinds in me that influence, and at times almost paralyze, my actions and even my thinking."

14 Born in Wisconsin under the name of Leota Loretta Brown, Elisabeth Severn (1879–1959) changed her name after a psychiatric internment and before starting a new life as a "Metaphysician and healer" in 1909. In the following years, she wrote two books on psychotherapy, with various case histories, published in 1913 and 1917, and was in analysis with Smith Ely Jelliffe and Joseph Asch. In 1924, she tried Otto Rank, but that didn't work out and so, in 1925, she went to Budapest to make a last attempt with Sándor Ferenczi. The analysis lasted

many years and was interrupted only in 1933, shortly before Ferenczi's death. See Rachman (2018), and especially Rudnytsky (2022).

15 Balint, Ferenczi's main pupil and his literary heir, refers precisely to this experience when he speaks of Ferenczi's "Great Experiment" as the one that introduced a new perspective on "regression" which was later developed in his clinical masterpiece, *The Basic Fault* (Balint, 1968).

16 "Under the influence of this analysis—he wrote—many things have changed, in my relationship and attitude, in every respect …" (Dupont, 1988, p. 193; August 8, 1932).

17 By Jeffrey Masson (1984), Appignanesi and Forrester (1992), and Rudnytsky (2022). Mikkel Borch-Jacobsen (2021, p. 122) hypothesized instead that she could be Anna von Vest, who, in 1885, at the age of 24, had undergone a castration (removal of the ovaries) after which she remained paralyzed for many years. Anna von Vest consulted Freud when she was 42, in 1903, and her analysis lasted until 1904. Following various relapses, analysis was resumed many times for short periods (1907, 1908, 1910, 1925). She died in 1936 as a result of an ulcer in his stomach, possibly a tumor. It is not clear on what basis Borch-Jacobsen identifies her with the patient in question. Borch-Jacobsen himself admits there is nothing in the information about Anna von Vest which tells us that after the removal of ovaries she had undergone a hysterectomy. Moreover, Freud wrote that the first analysis took place "in the earliest years of my work as an analyst" (Freud, 1937a, p. 222), and neither this detail nor the course of the case presented by Freud (successful treatment, relapse, and second treatment) fits with Anna von Vest's case history.

18 Paradoxically, Freud adduces the two case histories of Ferenczi and Eckstein to illustrate why "a constitutional strength of instinct" places certain patients beyond the reach of analysis (see Rudnytsky, 2022, p. 259).

19 Wilhelm Reich talks about it like this in the interview with Kurt Eissler in 1952,"When a child is born, it comes out from a warm womb … That's bad enough … Then the Jews introduced something six or seven thousand years ago. And that's circumcision. I don't know why they introduced it, it's a mystery. Take that poor penis. Take a knife – right? And start cutting. And everyone says: "No, it doesn't hurt." Everyone says "No, it doesn't hurt." Get it? … Now that's a murder. …"(Reich, 1954, positions in Kindle 443–453).

20 Kardiner's passage, perfectly in line with my research, was pointed out to me by Annie Topalov et Philippe Réfabert. I cannot even include here the book by Bruno Bettelheim *Symbolic Wounds* (1954), who also criticizes Freud's "androcentrism" and his theory of circumcision/castration. Like the psychoanalysts of his generation, he is very critical of Jewish circumcision. However, I find his attempt to highlight the positive and adaptive function of puberty rites very ambiguous (and violent). Furthermore, while Spitz and Bonaparte also talk about the use of clitoridectomy in the contemporary fight against masturbation, Bettelheim is completely silent on the subject.

Chapter 3

"Dark continent"

> "... after all, the sexual life of adult women is a 'dark continent' for psychology"
>
> (Sigmund Freud, 1926b, p. 212)

Castration of women

When the first volume of the correspondence between Freud and Ferenczi was published—the French edition came out first, in 1992—I was very impressed by the dreams that Ferenczi reports in his letter to Freud of December 26, 1912. I felt struck by the significance of the dream about the small erect penis served on a tray, more so than the Dangerous Coitus dream. It seemed to me that it was not only a dream of castration but also a dream *about* castration as a theoretical bastion of the Freudian system. I immediately associated this with *Thalassa*, Ferenczi's apocalyptic work whose hero, the phallus, is described as the *living monument of a catastrophe of cosmic dimensions.*

I began to wonder what catastrophe was being talked about. Beyond its manifest meaning, did this myth also have an unconscious meaning? And if so, what was the unspeakable element from which it drew its strength? What was the particular trauma intercepted and dramatized by Ferenczi with his universal myth?

Pressed by these questions I plunged into reading of *The Interpretation of Dreams*. Re-reading it from that perspective was a singular experience. The original edition consisted almost exclusively of Freud's dreams. This clamorous act of self-disclosure had been a hypnotic attraction for those who would soon become his pupils and followers. There is a great irony in the fact that in orthodox psychoanalysis the analyst will be described as an anonymous and impenetrable blank screen. Clinging to this fiction perhaps created a necessary dam to avoid being inundated by the images that came from Freud's unconscious. Be that as it may, I began to feel the

DOI: 10.4324/9781003353058-5

reverberation of a single catastrophic castration event—not symbolic or imaginary, but real.

This idea was particularly difficult to integrate because in psychoanalysis the word "castration" referred exclusively to something symbolic. No analyst used this term to refer to a real event. I still remember a passage by André Green (1990) in which the reader was warned that, in psychoanalysis, *it was never a question of real castration*. While trying to keep his warning in mind, this metaphorical dimension soon began to crumble before my eyes, as many of Freud's crucial passages took on a dramatic literal meaning.

I presented my idea to Michele Ranchetti, who was not at all surprised. He had recently made available in Italian two articles by Albrecht Hirschmüller based on the medical records of two female patients of Freud found in the Kreuzlingen hospital, and one case was about castration. Ranchetti set me an appointment with Prof. Gerhard Fichtner, Director of the Institute of the History of Medicine of the University of Tübingen, an undisputed authority in the field of Freudian studies, to discuss my hypothesis: namely, that the young Freud had been shocked by some cases of actual castration encountered in the course of his medical practice. Fichtner was at first perplexed, then, after a long silence, he got up and said: follow me. In a short time, he emerged from the institute's underground library with a large number of medical books and articles in German, all on the castration of women and the circumcision of children in the second half of the nineteenth century. At that point, a scenario opened up before me that had been systematically ignored by historians of psychoanalysis.

Let me give just one example. In an 1887 book by Freidrich Merkel entitled—for simplicity, I report here everything in English—*Contribution to the Study of Castration in the Neuroses*, the castration of hysterical women is indicated as the most discussed problem of those years in psychiatric circles. In the impressive bibliography, a number of studies were cited, all published in 1886, among which: *Castration in Hysteroepilepsy* by Böhmi, *Cure of Hysteria by Castration* by Forel, *Cure of Moral Insanity by Castration* by Heilbrunn, *Castration of the Woman* by Heydenreich, *Contributions to the Problem of Castration* by Prochownich, *Castration of Woman in Nervous Diseases* by Ruderhausen, *On Castration in Neurosis* by Schröder, *On Castration of the Woman in Surgery* by Tissier, and *Hysteria Cured by Castration* by Widmer. These are just a few of the 35 studies, including various university dissertations, all published within a few months, from the summer of 1886 to the end of that year, all on the castration of women. In those months the number of cases known and discussed in the medical literature increased from 180 to 215 (Merkel, 1887, pp. 54–55). Taking stock of the situation in 1896, the year in which the word "psychoanalysis" was coined by Freud, Krömer reviews the results of 300 operations: the success rate was 70%. His long (74 pages) article, titled *Beitrag zur Castrationsfrage* [Contribution to the Problem of Castration], began by saying that

> The question if morbid states and processes in the genital organs have an influence on the nervous system, and on mental illness, has been for 20 years in the middle of the psychiatric and medical controversies.
>
> (Krömer, 1896, p. 1)

This simple information is not found in any book on the history of psychoanalysis. In 1903, at the beginning of the book *Über die Wirkungen der Castration* [On the Effects of Castration] Paul Möbius wrote: "If before men were castrated often, while women exceptionally, now the castration of women is so frequent that the cases of busy operators are hundreds, while the castration of men is relatively rare" (p. 22). The reason for this disparity is discussed by Conrad Rieger in a book published in 1900 under the title *Die Castration in rechtlicher, socialer und vitaler Hinsicht* [Castration in Legal, Social and Vital Perspectives], written with the aim of contributing to "the emancipation of psychiatry from the superstitions of medicine" (p. 1), in an attempt to curb the *"furor operatorius chirurgicus."*[1]

According to Rieger, contemporary ideas about the sexual organs were subject to archaic beliefs, such as the idea that the testicles were a manifestation of "good" while the ovaries were a manifestation of "evil" (pp. 64–65). The issue also involved the legal status of castration. In Germany, the castration of a healthy man was illegal and, according to a few jurists, the removal of the ovaries in a healthy woman also was, in principle, a crime. Yet in practice, it was never considered as such, since a doctor's declaration that the patient was suffering too much, was too nervous or too feeble, and so on, would have been sufficient to turn the crime into a therapy. In short, while the castration of a male was perceived as a vital offense in a healthy body, that of the female was not. Her body was sick by definition!

This practice was not limited to Germany but was widespread in many areas of the civilized world. In America, at the turn of the century, Elizabeth Severn had been subjected to castration against her will, before changing her name and starting a new life as a "metaphysicist" and healer.[2]

A gynecological scandal

The year 1886, in which the *"furor operatorius chirurgicus"* exploded, is an important year in the history of our discipline. On Easter Sunday of that year, Freud opened his doctor's office and began his professional life as a neurologist, after returning from a long study trip to Paris and Berlin. The Freud we know begins to take shape only in 1892, when together with his mentor, Josef Breuer, he outlined the cathartic theory and therapy, revisiting a unique experience that Breuer had had more than ten years before, the famous "talking cure" of Anna O. from which the *Studies on Hysteria* developed (Breuer and Freud, 1895). But one can well imagine that the emergence of the word from the body was neither immediate nor simple.

Even Anna O.'s story had been more complicated than its actual presentation. We know this because Henry Ellenberger (1972) found her file at the Bellevue sanatorium in Kreuzlingen, which, in those years, had been a state-of-the-art clinic. Following an advice of Ellenberger, Albrecht Hirschmüller visited it again in search of other clinical material, just in time to save a couple of medical records from the papers ready to be trashed. One concerned a young woman of 24, Nina R., whom Breuer had sent to Freud (Hirschmüller, 1978). Freud had her in treatment for a few months in 1891 and then again at the beginning of 1893. After the worsening of her symptoms, he had sent her to Carl Fleischmann, a trusted gynecologist (he had followed the deliveries of Freud's children), who practiced a uterine curettage due to the excess of "vaginal catarrh." But it didn't help, and so Breuer and Freud took steps to send her to their trusted sanatorium.

The Kreuzlingen doctors diagnosed her as suffering from hysteria. Among the papers, there was also an earlier diagnosis by Krafft-Ebing, in which the pains in the abdomen were attributed to the left ovary. In January 1894, Breuer wrote to Robert Binswanger, the director of the sanatorium, for news. Since the patient was not improving and the vaginal catarrh had reappeared, they were considering castration. On March 12, Breuer replied that he did not consider the procedure legitimate: the catarrh certainly needed to be treated but it was not necessary to remove uterus and ovaries.

On March 23, Breuer wrote a long and detailed letter explaining his views on castration. He considered himself a "heretic" as he did not share the enthusiasm for this new practice which was spreading among doctors as an "epidemic." As proof of the collective madness that was going through the medical world, he told the following anecdote concerning a patient of his with persistent pain. Since she had one ovary larger than the other, Krafft-Ebing had recommended to remove it. The removed ovary had only cysts unrelated to the hysterical pains, as evidenced by the fact that the other ovary had the same cysts. Instead of acknowledging it, the surgeon decided to remove the other ovary as well to prevent the objection that the operation was unsuccessful because it was incomplete! Breuer had tried to save at least one ovary, but the "professional conscience" of the surgeon prevailed!

I stress this point because the themes of the "incomplete treatment" and of the "professional scruples" will re-appear in the dream from which psychoanalysis was born, the dream of Irma's injection. This reasoning was in fact paradigmatic of the medical attitude of the time: those who opposed castration risked being accused of lack of professional conscience, as it occurred to Dr. Israel years earlier. But here I must pause to explain the origin and the spreading of the castration of women, a treatment that, for a long time, will be used for all types of mental disorders.

Since ancient times the uterus had been considered the seat of hysteria, as indicated by the name, which in Greek designates the uterus. In the modern era, this idea resumed vigor around 1840, when Thomas Laycock advanced the hypothesis that the uterus was controlled by the ovaries. Shortly after, Romberg made the ovaries the key organ of the new and powerful psychiatric gynecology. In 1846, Romberg then redefined hysteria as a reflex neurosis caused by an irritation that from the genital organs spread upward through the abdominal sympathetic ganglia, arriving to cause convulsions, paralysis, and the typical hysterical bolus. In the new medical view of the body, the irritation of the genitals was the cause of a state of "irritable weakness" that makes the whole body sensitive to the spread of hysteric attack well beyond the moments of maximum irritation, such as the premenstrual period.[3] In 1872, the German gynecologist Alfred Hegar introduced a new surgical technique to remove the ovaries. In the same year, the same operation was introduced by Battey in America. Thus, in 1880, outlining the "constant effort to expand the range of local surgical treatments," James Israel caustically wrote: "The culmination of this effort is probably the bold attempt to conquer that protean demon of hysteria by the extirpation of both ovaries; that is, by the castration of women" (Israel, 1880, p. 241).

Dr. Israel considered it a folly. He had just become head of a surgery unit at the Charité of Berlin when a young patient of 22 years, who suffered from headaches, vomiting, and ovarian pain, arrived at the hospital with the request of being subjected to castration, after eight different physicians had each recommended that she undergo this procedure, as it was the only effective remedy. Initially, the girl was reluctant because she did not want to give up the possibility of having children, but then the pain had pushed her to entrust all hope of recovery to the remedy suggested by the authoritative group of doctors. Israel did not agree, but since the young woman was adamant, on December 31, 1879, after explaining all the risks she was facing, he performed the operation under anesthesia. The improvement was rapid and impressive, as he explained at a conference held a few weeks later in Berlin, when he surprised everyone by adding:

> Now, gentlemen, this would no doubt be a beautiful cure of a severe hysteria through extirpation of both ovaries had I in fact performed such surgery. But my operative procedure differed from Hegar's and Battey's in this fundamental way: apart from a simple skin incision made while she was under anesthesia, I did nothing to the patient. Both the operation and the postsurgical treatment were a mere pretense, a stage performance acted out in painstaking detail for the purpose of making the patient believe that a castration had truly taken place. This goal has been achieved with spectacular success.[4]

By staging a "simulated castration" [Scheincastration], Israel had demonstrated that the positive effect of the operation was solely due to suggestion. However, when the young patient understood from the hype aroused by the press what had really happened to her, she felt defrauded, the pains returned immediately and she took refuge in Hegar, demanding from the prominent gynecologist what she had been denied: a "true castration."

Of course, Hegar did not miss the opportunity to blame Israel in public for his lack of professional conscience (Hegar, 1880). The condemnation was unanimous and the new therapy of hysteria began to spread, becoming an elective treatment in 1885, following Hegar's new study on the relationship between sexual illness and nervous affection. The German gynecologist explained that the aim of castration was to "remove the cause of neurosis or at least a causal factor without whose elimination is impossible to achieve a cure or even a simple improvement" (quoted in Merkel, 1887, pp. 6–7). Although it encountered many opponents—including Charcot, who had become an ideal model for Freud in the course of his studies in Paris in 1885—this gynecological treatment of mental disorders became more and more widespread.

We can now return to Nina R. and to the letter Breuer wrote to Robert Binswanger on March 23, 1894, protesting vehemently: subjecting the young patient to such treatment, he wrote, would be a "gynecological scandal." However, since he was addressing a distinguished and esteemed colleague to whom he regularly sent difficult cases, Breuer added that, if he remained in his determination, he was ready to leave the question up to Hegar—the famous gynecologist who invented the technique to remove ovaries.

On September 4, 1894, after having examined the patient, Alfred Hegar wrote that he was in favor of her hospitalization even if there was no expectation of a cure with the treatment of the genital disorder alone. In any case, he added, the latter was too important to not eliminate it or at least partially cure it (in other words, there was nothing that advised against the operation). In October, Nina R. was transferred to Freiburg, to Hegar's clinic, but the operation was postponed because of a tuberculosis that had to be treated first.[5] At this point the documents are silent, but the story was not over. Nina had a brother whom, in July 1895, Breuer sent to Berlin to Wilhelm Fliess, for a new type of operation strongly advocated by Freud.

An alternative therapy

A close friend of Freud, Wilhelm Fliess was a specialist in diseases of the nose. In these difficult years, his relationship with Fliess was Freud's most important intellectual and emotional bond, as evidenced by their copious, sometimes almost daily correspondence, which took effect at the end of 1892. It became passionate in the years during which Freud was extraordinarily productive, but finally faded in the summer of 1900. Their friendship had been strengthened by a scientific alliance, based on a precise agenda: the search for the sexual causes of neurosis. It was Freud who pushed Fliess in this direction, receiving in return, in 1897, the idea of universal bisexuality. This idea will then have a central role in the breakdown of their association.

In his essay "Psychoanalysis and Psychiatry," which in 1919 won a prize awarded by Freud himself, August Stärcke argued that psychoanalysis belonged to a line of thought on hysteria which, starting with the ancient theory of the wandering uterus, was reorganized in the 1840s around the idea of uterine reflex neurosis, before being interrupted by the proponents of the cerebral localization. The theory of the nasal reflex neurosis developed by Wilhelm Fliess with the support and help of Freud was situated on the same trajectory. Thus, since 1893, while carrying out psychic treatment through the cathartic method, Freud enthusiastically embraced the theory of his dear friend, who had identified on the nose certain "genital spots" that acted by reflex. Thanks to this upward displacement of the *locus morbi* from the sexual organs to the nose, Freud was able to return to that sexual etiology which had, initially, and under the influence of Charcot and Breuer, aroused in him a profound aversion.[6]

The year 1894 then marked a period of great disagreement between Freud and Breuer, who was skeptical of Fliess' ideas. For Freud, it was also a period of growing pessimism about what psychotherapy could achieve. It was then that Freud formulated the theory of the somatic origin of anxiety, coming to the conclusion that, in certain situations, anxiety "turns out to be not further reducible by psychological analysis, nor amenable to psychotherapy" (Freud, 1894b, p. 97). At the same time, he intensely studied Hegar's books on the castration of women.[7]

He also wrote a review of Hegar's latest book, *The Sexual Instinct*, which was published in the *Wiener klinische Rundschau* on February 3, 1895. His review was not devoid of a subtle derision toward the highest authority of psychiatric gynecology.[8]

Shock, revelation, and conversion

Freud's boldness was supported by the pact that bound him to Fliess and their alternative project, which in those days made a qualitative leap. Until then Fliess had limited himself to intervening mechanically on the nose of masturbators, with probes, cauterization, or brushing of cocaine (all means also used by Freud), but now the decision had been taken: he will intervene surgically to remove a portion of the turbinate.[9] The patient chosen for the new operation was a female patient of Freud's whom Fliess visited in December. She was Emma Eckstein, a 30-year-old woman who would play a leading role in the untold history of psychoanalysis. Faced with the new therapeutic plan, Freud hesitated, but then the trust in his friend prevailed. Even though this operation today appears senseless, one could say that in the hands of another doctor the patient would have been subjected to a "castration," in the sense of removal of the ovaries, had Eckstein not already endured such a treatment. In fact, Freud later wrote: "Her condition was obviously of a hysterical nature, and it had defied many kinds of treatment" (Freud, 1937a, p. 222).

The nose surgery was performed in Vienna around February 23. It should have been harmless, but Fliess forgot a piece of gauze in her nasal septum. The situation worsened and at the beginning of March, when the gauze was finally removed by another surgeon, Emma Eckstein risked bleeding to death under the eyes of Freud who nearly fainted—the first in a long series of "fainting spells." As clearly demonstrated by the dramatic tone of the letters that Freud wrote to his friend Fliess in March 1895, it was not the corpselike paleness of his patient or the sight of blood that upset him. He had been shocked by the damage that, animated by the best of intentions, they had done to the "poor girl."

Over the following weeks and months, Freud will regularly look into Emma's throat to check on the healing process. However, the incident did not cast doubts on the validity of their choice, especially since at this point even Breuer began to support it. Breuer, who had been against Fliess' theory, sent several patients to Berlin in early 1895 to have their noses operated on by Fliess, including his daughter Dora, then 13.[10] On May 25, Freud wrote to Fliess: "Breuer is not recognizable ... He has accepted the whole of your nose [theory] and is promoting an enormous reputation for you in Vienna..." Apparently, the incident had no repercussions and Freud had new reasons to continue to look at Fliess as the prototype of the healer. In fact, he himself underwent nose operations several times at Fliess' hands.

In July, Breuer also sent a younger brother of Nina R. (the patient who had been placed in Hegar's hands) to Berlin to have his nose operated on and Fliess contacted Freud to inquire about the boy's family. Freud replied on July 13. A few days later he had the dream from which psychoanalysis was born.

Years later Freud would imagine the text of the marble tablet that should have celebrated it in this way[11]:

> Here, on July 24, 1895,
> the secret of the dream
> revealed itself to Dr. Sigm. Freud

The dream in question was the famous dream of Irma's injection, the guiding or paradigmatic dream from which *The Interpretation of Dreams* (Freud, 1900) unfolds. Irma is the fictitious name of a difficult patient who created troubles for her doctor. Today it would be called a "countertransference" dream (Langs, 1984; Lotto, 2001). But this subjective dimension was not considered by Freud, as suggested also from the name chosen by Freud for his patient. "Irma" comes from "ermen" and means "universal." As a matter of fact, in his dream a figure of woman surfaces of whom Freud will never cease to speak.

The revelation to which Freud refers was spread over time and took place in waves. The meaning of the dream continued to enrich itself as certain themes were taken up and amplified by other dreams, in the course of a process that lasted many years—Freud's self-analysis. However, in retrospect, this revelation appeared to Freud as the moment of a radical change, the beginning of a new time. This break in the linear time of history was well captured by Erik Erikson and Jacques Lacan in their readings of this dream.

In the first scene, Freud looks inside Irma's mouth, which in the dream merges with her vulva, and recoils with a feeling of horror. For Erikson (1954) Irma's oral cavity was a symbol both "of a woman's procreative inside, which arouses horror and envy" (p. 46) as well as of Freud's unconscious, fertilized, and ready to give birth to psychoanalysis. The act of looking in the horrible hole of Irma's throat is thus identified as the moment of an "initiation, conversion, and inspiration" that transforms Freud into a hero who in turn will be looked upon by mankind "with pity and terror, with ambivalent admiration and ill-concealed abhorrence" (p. 46).[12]

Although not knowing precisely what had aroused so much horror in Freud, Erikson perfectly grasped the transitive quality of the process: as in a ceremony of initiation, this "horrible" thing, which defies all capacity to think, invests Freud, takes possession of him, and changes him. Even if he cannot give a name to it, Erikson associates it with the "head of the Medusa" (p. 35). Naturally, he knew well that this mythological figure was for Freud the mark of the horror aroused by the woman's "castrated" genitals. For Erikson, the horror had been so intense that the dream could have been a nightmare. If it was not, it was only because in the end, as in a religious ceremony, the "solution" had appeared: the word "trimethylamine" printed in letters that float in the air before the eyes of the dreamer.

Also for Lacan (1954/1955), the act of looking into Irma's throat/vagina had been a de-structuring moment. He described it thus:

> There's a horrendous discovery here, that of the flesh one never sees, the foundation of things, the other side of the head, of the face, the secretory glands *par excellence*, the flesh from which everything exudes, at the very heart of the mystery, the flesh in as much as it is suffering, is formless, in as much as its form in itself is something which provokes anxiety.
>
> (p. 154)

In the view of both Erikson and Lacan, Freud was not annihilated by the anxiety because of the chemical formula of trimethylamine which appears to him, in his dream, as an "apocalyptic revelation" (p. 157), an enigmatic oracle similar to a religious formula. Lacan associates it with the Islamic formula *"There is no other God but God.* There is no other word, no other solution to your problem, than the word" (p. 158). In the next chapter, we will try to understand its meaning. But it must immediately be said that Lacan grasps well an ontological break: the *word* appears in place of the *body.* Until then Freud had been a physician and as such had had to take care of the body, but from now on this will no longer be the case. Psychoanalysis was born because the Unconscious had spoken. Describing the moment in the dream when Freud's ego is overwhelmed by anxiety to the point of fading away, Lacan wrote: *"And finally another voice is heard"* (p. 159; emphasis added). We will be concerned with this *"voice"* in the next chapter. For the moment, we will keep on sharpening the contours of the "dark continent."

The scene of the circumcision of a girl

Erikson and Lacan knew nothing about the botched operation on the nose to which Fliess and Freud had submitted Emma Eckstein in February 1895. Their reconstructions were in fact based on the first edition of Freud's letters to Fliess which appeared in 1950 (Bonaparte et al., 1950), from which all passages referring to this patient were deleted.

It was not until 1966 that new information became accessible. Max Schur, the doctor who had followed Freud in his last difficult years had also been Marie Bonaparte's personal doctor. From her, Schur received a copy of the Freud/Fliess correspondence, in spite of the prohibition to access to these letters. He needed it to write his biography of Freud, but the material he found in the letters was so interesting that, in 1966, he published some of the censored passages in an article entitled "Some additional 'day residues' of the specimen dream of psychoanalysis." These passages made it possible to identify Irma as Emma Eckstein. As a real person, Irma was another patient, Anna Hammerschlag, Anna Freud's godmother, but since in the dream Irma was a condensation of several women, as Freud repeatedly explained, it is correct to say that Irma was *also* Emma, at least with respect to the imagistic center of the dream: the mouth/nose that merges with the vulva/clitoris. Here too the choice of "Irma" as the name of her patient is significant: Irma=Emma, since both names derive from "ermen" (universal). For Freud, it was a representation of the figure of woman to which he refers in various other dreams, the *femme fatale* in which sexuality conjugates with death.

The access to the letters to which Schur referred was not made public by the Freud Archives. Consequently, his thesis hung in the air for many years, until it was picked up by Jeffrey Moussaief Masson, a brilliant young man who had been assigned the task of editing the complete edition of the letters of Freud to Fliess. He had obtained this prestigious and delicate assignment by gaining the trust of both Kurt Eissler, the founder of the Freud Archives, and Anna Freud. One year before the publication of the letters, Masson collided with his patrons by publishing a book entitled *The Assault on Truth. Freud's Suppression of the Seduction Theory*, which caused a great turmoil in the psychoanalytic world.

With this book Masson challenged a cornerstone of the official narrative of the birth of psychoanalysis, reviving the theory that Freud had abandoned in 1897, the idea that the specific cause of neurosis was a repressed memory of sexual assault endured in childhood. And he did so by linking this turning point to Eckstein's nose operation. Schur had already underlined how Freud's idealizing transference toward Fliess had led him to side with his friend in minimizing his surgical error to the point of attributing Emma's copious nosebleeds to her "hysterical desire." For Masson this alliance between two men at the expense of a victimized woman explained the suppression of the seduction theory: just as he had closed his eyes before the error of Fliess, similarly Freud disavowed the reality of sexual assault on children by adults.

This thesis presents, however, some inconsistencies, including the fact that the patient who had inspired Freud's idea of "infantile sexual shock" six months after the accident, was precisely Emma Eckstein. One would therefore be rather tempted to say that it was the feelings of guilt for the damage inflicted on the poor girl that allowed such a new idea to break through mind of her analyst.

Masson, then, did not seek or failed to clarify the relationship between the theory of infantile sexual shock and the shock stored in the dream from which psychoanalysis arouses—I am referring to the moment when Freud looks into Irma's mouth/vulva and recoils horrified. In his careful study of Freud's self-analysis, Didier Anzieu (1986) describes this scene as a "gynecological examination in disguise, a substitute for it" (p. 145). But Anzieu was speaking only in a metaphorical sense, since he simply neglected, with selective inattention, to acknowledge the practice of actual castration. In his monumental and indispensable study of Freud's self-analysis, he uses the word "castration" more than 60 times, but not once in the ordinary medical meaning it had in Freud's time. In fact, psychoanalysis has so radically changed the meaning of this word that today it is difficult to convince an audience of psychoanalysts that, in Freud's time, it denoted an attack on a female body disguised as "therapy." In the vocabulary of psychoanalysis, the word "castration" will, in fact, be defined entirely in the masculine, referring to an imaginary amputation of the penis. So, Anzieu, while recognizing the shock stored in the Irma dream as a "gynecological operation," was far from thinking that the operation on the nose performed by Fliess, *really* had such a value, as even Kurt Eissler and Harold Blum, both directors of the Freud Archives, eventually agreed.[13]

Moreover, Masson gave no weight to the scene of "the circumcision of a girl" that Emma Eckstein brings at the end of her analysis, despite the fact that Schur had identified it as the moment of transition from the theory of real trauma to the one of "pathogenic fantasies." The final result was that the epicenter of the drama was displaced from the genitals to the nose. The psychoanalytic audience fully adhered to this shift, with only one exception, Charles Rycroft, who wrote in his review of the book:

> Rather surprisingly, Masson does not refer to the fact that many child-rearing and surgical procedures involve literal violations of bodily integrity and must inevitably be experienced by small children as assaults, regardless of the conscious or unconscious motives of the parents and surgeons who inflict such traumas on their children. This is a curious omission, since it would be possible to resurrect the traumatic theory of neurosis on the basis of the mishandling of small children.
>
> (Rycroft, 1984)

Masson must have been struck by Rycroft's remark on his "curious omission." In the third chapter of his book, he had in fact reported the scene of her circumcision, treating it as a fantasy. But soon after Rycroft's review, he began researching this type of operation on children. Two years later he published a collection of German and French texts that appeared between 1880 and 1900, in a book entitled *A Dark Science: Women, Sexuality and Psychiatry in the Nineteenth Century*. The book captures and illustrates the "fallacies and contradictions underlying nineteenth-century gynecology and psychiatry" (Masson, 1986, p. 7), but in no way connects these practices to the case history of Emma Eckstein or to the dream from which psychoanalysis arose.

The great fear of masturbation

When, in 1992, I developed the hypothesis that the young Freud must have been struck and shocked by a real castration, I did not know anything about this background. A specialized literature on these practices did exist in the field of the history of medicine, yet their association to the birth of psychoanalysis was simply *unthinkable*. Alongside the texts of psychiatric gynecology, there were also articles written by pediatricians recommending circumcision in both males and females. The range of interventions practiced was vast. The clitoris could be cut or scarified, the labia minora cut or shortened, or, at once, the entrance to the vagina could be cauterized with "ferrum candens" (red-hot iron) or caustic substances, and so on. The endless horror of which Erikson and Lacan were speaking was beginning to have a concrete meaning.

　The practice of amputating the clitoris was introduced in England in the 1850s by Isaac Baker Brown as a cure for both masturbation and hysteria in young women and girls, causing a stir and heated debate that culminated in 1867 in his expulsion from his medical association.[14] Nonetheless, the intervention began to spread in both Europe and North America. As summarized by Norbert Finzsch (2018), "the cliteridectómial frenzy of the 18th, 19th and 20th centuries was deeply rooted in homophobic and gynophobic tendencies that identified the clitoris as an organ of bodily transgression" (p. 11).

The German term *Beschneidung* (circumcision), used by Freud when reporting the scene of Emma Eckstein, applied to both genders and in females included the excision of the clitoris. In the German pediatric literature, however, it was preferred to speak simply of the "operation." Everyone understood what it was referring to. In the German world the "operation" was imported by the pediatrician F. J. Behrend and disseminated in a work of 1860 in which he writes:

> Dr. Johnson advises to perform a small operation in order to provoke such a pain with its wound that it would leave in the child a lasting psychic impression and would make any attempt at masturbation painful. In boys the operation should be done on the prepuce, making a cut, etc. In girls it should, similarly, consist of a strong cauterization on the labia majora or inside the vagina entrance or, as Dr. Gros suggests, of small excisions all around the clitoris. With such scarifications, he succeeded in one case in really eliminating the evil.
>
> (Behrend, 1860, p. 328 ff.)

The context in which this practice took hold is the social phenomenon that historians of the mentality have called "the great fear of masturbation" (Stengers & Van Neck, 1984), a modern social phenomenon that can be considered as a side effect of, or a reaction to the secularization of morality prompted by the Enlightenment. Treatises against the "solitary vice" were circulating in Europe since 1700, but the qualitative leap took place with Tissot's famous treatise of 1760, which had extraordinary success and diffusion, becoming the main vehicle of propaganda for the "great fear," thanks to a series of exemplary case histories in which the "solitary vice" inexorably leads to illness and death.

Initially, the vice was found only in young men and was not tackled with particularly punitive measures. However, as reported in an impressive bibliographic survey authored by the Hungarian psychoanalyst René Spitz, "While up to 1849, masturbation was treated mostly with hydrotherapy, diet, etc., between 1850 and 1879 surgical treatment was recommended more frequently than any of the other measures." In the second half of the nineteenth century, Spitz tells us, "Sadism becomes the foremost characteristic of the campaign against masturbation," in line with the shifting of the frontline of the struggle against masturbation in the direction of women and children, both "suitable objects for retaliation."[15]

Michel Foucault, in the course at the Collège de France in 1974/1975, ascribed this attitude to the "medicalization of the abnormal" which marked a new phase of the Christian discourse of the flesh, determined on the one hand by the emergence of the nuclear family and on the other by the fact that in the modern state the body became a public health issue. The new family, to which all immediate power over the child was delegated but which was controlled by the medical knowledge and technique, then became a "principle of normalization," of "correction of the abnormal."[16]

An example of the new practices' extreme sadism is the long article "Onanism with nervous disorders in two little girls," which appeared in 1882 in the prestigious French magazine *L'Encephale*, and authored by Dr. Demetrius Zambaco, who later became correspondent of the French Academy of Sciences. This article, which was included in Masson's "dark science" collection, did not elicit any protest; on the contrary, was widely cited in the scientific literature of the time. Here I report only the conclusions to give an idea of the cultural climate:

> It is reasonable to presume that cauterization with red-hot iron deadens the sensitivity of the clitoris, and that if repeated a certain number of times, it can entirely destroy the clitoris. The second sensitive genital spot, the vulvar orifice, is also deadened by cauterization, and therefore one can easily imagine that children, once their genitals have become less sensitive, would be less likely to touch themselves there.
>
> It is equally probable that, once the clitoris and the vulvar orifice become the site of a more or less intense inflammation following the operation, touching there will be painful instead of a source of pleasure.
>
> Finally, fear at the sight of the instrument of torture, and the images that a red-hot iron produces in the imagination of children, should also be counted among the beneficial effects of curative cauterization.[17]

It should also be added that the same author vigorously protested against the use of similar means with males, as remarked in the introduction to the reprint of the article published in France in 1978.

Returning to René Spitz and his bibliographic survey of 1952, he engaged himself in this research on "the innumerable, varied and subtle practices of a refined cruelty," because it seemed to him that "in psychoanalytic circles one does not always realize how extremely cruel the persecution of the masturbator has been up to our day." But his plea went unheard; the imperative of those years was in fact that psychoanalysis must not concern itself with external reality. There are many traces of this trend. In an interview released in 1984, John Bowlby thus describes his psychoanalytic training, which took place in the 1940s,

> there was extreme pressure to turn your back on real-life events, and to give pure attention to the patient's internal world and way he interpreted

things. I was taught that to pay attention to real-life events was naive and irrelevant to psychoanalysis.

(Fortune, 1991, pp. 71–72)

In the 1950s, this trend was further strengthened. The systematic underestimation of the traumatic moment reflected an attitude of denial that the horrors of the Second World War had paradoxically reinforced. The tendency to downplay the consequences of the dramas of the civilian population, prison camps, forced migrations, and the Shoah, even seemed to grow with time, to the point that, in 1968, Ernest Rappaport found himself reiterating that "Traumatic neuroses are mentioned in the psychoanalytic literature especially after World War II almost only for the purpose of denying their existence" (p. 719). Having survived the Nazi extermination camps, Rappaport complained above all of the tendency to interpret the traumas suffered by the victims of the Holocaust according to the classical scheme, that is, explaining the effect of external events on the basis of predisposing factors, or, in psychoanalytic terms, on the basis of the Oedipal conflict.[18] This attitude was a consequence of the excessive traumatic pain produced by persecution and war. As it will be said later: "denial and repression reigned during this period of silence" (Jucovy, 1992, p. 267).

One exception was Niederland's research (1951, 1959a, 1959b, later collected in his 1984 book) on the famous case of President Schreber, whose delusional system was re-read by Freud in 1910. Niederland brought to light something that Freud had overlooked, namely, that Schreber's father, a physician transformed into a god in his son's delusions, had been a prominent figure in the crusade against masturbation in the second half of the nineteenth century. In order to save boys from this plague that made them "stupid and dumb," "impotent," "sterile," "*lebensmüde*" (suicidal), and predisposed to "nervous disorders [*Nervenkrankheiten*]," he had devised a series of mechanical instruments to prevent them from masturbating—mechanisms that shed light on many of the contents of his son's delusions.

The "secrets of childhood diseases"

In the second scene of the dream of Irma's injection, Freud examines his patient again, this time assisted by a group of men. Two of them were his assistants at the children's hospital where Freud worked. An important chain of thoughts then leads "from the sick child to the children's hospital" and the practice of examining children undressed. Freud, however, cut it short, saying: "Frankly, I had no desire to penetrate more deeply at this point" (Freud, 1900, p. 113). Irma herself "turned into one of the children whom we had examined in the neurological department of the children's hospital," as Freud added in a further passage very distant from the main text (p. 292). One of the assistants is presented as an able diagnostician of the nervous diseases of children, while the other, "Otto" in the dream, was the friend and pediatrician Oskar Rie.[19] The day after his death, which occurred on September 17, 1931, Freud wrote to Marie Bonaparte:

> My friend Oskar Rie died yesterday; 45 years ago, when as a newly married man (1886) I announced the opening of my office for the treatment of the nervous disorders of children, he came to me first as an intern and then as an assistant. Afterwards he became the physician of our children and our friend, with whom we shared everything for a generation and a half....
>
> (quoted in Schur, 1972, p. 430)

How is it possible that in 1886 Freud presented himself as a specialist of the nervous disorders of children? It was not part of his university studies. However, during his famous study trip in 1885–1886, when he was still in Paris, Freud received an invitation from Max Kassowitz to work in his pediatric polyclinic in Vienna, which he was enlarging and reorganizing. Freud then decided to stop in Berlin to attend, in March 1886, the polyclinic of Adolf Baginsky, a lecturer in pediatrics. Here, as he wrote to his sister Rosa on March 8, he had "a lot to do with small children." Two days later he wrote to his girlfriend Martha:

> As long as their brains are free of disease, these little creatures are really charming and so touching when they suffer. I think I would find my way about in a children's practice in no time... And now once more I have come to the end of my material and I ask you to be very patient with me; I cannot after all initiate you into the secrets of children's diseases....
>
> (Freud, 1960, March 10, 1886)

What "secrets" was Freud initiated into in Baginsky's clinic? In Freud's official biography, this chapter of his life is simply omitted, nor has the gap ever been filled. Even the indication offered by Jones of the place where Freud had his training is wrong, and, as a sign of neglect or disinterest, the error has continued to be repeated to this day by the most authoritative historians.

In 1877, Baginsky had published the book to which he owed his reputation, the *Handbuch der Schulhygene* (Handbook of School Hygiene), which had various editions until the end of the century. Baginsky was part of pediatrics that had continued to think of the child as an entity that could not be separated from the community to which the child belongs, and in which the causes of illnesses had to be first of all searched for. In the 1890s, his commitment to social hygiene led him to create the first isolation pavilion for infectious diseases in the world in a new pediatric hospital, the *Kaiser Friedrich,* which is still a renowned facility today, and at the forefront in the search for a therapy of diphtheria. But in the years of Freud's pediatric training, Baginsky's struggle against infections focused mainly on masturbation. In fact, he considered the latter to be "infectious" because of its transmission through "seduction."[20]

In the school hygiene handbook of 1877, he argues that "masturbation makes its appearance already in babies" and that the evil, usually caused by "certain external stimuli" and especially by "seduction" (p. 465), was apt to produce many illnesses given the greater fragility of the child's nervous system compared to the adult one. The difference depended on the higher "Reflexerregbarkeit" [the higher excitability of the reflexes], according to which the same "insignificant stimuli... which in the adult pass away without leaving traces... [in children] can provoke violent explosions" (p. 443). The most noxious "stimuli," claimed Baginsky, were "sexual excesses."

The latter, according to him, caused severe damages to the "central nervous system" (p. 451). While not excluding that in some cases the stimulus that pushed the hand toward the genitals could come from the brain, he believed that it was mostly peripheral and to be found "in the abuses of loathsome nursemaids and nannies who want to calm down the children playing with their genitals" (p. 466). And since evil sets in motion a vicious circle in which it was no longer possible to separate causes from effects, his conclusion was that "Every onanist represents a threat to [those who are] pure, because the imitation of onanism is infectious and masturbation tends to spread more than other evils" (p. 467).

In his *Handbook of Pediatrics*, he remarked that the frequency of hysteria in children in the superior social milieu was "terrific" while also stating that its main cause was to be searched for and found in "the bad example given by hysteric fathers or mothers" (Baginsky, 1883, p. 490). Despite his restraint, the impression one gets is that Baginsky believed that sexual abuse occurred within the family in the upper social strata.[21] Could this have been the "secret" Freud alludes to in his letter to Martha?

It must be said that the idea that masturbation in children was the effect of "seduction" was then widespread among pediatricians, partly because the idea of "infantile sexuality" as a normal developmental phase did not yet exist. However, the act of seduction was not conceived in "relational" terms, as we would say today, but purely in "physiological" terms. Divested of the character of an interaction between two persons, the act of seduction was placed within the paradigm of the reflex arc from a neurophysiological perspective that was completely indifferent to whether the "excessive stimulation of the genital part" was due to the action of a person or mechanical or chemical factors. Conditions such as an "inflamed and stretched clitoris" and others, can be read in a doctoral thesis inspired by the "practice of Prof. Baginsky" (Schäfer, 1884, p. 407). "All these conditions," wrote the graduate student, "are able to produce special nervous states by reflex, which can also be healed by the elimination of the cause." In short, within this mental space, in which the flattening of the causes was reflected in the indifference of the treatments, the girl who had become "impure" because she had been "seduced" was "cured" with the excision of the clitoris and similar methods. This paradox is well captured by what Freud will write in 1932, in the only passage in his entire work in which he refers to this practice. In fact, he will define circumcision as "cure or punishment."

There were also pediatricians who sought less bloody methods of treatment. For example, in October 1885 Maximilian Herz published in a medical journal, the *Wiener medizinische Wochenschrift*, an article on hysteria in children in which he reported that he had successfully experimented using the application of a brush of a 10% solution of cocaine on the entrance of the vagina of a seven-year-old girl twice a day (p. 1403). Onanism, he assured, had ceased immediately. Freud, who knew Herz, must have been more than interested, given that in those years he placed great hopes in cocaine. To be honest, I suspect that Freud came to Baginsky precisely through Herz, who, in 1877, had founded together with Alois Monti, professor at the University of Vienna and Adolf Baginsky the pediatric journal directed by the latter (*Centralzeitung für Kinderheilkunde*, renamed *Archiv für Kinderheilkunde* in 1880). Baginsky graduated from Berlin and spent a period of study in Vienna. He maintained strong relationships with a number of pediatricians who had risen to the top positions of the first pediatric wards when they opened in the Vienna General Hospitals. The third department was headed by Herz and the second by Monti. The first department had been opened in 1872 and was headed by Ludwig Fleischmann until 1878, the year of his premature death.

In 1878, the *Wiener medizinische Presse* posthumously published an article written by Fleischmann that had great resonance. It was entitled "On onanism and masturbation in babies." The author attributed the cause of the evil, especially to seduction. At the same time, he recommended the operation, that is circumcision and scarification or amputation of the clitoris for older girls, in whom the vice had been rooted a long time ago. With respect to babies, he suggested less drastic measures such as a simple "cauterization of the Labia or of the entrance of the vagina" or mechanical means able to prevent self-stimulation (p. 49). As director of the first pediatric ward of the General Hospital of Vienna, he was the right person for a bourgeois family to rely on in case the daughter presented signs of this dangerous vice. Emma Eckstein was born in Vienna in 1865 to a bourgeois family and throughout her life masturbation would remain a constant concern. In short, it is very likely that, as a child, she was brought to some Professor "Fleischman" (which literally means "butcher").

This was the state of the art when Freud opened his private practice in Vienna as a neurologist on Easter Day 1886, including the treatment of the nervous disorders of children among his services. In that year he accepted the position of neurologist offered to him by Max Kassowitz at the *Erstes Öffentliches Kinder-Kranken-Institut in Wien* (First Public Institute for Sick Children in Vienna). Freud held this position "for many years, working there for several hours, three times a week," making "some valuable contributions to neurology" (Jones, 1953, p. 233). Indeed, Freud published important studies on aphasia and infantile paralysis, and thus, in his biography of Freud, Jones described this commitment as purely "scientific"; however, the large numbers of a growing influx of patients suggest a different story (Bonomi 1994a, 2007). It is safe to assume that his long and diversified clinical experience with children, which lasted ten years, prepared the ground for his new version of the "seduction theory" as well as for his later theory of infantile sexuality.

However, this experience with children will never be fully metabolized. In the *Etiology of Hysteria*, the manifesto of the new theory of seduction, Freud presented himself as someone who was completely foreign to the world of pediatrics.[22] Of course he did not love the world of pediatrics. One of Freud's goals in writing the *Three Essays on the Theory of Sexuality*, which was published in 1905, was to present infantile masturbation as a natural phenomenon, demystifying the belief that it was an "exceptional" event and a "horrifying instance of precocious depravity" (Freud, 1905, p. 173). Nevertheless, in this monumental work, there is not a single reference to the contemporary "cure or punishment" of masturbation in girls. Later, in his essay *On the history of the psycho-analytic movement*, Freud wrote that his initial statements about infantile sexuality were based solely on the analysis of adults, since he "had no opportunity of direct observations on children" [Zu direkten Beobachtungen am Kinde fehlte mir die Gelegenheit] (1914a, p. 18).

Freud will profoundly and substantially modify the way of thinking about infantile sexuality, and through this, he will also modify the society and its mechanisms of repression. As put by the philosopher Arnold Davidson (1987), Freud gave a "conceptually devasting blow to the entire structure of nineteenth-century theories of sexual psychopathology" (p. 263). At the same time, however, by sticking to the fin de siècle notion of "perversion," Freud remained stranded in the old mental habits, in spite of having turned a creeping anxiety into a conceptual mutation, and provided a foundation for the newly emerging mentality (p. 275–6). Such a contradiction also characterized Freud's conceptualization of the child's sexuality as "polymorphously perverse"—a notion which, in Freud's intention, was disconnected from a "moral judgement" (Freud, 1925b, p. 38). With respect to female sexuality, the "dark continent," this was not true.

A last remark. In the first volume of the *Griechische Kulturgeschichte* (History of Greek Civilization), published posthumously in 1898, Jacob Burckhardt presented the castration of Uranus as the great crime from which misery and evil in human existence had begun. Was it easier to speak through myths?

Here I am reminded of Salomon Reinach's words which inspired Freud's title "totem and taboo": wherever a myth or ritual involves a dismembered or sacrificed hero and a masquerade of worshippers, "the duty of the informed exegete is to seek the word of the enigma in the arsenal of taboos and totems" (Reinach, 1905, p. IV).

Notes

1 Rieger (1900), supplement to p. 1, pp. 10 ff. Freud was well acquainted with Rieger's book: he recommended it to Fliess (see his letter of September 24, 1900) and then cited it in the *Three Essays on Sexual Theory*, where he pointed out that "the observations on castrated males merely confirm *what had been shown long before by removal of the ovaries*—namely that it is impossible to obliterate the sexual characters by removing the sex-glands" (Freud, 1905, p. 521, note 3; emphasis added). Incidentally, this is the only reference to the castration of women in the medical sense found in Freud's work. It was canceled in the 1920 edition of the *Three Essays*. Among historians of psychoanalysis, Rieger is known for having called Freud's theory of seduction an "'old wives' psychiatry" (Rieger, 1896).
2 This happened during her psychiatric internment. See Bonomi (2018, pp. 206, 209–210). A more precise reconstruction is offered by Rudnytsky (2022, pp. 57 ff. p. 65).
3 Romberg wrote his famous treatise (1840–1846) after having translated into German several fundamental works of British neuroanatomy and neuropathology. His theory is inscribed in the wake of the nineteenth-century tradition of the physiological or cerebral unconscious from which the idea of the psychological unconscious would later emerge. As reported by Marcel Gauchet (1992), it was in fact "in the context of research on the influence of the uterus and ovaries on mental states" that Laycock "was pushed towards the theory of the automatic action of the brain" (p. 46). In 1845, Laycock further developed the "law of reflex action" in an essay entitled "On the reflex action of the brain." The assumption of the uterus and ovaries conditioning the brain's automatic actions profoundly influenced the wave of research on "mesmerism" (hypnosis) that around 1850 spread from Edinburgh, Glasgow, and London (Gauchet, 1992, p. 44). This is the context in which the concept of "cerebral unconscious" was formulated in 1857. Finally, in 1889, certain phenomena such as catalepsy, which until then had been explained as "physiological automatisms," were explained by Pierre Janet as "psychological automatisms," i.e. as caused by embryonic ideas which do not to reach the threshold of consciousness.
4 Israel (1880, pp. 242–245). Here I am giving Jeffrey Masson's translation of this passage (Masson, 1986, pp. 142–143).
5 I owe this additional information to the courtesy of Albrecht Hirschmüller (correspondence from 1993).
6 Recalling the beginnings in his *Studies on Hysteria*, Freud wrote"… the expectation of a sexual neurosis being the basis of hysteria was fairly remote from my mind. I had come fresh from the school of Charcot, and I regarded the linking of hysteria with the topic of sexuality as a sort of insult [Schimpf]" (Breuer & Freud, 1895, pp. 259–260).
   Later, speaking of his rapprochement to the sexual etiology, he wrote: "The two investigators as whose pupil I began my studies of hysteria, Charcot and Breuer, were far from having any such presupposition; in fact, they had a personal disinclination to it which I originally shared" (Freud, 1896c, p. 199). The German expression translated into "a personal disinclination" is "eine persoenliche Abneigung entgegen," which is not only much stronger but also has a reactive meaning, as "a personal aversion." I discuss this aversion in Bonomi 1994a, 1994b.

7 Freud reads or rereads Hegar's most important book, *Der Zusammenhang der Geschlechtskrankheiten mit nervösen Leiden und die Castration bei Neurosen*, of 1885, the bible of castration of women for psychiatric reasons. The copy that belonged to Freud is full of comments. According to Kern (1975, p. 314), who consulted it personally, Freud had read and noted it while he was actively collaborating with Fliess in formulating the theory of the reflex nasal neurosis.

8 Freud wrote that he had found in the copy of the book a note written in pencil by a previous reader that says: "Mr. Hegar simply forgets the sexual instinct" (Freud, 1895a).

9 A shell-shaped network of bones, vessels, and tissue within the nasal passageways. Two years earlier Freud had already helped Fliess to formulate the reasons for treating reflex neurosis with nose surgery, in the presence of a reduced volume of the *corpora cavernosa* (a dense bundling of soft tissues also found in both the male and female sex organs that fill with blood and expand greatly during sexual arousal, causing the erection in the male) with a surgery. See the Minute C/1 of April 1893 and especially the Minute C/2, added in the German edition of the letters which appeared after Masson's edition, and the footnote 13 by Schröter, the German editor (Freud, 1986, p. 39).

10 See Josef Breuer's letters to Wilhelm Fliess in Hirschmüller (1986).

11 Letter of Freud to Fliess dated June 12, 1900.

12 This sentence contains an association by Erikson between Freud's Irma's dream, which marks the beginning of his self-analysis, and Freud's dream of self-dissection of his pelvis (self-castration), which marks the end, four years later, of his long journey. Erikson here establishes an implicit link between these two dreams. In the first Freud is the subject who looks, in the second he is also the object of the look.

13 Blum (1996, p. 519) noted that Fliess' operations on the nose were "similar to mutilating procedures of the genitals, to preclude and punish masturbation"; as for Eissler (1997, p. 1303), he wrote: "Inasmuch as ovariectomy as an intended cure for hysteria was performed with some frequency in late-nineteenth-century Vienna, the removal of a little bone must have appeared to Freud as innocuous." Both Eissler and Blum, however, failed to make use of this knowledge in their respective interpretations of the Irma dream.

14 A year earlier, an article appeared in an authoritative medical journal in which ironically it was pointed out that, given the new habit of doctors to amputate the clitoris in the treatment of most of the imaginary sufferings to which women are subjected ... soon it will be rare to find a woman whose sexual organs are complete. The article was ironically signed by Taliacotus, named after the Bolognese surgeon of the sixteenth century, Gaspare Tagliacozzo, who had described the operation to reconstruct severed noses (Shorter, 1992, p. 103). This ironic thought suggests that for the social unconscious of those years the anatomical complex clitoris/vulva was really equivalent and interchangeable with that of the nose/mouth.

15 Spitz (1952, p. 349). Spitz goes on to say that surgical treatment "is not limited to any one country, though its form varies according to the culture in which the anxiety about masturbation arose and led to hostility against its practice. The English advocated surgical intervention far more frequently than either the German or the French, in whose publications anodynic measures, as hydrotherapy and diet, are more prevalent. Nevertheless, drastic measures (surgery, restraint, severe punishment, fright) constitute at least fifty percent of the measures recommended in all countries until. ... the sadistic trend in anti-masturbatory retaliation died down in German- and French-speaking countries earlier than in the United States and England" (Spitz, 1952, p. 348).

16 Foucault (1999, p. 227). Foucault's lesson of March 5, 1975 (pp. 206–234) was on the fear of onanism, a topic to which he refers several times (pp. 235 ff., 260–286).
17 Zambaco (1882, p. 58). Here I have reported Masson's translation (Masson, 1986, p. 88).
18 Rappaport, who had been in a Nazi extermination camp with Bruno Bettelheim, wrote in this article in the *International Journal of Psycho-Analysis:*"I want to point out that the assertions made by psychoanalysts according to which 'external events , no matter how upsetting they are, they can precipitate a neurosis only when they collide with specific unconscious conflicts' (Rosenberg, 1943) need revision, at least with respect to extermination camp survivors" (Rappaport, 1968, p. 720).
19 Oskar Rie (1863–1931) was Wilhelm Fliess' brother-in-law and Freud's co-author of a study from 1891. Rie and Ferenczi were accepted as members of the psychoanalytic society of Vienna on October 7, 1908. One of his daughters, Margarete, married Hermann Nunberg, a prominent psychoanalyst whom I quote repeatedly in this book because of his classic study on "Circumcision and bisexuality," the other, Marianne Kris, became a famous psychoanalyst, as well as the wife of Ernst Kris, editor of the first edition of Freud's letters to Fliess.
20 Freud will use the same words, qualifying the hands-on sexual abuse in childhood as an "infection" [Infektion] (see Freud, 1896c, p. 209).
21 In a 1909 lecture on "children's nervousness," opposing the then-emerging idea of a sexual enlightenment of children, Baginsky said that sexual anomalies in children were a "confidential" issue, not to be discussed in public (p. 13).
22 Speaking of the exposure of children to sexual assaults, Freud wrote:"When I first made enquiries about what was known on the subject, I learnt from colleagues that there are several publications by paediatricians which stigmatize the frequency of sexual practices by nurses and nursery maids, carried out even on infants in arms" (Freud, 1896c, p. 207).

Part II

The code

Chapter 4

Amyl, trimethylamin = Brit milah

The Jew, like the clitoris, was considered to be primitive, savage, and vestigial; and it literally had no place in German civil society. The denigration of both Jews and women through the equation of their genitalia later became a significant factor in Freud's development of his theory of castration anxiety, penis envy, and the 'repudiation of femininity' as the 'bedrock' of psychoanalysis.

(Aron & Starr, 2013, p. 248)

Two separate worlds

The study of medical literature had brought to light the spread, between 1850 and 1950, of a practice unthinkable today, that of castration, and this mainly on women and girls. However, this historical reality has been altered and overwritten by the way castration is represented in psychoanalysis. A good example is the review, which appeared in 1961 in *The Psychoanalytic Quarterly*, of a follow-up study of 244 cases of castration on men and women, in which the author wrote:

From a psychoanalytic point of view, we must assume that castration in men re-enforces the fear of further loss—the loss of the penis; whereas castration in women does not interfere with the visible body image and thus has less or no traumatic effect.

(Gero, 1961, p. 589)

The psychoanalytic idea of castration, the fear that the penis will be cut off, is used here to erase the traumatic nature that castration can have on a woman—in this case, the removal of reproductive organs for eugenic reasons. But the same idea has been used to erase the traumatic character of Female Genital Mutilation based on the representation of the woman as "castrated man" supported by metapsychology and its many repercussions, primarily the belief that the woman, to become a woman, must give up her "imaginary phallus."

DOI: 10.4324/9781003353058-7

The gap between the historical reality of medical castration and the alternative reality created by metapsychology was the problem I faced after the study "Why did we ignore Freud 'pediatrician'?" (Bonomi, 1994a)[1]. It was a real puzzle. I soon became convinced that the moment when this cleavage had occurred was the dream of Irma's injection, but I was groping in the dark as to how the leap from medicine to psychoanalysis had occurred. It became clear to me, however, that what was at stake was none other than the origin and meaning of Freud's phallocentric system and that the puzzle could be summed up in the formula "From genital mutilation to the cult of the phallus" (*"Du sexe mutilé au culte du phallus"*), as I entitled a lecture presented in 2006 at the *Société Internationale d'Histoire de la Psychiatrie et de la Psychanalyse.*

The idea was this: Emma Eckstein's hysterical symptoms, her pelvic paresthesia, and her dreams of having a penis, were rooted in her genital mutilation, the circumcision she endured as a child. I was applying to a woman the classic thesis of Hermann Nunberg (1947), that the psychic reaction to the circumcision trauma served a single purpose: "preservation of the phallus" (p. 154). This simple and powerful thesis could well explain the construction of the Freudian system around the phallus. Nunberg had defined it in the masculine; I not only extended it to the feminine but, inverting the hierarchy between genders, I maintained that the true source of Freud's phallocentric doctrine had been Emma Eckstein's masculine fantasy. Emma's psychic reaction to the cut, her hallucination, survived the destruction of her carnal body (of her clitoris, I mean), as in the phantom limb phenomenon, finally becoming the relic preserved and secretly worshipped in the crypt of psychoanalytic theory. In other words, Freud, in his position of analyst, took possession of his patient's imaginary penis. There was a very strong clue suggesting it. The first anticipation of what will be Freud's notion of the Phallus bursts into the same letter in which he reports and comments on Emma's circumcision scene. On that occasion, he made use of a religious image: *der grosse Herr Penis,* the great Lord Penis.

I was sufficiently satisfied with the way I had argued my thesis to submit the text to *The International Journal of Psychoanalysis,* which had already published a rather unconventional work of mine. But this time the publication became an endless odyssey. The reaction of most *peer reviewers* was one of bewilderment. Nevertheless, the journal's editor was in favor, but since I was speaking of something completely unknown, she asked me to divide the article into two: now I had to limit myself to the medical context, including leaving out the possible impact on Freud of Emma Eckstein's castration. She convinced me that this was already a rich contribution and so, with her generous assistance I reworked the material that I had previously published in various forms. Even though my article contained only half of the message, the final product was well packaged and *The International the Journal of Psychoanalysis* was indeed the best place to air my ideas. But time passed and the article did not appear.

It happened that a board member was against its publication, even in this tamed form. Because of the editorial rules in force, he had veto power. In short, the publication had been blocked. The conflict within the editorial board lasted more than a year and it was only when the rules were finally changed that the article was given a green light.[2] It was published in the June 2009 issue with the title "The relevance of castration and circumcision to the origins of psychoanalysis. 1. The medical context," A few weeks later, on July 24 (the anniversary day of the Irma dream), I received an unexpected gift. In a long email, Adrian de Klerk, a Dutch psychoanalyst impressed by my paper, presented me with the missing key.

Brit milah

When I presented "Freud the pediatrician" at the Geneva symposium *100 Years of Psychoanalysis* in 1993, a question arose spontaneously: did Freud have his sons circumcised?

The first public statement that he did *not* is contained in a book that Sander Gilman had just published (Gilman, 1993a, p. 86). At the time, I did not yet know this. The only participant in attendance who appeared to have been acquainted with this topic was Peter Swales. He explained that Gilman's claim was based on an "ocular demonstration" which, for confidential reasons, could not be cited but only whispered. Apparently, no one at that time had consulted the *Matrikel* books of the Israelitsche Kultusgemeinde in Vienna. Of course, it was a naïve thought, but it is a fact that in the literature no one had ever reported the data of the register. I therefore asked Johannes Reichmayr if he could check these records once back in Austria. He confirmed that the space indicating the circumcision in the birth certificates of Freud's three sons was empty. At the same time, I received a note from the secretary of the community denying the value of evidence of the birth certificates because, in the Vienna of those years, Freud could have opted for a private ceremony.[3] Apparently, it was not easy to accept Freud's dissent.

In 1994, an article by Emanuel Rice, entitled "The Jewish heritage of Sigmund Freud," appeared in print. The author reported that attending a lecture by Swales he learned that none of Freud's three sons had received circumcision. Surprised by this "startling information," Rice immediately set about attempting to verify it. In an interview with Elliott Philipp (Martha Freud's first cousin), in July 1992, Rice asked if it was true, Philipp replied that it was.[4]

For many years this issue was discussed only in narrow circles, resurfacing later in a book by Franz Maciejewski (2002, p. 37, pp. 327–328, n. 13), in which the author recounts that when he asked Gilman for his source, the latter replied (referring to the birth certificates): "No record, no circumcision" (in the birth certificates there is a space that must be ticked, followed by the name of the mohel, the circumciser). Again in 2002, the archives of the Jewish community in Vienna were consulted by Adrian de Klerk (2000a, 2003b, 2008), who made a further discovery: Herbert Graf (Freud's Little Hans) too had been not circumcised (Klerk, 2004, p. 465). It was precisely in the essay on Little Hans that Freud had advanced the thesis that the castration complex was the most powerful unconscious root both of anti-Semitism and of the natural contempt that man has for woman, based on the equation Jew = circumcised = castrated = woman (Freud, 1909, p. 36).

The idea that Freud did not have his children circumcised is not yet fully accepted in psychoanalytic circles. To tell the truth, it is strongly opposed. Yet it is an important piece of the puzzle, which might concur to explain the widespread resistance to address the topic of circumcision. If the early psychoanalysts were the rebels who had subverted the tradition, today's psychoanalysts seem, on the contrary, even too loyal to a ritual that conveys a sense of affiliation and identity.

In the view of Adrian de Klerk, Freud had rebelled against this ritual as a boy and his struggle ran through his life and work. In Freud's dreams, de Klerk could read the traces of the shock experienced at age 10 while attending the ceremony of his brother Alexander's circumcision, mixed with shock at the birth, circumcision, and death of his brother Julius, who died at six months, when little Sigismund (Freud's Christian name) was nearly two years old, and with the somatic memory of the circumcision inscribed on his own body.

This was the way he had read the trauma inscribed in the dream of the self-dissection of the pelvis which occupied a central place in my reconstruction. De Klerk was convinced that circumcision operated as a secret organizer of Freud's system of thought. According to him, even the keyword of the Irma's injection, "Trimethylamin" had to be read as a transcription of the word (b)*rit milah* (circumcision in Hebrew, literally "Covenant of the Cut," the ceremony that takes place seven/eight days after birth, by which male babies are admitted into the Covenant with God)![5]

I focused on medical circumcision and de Klerk on religious circumcision. Our research was complementary and there was an intense exchange between us, until, not long after, in 2010, Adrian died.

I knew that the cross-contamination between these two areas was the central problem, but I was reluctant to address it. I knew that the scene of her circumcision that Emma Eckstein had brought into analysis had a double matrix and that the memory of her trauma was mixed up with her *brit milah* fantasy.[6] I also knew that this was the reason for the confusion not only between genders but also between reality and fantasy, yet I was unable to find an order. I must say that I was unable to overcome my resistance even when Adrian de Klerk generously presented me with his insight (trimethylamin = brit milah). I considered this idea too intellectual and disembodied, too "Freudian." Moreover, Adrian believed that the trauma in question was the circumcision that Freud had undergone at birth, while I believed that everything depended on Emma Eckstein's circumcision. Then problem was how to join these two perspectives together?

Withstanding trauma

For De Klerk, the problem posed by neonatal circumcision coincided to a large extent with that of the disavowal of the infant's sensitivity to pain. When anesthesia began to be introduced into surgical operations, in the mid-nineteenth century, it was believed that it was not useful with children because, as put in 1848 by Henry Jacob Bigelow, a distinguished professor of the Harvard School of Medicine at Harvard, children lacked the ability to "remember pain."[7] Supported by the discovery of the delay in the myelination process, the belief that the child was insensitive to physical pain dominated unchallenged for a century and a half. In this long period, it became common practice to perform on babies up to one and a half years more and more invasive surgical operations, even with open heart, without deep anesthesia. Only in the late 1980s, pediatricians realized that children feel pain from birth, reacting with high levels of stress up to and including sometimes dying from it.[8]

Of course, one may question whether physicians were really unaware of these effects of pain on babies, and how it was possible that the various signals pointing to them were overlooked. It is a problem similar to the pediatricians' blindness to the evidence that led Henry Kempe to introduce, in 1962, the concept of "battered child syndrome." According to Kempe, pediatricians were emotionally reluctant to acknowledge that the cause of multiple fractures was violence inflicted by parents (Kempe et al., 1985).

Only in the 1990s, a new awareness that newborns felt pain raised an alarm among pediatricians also with respect to neonatal circumcision, which, in addition to being practiced for religious reasons, in the course of the twentieth century had become a measure of mass social hygiene in North America (Goldman, 1997; Darby, 2003). Soon after the promotion of awareness and education campaigns in favor of the use of anesthesia among pediatricians, it became possible to demonstrate that operation without anesthesia did indeed produce long-term bodily effects.[9]

Of course, no one can remember his own neonatal circumcision. It is an event which is impossible to represent, in the same way in which Freud meant for one's own birth and death, all situations that require the mediation of the Other to be represented. The question that then arose was: who was Freud's Other? In my view, his "significant other" in the context of the birth of psychoanalysis, was Emma Eckstein. I must admit that De Klerk offered a good argument by bringing into the equation Alexander's circumcision ceremony, which Sigismund attended at the age of 10. In terms of biographical narration, it was very illuminating, giving a precise date to the beginning of young Freud's "masculine protest." Indeed, the latter surfaced shortly thereafter with Freud's repudiation of his father Jacob, suddenly perceived as too submissive and passive, and his substitution in fantasy with the more pugnacious Hannibal, as it is told in a well-known passage of *The Interpretation of Dreams*, that will be discussed in the next chapter.

Nevertheless, I remained convinced that the main role in this regard was played by the circumcision that marked Emma Eckstein in her body and mind, a trauma that Freud, as analyst, had felt it on his body and repressed it in his unconscious, despite the fact that the cutting of the clitoris was neither socially recognized nor categorized as a trauma. Because of repression, the trauma succeeded in being *preserved*, instead of fading into nothingness. Not only that, but the cutting of the clitoris had been transformed into a cult of the phallus. The phallocentric doctrine had to be conceived as a monument to memory, like a huge pyramid or an imposing cathedral, which are above all tombs.

Initially, I didn't know what to make of Adrian's insight. The equation trimethylamin = brit milah didn't speak to me. But two/three months after his first letter, a strange obsession about the analogy between body and architecture arose in my mind, something that I could not get rid of.[10] This analogy is relevant in the Irma dream. In the string of words that flow into the formula of trimethylamine ("Propylpräparat, Propylen... Propionsäure...") there was the word "Propyl." Freud associated it with propylaea, the colonnaded entrance to the Greek temple, which in the neoclassical age became a universal symbol of beauty. Both Erikson and Anzieu found here an allusion to the entrance to the vagina. For Erikson (1954) "Freud associated 'propyl' to the Greek word *propylon* (in Latin *vestibulum*, in German *Vorhof*), a term architectonic as well as anatomic, and symbolic of the entrance to the vagina; while 'propionic' suggests priapic—phallic" (p. 26). Similarly, for Anzieu (1986),

> "The dreamer moves from amyl (whose unpleasant smell is paralleled by that of the sexual secretions) to propyl (propylaea, in Greek architecture, are an entrance; it is also a word given to the labia majora surrounding the vaginal orifice ...)" [Anzieu obviously meant here "labia minora"]
>
> (p. 146)

This alignment of flesh and stone made me think. Did the dreamwork turn the horrible vision of Emma Eckstein's mutilated vulva into a magnificent colonnaded entrance to the temple? And the template of the "consecration" of the flesh was the Jewish ceremony of *milah* (cut) in which the male genital organ, the penis, is offered to God? It was then that I realized that Freud thought of psychoanalysis as a building under construction and that Emma Eckstein was, literally, the "stone rejected by the builders" that had become the "cornerstone" (Psalm 118: 22). "Eckstein" was the word chosen by Luther in his German translation of the Bible to refer to the concept of the cornerstone—*akrogoniaios lithos* in the Septuagint version or *"lapis angularis"* in the Latin version (Ephesians 2:20; 1 Peter 2: 6).

Freud was a materialist and wanted to build a science of the mind based on concepts such as "force" and "quantity." However, starting from the dream of Irma's injection, Freud's discourse began to be infiltrated by religious images and fantasies. This change has been well grasped by some of his most attentive readers. Erikson (1954), for example, found the echo of a religious rite in this dream, and, in his effort to fill the gap left by Freud, he came to associate the "secret" of Irma's dream with the dream of one of his women patients in which was embedded a visual shock: while walking in the Louvre Museum in Paris, she had been shocked by a painting titled "Circumcision of Christ" (p. 18). Isn't it extraordinary?

Erikson did not know that the founding dream of psychoanalysis really encoded Freud's reaction to the circumcision of a patient named "Cornerstone," just as Christ is represented in the Gospels. Yet, his unconscious managed to grasp pieces of a code that seems to flow throughout the work of Freud. Was Emma Eckstein's circumcision the "rejected stone" that becomes central to the new system?[11] Was it possible to reconstruct the architecture of psychoanalysis starting with this rejected stone?

In May 2011, I was invited to Budapest to inaugurate the newly purchased Ferenczi House. In the office where Ferenczi dictated his *Clinical Diary*, I presented a paper entitled "The future of Irma's dream and the overwhelming task of withstanding trauma." It seemed to me that this task, inscribed in the dream, was the legacy taken over by Ferenczi. So, while making de Klerk's intuition on the keyword of the Irma's injection dream (trimethylamin = brit milah) my own, I gave a different reading of it: what was encoded in Freud's unconscious was his reaction to the circumcision trauma endured in childhood by his female patient.

I reworked my presentation in the form of a paper and submitted it to the *International Journal of Psychoanalysis*, as the second part of the already published article on the "relevance of castration and circumcision" for the origins of psychoanalysis. However, it was not accepted. The main reason, according to the editor and two anonymous readers, was that I failed to give the evidence that Emma Eckstein had been actually circumcised. Note that it is Freud himself who gave the evidence by writing in brackets that one Labium minor was still shorter than the other. What kind of blindness is this, that leads to scotomize even the "ad oculum" testimony of the father of psychoanalysis? How is it possible that no psychoanalyst, I say no one because the problem goes far beyond the editorial board of the *International Journal of Psychoanalysis*, has been able to "see" something that, for those who were not under the spell of the "metapsychological witch," was completely evident?[12]

Since the tensions caused by the first part of the article were enough, I turned to *The Psychoanalytic Quarterly*, which in past had been even more orthodox, but at that time, under the direction of Jay Greenberg, was opening up. The revised text appeared in the issue of June 2013 under the title "Withstanding trauma: The significance of Emma Eckstein's circumcision for Freud's Irma dream."

Bridges and names

For the *International Journal of Psychoanalysis*, it was controversial also to claim that Freud did not have his male children circumcised. This is a comment of one of the *peer reviewers* of this journal, which is the most prestigious in our field: "The author also stated... that Freud's sons were not circumcised. This seems highly unlikely since Freud's parents were alive and along with Martha, would have been deeply disturbed."

I am very grateful to this anonymous psychoanalyst and reviewer for his observation of how Jacob, Freud's old father, would have been troubled by such a decision of the son. Pandering to his Father's wishes was not Sigmund's style. Isn't the Murder of the Father the pillar of his system? What better way could he have killed poor Jacob, if not by taking the decision not to have his children circumcised? This commentator seemed to ignore the ABC of psychoanalysis. And yet the question raised deserved attention. Isn't "the deferred obedience" to the slain father an equally fundamental pillar of the Freudian edifice? Doesn't the eternal oscillation between rebellion and submission flow like a river in Freud's work? Was I perhaps approaching the *caput Nili* of psychoanalysis?

When his first son was born, in 1889, Freud broke a tradition that had been handed down from father to son for generations: he did not have him circumcised. Nor did he give him a Jewish name, only a Christian name. He named him Jean-Martin in honor of Charcot, Freud's much admired teacher. The same thing was repeated in 1891, with the birth of the second son, named Oliver in honor of the combative General Cromwell. So, in that same year, his father Jacob, a pious and observant man of Hasidic tradition, decided to give his son, for his 35th birthday, the old family bible that they had read together years earlier, bound in a new skin. To remind him of who he was and what his duty was, commanded by God, Jacob added a dedication written in Hebrew (Freud's Jewish name was Schlomo, from the name of his grandfather, who was a rabbi).

It goes without saying that among his duties there was that of bringing his children into the Covenant (*brit*) with God, written on the organ of generation with the cut (*milah*). But Freud did not listen to him. Indeed, he did more. When his third son arrived, he named him Ernst, in honor of Brücke, the revered director of the laboratory of physiology he had attended as a student—as if to say that in his life, science had replaced religion. It was his answer to Jacob, or rather to the appeal to his religious duty conveyed by the gift of the old bible.

All this is recorded in a series of dreams that Freud reports in the *Interpretation of Dreams* and which culminate with the final dream of the self-dissection of the pelvis. This dream opens with a strange anatomical task that the revered professor of physiology had entrusted to him: to dissect his own pelvis. Of course, there is nothing "religious" in the manifest content of the dream; it is a "scientific" task. But didn't science replace religion? And didn't Brücke replace Jacob? Perhaps de Klerk was not entirely wrong in recognizing a "circumcision" in the image of the horribly eviscerated pelvis in the dream. But now the meaning was becoming clearer. What was at stake was the mandate that Freud had not fulfilled, the task that Jacob had reminded him of by giving him the old bible bound in a new skin.

This task is inscribed in the name Brücke which literally means "bridge." In his dream, to reach the end of the journey, Freud must pass over the chasm crossing a bridge. But when he realizes that the bridge consists of two children (the two sons who *had not been circumcised* when Jacob had reminded him of his duties), Freud wakes up in a mental fright. In the Jewish religion, circumcision of children is in fact a "bridge" between fathers and sons, the way in which a specific identity is transmitted from one generation to another.[13] But Freud had broken this bridge and was now falling in a bottomless chasm.

Here we must recall a precedent. In his study on *Aphasia* of 1891, in the place where Freud discusses the words that the aphasic continues to repeat in vain after a shock, we find a curious autobiographical insert. He remembers being twice suddenly in danger for his life and that both times he thought "Jetz ist es aus mit dir" [Now it's all over with you]. "In the moment of danger," Freud writes, "I heard these words as though someone were shouting them in my ear and *saw them at the same time as though they were printed on a fluttering piece of paper*" (emphasis added). This passage is reported by Isakower (1939, p. 347) in the first of a series of articles in which he develops the thesis that the human auditory sphere forms the nucleus of the superego. According to Isakower, "The super-ego character of these words is to be remarked, which sound like the pronouncement of judgement by a powerful authority, while at the same time the verdict can be read" (ibid.).

Even in Irma's injection dream, Freud sees a printed word floating in the air, the word trimethylamin. Had he relived a mortal danger? And was the printed word also the verdict of a powerful authority?[14]

Amyl/milah

Freud had six children, three boys and three girls. At the time of Irma's injection dream, he was on holiday with his family and his wife was pregnant. Freud did not know if the unborn child would be a boy or a girl. But he knew that in one case he would have named it Wilhelm, in honor of Fliess, in the other Anna, in honor of Anna Hammerschlag, widow of Rudolf Lichtheim, who will be the godmother of Anna Freud, Freud's sixth and last daughter.

Anna, was the daughter of Professor Samuel Hammerschlag, the teacher from whom Freud had received religious instruction until, at the age of 10, he entered the public school. As an adult, Freud will deny ever having known Hebrew, but Professor Hammerschlag had taught him until, at the gymnasium, the study of Hebrew was replaced with that of Greek and Latin. In more recent years, the old professor had also helped him financially, with great generosity. However, one can well imagine that, just like Jacob, the old religion professor was not at all happy with Freud's choice, namely, his refusal to let his children enter in the Covenant (*brit*) with God and receive a Jewish name during the ceremony of the cut (*milah*)!

The dream of Irma's injection was set in motion by a specific event the day before: a visit from his friend Oskar Rie (Otto in the dream), who tells him that Professor Hammerschlag had complained about the "incomplete treatment" of his daughter Anna, who was then being treated by Freud. It is a reproach that Freud does not like at all and that keeps him awake until late at night to write a clinical report in his defense. It is only when a rheumatic pain seizes him in the left shoulder that he throws in the towel and goes to sleep.

But in a dream Anna (the patient to whom Freud gives the name Irma) bursts into the hall of Freud's vacation house, where a party is taking place, like an unexpected guest and a real spoiler: she complains of the pains she feels in her throat and stomach. Freud takes her aside, reproaching her for she didn't accept the "solution." He says: "If you still have pain, it is your fault," as if projecting on her a guilt that he does not want to carry on his shoulders.[15] Then he thinks that perhaps he overlooked something organic and, worried, looks into her mouth/vulva, only to step back shocked and horrified by what he sees. Above all, he immediately feels to be in danger, since in the bottom of her mouth, he glances signs of necrosis that make him think of his own death.

It is clear that the rebuke for Anna's "incomplete treatment" merges and blurs with the far more serious rebuke of not having his sons circumcised, and with the dilemma of what to do now with the baby that is about to be born, an unplanned child, an unexpected guest. If it's a boy, will he have everyone against him again? Will only Fliess be, as always, by his side? What if the unexpected guest is a girl? *If it were Anna?*

As for the mouth, it is many things. As Erikson (1954) says, it is both the procreative feminine interior and the unconscious of Freud who, impregnated by Fliess, is about to give birth to psychoanalysis. Above all, it is Emma Eckstein's mouth, the mouth that Freud had anxiously inspected for weeks and months after the nose operation done by Fliess, a mouth that in the dream merges and confuses with the circumcised vulva that had shocked him when he examined it.

Of course, the theme of circumcision never surfaces in the manifest content of the dream, but remains in the background, giving the various elements of the dream their particular allusiveness.[16] Thus, in the accusation of not having "cleaned" the syringe (= penis), which in the dream is turned against the innocent Oscar Rie, we might read the reproach for not having circumcised his children. As Freud would recall in his book on Moses, those who have adopted this practice look with superiority at the uncircumcised, whom they consider "impure." In the dream, then Freud's *dissent* for this religious ceremony could not be expressed more strongly: the impurity is in fact magically eliminated with a shot of *dysentery*, in German *Dysenterie*, which contains the word *dissent* (in German *Dissens*).[17] Finally, Oscar Rie is properly repaid for having acted as an intermediary and messenger. All the blame passes on to him: in the end, it was discovered that the cause of Irma's pain was an injection given by Rie with a "dirty" syringe!

Besides bringing news from the Hammerschlag family, Oscar Rie had brought Freud a gift, a bottle of liqueur which Freud immediately gets rid of because of its disgusting smell of amyl. As Freud will further clarify in his short essay *On dreams* (Freud, 1901a), the word "amyl" had been the painful element repressed by the dream work and replaced with a string of words ("Propylpräparat, Propylen... Propionsäure...") culminating in "trimethylamin," the word which appears before the eyes of the dreamer fluctuating and in bold letters. It was the *solution*.

Everything becomes clearer if we read "amyl," the excluded and replaced element, as an oneiric transcription, by inversion of phonemes, of the Hebrew word "milah" ("cut," but also "word"), what makes, in its turn, of the word "trimethylamin" an almost literal transcription of "(b)rit milah" (pact of the cut). The magic word of the dream from which psychoanalysis was born did actually contain the Hebrew word for "circumcision," as speculated by Adrian de Klerk.

The attack on the "Jew"

In the central part of the dream, the examination of the patient is repeated by a group. While Freud is assisted by a group of male physicians it turns out that a portion of the skin [Hautpartie] in Irma's left shoulder was infiltrated. It is a crucial point in the dream, because all distance between doctor and patient is magically abolished: Freud feels the patient's body as if it was his own.

Freud's identification with Irma has been brilliantly drawn out by Jay Geller in a book entitled *On Freud's Jewish Body. Mitigating Circumcisions* (2007). Geller found a whole series of elements pointing to circumcision as the glue that unites Freud's body with that of Irma. He speaks of a "Jewish and gender-coded identification with Irma" (p. 91), since in an anti-Semitic context the mark of circumcision connoted the body of the Jews as a "feminized body."

Jay Geller elaborates his thesis in the wake of Sander Gilman's psychosocial study (1992), which revolves around the idea of circumcision as "the salient marker of the male Jewish body in fin-de-siècle medicine" (p. 159). In fact, the cut made of the circumcised penis not only a "truncated penis" but also an equivalent of the clitoris. In turn, the image of clitoris as "truncated penis" which is found in the writings of Freud, reflected "the popular fin-de-siècle Viennese view of the relationship between the body of the male Jew and the body of the woman. This clitoris was known in Viennese slang of the fin de siècle simply as the 'Jew' (Jud)" (p. 170).[18] In fact, the deep identity between the crippled bodies of the Jew and of the woman permeated the categories of the German medical culture and this sociocultural palimpsest had come to "place the 'Jew'—in its slang sense of the clitoris—into the body of the female" (p. 173).[19] In short, as well summarized by Gilman, "the 'Jew' is the male hidden within the body of the female for Freud" (p. 170).

Jay Geller has the merit of having found this palimpsest in the heart of Irma's injection dream, memorialized in the "Hautpartie," the "piece of skin" (a clear allusion to the "cut") that Freud feels on his own body. Note that Geller, a distinguished professor of Jewish studies, came to this conclusion purely on the basis of the textual analysis of the dream. Of course, everything becomes clearer if we consider the actual circumcision endured by Emma Eckstein, an attack whose traumatic significance had not been recognized by Freud, but which is nevertheless registered in his unconscious *as an attack on the "Jew."*

Reversal

Emma's circumcision and its dislocated repetition on the nose/mouth seem to awaken in Freud something deeply traumatic that in the dream breaks through images and thoughts of death. If in the external reality it was Emma Eckstein who risked death, in the dream it is Freud who is exposed to mortal danger. It is the irruption of a complex infantile traumatic experience whose various elements will continue to resurface in his dreams, deeply marking his self-analysis, as we will see in the next chapters.

This trauma experienced in childhood was the real unexpected guest. No precautions had been taken. As a physician and psychotherapist, Freud had not really expected it. Even though, from the beginning he had imagined cathartic psychotherapy as a repetition, he had not thought that he would be involved in it to the point of losing his status and role as a doctor, to the point of going over to the other side of the fence, finding himself in his patient's position, becoming her. For there is no doubt that, in that moment, Irma is Freud. The epochal importance of Irma's dream, the reason why it subverts logic, breaks with conventions, overcomes the categories of time and space, consists in the fact that the doctor has become the patient. That is why we can truly say that in this dream it is precisely psychoanalysis that is in gestation. However, one must immediately add that self-analysis will not be sufficient to bring the birth to term. Alone, Freud could not recognize himself in the position of the patient. As a "self-analyst," he remained condemned to remain in the middle of the road. In the end, the traumatic experience so powerfully awakened, will come to fester in the *Todesangst* (death anxiety) that will accompany Freud throughout his life.

There is also another essential feature of this dream that explains why Freud does not do the simplest thing, the thing we all would have done: why doesn't he go back to sleep, let his dream fade to nothing? Because in it the death anxiety dissolves. More, with a typical reversal, which we will encounter over and over again, the catastrophic experience is turned into a grandiose fantasy. Similarly, when fragments of the memory of sexual abuse by the Catholic nanny would emerge, their distressing character will be reversed into the fantasy of an early "conquest," and again, in the final dream, in which the scene of the horrible spectacle of castration will be his own body, the thought of death is reversed into a triumphant "wish fulfillment."

As both Erikson and Lacan noted, the dream of Irma's injection could have been a nightmare but it was not because the word "trimethylamin" finally appeared. In Irma's dream, the reversal of anguish is symbolized precisely by this magic word, which thus marks both the trauma and the fantasy that erases it, as is evident from a well-known exchange of letters with Karl Abraham.

In one of his first exchanges with the Professor, taking up Freud's doubt about his "oversight" regarding Irma's organic disease, Karl Abraham associated it precisely with "trimethylamin," going so far as to ask him if this word did not actually allude to a syphilitic infection (January 8, 1908). In his prompt reply (January 9), Freud wrote: "In the paradigm dream there is *no* mentioning of syphilis. Sexual megalomania is hidden behind it, the three women, Mathilde, Sophie and Anna, are the three godmothers of my daughters and I have them all!"[20]

If "brit milah" turns into the priapic fantasy of a grandiose "sexual baptism" it is because, as we shall see more fully below, *trimethylamin* contains "amen," indeed, "Three Amen." It is not only an overdetermined word, but, just as the word participates in the thing evoked, here it reproduces the "magic" of the Catholic nanny who had not only been "mistreated" but also "enchanted" little Sigismund. It becomes a vehicle for a part of the Catholic nanny that Freud incorporated, a part that transforms sexual abuse into "sexual baptism" and mortal anguish into a fantasy of conquest.

In the dream, it all begins with a reproach which Freud does not like and which engenders in him a thought of revenge on the "complete treatment" which would have been necessary for a widow, such as Anna (Irma). This allows Freud to connote the "injection" sexually, to make macho allusions about the right "therapy" and finally to find in the keyword of the dream, *trimethylamin*, an allusion to the "immense power of sexuality" shared in private with Fliess. Fliess is the friend in whom Freud found the same magic of the Catholic nursemaid, the same spell, the same promise of omnipotence.

It was with him that he made the pact, the "New Covenant," to replace the "pact of the cut."

As the seal of the new covenant, *trimethylamin* prefigures here the delusional core of psychoanalysis, its all-powerful project of transforming religion into science. For this magic word sums up both *brit milah* and *Three Amen* in a single "scientific" formula. All that remains to be said, all that we will say in the following chapters, is contained within the space these words circumscribe.

Of course, the moment the spell dissolves, considerable problems open up, since, in contrast to the virile image that Freud tries to give of himself, this chemical substance injects into the dream a *feeling of repulsion for female genitals*. Trimethylamine is in fact the substance that gives the female genitals the disgusting smell of rotten fish. Even Ferenczi refers to this in *Thalassa*.

The exchange

The gaping mouth/vulva, which in the dream throws Freud into terror, also consigned him to his own fate. The idea of "fate" that psychoanalysis would call "repetition compulsion" powerfully makes its entrance in this dream. Was the accident caused by the clumsy operation on the nose performed by Fliess just the result of chance, or had Freud repeated Emma's childhood trauma, delivering her, as her revered father had done, into the hands of the authoritative doctor who had circumcised her to cure her of masturbation? Be that as it may, Freud will not link the idea of fate to his patient's re-traumatization. His dream, rather, would speak to him of *his own* fate. It is he who is victimized by a "fate" that haunts him in many ways.

When Freud peers into Irma's throat, the scabs on the turbinal bone tell him of his concern for his own health: he is the one who is about to die. Freud believes he deserves it, for a whole series of reasons that he lists among the associations, among which is the fact that he hastened the death of a dear friend.[21] The most important association, the thought through which the whole irrational force of fate bursts, is Freud's association between the white spot that he sees in the throat of Irma and diphtheria, from the Greek διφθέρα, membrane, skin.

In fact, in the original text, Freud inserted this mysterious phrase: "Dysenterie klingt ferner an Diphtherie an, welcher Name ††† im Traum nicht genannt wird" ("Dysentery sounds not unlike diphtheria, a name ††† which is not named in the dream," Freud, 1900, p. 114). I report it in German because in the translations into other languages the three crosses have been omitted.

In classical philology the mortuary cross (†) is called *crux desperationis* or *obelos*, and is used to mark a *locus desperatus*, a non-amendable gap (lacuna) in the text of codices and papyri.[22] In his correspondence with Fliess, Freud would place the sign of the three crosses alongside "female sexuality."[23] Editors have traced it back to the peasant custom of tracing three crosses inside the front door to keep spirits away. Perhaps two meanings converge in Freud's gesture of repeating the *crux desperationis three times,* that of a non-amendable lacuna and the popular one of exorcism. As a matter of fact, "castration" will be for Freud a "hole" without remedy continually exorcised. In "holes," in turn, he would see the symbol of both female genitals and castration.

The magical thought of having contracted a debt with destiny will however resurface in other dreams, particularly in the dream of the Three Fates. Later this becomes embedded in a fantasy of "predestined death" that will accompany Freud throughout his life in strange and bizarre ways, well described by his biographers.

But what did Freud want to exorcise with the three crosses? "Dysenterie" (dysentery) naturally contained all his *dissent* (in German *Dissens*) toward his father's religion. As for the "Diphtherie," Freud brings it back to the moment when he had repeatedly looked into his daughter Mathilde's throat fearing that she had contracted this then often fatal disease.[24] Here the force of fate bursts through the names: the daughter's name was the same as that of a patient who had died of a new drug, sulfonal, which Freud had prescribed her when its lethal effects were not yet known. The identity of the names then forms a click: "this Mathilde for that Mathilde" (Freud, 1900, p. 112), the life of the one for the life of the other.[25] It is a completely irrational association, but very powerful. It is the most important knot in the dream and the key to the "name which is not named."

In a later dream, Freud dreamed that Mathilde was called "Hella," which in Hebrew corresponds to "Hannah," or Anna. The "name which is not named" in the Irma dream is indeed "Anna." It's not just the name of Freud's patient (Anna Hammerschlag) and the name he chose for his daughter (Anna Freud). It is above all the name of Freud's sister, that is, it is the name that will make the daughter *a reincarnation of his sister*: "*this Anna for that Anna.*"[26] It is here that the fate that will resurface in the Oedipal drama makes its entrance.

Another piece of the puzzle can then be deciphered. On the label of the bottle of liquor that Freud immediately got rid of because of the disgusting smell of amyl was written "Ananas," a word in which Freud recognized the sound of Irma's surname (actually first name). So, he read the word "Ananas" as a repetition of "Anna" (ana-ana-s).

Why this frightens Freud, why, as in a Greek tragedy, Freud ends up succumbing to the fate he is struggling against, we will see in later chapters.

What we can reiterate is that when this happens, the destiny from which Freud is trying to free himself is that of the religion of the fathers and its concrete symbol, circumcision. This particular resonance is best captured by bearing in mind that the word "Diphtherie" contained a reference to the

Bible wrapped in a new skin that his father Jacob had given him to remind him of his religious duties. *Diphtera* in ancient Greek meant both skin and books, which were then made with animal skin (parchment), and *diphtherai*, was the word used by Hellenized Jews to indicate biblical scrolls. Thus, as much as the "membrane" (diphtera) that is torn away in the rite of circumcision is a symbol of Freud's conflict with the father, the "skin," as a magical place of communion is also a symbol of the child's union with the mother.

Nunberg (1947) insisted on the symbolic identity between the "cut of the foreskin" and "the loss of the mother" (p. 146) staged in the rite of circumcision. So, one would say that precisely because the skin is a magical place of communion, cutting a piece becomes a symbol of a broken communion and, at the same time, an instrument of re-affiliation. In fact, the rite of cutting a piece of skin inscribes the newborn in the Covenant with God. The cut skin, the place of the lost fusion with the mother, becomes here parchment, book, biblical scroll, as if the sacred scrolls were a substitute for the maternal body and a reward for the lost piece of skin.

But Freud had rejected this trade. The skin had remained for him the place of an irreparable rupture, a *locus desperatus,* as clearly emerges from the image of the skin reduced to black scales that emerges powerfully in another dream of Freud, that of the Three Fates. Freud will here use the Latin word *epidermis*, enlarging what he had glimpsed in the throat of Irma: the idea that destiny took revenge by punishing him. But then, what was his trade?

In Freud, the cut piece of skin had not been exchanged for biblical scrolls, but with their equivalent, his dream book, a book invested with a salvific power precisely because the irreparable rupture it contains had been wrapped in a new skin.

The skin of destiny

For Lacan, looking into Irma's throat, the father of psychoanalysis had met his own Death, in a dream.

Sigmund Freud died in London on September 23, 1939. His assisted suicide was a calculated event. Suffering from mouth cancer for many years, he made a pact with his doctor, Max Schur: if his suffering was to become senseless, he would help him to end his life with an injection of morphine. It will then be Josephine Stross, a friend of Anna Freud, who will administer the injection (Lacoursiere, 2008).

The decision was made on September 21, and the last book Freud read was Balzac's *La Peau de chagrin* (literally: wild ass skin, but also "misery," *chagrin* in French). Translated under various titles, including "The Magic Skin," "Die Schicksalshaut," the skin of destiny, "Die tödlichen Wünsche," the mortal desire, the novel tells the story of a young man who, determined to end his life, is enchanted by an antiques shop while approaching the bridge from which he wants to throw himself. He enters and an old merchant, after having discussed the "great secret of life," offers him a magical piece of animal skin which has the power to fulfill any and all wishes of the person who possesses it. But he also warns him that it shrinks a little each time a wish is fulfilled until, consuming itself completely, it will take the owner's life away. Like Faust, our hero is tempted by the unlimited wish fulfillment and purchases the *peu du chagrin* to gain power, wealth, and prestige. But in this way, he also chooses his fate and destiny, inscribed in the second meaning of the word *chagrin*: pain, suffering, and misery. Eventually, he will find himself decrepit, miserable, and in despair.

Freud told Schur that this novel "about shrinking and dying" was the right thing to read. According to Kollbrunner (2001), Freud's words referred to his struggle against mouth cancer, the disease that had brought him so much suffering. Leukoplakia was discovered in 1923 and in the following 16 years, he had undergone more than 30 operations to eliminate the cancerous growths.

A letter that Freud wrote to his brother Alexander on August 2, 1923, confirms that from the beginning he had identified his condition with Balzac's novel: "My *peau de chagrin* (Balzac)," wrote Freud, "has also become short." Immediately afterward he composed the essay *The Economic Problem of Masochism* (1924), in which he returns once again to the problem of destiny, at the center of so many dreams and writings. Recalling how the figures of parents and then of the authorities come to form the superego, he writes: "The last figure in this series that begins with parents is the dark power of destiny, which only very few of us are capable of understanding in an impersonal way" (p. 168).

According to de Klerk (2008, p. 299), the magic skin of Balzac's novel must have reminded Freud of the piece of skin he had lost during his *brit milah*. The owner of the antiques shop is an old Jewish merchant and the parchment bore the Seal [Signet] of Salomon, a name which itself matched the same Hebrew name Schlomo that was Freud's name at the time of his circumcision that he later rejected.

That the portion of skin removed from the penis becomes, in a reunion fantasy, the talisman that magically renews the integrity of the organ of desire, the penis, and therefore the imaginary capacity to fulfill every possible desire, is intuitive. But why, wonders de Klerk, should the owner of the talisman be punished with death for satisfying his wishes? His answer is because circumcision marks an experience of deadly terror in the life of a child. Thus, the piece of skin lost by Sigismund was transformed into "a magical place of life and death," a true "skin of destiny." In support of his thesis, de Klerk recalls how Freud shortened his name from Sigismund to Sigmund (to which he switched back and forth between the ages of 13 and 22), a form of masculine protest against his circumcision, but also a repetition of the same displaced on the name, from which the phoneme "is" was ablated. Freud will do it again, later, with the term "Narzissismus," replaced with "Narzissmus."[27] In the disappeared phoneme, "is," Giovanni Foresti recognized the sound of the word that designates circumcision in Yiddish, *bris* (*brit* in Hebrew).[28]

Several times Freud repeats, in the dream book, that men grow in their names as in their skin and that the name is a precious part of a man's personality, even a portion of his soul.[29] And just like the "magic skin" of Balzac's novel, Freud's name got smaller and smaller, for example, in the practice of signing "Sigm." which de Klerk interprets in the light of the German "Sieg" (pronounced "Sig"), victory or triumph, as if, by giving himself a new name, he was trying to free himself "from his painful past by affirming himself as triumphant" (p. 298).

Already in the dream of Irma's injection, the "skin" or rather, the "piece of skin" [Hautpartie], designates the place of Freud's identification with his patient, turning it into a real *peau de chagrin* and "magical place of life and death." In fact, when Irma opens her mouth and Freud gazes at the signs of diphtheria announcing the "revenge of fate," he is struck by a "white spot." In Greek, "leukoplakia" means white plaque or spot.

Many commentators have been struck by this coincidence. To quote one for all, Levenson (1981, p. 498) wondered, "Isn't it extraordinary how his later life played out the prophecy of the Irma dream with its leukoplakic spots?"

The disease that will torment him until the end of his days would arise in the place marked by the three crosses †††, the *locus desperatus* of the dream that had brought him fame and success. Commenting on the white spot, he had in fact written: "Der weiße Fleck erinnert an Diphtheritis," *the white spot recalls diphtheria*. In 1923, Freud must have been greatly shaken by this coincidence. Indeed, the connection between the white spot in his dream and the cancerous lesion in his mouth is reflected in his association with the skin of destiny (Balzac) as well as in his meditation on the dark power of the superego. It cannot be a mere coincidence if in the difficult months that followed the discovery of the cancerous lesion, the same word, *Fleck* (stain) returns in a new context, this time in the sense of *patch or mending*. In the short essay *Neurosis and psychosis*, he writes that "the delusion is found applied like a patch [Fleck] over the place where originally a rent had appeared in the ego's relation to the external world" (Freud, 1924b, p. 151).

What Emma Eckstein's childhood trauma had reopened in her analyst, was a profound laceration, just as it was supposed by Ferenczi. One would therefore say that the delusion which was applied like a patch on this chasm was none other than psychoanalysis—a confirmation of Ellenberger's idea (1964) that psychoanalysis was the product of a *"Maladie Créatrice."*

The chasm's epicenter was the "mouth." Madelon Sprengnether (2003) rightly defined the injured mouth/vulva as the "imagistic center" of Irma's dream, which speaks to us of the impotence, passivity, and victimization that Freud tries to exorcise through a phallic and penetrating self-image. Thus, he casts out "the orally violated 'feminine' identification that runs, like a flashing subliminal message, through his dream," and yet, "with a vicious irony and fatality, Freud's disavowed identity with Irma returned to plague him in later life" (p. 271). Thus, becoming Freud's mouth, Irma's violated mouth offers "silent testimony to the legacy of trauma embedded in the dream of psychoanalysis" (p. 260).

In addition, we cannot fail to mention the imaginary marble tablet with which Freud celebrates the revelation of the secret of the dream in his letter to Fliess of June 12, 1900. "Mund," mouth in German, had been deleted from the name "Sigmund." This revelation makes Irma's dream a magical talisman which, will give Freud power, wealth, and prestige. It should therefore not be surprising that Freud would remember the *peu du chagrin* when discovering in his palate the "white spot" that will transform his life into an endless torture, nor that, when the time to take leave of life arrived, he felt the need to reread, once again, Balzac's novel. To put it in the words of Sprengnether (2003): "It's as though Freud's dream had turned to nightmare—one in which he was condemned to play the role of Irma until he died" (p. 273).

Notes

1 The work, which appeared in English, was at the time translated into French, language in which it had three separate publications. Recently, in 2020, it started to arouse new interest and was translated in Portuguese and Russian.

2 There was already dissatisfaction with the veto rule, but I have reason to believe that the discussion triggered by my paper was decisive. I received in fact a call from Antonino Ferro, who was then part of the board, asking me to "wait still a bit."

3 As I reported in a later article (Bonomi, 1994b, p. 73, note 25).

4 Rice later obtained additional confirmation from Albrecht Hirschmüller, who sent him a transcription of the birth records of Freud's sons taken from the records of the Israelitsche Kultusgemeinde in Vienna (Rice, 1994, pp. 251–252 and p. 257 n. 25). Here Rice adds: "Both Jacob and Amalia Freud were alive during the period when the three sons were born and one can correctly surmise that they could not have been too happy at the absence of this crucial religious ritual" (p. 252).

5 An excerpt from De Klerk's email of July 24, 2009 is reported in Bonomi (2015a, p. 122, note 7).

6 As I remarked already in an article that appeared in 1994 (Bonomi, 1994b, p. 83).

7 Promoter of the revolution introduced by anesthesia, Bigelow "hated all kinds of pain and cruelty," as stated in his obituary. He was also a strong opponent of vivisection. This shows even more the strength of the shared belief that children do not remember painful experiences, an idea that also conditioned the deep structure of nascent psychiatry, in which the belief that the child was spared from "madness" dominated (cf. Bonomi, 2007, 2009a).

8 Especially after the 1987 study by Anand and Hickey, "Pain and its effects in the human neonate and fetus." In a subsequent article, of 1992, the same authors demonstrated that deep anesthesia increased survival dramatically in surgical operations.

9 See Wellington and Rieder (1993). Taddio et al. (1997), found a significantly higher frequency of pain expressions at the time of vaccination in infants who had undergone neonatal circumcision than in the control group. Of course, this

is not about episodic memory. However, I must point out that recent clinical research suggests that even very young children, under one year of age, are able to link traumatic bodily experiences to certain events and to retain a sort of representative memory (Coates, 2016).

10 As I reported in the introduction of the first volume of *The Cut and the Building of Psychoanalysis*, these thoughts were organized around the formula "from flesh to stones," a sentence which began to repeat itself in my head as a sort of refrain.

11 Although fantasizing psychoanalysis as a building under construction, Freud had always been careful not to use the term "Eckstein." The words he used were, in order of frequency: "Grundfeiler" (basic pillar) "Grundstein" (foundation stone), and "Angelpunkt" (hinge), with one exception. In the summer of 1932, i.e., at the apex of the crisis with Ferenczi, a few pages after stating that women "cannot have any fear of castration," he wrote: "Both phenomena, sadism and masochism alike, but masochism quite especially, present a truly puzzling problem to the libido theory; and it is only proper if what was a stumbling-block [Stein des Anstoßes] for the one theory should become the cornerstone [Eckstein] of the theory replacing it" (1933a, p. 104).

12 For instance, Wilcocks wrote: "How on earth ... did Freud know that one half of the vaginal lips of Emma was shorter than the other half?" (2000, p. 102). After the publication of my articles and books, more and more psychoanalysts did acknowledge the actuality of the genital mutilation.

13 I'm here picking Freud's evocation of "the strange novel in which a person's identity is retained through a series of generations for over two thousand years" (Freud, 1900, p. 455).

14 Many years later Freud would argue that whatever the situation of mortal danger, it is experienced as castration anxiety, as the ego reacts by feeling abandoned by the protective superego, or destiny (Freud, 1926a, pp. 129–130). This thesis, which will be profoundly changed by Ferenczi's theory of trauma, I believe helps us understand something of Irma's dream, or at least how Freud understood it.

15 As highlighted by Mahony (1977, p. 91), the German word for "shoulder" (*Schulter*) "phonologically incorporates *Schuld* [guilt]." This is the place of Freud's identification with his patient, given that, as the dream continues, the infiltrated "portion of skin" will be found on Irma's left shoulder. It is not surprising that Freud feels it on his body.

16 Referring to Freud's Irma dream, Patrick Mahony (1977) remarked that the "extraordinary allusiveness of the reported dream is equally an elusiveness and an indication of strong censorship" (p. 94).

17 Furthermore, this word was at the center of a true phonemic concert—Rie, Diphte-Rie, Hyster-Rie, and Dysente-Rie—as pointed out by Mahony (1977, p. 89) in his textual analysis of the dream.

18 Also, Kurt Eissler (1977, p. 57) signals that the slang word that indicated the clitoris in Vienna at the end of the century was "der Jud" (the Jew).

19 "The entire medical vocabulary applied to the body of the female stressed her physical and mental inferiority to the male. And the terms used were precisely parallel to the discourse about the Jews" (Gilman, 1992, p. 170). See also Gilman (1991, 1993b, 1993b).

20 On the interpretation of Irma's dream disclosed by this statement see Appignanesi and Forrester (1992).

21 Ernst Fleischl von Marxow, Brücke's assistant at the Institute of Physiology, had contracted an infection in his hand that forced him to undergo surgery after surgery, turning his life into endless torture. To alleviate the pain, he had

become addicted to morphine and Freud, then an enthusiastic promoter of cocaine, had tried to help him by replacing morphine with this substance which was then believed to be not addictive. Then it turned out to be worse than the disease it was supposed to cure (Bernfeld, 1953), just like Emma's "harmless" nose operation.

22 I owe to Francesco Migliorino the mention of Rossetti's definition (1998):"The *crux desperationis* or *obelos* is the mortuary-type sign of the cross (†) which, according to a well-established convention, the editors of Latin and Greek texts use (A) to isolate one or those words (*lectiones*) which appear so dissonant with respect to the context that they can be considered corrupt and that, moreover, cannot be replaced with a convincing *emendatio*; (B) to mark a gap [lacuna] that cannot be healed with a sufficiently reliable *restitutio* (this in the case of *codices*, not also in the case of papyri: see the entry *Lacuna). The crux therefore indicates the locus desperatus*" http://www.rossettiweb.it/livio/glossario/r98crux.htm

23 Letter to Fliess of November 5, 1999. The three crosses will also appear alongside the idea of sexuality in Freud's letter to Jung of January 1, 1907, and in his letter to Ferenczi of January 19, 1910.

24 Freud writes that his daughter had fallen ill two years earlier, but this is an uncertain point. From his letters to Fliess we know that Mathilde fell ill with diphtheria, risking death, in early 1897, so that this association may have been introduced at a later time, when he wrote the *Interpretation of Dreams*.

25 Albrecht Hirschmüller (1989) also found the medical file of this patient, who presented a strong erotic transference. Trying to unravel the knot "this Mathilde for that Mathilde," he was struck to find that the heated debate on the pros and cons of the diphtheria vaccine reached its peak in 1895. He wondered, therefore, if Freud had not identified with Behring, the "savior of thousands of children" thanks to the discovery of the serological therapy of diphtheria. But diphtheria also brings us back to Adolf Baginsky, who, in 1895, had published the experimental study that validated the vaccine. For a more complete discussion see chapter 5 of the first volume of *The Cut* (Bonomi, 2015a).

26 The idea that the name given to a child makes it a reincarnation of the person bearing that name, is well present in *The Interpretation of Dreams*, as well as in the correspondence with Fliess. Freud's sister, Anna, will marry Eli Bernays, brother of Sigmund's wife, Martha Bernays. Anna and Eli Bernays will emigrate to America in 1892.

27 The explanation Freud offers is quite pretentious: he says that the neologism "is shorter and less cacophonous" (Freud, 1910b, p. 60, footnote). Significantly, he inserted this comment where he talks about the fact that the individual takes as an object of love, his own body and, in particular, his own penis.

28 According to Foresti: "if the word that designates circumcision is a word in which we find the cacophonic syllable 'IS' that Sig(is)mund gladly amputated, it does not seem out of place to imagine that the choice to eliminate it can having dealt with an anti-circumcision gesture. By amputating his Hebrew name of the disturbing syllable, Freud had somehow also eliminated the ritual amputation that had inscribed him in the Jewish community. In doing so, he affirmed his personal autonomy and his right to cultural self-determination" (Foresti, 2003, p. 161).

29 See in particular Freud's dream of the Three Fates, which we will discuss later.

Chapter 5

The great Lord Penis

We can only say: 'So muss denn doch die Hexe dran!'[We must call the Witch to our help after all!]—the Witch Meta-psychology. Without meta-psychological speculation and theorizing—I had almost said 'phantasy-ing'—we shall not get another step forward.

(Sigmund Freud, Analysis terminable and interminable, 1937, p. 225)

The mouth

In my 2013 article on the significance of Emma Eckstein's circumcision for Freud's Irma dream, I described her circumcision scene as a combination of reality and fantasy. Her mutilation was real, but her scene had been fabricated on the template of Orthodox brit milah, in which the mohel (the circumcisor), after cutting a piece of skin, sucks the blood of the circumcised penis of the baby. The scene was therefore the product of a contamination that crumbles all barriers between sacred and profane, medicine and religion, men and women, thus anticipating one of the most remarkable aspects of Freud's work.

Shortly after its publication, I received a letter from a New York lawyer who challenged my description of the Orthodox brit milah. She wrote to me:

I have been attending these ceremonies my whole life and have never witnessed a rabbi 'applying his lips' to a child's penis. Nobody I know among my numerous Jewish friends and family has ever witnessed an action of this kind either among the Orthodox or less observant segments.

This cultivated woman, who otherwise liked and enjoyed my text, had a specific interest in what is passed on from generation to generation. She nevertheless could not bring herself to accept the image of a rabbi "applying his lips" to a child's penis. She thought that it was ignorant on my part to highlight the fact, a blatant inaccuracy which had undermined the value

DOI: 10.4324/9781003353058-8

of my argument and even my credibility as a scholar and interpreter of psychoanalysis.[1]

Her unexpected e-mail made me suddenly understand how degrading and shameful this oral scene could be experienced, since the mouth is the organ of speech and words are the noblest products of our spirit. I also realized that my continued delay in writing the book in which I was collecting my research was largely due to the fact that I did not want to offend anyone or provoke hostile responses. At the same time, I remembered that one of the greatest achievements of psychoanalysis concerned oral fantasies of incorporation, and I consoled myself by thinking that these achievements had been made possible precisely by the symbolic meaning of these scenes so charged with shame.

Above all, I remembered that my inquiry was triggered by an "oral" scene. I mean the dream of Ferenczi in which a small penis is served with fork and knife. In my mind, I had not recorded it as a dream but as a *vision*, to the point of calling it from the beginning "epopteia," thus evoking the final phase of the initiation into the Eleusinian mysteries, namely, the "revelation," in the more generic sense of "holy play" used by Plato. At the end, the alignment along the oral axis allowed me to give a meaning also to the element that set in motion the analysis of Emma Eckstein: the "candy scene."

Sweets and candies

The first important reference to Emma Eckstein's analysis is found in a text composed about two months after Irma's dream. On two occasions when Emma was a child of eight, "she had gone into a small shop to buy some sweets, and the shopkeeper had grabbed at her genitals through her clothes" (Freud, 1895b, p. 354). The fact that she had gone back had left her with a deep sense of guilt, "as though she had wanted in that way to provoke the assault." Freud inserts this vignette into a paragraph of his unfinished *Project* entitled *The hysterical "proton pseudos,"* which, in the Aristotelian logic, is a false premise or first lie that is transmitted in the series of deductions that correctly follow from it. In Freud's meditation, it is clearly an extension of the crucial notion of "false connection" between affect and idea, which Freud widely explored in relation to obsessions and phobias, where an unbearable idea originally associated with a disturbing affect is replaced by another idea. But then, in March 1895 and thanks to Emma Eckstein, the notion of "false connection" was applied to hysteria as well, giving rise to the first formulation of the psychoanalytic idea of "transference," as it was proposed in the last chapter of the *Studies on Hysteria*.[2] The hysterical *"proton pseudos"* could therefore be translated as the hysterical "primal false connection" or "first transference."

What Freud meant has been the subject of various speculations. My interpretation is this: Freud considered the candy scene to be the transcription[3] of another much earlier scene, an *oral violation* that Emma did not remember and that was revived by the molestation she endured at the age of eight in the candy shop.

This would explain the close connection between the oral violation around which the Irma dream circles and the sudden revelation disclosed by the memory of the candy store. In October 1895, this "candy scene" precipitated a radical shift in Freud's thinking, a real conversion: the discovery of childhood as a period of life in which traumas, although not having visible immediate effects, determine the predisposition to hysteria that manifests itself later in life.

In mid-October, Freud introduced the concept of *infantile sexual shock* and during a few months of feverish work he elaborated the idea that traumatic seduction in childhood was the specific cause of "psycho-neurosis" (hysteria and obsessional neurosis). He found memories and scenes of abuses in all his patients, and presented his theory to the public, with two articles (Freud, 1896a, 1896b), in one of which the term "psychoanalysis" appears for the first time, and a lecture addressed to the psychiatrists of Vienna, the famous *Etiology of hysteria* (Freud, 1896c). It is a brilliant text that retains its value today. But it all happened too fast.

Freud did not give to himself the time necessary to emotionally digest his experiences and to verify his assumptions—just think that a year later he would complain with Fliess that he "had not yet finished a single case" (March 7, 1897). Above all, he had impressed on his idea the character of an all-encompassing revelation, prospecting it as the discovery of a "caput Nili" of neuropathology.

Since then, Freud seems driven to create a new version of the myth of original sin:[4] the repetition of a sexual abuse endured within the family was the vehicle by which a perverse action was transmitted from generation to generation, since the beginning of times. That is, his views emerged within an apocalyptic scenario. Freud was speaking more as a prophet inspired by dreams and visions than as a physician. But his lecture was addressed to an audience of physicians, who responded to his presentation with an icy silence that expressed disbelief and skepticism.

Presiding over the meeting of Viennese neurologists and psychiatrists was Professor Krafft-Ebing, who had just coined the concept of "pedophilia" for a new edition of his famous treatise on perversions. It was therefore not the denunciation of the ease with which children were exposed to sexual abuse that provoked this reaction, but rather the idea that sexual abuse was the only, specific and universal cause of hysteria—a "scientific tale," as it was defined by Krafft-Ebing. Not only that, but the belief spread that, rather than finding these memories of sexual abuse in his patients, Freud suggested them, which resulted in serious damage to his reputation and in a professional isolation.[5]

In addition, something troubling surfaced. At the same time, when he was working on the manifesto of the "seduction theory," Freud recognized

Emma Eckstein's bleedings as "hysterical" and caused by *Sensucht,* which we can translate as "nostalgic desire."

After Fliess' botched nose operation, Eckstein had had profuse bleeding, which later reappeared at such intervals that Freud was convinced they occurred according to the biological "periods" theorized by Fliess.[6] Later, a scene from the age of 15, in which she suddenly began to bleed from the nose in connection to her wish to be treated by a certain young doctor, convinced Freud that her bleedings following Fliess' surgical error were motivated by her "old wish to be loved in her illness" (May 4). Thus, following a suggestion from Fliess, he recognized that Emma's bleedings were "hysterical, occasioned by *longing*" (April 26), as also supported by the fact that "she has had several similar incidents, among them actual simulations [direkte Simulationen], in her childhood" (June 4).

What makes these statements incongruous is that Freud's theory of hysteria was then firmly grounded in the repressed memory of a childhood sexual assault. And if we may find in the term "Sensucht" an attraction to a forgotten trauma, it is more difficult to understand what Freud meant by "simulations," since this notion was not part of his vocabulary nor of his style of thinking, and would never be.[7] Did he mean that as a child she provoked her own bleedings by attacking her body with blades, spikes, or needles? On May 4th, he wrote to Fliess: "She has always been a bleeder [Bluterin], when cutting herself, etc."

Many years later, summarizing the reasons for her relapse in *Analysis Terminable and Interminable*, Freud traced it back to masochistic impulses "only incompletely resolved" in the course of the first analysis and wrote: "She fell in love with her surgeon, wallowed in masochistic phantasies about the fearful changes in her inside" (Freud, 1937a, p. 222). Emma Eckstein suffered from a particularly virulent form of traumatophilia that prompted her to repeat the attack she had endured, either alone or by undergoing surgery. It seems therefore that in 1896 Freud was very close to grasping what he will call "repetition compulsion." In fact, the term came out from his pen right at the end of the year, only to then disappear for a very long time.[8]

In summary, during 1895/1896, while analyzing the treatment of Emma Eckstein, Freud discovered the deferred effects of early sexual shocks, the phenomenon of the transference to the doctor in therapy, and concluded that that the disposition to hysteria is acquired in childhood, all elements which would characterize psychoanalysis in the years to come. Yet, Freud failed to see other things that are obvious to us today. The first is that the circumcision endured by Emma as a child was a sexual shock as well as a relational trauma, nor did he acknowledge that his participation in the nose operation had played a role in the resurfacing of Emma Eckstein's masochistic impulses and fantasies in the present doctor-patient relationship, nor, much less, that his own consent to the operation had itself been an enactment and a product of his countertransference. In any case, these unthought-of elements, will not remain silent: they will surface in a re-transcripted form through Freud's dreams, fantasies, and memories orienting both his self-analysis and the later construction of his theory. They will constitute an *après coup* to his patient's trauma and a case of inter-psychic deferred action (*Nachträglichkeit*).

Herr Zucker (The Candy Man)

At the end of 1896, the seduction theory was undergoing a transformation. It was sliding toward a "theory of the father," in the sense that at the onset of a chain of abuses spreading among brothers and sisters, there always was a "Pater." Freud also calls it the "unforgettable prehistoric other." He was then collecting clinical material for a book on the theory and therapy of hysteria which would never be written.

The "theory of prehistory" should have marked a substantial advance with respect to the view presented in the *Etiology of hysteria*. Freud's new idea was that the sexual abuse might occur at such an early age that it cannot be recalled as an actual memory located in time and space, eventually coming into representation only in imaginary scenes. Ferenczi and Severn would call these memories "emotional memories." For Severn they were a clinical phenomenon that Freud belittled to "mere fantasy" (Severn, 1933); for Ferenczi they were special mental states which had to be treated with the dramatic technique described in *Child-analysis in the analysis of adults* (Ferenczi, 1931), requiring from the analyst a kind of participation which Freud had rejected as forbidden. In order to understand these mental states within a clinical-theoretical framework, Balint (1968) would provide a powerful description of the therapeutic process in terms of regression toward the "basic fault," an area of the psyche characterized by turbulence and compulsiveness, in which the language loses its common and shared sense, while the boundaries between patient and analyst fade away.

Emma Eckstein had entered this phase of the therapeutic process. On January 17, 1897, Freud wrote to Fliess: "Eckstein has a scene where the diabolus sticks needles into her fingers and then places a candy [Zuckerl] on each drop of blood." Evidently, this scene awakened in Freud the memory of the bloody disaster of two years before, because he immediately added, as if his association was completely obvious and transparent: "As far as the blood is concerned, you are completely without blame!"

By saying "Eckstein has a scene [hat eine Szene]," Freud leaves us with an unresolved ambiguity. What kind of scene was it? Certainly, it wasn't a memory located in time and space like that of the shop where Emma had gone to buy sweets and the shopkeeper had touched her genitals. And yet we find here a more essential version of the same "candy scene." Freud immediately aligns it with the nose operation performed by Fliess that had re-actualized Emma's childhood trauma, as it would become clearer with the ensuing scene, that of the circumcision of a girl. But the most interesting thing is that Freud dreamed of the "candy scene" himself. The word, *Zuckerl* (sugars, candies), had in fact a deep resonance in him: he dreamed of a certain "Mr. Zucker," the candy man from whom children should beware. But here we need to broaden the focus and clarify the context in which we are moving.

Freud's dream was part of a series of dreams about Rome with which were resumed, a year and a half after Irma's dream, the journey that unfolds along *The Interpretation of Dreams*. In this book, Freud's dreams are not found in chronological order, but the work of Didier Anzieu (1975, 1986) and of many other scholars has made it possible to date most dreams, restoring a chronological order. However, neither Anzieu nor the other authors have associated Freud's self-analysis with his analysis of Emma Eckstein. Seeing things from this perspective changes everything.

In those years Freud had many patients in treatment for short periods of time, but very few in treatment, which lasted long enough to be considered "analyses": only three. Two patients were males, while Emma Eckstein was the only female. Her analysis would terminate not long after the scene of circumcision, and only then, in the summer of 1897, would Freud inform Fliess that he had become his own main patient. Freud's self-analysis will later be narrated as the intrapsychic adventure of an isolated individual, but the starting point of his self-analytic journey is to be found here, in the final phase of Emma Eckstein's first analysis, jointly with an intensification of his emotional involvement.

Behind this resumption of Freud's dreaming there was also another trigger, which was later acknowledged by Freud himself in his preface to the third edition of *The Interpretation of Dreams*: the death of his father Jakob, on October 23, 1896. In the ensuing weeks, he began to have the fantasy of meeting Fliess in Rome on Easter Sunday. It was around this curious fantasy that his series of dreams about Rome took shape between December 1896 and January 1897.

In the first, he finds himself on a train that leaves Rome without having succeeded to set foot in the city. Together with nostalgic longing for his first three years of life in Freiberg, Moravia, this dream signifies the traumatic rupture of his childhood: the moving of his family to Vienna, by train, when he was three years old. In the second dream, Rome appears as "the Promised Land seen from afar" (Schorske, 1974), a reference to Moses condemned by God to die before his mission was accomplished (Deuteronym 34). Finally, in the third dream, Freud almost reaches Rome. The place, however, is another. Starting with Grigg (1973), commentators have recognized it as the country where little Sigismund spent the first three years of his life. "Rome" condensed various things, among which the "Roman Catholic" nanny who Freud would later describe as his "initiator" and "teacher in sexual matters." For Grigg, moreover, "sweets represent sexual favors, valleys and throats symbolize the vagina, and rocks symbolize the lips" (p. 115). It is precisely in this dream that Freud asks "Mr. Zucker" directions to the city (Freud, 1900, p. 194), the candy man at the origin of the seduction theory.

Freud's dream seems to register his emotional response to Emma's scene where the devil puts a *Zuckerl* on each drop of blood. Freud associates sugar with Karlsbad, where patients suffering from "Zuckerskrankheiten," literally sugar diseases (diabetes), went for treatment, and speaks of the trip to the spa as a "Leidensstation," a via dolorosa or via crucis, the annual repetition of the passion and crucifixion of Christ. Freud does it with a certain self-irony, but isn't it a perfect metaphor for the compulsion to repeat a trauma? It brings us back not only to Emma's repeated bleedings but also to analysis as the place where the traumatic attachment to the "unforgettable prehistoric other" that relives in dreams and fantasies is staged and repeated: Herr Zucker.

Executioners and victims

We can now focus on the letter in which Freud reports to Fliess the scene of Emma Eckstein. The letter, dated January 17, 1897, begins with a reflection on the new idea of the "prehistory of hysteria," which Freud here links with the "theory of the foreign body and the splitting of consciousness" [Fremdkörpertheorie und Spaltung des Bewußtseins], that is with the idea of "dissociation" that nowadays powerfully reentered into debate. Freud had derived it from Janet. In his 1894 article *The neuro-psychoses of* defence, Freud then criticized Janet's notion essentially because it implied a congenital weakness of the ego, whereas for Freud the splitting of consciousness was the result of a psychic defense. Guided by obsessive neurosis, he had introduced the dynamic model of repression, which will then impose itself on that of dissociation also for hysteria, at least until Ferenczi will reintroduce it contextually to his rediscovery of the hystero-traumatic basis of every neurosis.

In this letter, Freud refers to dissociation for the last time. It would seem, that is, that it was his emotional reaction to Eckstein's last scenes that determined a fatal turning point in the history of psychoanalysis, the definitive abandonment of the dissociation model, together with that of the traumatic etiology of hysteria.

On January 17, 1896, Freud wrote to his friend:

> Do you remember that I always said that the medieval theory of possession held by the ecclesiastical courts was identical with our theory of a foreign body and the splitting of consciousness?[9] But why did the devil who took possession of the poor things invariably abuse them sexually and in a loathsome manner? Why are their confessions under torture so like the communications made by my patients in psychic treatment? ...

Incidentally, the cruelties make it possible to understand some symptoms of hysteria that until now have been obscure. The pins which make their appearance in the oddest ways; the sewing needles on account of which the poor things let their breasts be mutilated and which are not visible by X-ray, though they can no doubt be found in their seduction stories! Eckstein has a scene where the diabolus sticks needles into her fingers and then places a candy on each drop of blood. As far as the blood is concerned, you are completely without blame! ... In regard to cruelty in general: fear of injuring someone with a knife or otherwise.

Once more, the inquisitors prick with needles to discover the devil's stigmata, and in a similar situation the victims think of the same old cruel story in fictionalized form [Dichtung] ... *Thus, not only the victims but also the executioners recalled in this their earliest youth.*

(emphasis added)

In these years, Freud let himself to be guided by the "intense emotional reactions" of his patients, and we will do the same. The marker of Freud's intense emotional reaction in this letter is the word *Nadeln*, (needles), which in a few lines appears five times alone or in compounds. This makes me think of Irma's *injection*. Is it possible that already in that dream something broke through that belonged to the world of Emma Eckstein, something which now powerfully resurfaces in the image of needles stuck in the body that escape "X-ray"? It must also be said that Freud had stuck needles in patients who, like Emma Eckstein, had pain in the legs, to find those anesthetic areas that in Middle Ages were called *stigmata diaboli*.[10] In short, the scene produced by Emma is so full of resonances that it tears the analytic couple from the present and throws it into a medieval "ecclesiastical" scenario which, while illuminating the dynamics which are unfolding in the consulting room, evokes and heralds the surfacing of dreams and memories about the "bad treatment" suffered by Freud from his Catholic nanny. Just as the patient remembers her abuse through images and fantasies that offer a fictionalized version of it, the same occurs to the analyst.

In this way, Freud seems to come across a crucial node rediscovered by contemporary psychoanalysis, that of the encysting of the memory of childhood abuse in the form of a "victim-executioner" dyad, which is then relived in the therapeutic situation in ways that involve the analyst through both corresponding (with the victim) and complementary (with the executioner) identifications. Prompted by these role identifications, the Freudian "Dichtung"—the fictionalized form of memories of his native village—began to emerge. In particular, as noted by other authors, we find here the emerging of the memory of the "mistreatment" of Pauline in the company of John. It seems that this is what Freud alludes to when he writes that the executioner/

analyst remembers his youth. Freud would evoke this memory in his letter to Fliess of October 3, 1897:

> I have also long known the companion of my misdeeds between the ages of one and two years; it is my nephew, a year older than myself, who is now living in Manchester... The two of us seem occasionally to have behaved cruelly to my niece [Pauline], who was a year younger.

This memory became so important for Freud that we find it at the center of his essay *Screen Memories.*[11] It is the scene of the meadow in Freiberg, where little Sigismund and his two companions are picking yellow flowers, when the two boys, "as though by mutual agreement ... fall on her and snatch away her flowers" (Freud, 1900, p. 311). Besides mirroring the male alliance between Freud and Fliess and their cruel behavior to Emma Eckstein, this scene describes the two boys' "misdeed" as a "defloration," implicitly assimilating it to the cutting of an imaginary penis, thus anticipating the essay on *The Taboo of Virginity*, in which defloration is equated to the stealing of an imaginary penis and punished with "castration."[12]

In short, Emma's scene with the devil triggered memories and fantasies in Freud that would for years feed both his self-analysis and the construction of his theory. Above all, this scene was heralding the next scene—the circumcision scene—which Freud reported to Fliess only one week later. The image of the devil piercing Emma's fingers introduces in fact the theme of the *punishment for masturbation* (the fingers of the hand) and therefore of the circumcision that Emma had undergone as a child, the violation that was repeated with the operation on the nose. Yet, while describing the devil's scene Freud's identifications with both the victim and the perpetrator were still fluid, but before the new scene Freud stepped back from involvement. All the distance between doctor and patient is abruptly reestablished: the doctor returns to be the Judge and the patient is definitively cast in the role of the Witch. This stepping back produces Freud's great turning point. In the following months, his doubts about his seduction theory would increase until morphing into a new system of thought based on drives and pathogenic fantasies. Namely: innate fantasies, inherited, and rooted in traumatic events that occurred at the dawn of mankind.

The "theory of prehistory" on which Freud was working, parted then from the patient's personal history, only to be placed into an archaic past where Freud's interest for trauma took refuge. Sheltered from the emotional exchange within the analytic dyad, "traumas" will then maintain an exclusively "scientific" interest for Freud. They will be acknowledged as actual events in the archaic family, and categorized as hereditarily transmitted traumas that became predisposition, phylogenetic schemata, and "primary fantasies" (Freud, 1916–1917, pp. 368–371), "categories which *a priori* inform every individual experience" (Laplanche, 1992, p. 430). This step, heralded in many ways, would be completed in a definitive way with the case history of the Wolf Man. We will deal with that in the last chapter.

The great Lord Penis

The ensuing letter, of January 24, 1897, has two narrative focal points. The first was generated by Emma's devil scene and today it would have been called a "rêverie." It's Freud's new brilliant idea that the broom on which flying witches furrow the sky, is nothing but "the great Lord Penis" [der grosse Herr Penis].

In her essay on Freud and the devil, Luisa De Urtubey (1983) found in this image an essential ambiguity: to whom does this magical penis belong? To the witch or to the devil? (p. 34). We can add: to the patient or to the analyst?

Significantly, Freud hastened to inform his friend that he had ordered the *Malleus Malleficarum*, a well-known witch-hunting treatise published in 1486 and the most misogynistic of all. Did Freud order it because a chapter of this treatise explains how witches make men impotent by stealing their penises, which are then hung on the branches of the tree around which they gather for the Sabbath? Had Emma's genital mutilation taken possession of Freud to the point of making him feel "castrated"?

What is sure is that the image of the great Lord Penis heralds the disembodied and transcendental dimension that the Phallus will have in the mature Freudian system. There it would designate what comes first, as the God of medieval philosophers, but also in the rational, Kantian sense, of the condition which makes experience possible. This philosophy will be presented as the product of infantile thoughts confirmed by science. Thus, in the essay *On the sexual theories of children*, the first "theory," the one which directs all other theories, consists *"in attributing to everyone, including females, the possession of a penis"* (Freud, 1908, p. 215). The difference between sexes unfolds then from the opposition "has a penis/does not have a penis" (Freud, 1923a). The immediate fallout is that female genitals are intellectually categorized and emotionally experienced as a mutilation, even if this idea is rejected by all means, by both females and males. In the girl, it is the sensitivity of the clitoris that fuels the belief that her small penis will grow, becoming a real penis. As for the boy, he rejects this idea because it announces that he too could be deprived of his penis. It is only then that the threat of castration that accompanies that exhortation not to touch, to which the boy paid no attention, becomes effective. In a footnote added in 1920 in the *Three Essays*, Freud would summarize the entire question in this way:

> Both male and female children form a theory that women no less than men originally had a penis, but that they have lost it by castration. The conviction which is finally reached by males that women have no penis often leads them to an enduringly low opinion of the other sex.
>
> (Freud, 1905, p. 195)

Isn't this the core of the paleo-biologic tale invented by Ferenczi while he was in analysis with Freud? This core has a precise origin: it is the "great Lord Penis" which January 24, 1897 Freud saw flying in the sky.

The circumcision scene

And now let's move on to the second focal point of Freud's letter to Fliess, the circumcision scene. It was reported in this way:

> I am beginning to grasp an idea: it is as though in the perversions, of which hysteria is the negative, we have before us a remnant of a primeval sexual cult, which once was — perhaps still is — a religion in the Semitic East (Moloch, Astarte). Imagine, I obtained a scene about the circumcision of a girl [Denk Dir, dass ich eine Szene von Mädchenbescheidung bekommen habe]. The cutting off of a piece of the labium minor (which is even shorter today), sucking up the blood, after which the child was given a piece of the skin to eat. This child, at age 13, once claimed that she could swallow a part of an earthworm and proceeded to do it. An operation you once performed was affected by a hemophilia that originated in this way.
>
> Perverse actions, moreover, are always the same — meaningful and fashioned according to some pattern that someday will be understood.
>
> I dream, therefore, of a primeval devil religion with rites that are carried on secretly, and understand the harsh therapy of the witches' judges. Connecting links abound.
>
> (Masson, 1985, p. 227)

The patient in question was Emma Eckstein. As happened in other situations, Freud here pressures the patient to pull out of the scene, as the German verb "bekommen" suggests. That is, he knew she had been circumcised (preliminary examination of the genitals was routine, especially in cases of hysteria) but until then Emma had never spoken of it. We can imagine that the previous scene, the one in which the devil sticks needles into Emma's fingers, evoking punishment for masturbation, had convinced him that the time to get the memory of punishment had finally arrived. But Emma startled him. What she gives him is a scene fabricated from an element of Jewish ceremony (the sucking of blood) in which Freud can also mirror himself, a scene that disrupts every distinction of gender and between the sacred and the profane. In short, as in Freud's Irma dream, in this scene too there is a conflation between the medical circumcision Emma had undergone and the brit milah. One wonders if Emma knew that her therapist had not circumcised his children.[13]

Freud is evidently impressed. Not only does he not dwell on the damage and suffering that the real event has caused to his patient, but, on the contrary, he makes her fantasy his own and projects it into an absolute time. He identifies himself with his patient to the point of appropriating her scene, making it the place from which his work will draw strength and nourishment in the decades to come. In short, he is the one who steals her magic penis from the witch, and wraps it in a metapsychological suit, as he would candidly confess in *Analysis Terminable and Interminable*, when describing his metapsychology as the inspiration of a "witch."[14]

It is something more than a reverie. It is the moment when Freud discovers the unconscious as a foreign language with its own grammar, of which he begins to grasp the rules, even though it remains obscure. In the quoted passage there are two keywords, Moloch and Astarte, which are so dense and important that unpacking them right now would take us too far. But even without them, we can recognize in the "primeval sexual cult" the scenario from which *Totem and Taboo* would bloom. Then Freud will decode the Christian rite of the Eucharist by tracing back to cannibalism, that is, to the idea that by incorporating parts of a person, by eating them, one acquires the qualities of that person (which is what is here happening inter psychically between Freud and Emma). But the scene produced by Emma also anticipates *The Taboo of Virginity*, in which Freud suggests that defloration is experienced by the young woman as a "castration" that triggers in her the desire to take revenge on the man, castrating him and taking his penis for herself. Karl Abraham (1920) will expand on this point by explaining that the woman reacts to the "wound" by fantasizing about robbing the man of his penis by biting and devouring him. This is precisely what we find in the second fragment, the epilogue of the circumcision endured as a child.

When, at 13, she challenges boys by swallowing a worm, Emma is no longer a frightened child, rather she is scary. The reversal of her position from passive to active, "masculine," is definitive. She is no longer a "poor victim" but a threatening phallic female who, having orally incorporated the penis and its power, challenges her playmates. A real witch.

As long as Freud perceived her as a victim, he had been close to her, but when he is confronted with the "witch" that the poor victim has transformed into, then everything changes. It is as if Emma's scene transported Freud to the overdetermined place of his childhood trauma at the hands of the Catholic nanny who will soon begin to populate his dreams and memories.[15]

Until then, Freud had believed that Emma Eckstein had been victim of sexual abuse by her father. Everything suggests that from the beginning he had in mind a *fellatio*, as suggested by the image of the wide open mouth of Irma's dream. But, as if panicked, Freud here transports everything into a prehistory, in an archaic "Semitic East," evidently reinterpreting in his own way the proto-religion at the origin of the Jewish and Christian rites that Robertson Smith, an author who he greatly admired, had reconstructed in his famous lectures on the religion of the Semites of the years 1889–1890. Which was the rite of the primeval sexual cult that Freud has here in mind? I think that by putting together the salient features of Moloch (the wide open mouth) and Astarte (the sacrifice of male genitals) it can be determined with a certain precision: it was a cannibalistic rite, and its object was the "great Lord Penis."

In *Totem and Taboo*, Freud will attach great importance to Frazer's thesis of the killing of the king/priest ritually sacrificed to rejuvenate the world, but even more so to the totemic banquet from which Robertson Smith derived the origin of the religion of the Semites. Freud will then direct the spotlight over the Eucharistic rite, omitting to mention the Orthodox rite of Jewish circumcision, even though the fantasy of incorporating the ancestor's penis would have clarified the meaning of the totemic banquet and made Freud's argument transparent. As Nunberg (1947) would point out in his essay "Circumcision and problems of bisexuality," sucking the penis' blood in the Jewish ceremony of the brit milah is a "relic of the totemic meal" (p. 172). Since "Orthodox Jews, at the circumcision ceremony, usually name their son after their deceased father" this makes the son a "reincarnation" of the grandfather (p. 168).

> Since the son is a reincarnation of his father's father, sucking blood from his penis at the circumcision ceremony is a relic of the totem meal.
> (p. 172)

It is therefore this detail of Emma's account that arouses in Freud the thoughts and fantasies about the beginnings of the human family that will constitute such an important part of his metapsychology. The blood-sucking fantasy not only acts as a protective screen with respect to the experience of his patient but also creates an isolated place within his psyche where the traumatic experience will remain encapsulated in time. From this place, his later phylogenetic speculations will germinate, first of all, the conviction that castration was carried on by the father of the primeval family on his grown up boys,[16] and that circumcision was "a clearly recognizable relic of it" (Freud, 1933a, pp. 86–87). It is as if, reading Freud's reaction to Emma Eckstein's two last scenes, we have the privilege of witnessing live the change without return that generated metapsychology. Not only does Freud not pause to reflect on what Emma's circumcision has stirred in him, a Jew in conflict with his father precisely about circumcision, but this is also the moment when Freud identifies with the aggressor and "understands the harsh therapy of the witches' judges" (which, we can translate as follows: "I finally understand the reasons for that therapy of circumcision of girls that has always aroused so much horror in me") and, having stripped his patient of her brilliant idea, he abandons her to her fate.

Notes

1 This episode is related in the first volume of *The Cut*. In his review of the book, Jonathan Sklar (2016) commented in this regard: "The practice of *metzizah b'peh* was even described by a New York lawyer, writing to Bonomi, as impossible and

wrongly described. Yet in 2004 out of concern for the potential spread of herpes infection the New York City of Health and Mental Hygiene advised parents and *mohelim* that *metzizah b'peh* with direct oral suctioning of the circumcision wound should never be performed."

2 Discussing "The therapy of hysteria," Freud stated that the patient can transfer to the figure of the doctor a disturbing idea that is emerging in the course of the therapy, adding: "Transference onto the physician takes place through a false connection" (Breuer & Freud, 1895, p. 302). Freud wrote this chapter in March 1895, just in the days when Emma Eckstein had almost bled to death from the complications of the clumsy nose operation. Ann Salyard (1992) convincingly contended that "Freud discovered transference in connection with material derived from his treatment of Emma Eckstein," while in the midst of a crisis, as both a defense and a means to work through the crisis.

3 One year later, on December 6, 1896, Freud would write to Fliess:"As you know, I am working on the assumption that our psychic mechanism has come into being by a process of stratification: the material present in the form of memory traces being subjected from time to time to a rearrangement in accordance with fresh circumstances — to a *retranscription* [Umschrift]."

4 This shouldn't be too surprising. Even the theory of progressive degeneration, introduced a few decades earlier by the French psychiatrist B. A. Morel, a fundamentalist Catholic, was explicitly inspired by the myth of the Fall. Freud, who was then fighting against the concept of "degeneration," translated in terms of "seduction by the father" according to the formula "heredity is seduction by the father" (see Freud's letter to Fliess of December 6, 1896).

5 See on this point Schröter and Hermanns (1992a, 1992b).

6 Freud noted the dates of Emma's bleeding and sent them to Fliess, who was collecting data for his theory of biorhythms (in addition to the 28 days female cycle, Fliess found a male cycle of 23 days). There is no doubt that this conduct by Freud was an obsessive defense, as also pointed out by Schur (1972). After all, Freud considered himself a neurotic of the "obsessive" type.

7 In his early writings, Freud vigorously rejected the theory of simulation and, in his 1888 article on "Hysteria," had written: "The poor hysterics, who in earlier centuries had been burnt or exorcized, were only subjected, in recent, enlightened times, to the curse of ridicule; their states were judged unworthy of clinical observation, as being simulation and exaggerations" (Freud, 1888, p. 41).

8 See Freud's letter to Fliess of December 17, 1896. The term used here by Freud is *Wiederholungszwang*. He would later use *Repetitionszwang*. Freud will return to the concept in *Remembering, repeating and working-through* (1914b) and then in *Beyond the pleasure principle* (1920). In the latter, the notion would be plagued by unsolvable ambiguities: a figure of the traumatic and a product of the death instinct, a universal attribute of organic life, and a "demonic" phenomenon.

9 The term used here by Freud is "Spaltung," splitting, which is the term he used until he introduced the notion of repression to differentiate himself from Janet's theory (Freud, 1894a). Since his doctoral thesis, dated 1889, Janet spoke of the phenomenon of psychic "disaggregation," a term translated with "Spaltung" in German and "dissociation" in English.

10 See the initial examination of Elisabeth von R. in 1892, in Breuer and Freud, 1895. Freud referred to the *stigmata diaboli* in his 1888 article "Hysteria."

11 This essay, built around an articulated palimpsest, was identified by Bernfeld (1946) as a disguised autobiographical essay.

12 In Freud's essay *Screen memories*, the scene then moves to the house of a peasant woman who consoles the little girl and offers everyone a delicious piece of loaf

that she cuts with a "long knife." All commentators recognized in the long knife a threat of castration—a retaliation for the "defloration" (= stealing of the penis). The oral element, here represented by the delicious loaf, will return in subsequent dreams.

13 Both families were Jewish and one of Emma's brothers was a close friend of Freud's: philosopher Friedrich Eckstein was a Tarot companion of Freud, his favorite card game, along with oculist Leopold Königstein and pediatricians Oskar Rie and Ludwig Rosenberg.

14 Freud (1937a, p. 225). On this subject, see the fine essay by Robert Holt (1982) who traces back the figure of the "metapsychological witch" used by Freud in 1937 to his letters to Fliess of January 1897.

15 In the figure of the witch evoked by Freud in these letters, Robert Holt (1982, pp. 247–248) found the Catholic nanny who fascinated and at the same time mistreated him as a child. Freud had been breastfed by his mother, yet, strangely enough, he sometimes calls this nanny "Amme" (wet-nurse), as pointed out by several authors (Grigg, 1973; Mahony, 1977; Vitz, 1988), a term that brings to mind "Emma." On Emma/Amme we will return in Chapter 8.

16 This "audacious thought" was expressed for the first time in Freud's letter to Ferenczi of February 1, 1912. Freud exposes it in response to the case of Ferenczi's "little Rooster-Man," a child whose penis had bled from a bite by a rooster, and who later behaved like a rooster, as if he had identified himself with his aggressor (see Bonomi, 2018a, pp. 170–171, 17–178). Freud will use this case history in *Totem and Taboo*, in the chapter on the return of totemism in the development of the individual.

Chapter 6

The blood bride

...I'm thinking of ...Zipporah, the one who repaired the failing of a Moses incapable of circumcising his own son, before telling him, 'You are a husband of blood to me,' she had to eat the still bloody foreskin, I imagine first by sucking it, my first beloved cannibal, initiator at the sublime gate of fellatio, like so many mohels for centuries had practiced suction, or mezizah, right on the glans, mixing wine and blood with it, until the thing was abolished in Paris in 1843 for reasons of hygiene ...

(Jaques Derrida, *Circonfession*, Period 13)

The cornerstone

Freud had another dream. While the dream in which he asks Herr Zucker the way was encoding his reaction to the devil scene, the fourth and final dream of the Rome series encodes Freud's reaction to the last scene produced by Emma, the scene of the circumcision of a girl.

This dream consisted of a single scene set not in Rome but in Prague, where, at that time, a revolt against the empire and the imposition of German language was going on. In his dream, Freud finds himself in front of a street corner (*Strassenecke*), surprised to see so many posters and proclamations in German on the walls.

This dream is considered by commentators to be the most important crossroads of Freud's self-analysis. For Anzieu (1986) it was the "Rosetta stone"[1] of psychoanalysis, since the Freudian theory of dream as a riddle or cryptogram to be deciphered derived from it. It seems that it inspired Lacan's idea that the unconscious is structured like a language. Anzieu, who had been a pupil of Lacan, devoted many pages to this dream, coming to imagine it as the moment in which Freud/Moses receives "the Tables of the Law of the Unconscious" (pp. 203–204). For him, the most important element was the "street corner" as a place where several lines and systems converge and unite, starting from the various languages (German, Czech, Yiddish) and religions (Hebrew and Catholic) in which Freud had grown up. This stratified intersection signals, according to Anzieu, the emergence

DOI: 10.4324/9781003353058-9

of a new type of mental space that prepares and anticipates the discovery of the Oedipus complex.

What Anzieu had missed is that the street corner (Strassen-*ecke*) encodes the family name of Emma, *Eck*-stein (cornerstone), as it also occurs in a dream that Freud had in April 1897. In the dream book, Freud placed it immediately after having explained how the figure of Irma was condensing more people and remarked that the work of condensation in dreams "is seen at its clearest when it handles words and names," as "words are frequently treated in dreams as though they were things" (Freud, 1900, p. 295).

The dream in question is "norekdal," which is one of his most condensed dreams. The day before, Freud had received an article from a friend (Isidor Sadger) in which Paul Flechsig's scientific discovery that the "architecture of the mind" mirrored the "architecture of the brain" was exaggeratedly praised.[2] That night Freud dreamed the sentence "It's written in a positively norekdal style," where the latter word, fabricated with the names of characters taken from works by Ibsen (Nora and Ekdal), stood for a superlative such as *colossal, pyramidal*. The theme of Ibsen's work was a deception perpetrated by women who do not tell the truth (Grinstein, 1980, pp. 218–219), while the syllable "ek," that in the dream's verbal architecture is the pinnacle of a pyramid, alluded to the name of a patient of Freud: "Eck-stein" (Anthi, 1990, p. 147). The dream thus signals the simultaneous collapse of Freud's belief in his seduction theory and the fact that, in any case, "Eckstein" still was the cornerstone of a system under construction. The reason is simple. As is known, Freud will connect his abandonment of the seduction theory to the discovery of spontaneous masturbation in children. Behind this discovery there was, again, Emma Eckstein, who underwent circumcision precisely because of her masturbating. A few weeks later Freud drew his "architecture of hysteria" (Draft M and N in Masson, 1985, pp. 278–285), bridging the transition to a new paradigm, the one of drives and pathogenic fantasies. The Oedipus legend will soon be placed at the center of the new system, slowly becoming its cornerstone. A new metapsychology, based on the concept of drive, "Trieb," was being set up, drawing a parable of the alliance, "Brit" but in reverse, as Philippe Réfabert acutely noted.

If up to that moment Freud had considered Emma as the innocent victim of a "seduction," the "perverse" suction fantasy had produced in him a reversal of moral judgment as well as justified doubts as to whether fellatio with the father had really taken place. Now, it seemed more likely to him that the scene at the origin of his inferences had been constructed from things "heard" or seen, or from a combination of experiences and "past events from the history of parents and ancestors" (Masson, 1985, p. 240). And so, in May 1897, Freud drew his "architecture of hysteria" (Draft L, M, N in Masson, 1985, pp. 240–253), which accompanies the transition to the new paradigm of pathogenic impulses and fantasies, at the center of which will be placed the legend of Oedipus, the new cornerstone of the system. In this chapter, we will try to understand how this transition was accomplished and what was repressed or dissociated on the way.

The crossroads

The street corner (Strassen-*ecke*) of the fourth dream of Rome is not the only place where several systems, such as Judaism and Christianity, intersect, as rightly noted by Anzieu. It is also the place where the lives and the unconscious of Emma Eckstein and Sigmund Freud crisscrossed. The upheaval caused in him by the circumcision scene can be found also in the following. Two weeks after, on February 8, 1897, Freud wrote to Fliess that also his father was a "pervert" who had abused his children, especially Alexander, his younger brother, whose symptoms now appeared as the result of an identification with his father. Everything suggests that Freud had in mind here too a specific "perverse action," a *fellatio*.

There are reasons to believe that Alexander's circumcision was among the memories that the scene of Emma had awakened in Freud. That ceremony was performed with the oriental rite, which included the *metsitsah b'peh*, that is, the sucking of the drops of blood from the penis (Gilman, 1993a, pp. 67–70). This rite was practiced by Eastern Jews and, in the anti-Semitic perception of the late nineteenth century, stigmatized the Jewish male as "feminine" and "primitive." This historical context has been well reconstructed by Gilman.

In contrast to Western European Jews, progressively assimilated and integrated into German culture, Eastern European Jews were seen by most Viennese as vulgar, crude, and uncivilized. As anti-Semitic intolerance intensified, the assimilated Jews of Vienna tended to distance themselves from the large *Ostjuden* community. Freud was part of the latter. He was born to Galician parents and grew up in the second district of Vienna, the one in which most of the Eastern Jews who arrived in Vienna after the democratic reform of the 1860s converged. Growing up, Freud progressively dissociated himself from the "primitive" and "barbarian" rituals which, in the imagination of both non-Jews and Western Jews, exemplified the anti-Semitic stereotypes projected on Jews as a whole. Freud had distanced himself from this legacy by studying Greek and Latin at the gymnasium and eventually becoming part of the bourgeois intellectual elite. Yet, it is precisely this repressed legacy that powerfully returns through the circumcision scene that Emma produced in analysis, taking Freud to a distant "Semitic East" and precipitating him in thoughts about his father's "perversion."

His doubts were not limited to his brother Alexander: Freud was tormented by the thought that he himself had been abused by his father. According to many, it was precisely this doubt that made the theory of seduction waver. Indeed, the two things go hand in hand. Some months later, in his famous letter to Fliess of September 21, 1897, Freud would reject his theory of the seduction, while exonerating Jacob from all accusation of perversion, partly by acknowledging that he'd projected onto him something that was boiling within himself. Immediately after, on October 15, 1897, he would grasp in the Oedipus legend a universal element that gave new meaning to his conflict with his father, which would then become an "Oedipal conflict."

In orthodox narrative, this is celebrated as the glorious moment of the birth of psychoanalysis. The same narrative glorifies Freud's self-analysis as the enterprise of a solitary hero and the fruit of an isolated mind, eradicating it from the emotional turmoil produced by Emma Eckstein's analysis. It is true that her treatment terminated not long after the circumcision scene, perhaps on Easter 1897, but Freud's subsequent need to analyze himself, becomes clearer considering his need to find an order in the inner turmoil that this experience had left him with.

Early 1897 Emma Eckstein's analysis sucked Freud into a vortex of horrible cruelties projected in the "Semitic East." In order to rebalance himself, Freud would turn toward classical Greece and the vision of "beauty" he had learned at school under the influence of Winckelmann and neoclassical culture. William McGrath (1986) well describes Freud's "aesthetic turn," his turning away from gloomy medieval landscapes crowed by the devil, witch hunting, and atrocities to pursue the ideal of beauty in the footsteps of Goethe's Faust—as when, at the end of May, the word "Hella" appeared in a dream. For McGrath Hella was "Helen of Troy," the "archetypal representative of Greek beauty symbolizing the balance, restraint, and proportion that Goethe and other great German classicists saw as the essence of Greek art" (p. 202). Just as Faust had landed under the sun of classic Greece in search of absolute beauty, Freud too, traveling across Italy in the summer of that year, wrote to Fliess that he was now feeling close to his idea of *Absoluteschöne*, "absolute beauty." A few days later, he wrote to him, from Siena: "As you know, in Italy I am seeking a punch made of Lethe; here and there I get a draft. One savors the strange kind of beauty and the enormous creative urge ..."

This shift from the Semitic East to Greek-Roman world was a leitmotif for his family romance. During Alexander's brit milah, Jacob had given his son the name of his grandfather, Ephraim, but Sigismund had imposed himself in the choice of the Christian name by reciting in the family, like a child prodigy, the victories and triumphs of the greatest military leader of antiquity, Alexander the Great. It had been an anticipation of the heroes he would choose as ego ideals. In fact, it would be shortly after that the boy, disappointed by his submissive father, would replace him, in imagination, with the pugnacious Hannibal.

Freud recalled this replacement in association with his fourth dream of Rome. Indeed, it was his most important association in the street corner dream (Strassen-*ecke*). It is a stratified association, which would fully emerge only after the trip to Italy in the summer of 1897, following his great turn. Thus, in *The Interpretation of Dreams*, associating his dream to his wish to conquer Rome in the footsteps of Hannibal, Freud would write:

> To my youthful mind Hannibal and Rome symbolized the conflict between the tenacity of Jewry and the organization of the Catholic church. And the increasing importance of the effects of the anti-Semitic movement upon our emotional life helped to fix the thoughts and feelings of those early days. Thus the wish to go to Rome had become in my dream-life a cloak and symbol for a number of other passionate wishes.
> (Freud, 1900, pp. 196–197)

Here Freud recalled his juvenile infatuation with Hannibal, which was rooted in his sudden disappointment in his until then admired father. When he was 11 or 12, Jacob had told him a mishap of his youth. One Saturday, he was walking to go to synagogue with a new fur cap, when a Christian had blocked the sidewalk and with a single blow knocked his cap to the mud, while shouting: "Jew! Get off the pavement!" "And what did you do?" the boy asked. "I went into the roadway and picked up my cap" was Jacob's quiet reply (p. 186). The boy's disappointment at (what he had then interpreted as a sign of) his father's passivity was such that in his eyes he lost all value. The father was soon replaced, in fantasy, with the pugnacious Hannibal who, as he had learned at school, had the courage to challenge Rome.

This memory brings on the stage the boy's "masculine protest" to the anti-Semitic attack and a reversal of passivity into activity. Yet, Freud's lack of empathy for the story of the father who suffers without reacting raised lively discussions among readers. But Freud's repudiation of "passivity" contained in his memory of Jacob's "un-heroic" conduct appears much clearer if we insert this memory in the chain of thoughts and fantasies triggered by Emma Eckstein's circumcision scene: the story of the anti-Semitic attack on Jacob replaced the attack on the "Jew" in Emma's body.

Freud's defense against his identification with the circumcised girl took advantage of his rebellion against the father. By reversing roles, Jacob was in fact put in the passive position of the circumcised child (the knocked-off "cap"), according to a typical inversion that will become a mark of Freudian reading of the Oedipal conflict with the father. Letting go the orality inscribed in the word games of school boys (Hannibal/Cannibal), there is an evident continuity between the identification with the pugnacious Hannibal and that with Oedipus.

According to several commentators, by embracing the Oedipus myth Freud managed to dissociate himself from his subjective experience of circumcised, effeminate, and passive Jew. For Feldman (1993), Freud made use of the Hellenic narrative to distance himself from the biblical one. According to Boyarin (1997), his identification with the phallic hero of the Greek myth had sheltered him from the subjective experience of "circumcised," that is, of a feminized Eastern European Jew. The Oedipal narrative enabled him to construe a "family romance of escape from Jewish queerdom into gentile, phallic heterosexuality" (p. 215), denying to be son to Jacob Freud, while fantasizing himself as "Oedipus, son of Laius" (p. 250). Aron and Starr (2013) as well, consider Freud's choice to base psychoanalysis on the Oedipus myth, instead of the Jewish narrative, as a defense from the idea that Jews are passive, feminine, and homosexuals. More precisely, disavowing his own origin and renouncing the traditional Jewish understanding of what it meant to be a man transmitted by his father's passivity, he "was disavowing his own vulnerability, passivity, dependence, and femininity, a disavowal that was then unconsciously embedded in his psychoanalytic theories" (p. 258).

Experimenta crucis

Although shareable, these comments set Freud in a world populated only by men. But Emma Eckstein had scrambled the rule "men with men, women with women," messing everything and forcing him to relive what Freud called his "sexual initiation."

Velikovsky (1941, p. 492, note) suggested reading *Trimethylamin*, the keyword of the Irma dream, as "Three Amen." This keyword, besides reflecting the aim of changing religion into science (it is a scientific formula), would then mark the place of an intersection between Judaism (brit milah) and Christianity (Three Amen). "Amyl," the unpleasant element that is replaced in the dream with the verbal string we know, does not only recall "milah" (cut and name) but also the name of Freud's mother, "Amalia," so that in the substitution of "amyl" for "Three Amen" we find a piece of Freud's family romance that paved the way to his identification to Oedipus. It is the substitution of a Jewish mother for a "Roman Catholic" nanny who, on Easter Sunday, 1858, the days of the illness and death of his brother Julius, had taken little Sigismund to church and taught him to pray.

In his dense letter to Fliess of October 3, 1897, there are various fragments of Freud's main memories stemming from his first three years of life, including the germ of remorse left in him by Julius' death and the mistreatment of Pauline in the company of John. Then, explaining to Fliess that, in his case, the culprit had not been the father, Freud added that his "prime originator" was his nanny, "an ugly, elderly, but clever woman" who told him "a great deal about God Almighty and Hell."

The word used by Freud, *Urheberin*, was the same he had used in reference to the "theory of the father" (*Urheber*). Thus, despite having heralded two weeks before his dismissal of the seduction theory, he was keeping it alive—one of the many contradictions to which Freud repeatedly exposes us. The point is that to Freud it was not a contradiction. It is as if, moving from father to a mother substitute, his sexual initiation lost in his eyes its passive and humiliating quality, becoming in fantasy an early "conquest." But just as Freud's desire to "conquer Rome" in the footsteps of Hannibal was jeopardized by a series of inhibitions and failures (he will overcome his irrational fear of the eternal city only in 1901), similarly, in his dreams, his exhibited masculinity was repeatedly challenged by ugly, elderly women that scolded and humiliated him.

The Catholic nanny began to make her way in Freud's dreams with his fantasy of going to "Rome," but it was only when the analysis of Emma was over that the figure of the "prehistoric nanny" who harshly punished little Sigismund for his lack of cleanliness,[3] became a central element of his self-analysis. Her first appearance was in the "exhibitionist" dream, where Freud is nearly undressed. He is running upstairs, three steps at a time, when a maidservant stood in front of him and he found himself glued to the steps, paralyzed and, at the same time, excited.

This dream, included in *The Interpretation of Dreams*, was reported in the letter to Fliess of May 31, 1897, along with the Hella dream, which was not included. Now, this juxtaposition is extremely important because both dreams took up, and expanded upon, elements of Irma's injection dream.

The staircase of the first dream was the same Freud had to climb twice a day for years, to make a morphine injection to a 90-year-old lady. Also analyzing his Irma dream, Freud associated the injection with the one he was giving the "old woman." He wondered if he had caused phlebitis with a dirty needle, coming to the conclusion that he had taken every precaution to ensure that the needle was "clean." But the matter was far from settled. Freud, in fact, climbed the staircase of the elderly lady sometimes with muddy shoes, sometimes spitting on the stairs, and each time the maidservant stopped and reproached him. She scolded him for tracking mud into the carpet or made him wait for a too long time in the waiting room, where every day Freud saw the beautiful reproduction of the Tiber River that had given way to his dreaming to meet Fliess in Rome on Easter day.

Climbing the staircase twice a day was rather painful, since it reminded him of how poor and miserable he was. And so, stepping up, Freud often was daydreaming of "going higher and higher." In his "exhibitionist" dream, this sense of elation is combined with the maidservant's reproaches. For Freud, climbing stairs was a symbol of copulation. Indeed, as Risto Fried (2003) explains when commenting on this dream, if the house "represents the woman's body, and the stairs her vagina, the dreamer's entire body becomes a phallus" (p. 481). Freud's dream thus brings his identification with the phallus onto the scene. His conquest fantasy, however, was full of aggression, not only phallic (the injection) but also pregenital. Spitting (urine) and mud (feces) brought a feeling of hostility and degradation into the sexual act.

In the other dream, Freud experiences "over-affectionate feelings" for his daughter Mathilde, who had fallen ill with diphtheria. In the dream, her name was Hella, a word that also appeared to him in clear print in the dream, just like the word trimethylamine in Irma's dream.

Hella was the name of his sister Anna's daughter, whose photograph Freud had just received from America, where the family had moved. As Barbara Mautner (1991) noted, he must have been struck by the child's resemblance to his sister at the same age, as well as the identity of the name, since "the Jewish name for both Hella and Anna is Hannah" (p. 283). According to Mautner, the photograph had awakened in Freud an "erotic memory" of when Sigismund was 5 and his sister 3 that would constitute the "latent skeleton" of Irma's injection dream (p. 275).

In short, if the mixture of paralysis and sexual arousal in the "exhibitionist" dream suggests sexual abuse by the nanny, the Hella dream brings into play its repetition with his sister, according to what Freud had recently written in the *Etiology of Hysteria* about the little boy who, having been previously seduced "by an adult of the female sex" turns into an aggressor and "under the pressure of his prematurely awakened libido" tries "to repeat with the little girl exactly the same practices that he had learned from the adult woman" (Freud, 1896c, p. 208).

Peter Rudnytsky (2012) called attention to how for Freud the psychic consequences of such repetition were "extraordinarily far-reaching." Indeed, Freud (1896c, p. 215) had added that brother and sister "remain linked by an invisible bond throughout the whole of their lives." In light of the growing importance that the theme of brother-sister incest would assume in Freud's meditation, Rudnytsky rightly asks: had little Sigismund actively repeated his "sexual initiation" on his sister Anna? Had Sigismund and Anna remained linked by such an "invisible bond"?

Of course, this would clarify the importance that the name "Anna," the "name which is not named," has in Irma's (=Anna's) dream, as well as the breaking into it of the idea of destiny. We have repeatedly wondered how it is possible that in this dream the retraumatization of Emma Eckstein consigns Freud to his destiny.

In this dream, there is an obscure point at which Irma becomes or rather is felt by Freud to be a child (Freud, 1900, p. 271). This child evokes Emma on the one hand and Anna on the other. It is as if the repetition of Emma Eckstein's circumcision with the operation on her nose had awakened in Freud the sense of guilt for the sexual assault on his sister together with a long series of justifications and the memory of the abuse he had previously endured. Summing up the meaning of the dream, Freud will say, simply, that it fulfilled the desire not to be guilty.

It is as if in the moment when Emma is about to bleed to death in front of Freud's eyes, these thoughts and the many others that would unfold through the various dreams, had all presented themselves in a single moment, as is said to happen when, plummeting in a ruinous fall, one sees his entire life unfold before one's eyes. Only later will the traumatic progression caused by the shock turn into regression, until the figure of the nursemaid of his childhood emerges, the old woman who made him feel ashamed and clumsy, as in the dream of Bad treatment. Freud had it the night between October 3 and 4, 1897, immediately after informing Fliess that his "prime originator" was not the father but the nanny who spoke to him of God and Hell. It is one of the few dreams among those reported to Fliess which was omitted from *The Interpretation of Dreams*:

> she was my teacher in sexual matters and complained because I was clumsy and unable to do anything. ... The whole dream was full of the most mortifying allusions to my present impotence as a therapist.....
> Moreover, she washed me in reddish water in which she had previously washed herself. ... The dream could be summed up as "bad treatment."
> Just as the old woman got money from me for her bad treatment, ...
> A harsh critic might say of all this that it was retrogressively fantasied instead of progressively determined. The *experimenta crucis* must decide against him. The reddish water would indeed seem to be of that kind.

Commentators were deeply impressed by the contents of this letter and by the reference to reddish water. In a famous essay on "Freud and archeology," Suzanne Cassirer Bernfeld (1951, pp. 122–123) associated it with the blood of Christ, as did Robert Holt and Robert Vitz (1988). For Wendy Colman (1994, p. 613) the reddish water in which little Freud had been washed by the nanny was the blood of a Jewish ritual circumcision, perhaps of Julius, the little brother who died at six months. For Maciejewski (2002, pp. 47–49) at the origin of the entire group of fantasies there was Freud's own circumcision, of which he couldn't have any memory but had nevertheless come into representation through the circumcised boy's fantasy to be "bridegroom of blood to his mother," a fantasy embedded in the legend of Zipporah, Moses' Midianite wife: "Then Zipporah took a flint, and cut off the foreskin of her son, and cast it at his feet; and she said, surely a bridegroom of blood art thou to me" (Exodus 4:25). For Maciejewski, this fantasy of the "bride of blood" was dramatized in the bad treatment dream, paving the way to the discovery of the Oedipus complex, to finally return in the dream of Freud's self-dissection of the pelvis.

Can the enigmatic Zipporah legend, object of most diverse biblical interpretations, help us to put together Freud's various dreams? Perhaps yes, for several reasons. The main one is that Freud had a valid reason to identify with Moses. In the most accredited reading of the story of Zipporah, God was so angry with Moses to the point of wanting him dead because he failed to have his son circumcised, and here we find all of Freud's inner torment caused by his conflict with his father. In addition, Emma Eckstein's copious nose bleedings had turned her into a "bride of blood." Finally, the sado-masochistic aspects of this tie came to the foreground in the last phase of her analysis, when the entire analytic scene was colored by blood. The bad treatment dream was the heir of this world of sublime atrocities, which continued to reverberate in the inner world of Freud even after the end of Emma Eckstein's analysis, supported by the figure of his prehistoric nanny that had simultaneously "enchanted" and "mistreated" him.

As pointed out by other authors, the Bad treatment dream is in fact the Irma dream in reverse: in one it is the nanny who mistreats Freud, in the other it is Freud who mistreats his female patient (Swan, 1974, p. 39). Freud himself in some way realized his identification with the aggressor when, coming back on an emblematic episode of his relationship with the "old nanny," he noted: "the correct interpretation is I = she [Ich = sie]." Freud wrote this in his letter to Fliess of October 15, 1897, the same in which his discovery of the psychological meaning of the Oedipus tragedy was heralded!

Freud tells us how he came to this discovery in *The Psychopathology of Everyday Life*. The setting was the same one of the Exhibitionist dream, the house of the very old lady where Freud went twice a day to give her a morphine injection and to put a few drops of eye-lotion into her eye. But one day he got confused and was greatly frightened. It came then to his mind that "to make a blunder" was "to commit an assault" ("vergreifen" in German has both meanings).

He had come to the old woman while thinking of a dream of one of his patients who was in the habit of accusing himself of all sorts of crimes. Absorbed in this dream, which alluded to sexual intercourse with mother, Freud grasped "the universal human application of the Oedipus myth as correlated with the Fate which is revealed in the oracles; for at that point I did violence to or committed a blunder on 'the old woman'" (Freud, 1901b, p. 178; Rudnytsky, 1987, p. 63).

It is evident that here Freud reads the dream of Irma's injection as a prophecy, as an oracle that had continued to pursue him through a series of dreams that spoke of his trauma, from which, however, he once again distances himself by reversing it. According to Appignanesi and Forrester (1992, p. 133), Freud had displaced his aggression from his mother, to whom he went to lunch every Sunday, onto the "old woman." Wondering "How did Freud convert such anger, here directed at the old woman, to 'the love for the mother' he claimed as part of the Oedipus complex?" Jennifer Eastman (2005, p. 339) summed up the matter by saying that Freud "did not feel his feelings, he somaticized them," experiencing "gastrointestinal symptoms, endured every Sunday throughout his life while visiting his mother" (p. 342).

Indeed, Freud never abandoned the view that the relationship between mother and child was "the most perfect, the most free from ambivalence of all human relationships" (Freud, 1933a, p. 133). According to Otto Rank, it was a "blind spot" which conditioned his theory: all his impotent rage toward his mother had been dissociated and redirected to the father, to be finally boxed up in the myth of parricide Oedipus (Rank, 1926, pp. 142–143; Kramer, 1995).

Oedipus, Isaac, and Christ

According to Rudnytsky, Freud "transformed his molestation by his nurse into an oedipal romance" (2022, p. 282), a romance, moreover, which provided him with both a "refuge from Jewishness" and a "bulwark against the realm of the mothers" (2002, p. 55).

This is how, after having found in himself his "being in love with my mother and jealous of my father," Freud announced to Fliess, on October 15, 1897, his discovery of the universal value of the Oedipus legend:

> I now consider it a universal event in early childhood, even if not so early as in children who have been made hysterical. (Similar to the fiction of parentage [Abkunftsroman] in paranoia — heroes, founders of religion)

Why did Freud find paranoia in such simple and natural feelings? And to which "founders of religion" was he referring?

On the one hand, he seems to have touched, in Ferenczi's words, the hysterical-traumatic basis of his obsessive neurosis. On the other hand, he defends himself from his traumatic core by wrapping it in universal concepts just as Emma Eckstein's circumcision scene had disappeared under a universal fantasy. "Moloch, Astarte" are part of the same covering mechanism. At the same time, they illuminate the palimpsest of Freud's thoughts.

The association was more than motivated. In Jewish religion, the practice of sacrificing children to Moloch had in fact been replaced by circumcision, as is well recorded in the legend of Abraham and Isaac.

The story is well known: the Lord orders Abraham to sacrifice his son and only when Abraham shows himself obedient and has already tied Isaac to the altar of sacrifice, the Lord sends the Angel to block his hand. It is then that God establishes the Covenant with Abraham and his people, the pact signed with circumcision: human sacrifices will be replaced from now on with a symbolic sacrifice, the cutting of the skin that surrounds the glans. The part for the whole. As summarized by Martin Bergmann in his book *In the Shadow of Moloch: The Sacrifice of Children and Its Impact on Western Religions* (1992), circumcision is "a memorial to, a replacement for, and a prevention of the sacrifice of the child" (p. 104).[4]

Freud's attitude to this tradition was ambivalent. In his last great work, *Moses and Monotheism*, where he discloses to value circumcision a "key-fossil" (*Leitfossil*),[5] Freud dismissed the myth of Abraham and Isaac as a clumsy invention, destroying one of the cornerstones of his ancestors' religion. At the same time, there is a profound continuity, as in the Jewish circumcision Freud would continue to recognize the memory of an archaic time dominated by unbound violence. So, he will say:

> Circumcision is the symbolic substitute for the castration which the primal father once inflicted upon his sons in the plenitude of his absolute

power, and whoever accepted that symbol was showing by it that he was prepared to submit to the father's will, even if it imposed the most painful sacrifice on him.

(Freud, 1939, p. 122)

In the absolute power of the primal father, we can recognize the shadow of Moloch, mentioned in Freud's letter of January 24, 1897, even if from that precise moment on the name Moloch will disappear from Freud's pen. It will never be mentioned again either in public or in private. Moloch's identification with Israel (Robertson Smith, 1889–1890), the use of the accusation of ritual infanticide in anti-Semitic propaganda, the proliferation of the equation Judaism = Molochism among nineteenth-century intellectuals and philosophers (Rose, 1990, pp. 251–262), are sufficient elements to explain Freud's *political choice* to delete Moloch from his vocabulary.

But Moloch was not just canceled. It was replaced with its Greek equivalent, Kronos, to which Freud will continue to refer in many works as the reliable evidence of the brutality of primal age and of the harsh actuality of castration.[6]

In this shift, passivity was replaced by activity, in accordance with the pugnacious character of the overcoming of primeval age in Greek narrative. If in Jewish narrative the overcoming of the primal age of "monsters" is recalled by a suspension of action (the suspension of the sacrifice of Isaac), in Greek narrative it is celebrated by the triumphant battle of the Olympians gods against Monsters and Giants, who are defeated and pushed back into the womb of the earth. Shifting from one narrative to another, Freud substituted oral passivity (Moloch) for phallic activity. Yet, in the process he stumbled upon a "Freudian" slip, that is, a non-random error, which years later he will trace back to the legend of Isaac.[7]

Since *The Interpretations of Dreams*, Freud used Kronos as a window on the archaic, which transports him from the nineteenth-century Vienna to the gloomy landscapes of the primeval ages of human society in which "the father's despotic power" commands and "the ruthlessness with which he made use of it" (Freud, 1900, p. 256). In *Totem and Taboo*, this absolute tyrant will reappear as the head of the primitive family who is assaulted by his rebellious sons, thereafter rising to God in the memory of the crime. This endless struggle with the tyrant that flows through Freud's work, supporting it like a backbone, was thus rooted in the place of Emma Eckstein's dreamy circumcision scene—our "key-fossil."

Together with the replacement of Moloch with Kronos, the shift of the narrative axis from the "Semitic East" to the Hellenic one, produced a new, decisive effect: the replacement of Isaac with Oedipus. Starting with Erich Wellisch (1954), who compared their respective myths in the light of infanticide, the primordial crime of mankind, many authors have pointed out the similarities between Isaac and Oedipus, wondering why Freud did not rely on biblical narrative. Both are brought to a mountain, and tied up to be killed, surviving death. Like Isaac, also Oedipus is "almost sacrificed." They are both survivors.

Isaac was also an equivalent of Christ. The sacrifice of Isaac, which according to Jewish tradition took place at Passover,[8] prefigures the sacrifice by the Lord of his son. If in Jewish tradition is celebrated the Akedah (the act of binding), emphasizing the fact that the sacrifice of Isaac did not take place, the apostle Paul advocated in the letter to the Galatians the doctrine that Christians were descendants of Isaac sacrificed and risen again. In this tradition, where Isaac's sacrifice did take place, Christ is the second Isaac: God sacrificed his only son to redeem men and free them from the original sin. Thus, with the supposed arrival of the Messiah and his universal message, circumcision, the seal of the Old Covenant, lost its function. In Paul's discourse, it became a simple metaphor (Romans 2: 28–29), in Freud's a "fossil."

This articulated palimpsest illuminates the background from which emerges, in Freud, the recognition of the "universality" of Oedipus, which from the beginning is set as an equivalent of Isaac and Christ, the "founders of religions," giving to Freud's discourse a complex character, irreducible to simple psychology.[9]

Freud's will to deconstruct religious discourse, rewriting it into a secular story, would fully manifest itself in *Totem and Taboo*, where, however, the bridges and junctions are missing that would have brought to the surface the role played by Jewish circumcision in the construction of his arguments. Precisely because it is not explicit, this shift of the narrative axis creates a sub-text, a sort of semantic unconscious which endows Freud's texts with a peculiar allusiveness, further feeding them like an underground river from which new interpretations continuously spring.

Fishing in this sub-text, Moises Tractenberg would explain, in his 1989 article "Circumcision, crucifixion and anti-Semitism," how the image of Christ, the sacrificial Lamb and the Lord "nailed to the cross with a crown of thorns on his bleeding head represents the circumcised Phallus" (p. 464). In turn, the nailed feet of Christ evoke and overlap the figure of Oedipus, the child exposed on Mount Cithaeron with pierced and tied feet. Of course, the pierced and tied feet also make of Oedipus an equivalent of the bound Isaac. But all this disappeared from Freud's manifest discourse, which will be built around the figure, apparently free from all legacies, of Oedipus.

The reorganization of his thought will be a slow process. Indeed, it was only in 1909 that the idea of a "nuclear complex of neuroses" was formulated. The term "Oedipus complex" was introduced the following year, 1910. Finally, in 1920, in the fourth edition of the *Three Essays on the Theory of Sexuality*, Freud inserted the famous claim that the recognition of the importance of the Oedipus complex "has become the shibboleth that distinguishes the adherents of psycho-analysis from its opponents."[10]

Throughout the twentieth century, psychoanalysis will be identified with the Oedipus complex, despite the large number of unsolved problems, well summarized in 1991 by Bennett Simon in the article "Is the Oedipus complex still the cornerstone of psychoanalysis?" No less severe criticisms have been addressed to Freud's reading of the myth. According to George Devereaux (1953), his reading was "half blind," having canceled all the impulses and desires of adults, starting with Laius' homosexuality at the origin of the prophecy with which the legend begins. No less surprising is Freud's blindness for the traumatic elements in Oedipus' tragedy. Sander Gilman (1993b) was baffled by Freud's overlooking one of the most salient features of the legend, the somatic symbol of Oedipus early trauma: his pierced and deformed feet.[11]

This somatic symbol is indeed the axis around which the story unfolds. Exposed to die at birth, he was found by a shepherd with pierced and tied ankles and rescued. Yet he was marked by his wound (in Greek "trauma") both in his body (the pierced ankles) and in his name ("Oedipus" means "Swollen feet"). As a young man, the somatic memory of his early trauma was re-awakened at the fatal crossroad, when the wheel of an arrogant stranger's chariot ran over his foot. Then, in a fit of anger, he killed the stranger, unaware that he was his father Laius. Again, his foot sensitivity, this time in form of intelligence accelerator—Ferenczi called this side of trauma "traumatic progression"—enabled him to find the solution of the famous riddle of the Sphinx ("What walks on four feet in the morning, two in the afternoon, and three in the evening?"), to marry Jocasta and to become king. Finally, when all veils fall and he realized that he has killed his father and married his mother, fulfilling the oracle's prophecy, Oedipus pierces his own eyes repeating on his body the wound that had determined his fate. The horror of his pierced and bleeding eyes is the image by which he is best known. In short, his story is indeed paradigmatic, but of the compulsion to repeat an early trauma inscribed in the body.

According to Maciejewski (2002), mirroring himself in Oedipus, Freud unconsciously assimilated Oedipus' pierced ankles to the circumcision which marked his own body, a repressed trauma which returns in the Oedipus complex theory in form of symbolic castration. Circumcision would then be the somatic archive of psychoanalysis and "a crypt of the repressed sufferings of the young Oedipus" (p. 28).

Astarte

The circumcision scene had made him think of Astarte as well. In his letter to Fliess of January 24, 1897, Freud had evoked Moloch and Astarte, the idols of popular religion suppressed and destroyed by Torah Judaism. Both referred to the original violence attenuated and mitigated in the course of civilization. Both will disappear from Freud's pen, while remaining omnipresent.

It seems that the name Astarte derives from the Phoenician word for the uterus or "what comes from the uterus" (Patai, 1978), but the most distinctive feature of the cult of the Goddess Syria, as she was known in the Roman world, was the orgiastic rite at the apex of which the new adepts and priests tore their genitals to offer them as bloody sacrifice on the altar of the obscure Lady of Birth, Sex, and War. The Eastern cult of the Great Mother Goddess, in fact, "explicitly stressed and actually demanded a perfectly real castration" (Brenner, 1950, p. 322).

At the time of my archive searches in Berlin, I wanted to check if this detail was known to Freud and so I consulted Roscher's *Lexicon* of Greco-Roman mythology to which Freud often referred, and here, under the heading "Astarte," I found a reference to the "castration by which the sacrifice of emasculation is offered to the obscure Goddess, who sends death and destruction" (Roscher, 1884–1890, I, p. 654). So, this was the reason why Emma's scene made Freud think of Astarte. Actually, Eckstein was the "castrated" one, yet Freud experienced and felt the castration on his body, as it would powerfully emerge in his dream of the self-dissection of the pelvis.

The psychoanalytic idea of castration, centered on the ablation of the penis, is this. It is not a new idea. Indeed, it has a long history that intersects with ritual circumcision.

In the Bible, the "obscure Goddess, who sends death and destruction" is called Ashtoreth (1Re 11:5, 11:33; 2Re 23:13), a fusion of the name Astarte and the suffix *bosheth* for contempt for worship. The Judaism of the Torah was in fact "uncompromisingly hostile to everything that had anything to do with the Astarte-Adonis belief and cult. All its sanctuaries and cult objects were commanded to be ruthlessly destroyed, root and branch" (Feldman, 1944, p. 376). "The belief and cult of Astarte-Adonis was abandoned, sacred prostitution entirely ceased, idolatry disappeared, child-sacrifices were given up, and other immoral and condemned practices were relinquished by the Jews in the centuries after Ezra" (p. 383).

Some authors trace the origin of circumcision back to the worship of the Great Mother Goddess to whom the sacrifice of male genitals was offered and believe that in the biblical story of the "blood bride" might be the remnant of a time when it was the mother to circumcise the child.[12] In the reconstruction of Feldman (1944), together with the cult of Astarte, the scribe Ezra also abolished this archaic form of circumcision, which was reintroduced later by the Pharisees, but canceling the role of the mother, separating it from the sexual rites of the puberty and adopting a compromise solution: the rite was brought forward to the eighth day after birth.[13] Even Nunberg, an author very close to Freud, seems to move in this direction when, in his classic study "Circumcision and problems of bisexuality" of 1947, he writes:

The opinion has been expressed that in pre-biblical times Jewish women circumcised their sons. Elderly women of maternal type are represented on Egyptian sculptures assisting in the circumcision of the boys. Most important, however, is the fact that in the religions of the ancient Middle East, the cradle of Western civilization, men castrated themselves in religious ecstasy and offered their genitals on the altar of the Great Mother, the goddess Astarte, also known under other names. What men really did in ancient times, *they dream and fancy in modern times.*

(p. 175, emphasis added)

Isn't it this remark about what modern men do in dreams, a subtle allusion to the dream in which Freud enacts the sacrifice of his genitals? In this dream, which we will examine in detail in the next chapter, castration is accomplished with the concurrence of a woman who, like the protagonist of Rider Haggard's novel *She*, embodies destiny. She, in fact, stands for "She-Who-Must-Be-Obeyed." Lady and Domina of a sepulchral realm, She is "a magna mater of ancient times" (Grinstein, 1980, p. 402), an Astarte who treats her lover-son, her Adonis, as the embodiment of her own phallus.

Freud "normalizes" this passivity when he asserts: "A mother is only brought unlimited satisfaction by her relation to a son; ... she can expect from him the satisfaction of all that has been left over in her of her masculinity complex" (Freud, 1933a, p. 133). In the surrender of the son to the authority of the mother, Freud finds nothing problematic. It seems that in real life Freud was amazingly submissive to his mother, who was often described as "tyrannical" (Roazen, 1993). On the theoretical level, Schafer (1973) pointed out how the absence of the mother shines in Freud's discussion of resistance. In fact, behind the shell of "masculine protest," we find a total surrender to a female figure experienced as omnipotent, a figure that gives and takes away everything.

Freud's clearest reference to this female figure is found in the essay *The theme of the three caskets*, in which his dream of the Three Fates is synchronized with themes of myth, folklore, and literature. Freud, then, will explain the power of destiny starting from the ancient identity between the goddess of Love and the goddess of Death, an identity, so he writes, dating back to the "great Mother-goddesses of the oriental peoples ... both creators and destroyers" (Freud, 1913b, p. 299). He doesn't call her by her name, but there is no need: she is again and always Astarte. Yet this female figure who guides and organizes his thoughts will be continually erased by Freud.

His need to turn away from this powerful, destructive and magical figure is very clear in *Totem and Taboo*, where the myths of the Great Mothers and their consort sons are hastily treated and relegated to a secondary position.[14] Freud's tendency to diminish and even cancel the figure of the Great Mother has raised perplexity in many authors. In an essay on the meaning of castration anxiety in rabbinic mythology, Richard Rubenstein (1963), a scholar of Jewish theology, notes that the punishment most frequently inflicted by God is that of incorporation, which not only reflects "fear of the pre-Oedipal mother rather than the father" (p. 145), but induces an infinitely greater terror than castration, the terror of being incorporated by the Mother Earth who swallows like a mouth, a uterus and a grave: it is the "mouth of the earth" that it opens wide to swallow up unrepentant sinners. And quoting Erich Neumann's *The Great Mother* (1955) he recalls how this Terrible Mother who gives life and takes it away is "the hungry earth, which devours its own children and fattens on their corpses" (p. 149). According to Rubenstein, there was a continuity between Jewish monotheism and Freudian psychoanalysis: both had sought to replace an archaic, irrational and terrifying female figure with a more controllable father god.

According to Roy Schafer (1973), Freud emerged from his self-analysis with a painful personal knowledge of what it means to struggle against the archaic father, "but he taught us virtually nothing directly about what it is to struggle endlessly with the archaic mother" (p. 278). In fact, Freud does not struggle. He succumbs. As hypnotized, he surrenders himself to the object of terror without perceiving any terror, indeed with that sense of relief that accompanies the return into the mother's arms.

Notes

1 The Rosetta stone had made it possible to decipher the Egyptian pictographic writing thanks to the inscriptions in three languages.
2 Flechsig, known for his studies on the pyramid system, is in fact compared to the radiant Moses coming down from Mount Sinai (May 2003, p. 128).
3 Freud in fact wrote about the Catholic nanny: "From what I can infer from my own dreams her treatment of me was not always excessive in its amiability and her words could be harsh if I failed to reach the required standard of cleanliness." (Freud, 1900, pp. 247–248).
4 Already Bakan (1958) suggested that the essence of Judaism was the control over infanticide, preventing [binding] that the father enacts this impulse (p. 354).
5 In geology, key-fossils permit to determine the age of the rock through the organisms that have settled there (the Trilobites for the Paleozoic and the Ammonites for the Mesozoic). This powerful metaphor resonates with Freud's image of the "bedrock" in the final page of *Analysis Terminable and Interminable.*
6 Many direct and indirect references to Kronos are spread throughout Freud's work. See especially Freud (1926b, pp. 211–212).
7 See Freud (1900, p. 256), footnote. Freud will return on his error in *The Psychopathology of Everyday Life*, explaining it as the leap of a generation. In private, he will return on it again in a letter to Ferenczi in which he associated his error with the legend of Isaac. It seems that Ferenczi worked on the myth of Isaac in 1909, while having in mind the "castration-circumcision" complex (letter to Freud of 9 July). The only trace of this lost manuscript is Freud's commentary. Freud wrote: "Isaac just as nice. Analogous to my mistake in telling the story of Kronos' castration by Zeus, put forward against mythology, *only now explains this mistake to me* (Interpretation of Dreams)." (Freud's letter to Ferenczi of November 21, 1909; emphasis added).
8 Following James Frazer and other authors, Bergmann (1992) argues that children were originally sacrificed during Passover (*Pesach*, meaning the act of

passing over), which commemorates the day the Angel of Death passed over the houses of the Jews, sparing the life of the firstborn (Exodus 12).

9   According to Gilman (1993a) what made of the Freudian Oedipus a "universal" figure was the "overcoming" of circumcision as a distinctive element of the "racial" anti-Semitism of the late nineteenth century, thanks to "symbolic castration."

10   Freud (1905, p. 226) footnote. The *shibboleth* is a test based on a word that betrays the speaker's ethnic origin. In the biblical account whoever betrayed himself in pronouncing it was identified as a stranger and killed (Judges 12, 5–6). We can consider it as the linguistic equivalent of circumcision as a distinctive element that separates the pure from the impure ones, we from others, or vice versa. On this issue see (Aron & Starr, 2014, pp. 367–369). The "purism" folly in psychoanalysis, with its continuous projection of the "impurity" on the others, was, and still is, the scourge of "true psychoanalysis," an idea fueled solely by exclusion.

11   According to Gilman, this repression had to do with the toxic and virulent anti-Semitism of the turn of the century, in particular with the delusional idea of deformed feet of Jews.

12   Daly (1950), Dreifuss (1965) and Hobson (1961) report that, according to Barton (1932, p. 679), Semitic circumcision was originally a sacrifice to the goddess of fertility, aimed at placing the child under her protection and consecrating his generative power, putting him at her service.

13   Nunberg (1947) explains the choice of the eighth day thus:"The Jewish year is a moon year, each month being divided into four sevenday weeks. The seventh day, the Sabbath, was observed by Israelites even before monotheistic times. The term 'Shabath' is akin to the Babylonian 'Shabattum', the name given to the nefasti or evil days. On these days no work was done because no blessing went with it. ... The eighth day, i.e. the first day of the second week was considered the day of resurrection (The Jewish Encyclopoedia). Since the circumcision was regarded as symbolic rebirth, the choice of the eighth cay seems to correspond to a regression to an older premonotheistic religious belief, which in disguised form could easily be adopted by the adherents to circumcision. Christ's circumcision on the eighth day after his birth coincides with New Year's Day, the re-birth of the year, indeed" (p. 176, note).

14   Freud reads them in an Oedipal key as a belated expression of the incestuous libido, stimulated by the introduction of agriculture, which is reflected in the growing desire to replace the religion of the Father with that of the Son (Freud, 1913a, p. 152).

Chapter 7

The tomb

... the 'dead', 'murdered' part of the person – like a child – nursed, wrapped up in, by the parts which remained intact.

(Sándor Ferenczi, *Notes and fragments,* 24 August 1930)

Finis mundi

In his prehistoric life in Freiberg, Freud experienced another disappearing, after his brother Julius' death. At the end of 1858, both mother and nanny disappeared, the first to give birth to his little sister Anna, the other imprisoned for robbery. Freud did not keep conscious memories of these events, and yet from time to time an enigmatic scene came to his mind: he was desperately crying over the disappearance of his mother and then Philipp, his 20-year-old half-brother, opened a cupboard, or box (Kasten), but it was empty and this threw him even more into despair, until his mother came in through the door "slender" (=no longer pregnant) and "beautiful."

Freud reported this memory in the letter of October 15, 1897, the same in which the universal value of the Oedipus tragedy is claimed, offering an explanation: Philipp, who liked to play with words, must have told him that the nanny had been locked up ("eingekastelt," boxed up in the "Kasten," cupboard or wardrobe). The memory was thus manufactured around a pun, later contributing to the overdetermination of the *Box* [Kasten] as *Coffin* and *Womb*, which flows through life, dreams, and work of the father of psychoanalysis, shedding light into the private meaning that archeology had for him, as remarked by Suzanne Cassirer Bernfeld in a nice essay on "Freud and archeology" (1951).

Freud's passion for archeology was perhaps rooted in the evocative images of the Philippson Bible, an illustrated bible that had impressed him as a child. At least this is what suggests his dream of the "dead mother," the only dream stemming from his childhood that Freud reports in *The Interpretation of Dreams*. At the age of nine and a half, when Amalia was

DOI: 10.4324/9781003353058-10

pregnant with Alexander, Sigismund dreamed that his beloved mother was carried, motionless, by bird-beaked figures derived from an ancient Egyptian funerary relief of the illustrated bible (Freud, 1900, pp. 583–584). As is well known, Freud will become a great collector of antiquities, objects "found in a tomb" (as he will say to the Rat Man and other patients) and objects which he surrounded himself with and which gave him a unique pleasure.

In real life, his passion for archeology took shape in the summer of 1897, while wandering between Tuscany and Umbria searching for "absolute beauty." On September 9, 1897, he arrived in Orvieto in company of his brother Alexander. That morning he visited the majestic cathedral dedicated to Santa Maria Assunta. Its construction began in 1290, lasting nearly three centuries; its Gothic facade is one of the great masterpieces of Late Middle Age and an impressive testimony of the "organization of the Catholic church." The bas-reliefs that decorate the lower pillars tell the story and destiny of man, from Creation to Last Judgment, a theme taken up and expanded in the apocalyptic cycle of frescoes in the New Chapel that Luca Signorelli painted around the year 1500, a time when the arrival of *finis mundi* was anxiously expected. The central fresco, the *Resurrection of the Flesh*, illustrates one of the central tenets of Christian faith, the promise of Christ's death and resurrection to all individuals who believe in him that they will be resurrected in the flesh on the Day of Judgment, and received in the Kingdom of Heaven, the New Jerusalem for the Elects. The scene is a cosmogony in reverse: by hallucinatory fulfilling the desire of a happy reunion at the end of times, it repairs the rupture from which the world was born.

Usually, Freud got angry at the scandalous lie of Resurrection, but this time it was different. The apocalyptic cycle impressed him so deeply, that he will remember it as the most beautiful thing he had ever seen. Is it possible that his idea of religion as an unconscious psychology projected into the beyond was triggered by this scene where dead bodies return to life as a phallus in erection which is admitted into the womb of the Queen of Heaven? Years later he confided to Jung that carnal template of Resurrection was the erection of the penis, the latter being personified by Adonis in the myth of the god's death and resurrection.

Then, full of his visions, he undertook a long way to the base of the rock on which the city of Orvieto is built, to visit the Etruscan necropolis still known as "Necropolis of the tuff Crucifix," and here he entered a tomb carved into the tuff rock. The emotional impact was extraordinary: the Etruscan tomb, which replaces the womb of the Queen of Heaven in Freud's reunion fantasy, will mark the end of the long journey initiated with his Irma dream. As for Signorelli's apocalyptic scenes, they will be the background to a curious "memory disturbance" about the artist's name (or rather a part of it, "Signor," Lord in English).

Imposed suffering

The "systematic" phase of self-analysis, as Anzieu called it, lasted only a few months, from September to December 1897. Freud then understood that self-analysis was "impossible," as he wrote to Fliess toward the end of the year. The work of interpreting his own dreams will continue, but pursuing a new aim, that of writing the *Traumdeutung*, the dream book.

At Christmas 1897 Freud met again Fliess, this time in Breslau, where his friend picked up again the theme of innate bisexuality, which was introduced in the course of their previous encounter. Unexpectedly, Fliess had interpreted a recurring dream of giant snakes of a female patient of Freud as an expression of her "masculine" part. At Christmas, then, he had tried to combine bisexual constitution and bilateral symmetry in human anatomy. Just as lateralization divides the body into a right and a left half, similarly in everybody there is a male and a female part, one dominant and one repressed. Though interested in the subject, Freud became confused and could not follow him. In an effort to clarify his view, Fliess began to say "If we had an eye in the middle of our foreheads like a Cyclops [Zyklop]…" but at this point, Freud froze completely and Fliess lost his temper.

Freud had then a dream that he called "My son the Myop," where "Myop" is created on the model of "Zyklop" (short-sighted in German is "kurzsichtig"). The dream was built, Freud explains, on a tangle of thoughts prompted by a play that he had seen, *The New Ghetto*.

The dream opens with the declaration that something had occurred in the city of Rome, and had become necessary "to remove the children to safety." Thus, this dream echoes the dreams of the Rome series of the previous year, but the sense of catastrophe now being sharper. Even if at the end of his associations Freud assumed a fool's cap, this is one of his few dreams in which a genuine feeling of pain, I would say of mourning, transpires. "I was sitting on the edge of a fountain and was greatly depressed and almost in tears," writes Freud, quoting the Psalms ("By the waters of Babylon we sat down and wept"). Then a strange figure, a combination of his Catholic nanny and Emma Eckstein (a "nun" with a "red nose"), brings him two boys, his children. Taking leave from the older boy, the woman asks him for a goodbye kiss, the boy instead, writes Freud, "says AUF GESERES to her, and then AUF UNGESERES to the two of us (or to one of us). I had a notion that this last phrase denoted a preference" (Freud, 1900, p. 441).

Authoritative commentators have recognized in this formula the conflict between Judaism and Christianity. In the farewell "auf wiedersehen" (goodbye) the verb "sehen" (to see) is replaced by the Hebrew word *geseres*, from *goiser*. Freud says that he did not know its meaning and that he had been told that it meant "imposed suffering," "doom," and "weeping and wailing." The verb "Goiser" actually means to cut, fell, or clip, as noted by Wendy

Colman (1994), who came to the conclusion that Geseres-Ungeseres stood for "beschnitten-Unbeschnittensein" (circumcised—not circumcised).[1]

Colman also found in "geseres" the plural of "geserah," which is "a very strict ordinance or edict developed and imposed by rabbis to reinforce the religious law of the Talmud" a word that is often

> associated with persecution, following its use with a story of a massacre of Jews in Russia in 1648 ... Used in this way, geserah embodies a history of sentences imposed by rulers that signified doom through impending torture or disaster for the Jews.
>
> (p. 613)

What was anchored to circumcision was therefore an infinite disaster. In the years to come and throughout his work, Freud will remain faithful to this anchoring which turns the penis into the hero and monument of a cosmic drama in which the echoes of an unfinished mourning are preserved.

For Colman, at the root of the dream, there was a shock related to circumcision, perhaps the memory of the circumcision of Julius, the young brother who died prematurely. But it is not only religious circumcision that circulates in the dream. In Freud's associations, a whole series of allusions point to the danger of masturbation for school-going boys, an evil that results not only in a shorter sight but also in a shorter (cut) penis. Finally, we find a powerful allusion to the "massacres" by pediatricians.

Freud recalls that, while walking with Fliess, a girl had asked them the way, eliciting his apprehension for the reckless child. Soon after, he saw a doorplate baring the words "Dr. Herodes. Consulting hours: ..." "Let us hope," he then remarked, "that our colleague does not happen to be a children's doctor," thus associating the world of pediatricians with the massacre of the Innocents ordered by the infamous King Herod. In short, coming across a "Herr Zucker" creates troubles, but ending up in the hands of a pediatrician was even worse!

We find here a condensation of child sexual abuse and of circumcision as a "cure" for the abused child, and that alignment between personal history and biblical story, secular and religious world that makes the work of Freud truly unique. It seems that he is talking about some private event and instead he is making a political speech, it seems that he is talking about science and instead he is dueling with biblical texts.

However, in this dream triggered by the "bi-bi" (bisexuality-bilaterality) Freud is clearly divided in two. In an attempt to clarify himself with Fliess, on January 4, 1898, he revealed to him that he could not distinguish right from left.

Freud suffered a disorder of lateralization, perhaps a type of dyslexia, which forced him to compensate his deficit by abstract strategies. According to Anzieu (1986, p. 206), this confusion was the product of the multicultural context in which he grew up and of the fact that he had multiple "mothers" (the Jewish mother and the Catholic nanny), so that the mixed codes had been the cause of "difficulties in reading and learning."

If we consider that the coding rules of alphanumeric symbols in Christian writing are from left to right, while in Hebrew writing they are from right to left, one should also ask whether it was for this reason that in certain dreams the sequence of numbers was easily changed (as in "absurd dreams") and the order of phonemes (milah-amyl), or, again, if this was not the reason why he was delighted with palindromes, such as "Anna," which remain the same whether read from left to right or from right to left. Some have even suggested that for Freud "Roma" (Rome) coded secretly "Amor" (love). I wouldn't be surprised, considering how deeply Freud mirrored himself in Leonardo da Vinci, who kept a secret diary written from right to left. In the course of 1898, he would signal Leonardo to Fliess, for his research on the connection between left-handedness and sexual inversion.

The psychic block, however, did not disappear, on the contrary, it took the form of a memory gap. Freud will be unable to keep in his head the moment when Fliess had told him about bisexuality, he "forgot" it repeatedly, while entertaining at the same time the desire, and sometimes the illusory belief, that he had been the first to seize it.[2]

In a passage of his self-analysis of the end of 1898, this rivalry with Fliess was transported to his mythical childhood. It is the story of Sigismund's first conflict with John, the prototype of all male friendship in which the friend coincides with the enemy. In this passage, which is part of the thoughts aroused by another dream, Freud says that "The two children had a dispute about some object. … Each of them claimed to have got there before the other and therefore to have a better right to it. They came to blows and might prevailed over right." Even though he was in the wrong, Freud wrote: "this time I was the stronger and remained in possession of the field" (Freud, 1900, p. 483). Put in the present, the "object" of the dispute between Freud and Fliess was, in abstract, the brilliant idea of bisexuality; in concrete, it was Emma Eckstein's imaginary penis.

The giant snake that inspired Fliess' theory of bisexuality was about to become, in Freud's fantasies, a magic talisman protecting against pain, loss, and mourning. Even though the traumatic significance of Emma Eckstein's circumcision had failed to make its way into Freud's psyche, it was nevertheless admitted and recorded through its negative, the "great Lord Penis." Which, in turn, would have made the Phallus a reminder of castration.

Defloration fantasies

In 1898, Freud tirelessly worked on *The Interpretation of Dreams*. In March, the book even appeared to him in a dream through a shop window: it was a Botanical monograph. For Anzieu (1986), this dream with endless branches was modeled on a simple equation: "flowers = female genitals" (p. 293). At its center stood a plastic memory of when Freud was five, an image of himself with his three-year-old sister Anna, blissfully pulling a book with color plates into pieces "*leaf by leaf,* just like an artichoke [Artischocke]" (Freud, 1900, p. 172). According to Anzieu, it represented "an intellectualization of a past, carnal action—opening the folded 'flower' of a little girl, in other words her sexual organs, ... where the little boy imagines he can see the results of castration" (1986, p. 288). For Grinstein (1968), the scene suggests the presence of "forbidden incestuous feelings toward his sister Anna" (p. 67). For other commentators, it displayed a destructive action that resonates with the word "schockieren"—to shock, offend, and dishonor—contained in the word "Artischocke," as suggested by Barbara Mautner (1991, p. 283). As for the action of pulling into pieces the plates (Tafeln), Lippman (2009, pp. 581–582) recognized an allusion to the blasphemous act of breaking the Tables of the Law (*Die mosaischen Gesetztafeln*).

At Easter 1898, Freud was again in Italy with his brother Alexander, where he is seized by euphoric fantasies of deflowering while venturing deeper and deeper into the "holes" (caves) of Carso, as he wrote to Fliess on April 14. He had just visited the Etruscan Museum of Aquileia, where he was struck by the large number of "priapic statues." In his letter to Fliess, he made a long list of those statues, coming to the conclusion that "Priapus stood for permanent erection, a wish-fulfillment representing the opposite of psychological impotence." It is the first explicit statement about the *apotropaic* meaning that the erect penis had for Freud.[3] Then he took a memorable boat ride in the lagoon, celebrating with his brother and some good Istrian wine, the *joie de vivre*. The memory of this exciting day underlies an important dream in which Freud finds himself with his brother facing an attack in a castle by the sea. This dream was triggered by concerns about Freud's sister Anna, and Anzieu dated it May 10, 1898,[4] but it could have been of three or four days later, marking on the anniversary of his brit milah (Freud was born on May 6).

Freud dreamed that he had taken the place of the commander of the castle, who died in the course of the attack. He and his brother were observing the warships in the channel through a window and noticing that a large warship was returning, they were both scared to death. The terror was, however, magically dispelled at the sight of another ship, small and cut off short. The two brothers called out with one voice (in German: *aus einem Munde*, with one mouth): "Here is the breakfast ship [Frühstücksschiff]!" (Freud, 1900, p. 464). Freud's conclusion was that the "breakfast ship" recalled of the most cheerful *joie de vivre* experienced in the Grado lagoon, behind which, however, "the gloomiest thoughts" were concealed (Freud, 1900, p. 466).

The "breakfast ship" re-proposes an oral scene. Its magic power to dispel anxiety might evoke the magic that the nipple has for a newborn ("Frühstück," breakfast, literally means "early bite"), however, it is more akin to a talisman. It recalls, in fact, the greatest bliss that accompanies the archaic illusion that the mother is endowed with a penis, a fantasy that begins to form when the baby takes the nipple in his mouth and sucks it, as Freud wrote in his essay on Leonardo da Vinci (Freud, 1910b, p. 87).

The saving "Breakfast ship" had the same shape of an object that, the previous summer when he and his brother visited an Etruscan Museum on the way to Orvieto, attracted their interest: a rectangular cup of black pottery. It looked like a modern breakfast-set but it was the toilet-set of an Etruscan Lady who had been put in her tomb to make life after death comfortable for her. Commenting on this strange object, Freud wrote that it meant "black toilet, mourning," referring to "a death." As the dream-object reminded him of "the funeral boats in which in early times dead bodies were placed and committed to the sea for burial." Since the ship was broken, Freud concluded that it represented "the return after a shipwreck" (*Schiffbruch*, literally "broken ship"; in English: "ship-break," hence "break-fast," breakfast).

Reading the dream in the light of the fantasies of defloration that surfaced in the previous months, Anzieu writes:

> The power of the 'bombardment' was such that it cut off the small ship in the middle: the defloration is phantasied as sadistic and destructive. ... When looked at from the angle of the body image, the dream effects a symbolic exploration of the female body ... [which] culminates with the act of taking possession ... a source of both anxiety and intense pleasure.
>
> (Anzieu, 1986, p. 318)

While being a symbol of the female genitalia, the truncated vessel is also a depiction of the circumcised penis. Thus, in addition to the attack on female genital highlighted by Anzieu—an attack that is illuminated by Emma Eckstein's circumcision—I believe that in the dream circles also the memory of Freud's brother Alexander's *brit milah*, an experience that had probably awakened in the ten-year-old boy the condensed memory of Julius' circumcision and death. The Lady in black seems to refer to Amalia's mourning for the death of her child; the squat and truncated vessel is then both the circumcised penis and the child whose life was prematurely broken (in his work Freud will strictly adhere to the equation penis = child).

I reported this dream because, in my opinion, Ferenczi unconsciously drew from it the material to create the dream in which a small penis (extraordinarily erect and horribly mutilated) is served with utensils on a saucer. Indeed, the German word used by Ferenczi will be "*Tasse*," cup, but in his letter to Freud he also made a sketch of it (I will report Ferenczi's drawing in a later chapter), and what he sketched was a rectangular saucer—therefore a singular "rectangular cup," just like the breakfast ship!

In Freud's dream this amputated ship, in which all possible catastrophes are condensed, becomes a magical talisman that dispels anxiety, a bit like what it happens in popular religions where the relics of martyrs are venerated and perform miracles. However, the saving function of this fetish is not without cost. Soon after, Freud dreamed of being trapped in a sort of hospital with machines, similar to "a Hell with its diabolical punishment tasks," where he is accused of having "appropriated" a missing object and is subjected to an "inspection" in the double meaning of medical examination and judicial investigation. Then they say he can go, but he can't find his "hat" and can't get away (Freud, 1900, p. 36).

For Wendy Colman (1994), the dream repeats the "ritual of circumcision" and the missing hat is "the penis or foreskin on the penis, removed in circumcision" (p. 615). Since Freud associates his dream with birth and death, Colman finds there the echo of Julius' birth, circumcision, and death. This too seems to be an anniversary dream of Freud's brit milah. As to the charge of embezzling something, one cannot avoid to think of Emma Eckstein's imaginary penis which, as a magic talisman, can undo every mutilation and loss.

Femme fatale

In his travels, Freud moved constantly because he wanted to see more things in a single day. After the Easter journey, his brother was so tired of his frenzied way of traveling that he no longer wanted to accompany him. But Freud's phobia of trains prevented him from traveling alone and so he began to think of another accompanying person: his wife's younger sister, Minna, who two years before had moved to their home to help out with their children. She was once engaged, but her betrothed died and afterward she never married. Freud liked her, she was intelligent and open, to the point that she was the only person, apart from Fliess, with whom he discussed his work. Moreover, as Jones says, she was of the "masculine" type that Freud liked.

Elisabeth Roudinesco (2014, p. 68) calculated that Freud's sex life during his marriage lasted no more than nine years; for the rest he had practiced abstinence, which probably fueled his creative energy. Nevertheless, Freud was not proud of it; like Nietzsche, he saw abstinence as a sign of weakening and decay. It was not a virtue but a burden of "aging" that Freud accepted with resignation. Together with his constipation, it fed his pessimism and the image of himself as an old man drained of all energy. Deflowering fantasies had a revitalizing effect on him. Imagining of taking possession of the woman's magic penis did not only compensate him for his "wound" but was also an antidote to his depressed mood.

In the summer of 1898, these deflowering fantasies began to have as object Minna who was both a virgin and a "sister" (in-law). According to Anzieu (1986, pp. 328; 542–543), the trips he made with Minna revived the incest taboo in Freud. In fact, in the summer of 1898, Freud began to deal more and more intensely with the topic of brother and sister incest. Fantasies on this theme broke into important dreams, crossed by a growing euphoria, such as "Hollthurn," named after a marine animal that has the shape of a phallus (it is also called "sea cucumber"), "Count Thun," a revolutionary dream in which he challenges every possible authority, and "Open air closet," in which he has now become a Nietzschean "superman," beyond and above morality. A day or two after this dream Freud and Minna left for their first vacation alone. Between August 4 and 15 they crossed the Austrian Tyrol, Italy, and Switzerland. On August 8 they were in Trafoi and on August 13 in Maloja where they slept in the same room at the Hotel *Schweizerhaus,* registering as "*Dr. Sigm. Freud und Frau* [and wife]" (Maciejewski, 2006).

According to the editor of the correspondence between Freud and Minna Bernays, published in 2005, the picture they reveal is hardly compatible with a secret *liason*. Other Freud scholars came to the conclusion that a couple of years later (by 1900), Freud did eventually engage in an affair with his sister-in-law.[5] In any case, sleeping together was probably not easy. It would seem an experience to forget about. As a matter of fact, Freud began to run into strange forgetfulness and finally found himself unable to remember the name "Signorelli."[6] Shortly after, Freud had the dream of the Three Fates.

Hungry, he went to the kitchen in search of a piece of cake and found three women there. The first wriggles her hands, like doing Knoedels (dumplings), but she tells him that he has to wait, and so he goes away, hungry, and resentful. In the second scene, which has a homosexual flavor, he consoles himself by wearing the overcoat with a fur collar of another man. In the associations, he then revolves around the idea of "plagiarism." Together with Freud's desire to take possession of Fliess' brilliant idea (bisexuality), it also takes shape the idea that transference is nothing else than a "change of skin," an idea which will be confided to Ferenczi as something to keep secret.[7] The symbolic exchange ("this Mathilde for that Mathilde") is here aligned with the skin lost in circumcision, leading to the view of life as incessant search for substitutes, a fair of barters that inevitably ends with the last exchange: the one with death, animistically imagined on the model of the mother and her substitutes (sister, daughter).

In the essay "Circumcision and problems of bisexuality" (Nunberg, 1947), to which we will return several times, Herman Nunberg will clarify that the trauma of circumcision stirs unconscious fantasies that have the same structure as cosmogonic myths, in which a whole is divided into two parts. Such parts are often imagined as brother and sister, thus generating the fantasy that the sexual union of the separated fragments can repair the wound.

In his first association to his dream, Freud recalls a historical novel (Hypatia) in which the monk Philemon falls in love with Pelagia, a Greek beauty who plays the role of Aphrodite in pagan ceremonies. Freud omits, however, to mention the central moment of the novel, when the monk discovers with horror that the woman he fell in love with was his own sister and, in front of her erotic dance, utters "Pelagia! Sister! My sister! ... ." For Grinstein (1980, p. 183), this detail, on which Feud was silent, informed both his dream and his associations. In his turn, Grinstein omitted to say that what makes this uttering significant is the role of *femme fatale* that Minna, the "sister," was now playing in Freud's fantasy world. This, by the way, explains why Freud recognized the three women of his dream as the "sisters" who personify "fate" in Greek mythology.

The three women in the kitchen reminded him "of the three Fates who spin the destiny of man." The first "was the mother who gives life, and ... its first nourishment. Love and hunger, I reflected, meet at a woman's breast" (Freud, 1900, p. 204). Finally, one might say, Freud confronts that recurring oral element that breaks out like a dull scream from the dream in which Irma opens her mouth. But a childhood memory resurfaces powerfully. He rushed hungry into the kitchen toward his mother, who apparently was making dumplings. However, instead of making good food, she rubbed the palms of her hands together, showing him me the blackish scales of *epidermis* (skin) produced by the friction as *ad oculos* demonstration that we are made of earth, and to the earth we will return. Just like the diphtheria (from *diphtera*, skin) in the Irma dream, the epidermis reminds him that he "owed a death." It is the moment when, in Freud's thought, castration, and death are aligned—along with the rest of his work, the one will be an equivalent of the other—by tying in with the theme of incest.

At the end of the long analysis of his dream, Freud notes that his thoughts were telling him, on the one hand, that "one should never neglect an opportunity, since life is short and death inevitable" while presenting him, on the other hand, "restraining thoughts of every kind and even threats of the most revolting sexual punishments" (Freud, 1900, pp. 207–208). If the missed opportunity brings us back to the trip with Minna, the allusion to "repugnant sexual punishment" brings Emma Eckstein back on the stage, as if the shocking demonstration *ad oculos* offered by her mutilated vulva was slowly transmuting, in Freud's mind, into an obsessive admonishment. This is the moment when the thought of castration is welded to incestuous desire in such a way that the individual history and the traumatic are erased. Freud had given himself a new foundation.

Irma, the "universal woman" that in the dream of the Three Fates is projected in the three figures of mother, sister/lover and death, in the final dream, will return to be a single figure without a name: "She." *She* is the *femme fatale* and it is Minna who embodies her.

Freud had it in May 1899 when he was revising the last chapter of *The Interpretation of Dreams*, the chapter of the ultimate explanations. Minna (in the dream Luise N.) had asked him for something to read and Freud offered her a novel by Rider Haggard entitled *She*, "A *strange* book, but full of hidden meaning... the eternal feminine, the immortality of our emotions ... ." Minna, however, wanted to read something written by Freud. Since Freud replies: "my immortal works are not yet written," she presses him, stinging him with sarcasm: "So, when will the so-called 'ultimate explanations' come out...?" And Freud once again freezes and falls silent. That night he dreamed that his old professor had entrusted him with a task, an "anatomical preparation":

> Old Brücke must have set me some task; *Strangely Enough*, it related to a dissection of the lower part of my own body, my pelvis and legs, which I saw before me as though in the dissecting-room, but without noticing their absence in myself and also without a trace of any gruesome feeling. Louise N. [Minna] was standing beside me and doing the work with me. The pelvis had been eviscerated, and it was visible now in its superior, now in its inferior, aspect, the two being mixed together. Thick flesh-coloured protuberances (which, in the dream itself, made me think of haemorrhoids) could be seen. Something which lay over it and was like crumpled silver-paper1 had also to be carefully fished out. ...
>
> (Freud, 1900, p. 452)

Confronted with this scene, Freud's followers will remain speechless for a long time. When Erikson (1954) described the act of gazing the horrible gap of Irma's throat as the moment of an "initiation, conversion, and inspiration" which transforms Freud into a hero who, in his turn, will be looked at by men "with pity and terror, with ambivalent admiration and ill-concealed abhorrence" (p. 47), he had implicitly superimposed these two scenes.

As for Freud, he merely said that the self-dissection represented his self-analysis and the sacrifice of making it public. Only recently have some authors explicitly recognized in this scene a representation of his circumcision, mediated by the fantasy of the "bride of blood" (Maciejewski, 2002) or by the memory of his brothers' circumcision ceremony which had awakened the somatic memory recorded on his own body (de Klerk, 2008). If we consider that Freud was born on May 6, one would even think that he had this dream on May 13 or 14, i.e., on the anniversary of his brit milah, just as, one year before, he had the dream of the Breakfast-ship and of the Hellish machines.

And yet the fabric of this dream arises at the intersection of several lines of thought. The first is the paternal reproach for not having fulfilled his religious duties. Freud had not listened to him and indeed at the birth of his third son he had called him Ernst in honor of Brücke, to reaffirm that in his life science had replaced religion. The task assigned by Brücke, the paternal substitute, is therefore a scientific task, an anatomical dissection, but also a perfect equivalent of the religious ritual from which Freud had rebelled.

Moreover, the dream also picks up on the "Bad Treatment" dream in which the Catholic nanny, the prototype of the femme fatale, washes him in blood-soaked water. Thus, his own castration is also an *imitatio Christi*.

Freud offers his flesh and blood as a Christ on the cross. The allusion to the Eternal Feminine [das ewig Weibliche], brings Faust on the stage and his burial, imagined by Goethe in imitation of the Deposition and Resurrection of Christ. When Faust dies, the abyss of hell opens up before him as a horrible jaw (Faust, 1644), and then his soul is drawn up by the Eternal Feminine and saved. Like Faust, the modern hero who does not believe in sacred scriptures, Freud also imagines himself in imitation of Christ, but in his dream, there is no resurrection or salvation. There is only an empty Tomb.

In the second part of the dream, Freud begins a long and perilous journey toward the center of the world with aching legs, guided by a woman who has to bring him in arm, from time to time. The journey ends in a small wooden house that Freud recognizes first as the coffin and then as the empty Etruscan tomb, he had entered in Orvieto.

It is one of the high points of that equation between Box, Coffin, and Womb that runs through his life no less than his work. At the end of his long journey, Freud chooses as his domicile this place that recalls the empty box (Kasten) in which, in his childhood memory, his mother had disappeared. For the rest of his life, he will continue to stage his death with a mixture of fear and desire, as Ernest Jones wrote in his biography (Jones, 1957, p. 301), and with powerful obsessive ceremonials well described by Max Schur, his last doctor, in his book on Freud's living and dying (Schur, 1972).

Coffin = womb

At the end of the perilous journey in which life, self-analysis, and writing converge, as if they were one thing, Freud finally arrives in a wooden house in which he finds himself trapped, as in a womb. He immediately finds a window from which he could get out and overcome the chasm using two axes as the bridge. But when the thought surfaces that he should pass over two children (instead of the two axes), he wakes up in the most profound anguish. It is the return of the nightmare that in the Irma dream was exorcised by the formula of the trimethylamine. Now he could really say "Jetz ist es aus mit dir" [This is your end]. And yet, while recognizing the wooden house as the coffin, in his reading of the dream Freud turns his nightmare into a "wish fulfillment":

> The 'wooden house' was also, no doubt, a coffin, that is to say, the grave. But the dream-work achieved a masterpiece in its representation of this most unwished-for of all thoughts by a wish-fulfilment. For I had already been in a grave once, but it was an excavated Etruscan grave near Orvieto, a narrow chamber with two stone benches along its walls, on which the skeletons of two grown-up men were lying. ... The dream seems to have been saying: 'If you must rest in a grave, let it be

the Etruscan one.' And, *by making this replacement, it transformed the gloomiest of expectations into one that was highly desirable.*
(Freud, 1900, pp. 454–455, emphasis added)

Freud seems not to understand that a part of himself is already "dead" and that the "coffin" signals the resurfacing of his childhood trauma, which, however, finds no "empathic witness" (Ferenczi) in self-analysis.

Even though the fantasy of returning to the womb is one of Freud's most important discoveries, within his system of thought it remained prisoner of a "confusion of tongues." Here is how Freud talks about it in his letter to Ludwig Binswanger of May 17, 1909: "coffin = womb; being buried alive = life *in utero*. Thus, the phantasies show that what is involved here is a return to the womb of the mother." And later, in *The Uncanny*, Freud traced the "terrible fantasy" of being buried alive to the fantasy of "intra-uterine existence" (Freud, 1919). Indistinguishable from bliss, this "terrible fantasy" will be dramatized in his fainting spells and theorized in the idea of death instinct, leaving us dismayed, as indeed his erasure of any distinction between dream and nightmare, wish fulfillment and trauma, desire and incest, life and death.

Abandoned to himself, Freud is unable to rediscover those pleasurable sensations of flying and floating which, in the wake of Ferenczi, Michael Balint will trace back to the child's feeling of being kept safe in the mother's arms and explore extensively in the light of the theory of primary love.[8] Similarly, discussing the concept of "oceanic feeling," he will admit: "I cannot discover this 'oceanic' feeling in myself."[9] More than a return to the womb, what is staged here is the repetition of his childhood trauma. It is the moment in which the open mouth of Irma, the matrix of everything, closes like a sphinx. Better, as an indecipherable Etruscan grave. It is then that the nightmare continually pushed away, rejected, exorcised, becomes real.

Here I am reminded of what Elisabeth Severn writes in the chapter "Nightmares Are Real" of *The Discovery of the Self*:

The imagination fails utterly to act as a "shock absorber" and what remains is *pure shock*, unadulterated by any fantasies of relief, escape, or amelioration. These dreams are always of painful content and intensity, and constitute what is called *nightmare*. They might be instigated by current events, as most dreams are, but they have, in my opinion, a distinguishing and significant quality. It is that they are *historical* and tell always of some *decisive and disintegrating event in the past*. They are records of personal catastrophes, the consequence of which was disruption of the whole mental machinery. Such shocks destroy the inherent integration of the psyche and leave permanent scars.
(Severn, 1933, pp. 89–90)

Taking then a stand against Freud's belief that the psyche cannot have any experience of death, Severn recalls a recurring dream of her's in which, split in two, she attends her own funeral watching her being buried in the tomb. And if, as she writes in *The Discovery of the Self*, for Freud "no one really dreams of his own death because, if he is present as an observer, this is sufficient proof that the dream is a 'fantasy'..." (p. 108),[10] for Severn it was instead perfectly possible "for a person to be psychically 'killed', or at least, that a part of the person can be killed, while another part of him continues to live in the flesh" (pp. 108–109).

This split, between a destroyed or dead part and an observing part, a lucid, insensible, and omniscient intelligence that detached itself from the ego and calculates the damage by looking at it from the outside, was for Severn a psychic mechanism of the "utmost importance." This is what Ferenczi writes in the *Clinical Diary*: "The person splits into a purely cognitive psychic being, which observes events from the outside and into a totally insensitive body" (Dupont, 1988, p. 177; May 10, 1032). This splitting, which for Ferenczi was the hallmark of trauma, was the salient characteristic of Freud's final dream.[11] But it is also a constant trait of his personality divided between a part always on the verge of dying, perhaps already dead, and a grandiose, omnipotent, triumphant part, which from time to time presents itself as the leader who has a mission to accomplish, the prophet to whom the "secret of dreams" is revealed, the "founder of religions" who will end up imprinting psychoanalysis precisely with the character of a new religion, a "scientific" one (as heralded by the word "trimethylamine").

The task

While observing his eviscerated pelvis, Freud understood his task: something had "to be carefully fished out." This something is represented in the dream by a piece of tin foil, which is immediately understood by Freud as an allusion to the name of the author of a study on fish and to his first publication, a scientific study on a fish, which had been assigned by Professor Brücke when he was a student. He doesn't say anything else.

It is clear that what the father of psychoanalysis "observes" in this dream is his infantile trauma, as if the shock experienced at the sight of Emma Eckstein's mutilated vulva[12] made him fall back on himself. The external reality disappears and, in its place, Freud looks, astonished, at his own disappeared penis. In the final dream, this shock becomes "traumatic progression,"[13] revelation: in place of the penis there is a fish, a symbol of "phylogenetic childhood." In a passage added to the dream book in 1919, Freud will take up Nietzsche's assertion that in dreams "some primaeval relic of humanity is at work which we can now scarcely reach any longer by a direct path," further claiming that "the analysis of dreams will lead us to a knowledge of man's archaic heritage, of what is psychically innate in him" (Freud,

1900, pp. 548–549). Dreams are therefore a window on the unconscious that goes beyond individual childhood, giving "a picture of the development of the human race, of which the individual's development is in fact an abbreviated recapitulation" (ibid.)

According to Haeckel's recapitulation theory, which had profoundly impressed Freud as a student, the human embryo passes from a stage where it first resembles a fish and then a reptile, thus repeating the history of the organism's biological evolution. Besides being a symbol of the distant phylogenetic past, the fish is also a widely spread religious symbol in the pagan world, where it represented fertility. Many mother goddesses were represented through the symbol of the fish, or with a fish instead of the head, or with a part of the body in the shape of a fish. In the entry "Astarte" of the mythological *Lexicon* that Freud regularly consulted, we read that the fish was a symbol of the "mysterious life of nature." In parts of Syria, where the eating of fish was forbidden, fish was served as ceremonial food in pagan rituals in which priests tore their genitals and offered them to the fish goddess Atargatis, whose son was called Ichtùs (fish). And, of course, the fish was a Christian symbol.[14] Tertullian called Christ "our fish" and baptized Christians as "little fishes," making use of a symbol of the early Jewish tradition, where "eating the fish represented a mystic sharing in the divine power which would be fully manifest in the Messianic age, and in which each faithful Jew placed his hope for resurrection and future life" (Friedman, 1960, p. 257).

Our story could terminate here. Yet, the task of carefully fishing out something from the eviscerated pelvis will be taken over by Ferenczi. The fish as a mysterious symbol of nature will in fact be the hero of *Thalassa*, a scientific fantasy by which he will try to carry out Freud's theory of genitality, drawing, then, a new apocalyptic scenario.

Notes

1 Colman (1994, p. 615); same conclusion in Maciejewski (2002, pp. 50–53).
2 The question is not that simple, given that even in previous years the topic was present. See Freud's letter to Fliess of December 6, 1896. However, the theory of bisexuality that Fliess presented to Freud at Easter 1897 was different. We will return to this point in the penultimate chapter.
3 As suggested by Erickson, an allusion to Priapus (Proprion…) was already contained in the sequence of words that in Irma's dream exorcise the sense of helplessness and death. The stone phallus Priapus will be mentioned again in *The Taboo of Virginity* (Freud, 1918b), in connection with the rites of defloration through a paternal surrogate. It seems that, in the spring of 1898, Freud was fantasizing defloration ceremonies as a feminine equivalent of brit milah.
4 On May 10 in the Neue freie Presse, a long article was published on the Spanish-American naval battle to which Freud refers in his associations to the dream, linking it to his concerns for the family of his sister Anna who lived in New York.
5 Peter Swales (1982), first of all. An exhaustive review of the debate is provided by Peter Rudnytsky (2012) in a still unpublished manuscript in which he further

develops Swales' thesis, clarifying the infantile origin of the "sister theme" in Freud's life and work. In this work, I do not take a position on whether or not Freud's incestuous fantasy was enacted at a genital level as well, but I do acknowledge that the "sister" theme played an essential role in structuring Freud's theory of castration as punishment for incestuous desires.

6 Freud was about to tell an occasional traveling companion from Berlin that Luca Signorelli's cycle of apocalyptic frescoes was the most beautiful thing he had ever seen, when the artist's name faded. He remembered "Luca," but for several days only "Botticelli" kept coming to his mind. I explore this substitution in *The Cut* volume 2 (Bonomi, 2018a, pp. 106–109).

7 See Freud's letter to Ferenczi of January 10, 1910.

8 See Balint (1955, pp. 229–231, 1968, p. 74). For Balint (1960) "The ultimate aim of all libidinal striving is thus the preservation or restoration of an original harmony" (p. 41), namely, the merging with the good object, as the matrix of the *"unio mistica."* In his view "the re-establishment of the original harmony between the individual and the most important parts of his environment, his love objects" was "the desire of all humanity" (ibid.). This passage is also reported, slightly modified, in Balint (1968, p. 74). See in particular chapters 11 and 12 of *The Basic Fault*, and in general Balint's revision of the theory of primary narcissism. As for life in utero, Balint speaks of a greater and more intense investment of the environment by the fetus, naturally an environment without defined boundaries, well exemplified by the water that is found in the gills of the fish: "It is an idle question to ask whether the water in the gills or in the mouth is part of the sea or of the fish; exactly the same holds true about the foetus" (Balint, 1968, p. 66).

9 Freud (1930, p. 65). According to Balint, Freud's misunderstanding of the "oceanic feeling" was closely connected both to his lack of *Flugtraume* (dreams of flying) and to his *Reisefieber*, his neurotic anxiety related to travel (Balint, 1959, p. 55).

10 According to Freud (1926a), "the unconscious seems to contain nothing that could give any content to our concept of the annihilation of life" (p. 129), "nothing resembling death can ever have been experienced" (p. 130). This position has met with several objections (cf. Stern, 1968; Becker, 1973; Hoffman, 1979).

11 I would like to call attention on an important point, which helps us to understand the abysmal difference between Freud and Ferenczi. At the time when he had his dream of the self-dissection of the pelvis, Freud argued that the fact that in the dream the ego observes a scene in which he himself is the protagonist, indicated that the content of the dream was not an actual trauma but a retrospective fantasy (Freud, 1899, pp. 321–322).

12 Of course, this is a narrative simplification. The most precise reconstruction is as follows: when Freud took charge of Emma Eckstein Freud, he made a gynecological examination, as was the practice at the time, without having any emotional reaction. Only after the operation on the nose, at the precise moment when Emma risked bleeding to death, the emotional reaction that did not take place at the time of the gynecological examination broke in as a shock.

13 According to Ferenczi, a trauma doesn't result only in a regression but sometimes also in a "progression," when "the traumatized and split child suddenly develops astonishing faculties of intelligence and wisdom" (Dupont, 1998).

14 As is well known, the letters of the word fish, in Greek, form the acrostic: Iesùs Christòs Theòu Uiòs Sotèr = Jesus Christ Son of God the Savior.

Part III

Transmission

Chapter 8

A gap as heredity

> What we call heredity is perhaps, therefore, only the displacing upon posterity of the bulk of the traumatically unpleasurable experiences in question.
>
> (Sándor Ferenczi, *Thalassa*, 1924, p. 66)

The will

The dream of the self-dissection of the pelvis marks the end of the self-analytic journey that unfolds along *The Interpretation of Dreams*, a journey that began with the fantasy of meeting with Fliess in Rome on Easter Day. Eventually, Freud had met his own trauma, but it will be continually projected onto his followers.

In this dream, together with the thought of his death, the thought makes its way into Freud's mind that he "should have to leave it to his children to reach the goal of his difficult journey" (Freud, 1900, p. 478). The idea "that children may perhaps achieve [erreichen, reach] what their father has failed to" arises when he realizes that the bridge over the abyss is made of two children, an image that while evoking the act of "passing over" celebrated by the Jewish Passover (Pesach), Freud presents as "a fresh allusion to the strange novel in which a person's identity is retained through a series of generations for over two thousand years" (Freud, 1900, p. 454).[1]

If Grinstein (1980) found in this allusion a "connection between the theme of repetition-compulsion... and the wish to master a traumatic event" which foreshadows "Freud's concept of the death instinct in the years to come" (p. 402), McGrath (1986) found in it a reference to "the image of Moses being denied entry into the promised land," and to Joshua and Caleb (Numbers, 14), the two boys who will complete his mission. In Freud's dream the two children/bridge foreshadows then his followers and the foundation of the psychoanalytic movement in the years to come:

> Freud hoped to secure intellectual followers to spread the understanding and practice of psychoanalysis, and the image of Moses was

DOI: 10.4324/9781003353058-12

extremely appropriate to such an enterprise. Freud used it specifically with reference to himself and his movement ten years later in a letter to Jung. He wrote, "If I am Moses, then you are Joshua and will take possession of the promised land of psychiatry, which I shall only be able to glimpse from afar."

(McGrath, 1986, p. 302; Freud's letter is dated January 17, 1909)

McGrath's intuition is made even more complete when we consider that Freud will appoint not one but two heirs: Jung and Ferenczi.[2]

Freud will slowly begin to overcome his isolation in the first years of the new century, but it will be above all through Carl Gustav Jung that his most important followers will reach him. His intense and passionate relationship with Jung will begin in 1906, reaching its peak in the spring of 1910, when the International Psychoanalytic Association was founded and Jung was elected president. Growing tensions will surface not long after and will lead, at the end of 1912, to an irremediable break. Theoretical differences will have their weight, but not as much as other factors which can be grasped starting with Freud's legacy dream.

With *The Interpretation of Dreams*, the real cradle of psychoanalysis, Freud not only developed a theory but also made a spectacular *self-disclosure*, as we use to say nowadays, exposing his own dreams and the events in his private life that the dream images remind him of, expanding each of these images as if through a magnifying lens.

Shouldn't we wonder how Freud's dreams spoke to his followers, what was transmitted to them and which form did it take in their fantasies and dreams?

Is it possible to privilege this transmission that operates through the unconscious and try to tell the story of psychoanalysis as the acephalous story of a "transmission" that passes from one generation to the next like a nightmare, which aims to be transformed into a dream? Long ago I wrote that "the closest followers of Freud were unavoidably attracted by the verbal tombs of the master, and unconsciously driven to excavate them. By restlessly enacting his own burial, Freud facilitated the duty" (Bonomi, 1996, p. 168). In this chapter, we will see how the "Etruscan tomb" spoke to the two men appointed by Freud as his successors and heirs.

In 1909 Freud appointed both Jung and Ferenczi to this role, but with different functions. Jung received a public office, as he was made president of the International Psychoanalytic Association (Freud wanted him as "president for life"!). The choice of "Christian" Jung as his successor was motivated not only by his personal charisma and his prestigious position at the Burghölzli, then the world center of psychiatry, but also by Freud's firm determination to prevent psychoanalysis from being identified as a "Jewish science." Ferenczi was instead appointed by Freud as his "secret Grand Vizier."[3]

After the break with Jung, Ferenczi didn't take his place because the leadership was taken over by a group of people, the so-called Secret Committee.[4] Nevertheless, since their first meeting, in 1908, Ferenczi conquered the heart of Freud, who considered him as a son, would have liked to see him married to one of his daughters, and in secret appointed him his crown prince. Moreover, he was the only one that was invited by Freud to accompany him in his travels, just as Freud's brother Alexander used to do before. Sándor will take his place in name and deeds. He will also accompany Freud on his famous trip to America, from August 19 to September 29, 1909, when Freud was invited to speak about psychoanalysis on occasion of the twentieth anniversary of Clark University.

Jung was invited as well and, as is well known, during the long journey Freud and Jung underwent a sort of mutual analysis, interpreting each other's dreams. This short experience left deep traces in all of them. It was also the only time Freud abandoned the position of analyst to let himself be analyzed—and then he immediately took a step back.

The legacy

Freud calls Jung his "eldest son" and his "successor" in the letters he wrote to him in early 1909. In April they met in Vienna, where it happened something strange that aroused in Freud a strong emotional reaction which flows in the long letter he wrote to Jung on April 16. In this letter the father of psychoanalysis shared with Jung his most irrational fears, disclosing himself with no hesitation, as he had previously done only with Fliess. Thus, he explained that, when he finished *The Interpretation of Dreams*, he had the feeling of having completed his life-work and that he might "lie down and die"—a clear allusion to the journey ended in the "Etruscan tomb." Freud then added some elements that illustrate how his magical thinking had developed. He recounted that, soon after he discovered within himself the conviction that he "would die between the ages of 61 and 62," as suggested by the new telephone number he had just received. Later, in the course of his 1904 trip to Greece, he was haunted by premonitions of his fated death which "kept cropping up in all sorts of numbered objects," not only the number 61 but also 31, the number of his hotel room in Athens, which was half of 62. Veiled references to this obsessive thought, with which he tried to keep under control a feeling of imminent catastrophe, are also contained in the essay on *The Uncanny*, which Freud composed precisely at the age of 62, the supposedly fatal year. The uncanny experience of his only trip to Greece will be the subject of his last self-analytic study, the famous *A Disturbance of the Memory on the Acropolis*, composed in 1936. We will go through it in a later chapter.

In his letter to Jung, full of disconcerting details, Freud appears torn between belief and disbelief at his "madness," since in it there was also "method" and was not "so absurd" ("You will admit that after this substitution it no longer sounds so absurd"). At the end of his letter, he also called in question a second unconscious factor, similar to the inclination to see "Helen in every woman." How did Jung react?

Jung began to have disturbing fantasies and dreams about graveyards, ghosts, and skulls. Already in April, he had his "great dream" in which Freud appears to him as a customs official, dead since centuries and wanderings like a ghost (see Kerr, 1994, pp. 213–214). In Bremen, where Jung joined Freud and Ferenczi to embark for the trip to America, the Swiss psychiatrist was seized by a strange obsession with the mummified bodies that had recently been found nearby. Freud was so disturbed that he had a fainting spell (Jung, 1961, p. 156). Later, on the ship, after wondering on the foundation of Freud's psychology, Jung dreamt of a house on several floors with a cellar of Roman age, under which there was a cave with remains of a primitive civilization and two skulls (p. 161). In the course of the trip, the conviction grew in Freud that Jung's deadly fantasies and dreams all referred to him. Wasn't indeed Jung re-dreaming the place that Freud had chosen as his own residence, the "Etruscan tomb"?[5]

While presenting himself as "dying," Freud was particularly insistent on one point: he wanted that Jung recognized his deadly wish toward him and his desire to take his place. Jung didn't find, however, this "Oedipal" wish in himself and so, in part to shield himself, in part to repay Freud with the same coin, when Freud asked about the meaning of the two skulls, he replied: "wife and sister-in-law." He was in fact convinced that Freud had a secret relationship with his sister-in-law, Minna. For Jung "wife and sister-in-law" were the skeletons in the closet of Freud.[6]

It is not clear how this belief, of which we have only indirect evidence, did originate in Jung's mind.[7] In my opinion a careful reading of Freud's dream of the self-dissection of the pelvis is sufficient to generate this thought. Indeed, this is what occurred, years later, to Anzieu.[8] And if Anzieu had such a fantasy, why not Jung, who plunged himself in Freud's dreams to teach them in his university courses? Indeed, one should ask: who, in Freud's intimate circle, had not understood that the mysterious "She" of his dream was Minna? Ferenczi will have the same "infantile thought."

During his stay in America, the question reappeared after an unfortunate incident of urinary incontinence that seized Freud on the Riverside Drive. Embarrassed by the episode, Freud, who was then 53, interpreted it as a sign of senility. Since he was afraid that it might happen again, Jung tried to reassure him that it was only a neurotic symptom that could be cleared with a short analysis.[9] Freud accepted, but when Jung asked for additional details from his private life, he stepped back because, as he said, he could not risk his "authority." It was a decisive moment: those words, Jung would say later, remained carved in his mind.

Ferenczi too was impressed by these events. In the summer of 1910, he will tell Freud that that experience had reactivated his "infantile complexes." As it will become apparent two years later, his "infantile thoughts" were about Minna, as he wrote interpreting his own dream of the Dangerous coitus.

In the archaic

Before the trip to America Jung had no interest in "archeology," but once back home he was seized by a real obsession. He had begun to dig the "Etruscan tomb." On November 8, 1909, he wrote to Freud:

> One of the reasons why I didn't write for so long is that I was immersed every evening in the history of symbols, i.e., in mythology and archaeology. … All my delight in archaeology (buried for years) has sprung into life again. Rich lodes open up for the phylogenetic basis of the theory of neurosis… I have discovered a capital book in Knight's *Two Essays on the Worship of Priapus*…

On November 11, Freud replied: "I was delighted to learn that you are going into mythology. … I hope you will soon come to agree with me that in all likelihood mythology centers on the same nuclear complex as the neuroses." On November 15, Jung declares himself convinced that the most ancient myths "speak 'naturally' of the central neurosis complex" and reveals the epicenter of his interest:

> These flagellation scenes are repeated in the Isis cult, in the cult of Cybele, where there is also self-castration, of Atargatis (in Hierapolis), and of Hecate: whipping of youths in Sparta. The dying and resurgent god (Orphic mysteries, Thammuz, Osiris [Dionysus], Adonis, etc.) is everywhere phallic. At the Dionysus festival in Egypt the women pulled the phallus up and down on a string: "the dying and resurgent god." …
> … A counterpart of the nunlike Vestal Virgins would be the self-castrated priests of Cybele. What is the origin of the New Testament saying: "There be eunuchs which have made themselves eunuchs for the kingdom of heaven's sake"? Wasn't self-castration practically unheard of among the Jews? But in neighbouring Edessa self-castration of the Atargatis priests was the rule…

The enigmatic dream of Freud's self-dissection of the pelvis was entered in his skin and now Jung did not just revolve around the theme of self-castration, but he was going through its psycho-historical stratification as well. He was on the trail of the "great Lord Penis" and "Astarte"—the images that epitomize Freud's reaction to the circumcision scene produced by Emma Eckstein.

Though in Jung's letter Astarte was not mentioned, the cult of Atargatis was mentioned, which explains even better some elements of Freud's dream. As for the Lord Penis, here we find it in the version of the "dying and resurgent god" at the center of James Frazer's grandiose attempt to unify the infinite variations of the entire mythology.

In the first edition of *The Golden Bough*, which appeared in 1890, the figure of Adonis had a special role precisely because of the alternation of the greatest despair for the death of the god and the festive joy for his resurrection during the feast that was celebrated every spring in Byblos, Syria, when the river was tinged with red following the thundering rains on the clayey soils. In the popular imagination, the river was colored by the blood of the god. Frazer claimed that the central theme of all world mythologies featured a prototypical rite that served to rejuvenate the world, the periodic sacrifice of a king who died and was resurrected in Spring, following the model of the annual cycle of vegetation. The cycle of the dying and rising Lord staged in the Adonis myth was then passed into the Easter celebration of the death and resurrection of Christ—a thesis so desecrating for the time, that Frazer avoided including it in the first editions of his famous study.

For Frazer, these rituals served to exorcise death by celebrating the rebirth of divine life embodied in a material body, yet in the Freudian translation, the "divine life" was libido. Incarnating in the erect penis, it had the function of exorcising castration or its equivalent, death. Oedipus himself, who takes the place of Adonis and Christ in the Freudian system, was a personification of the tumescent penis, as indicated by the name ("swollen foot"). This is *the axis around which it organizes that alignment between mythology and neurosis* that makes it so powerful, heuristically speaking, the Freudian system, which, different from religion, not dished up the "lies" of Resurrection: Oedipus was not a dying and resurgent God, but a tragic hero.

Freud could not bear the "lie" of the Resurrection, but recognized in mythology and religion a product of the unconscious, indeed a precious source of knowledge of unconscious processes. He considered them "psychology projected into the external world," on the paranoia model, as explained in a famous passage of *The Psychopathology of Everyday Life*.[10]

The correspondence we are examining shows how, in November 1909, Jung was sucked into this system. It's like the grammar of a new language: one learns it by speaking, and Jung was speaking it, yet what he says reveals something that Freud had not considered. Thus, he pointed out that the self-castrated priests of Cybele were the "counterpart" of the Vestal Virgins, meaning that they were the bridegrooms of the Mother. This was the moment when Jung began to make a link between self-castration and the veneration of the Mother. Freud had not considered this side of the question and was astonished by it. On November 21, he replied: "Much of what you write is quite new to me, e.g., the mother-lust, the idea that priests emasculated themselves to punish themselves for it," adding:

> Since castration was of course unheard of among the Jews, I can't see the point of the New Testament passage. ... In private I have always thought of Adonis as the penis; the woman's joy when the god she had thought dead rises again is too transparent![11]

The theme of the desire of the incestuous and castrating mother (the "blood bride") will not be taken up and worked through by Freud, while for Jung it will form the basis of a new vision of the "sacrifice" that will lead him on a collision course with Freud in relation to the meaning of libido (the divine life). For Freud libido was and will remain exclusively "masculine."

It must be said that what begins to take possession of Jung was not a mere intellectual vision. From this moment on, he would relive "the agony and ecstasy over the dying and resurgent god" (February 11, 1910), inform Freud about his "self-castration" (February 20: he injured his thumb and then dreamed that his wife had her right arm chopped off), struggle with homosexual fantasies and finally get lost in the "religious-libidinal cloud" of the intertwined symbols of phallic potency, self-castration, and the cross (June 26). At the height of this exchange, Freud addresses Jung as his "dear son Alexander" (March 6). Later he would say that he and Jung had met each other "in the archaic" [im Urtumlicher].[12]

Freud's final dream had been like an appointment in the dark that Jung had gone to just to find within himself the fantasy of the son who sacrifices his genitals to the incestuous and castrating mother. On February 25, 1912, after a prolonged silence, Jung explained his *catabasis* (descent into the underworld) to Freud as follows: "This time I have ventured to tackle the mother." Wasn't Freud's unconscious mandate precisely this, namely, to achieve what the father of psychoanalysis had failed to?

Jung's descent into the "Etruscan tomb" was not easy, nor was it a mere intellectual pursuit but, rather, a lively and compulsive process that took the form of an "incestuous intercourse" (Hannah, 1976, p. 110). The *catabasis* was accompanied by fantasies of dismemberment, intense depression, and dissociative states (a real psychosis of which Jung himself spoke at length), taking on the form of a conquest of the "destructive" or "terrible" mother-imago, a new concept, unknown to Freudian vocabulary. Especially in the chapter on "The Sacrifice" of *Wandlungen und Symbole der Libido* [Transformations and symbols of the libido], which was published in 1912, the sacrifice of the hero's self-castration is described as a votive offering to the "Terrible Mother." Here the paths of Freud and Jung, which still met in the archaic, diverged once again. In the summer of 1911, Freud began to work on *Totem and Taboo* with the aim to reaffirm that the earthly template of God was the tyrannical Father that, after being torn apart and devoured, rose in memory to God.

When, years later, Rank wrote *The Trauma of Birth*, he will be accused of repeating Jung's heresy: replacing the Father with the Mother as the fulcrum of the neuroses. What both of them had done was to give voice to what was clearly inscribed in Freud's dreams and fantasies, though in a dissociated way. By naming the Terrible Mother (Jung) and finding the origin of anxiety in the relationship with the mother (Rank), these authors had given a name to the abysmal anxiety that overwhelms Freud when, in the dream from which psychoanalysis was born, Irma opens her mouth/vulva. Only later the mother's womb will be then made a habitable place and a vital container by the Hungarian school of psychoanalysis. Ferenczi, of course, will be in the front row, but he wasn't alone. Among the contributions that must be remembered are those of Imre Hermann, with the concept of "dual unity," Alice Balint, with that of "primary love," and Michael Balint, with the idea of an original "harmonious interpenetrating mix up" predating object relatedness and his vision of trauma as an early distortion of the balance between the organism and its environment.

The black hole

In his interpretation of the Irma dream, Erikson (1954) offered us a number of brilliant observations. One of these, also taken up by Lacan, is that the dream from which psychoanalysis was born could have been a nightmare and if it had not been, it was because the word "trimethylamine" appeared before the eyes of the dreamer. I see the question in this way: when Irma opens her mouth wide, Freud falls into a black hole, in the sense suggested by Grotstein (1990), when he describes the psychic death experienced by schizophrenics.

According to Grotstein, this is the moment in which schizophrenics become acquainted with the "basic language" [Grundsprache] (a concept that Freud borrowed from the paranoid Schreber), as a reaction to the catastrophic experience of psychic extinction. Threatened by psychic death, such individuals experience the terror of falling into a cosmic abyss, or "black hole," and substitute "archaic, apocalyptic (meaningful) scenarios in order to prevent their minds from dissolving into the maelstrom of nothingness" (p. 265). Isn't that exactly what happened in the dream from which psychoanalysis was born? Isn't Irma's gaping mouth a bottomless abyss? Didn't Lacan recognize in the word trimethylamine an "apocalyptic revelation"? It is not an archaic scenario, full of meaning, that starting from the Irma dream begins to take shape in the mind of Freud?

Something similar occurred in the dream of the Breakfast-ship, which could have been a nightmare, but it hadn't been because, at the culmination of terror, Freud was saved by the small cut-off-ship that was called out with one voice with his brother Alexander: "Here is the breakfast ship!"

Bliss

This *fetish* will be at the center of the essay on Leonardo that was composed by Freud in the period when he met Jung in the archaic. It is as if the magic embedded in Freud's intense friendship with Fliess was reviving in his no less intense relationship with Jung. If we add that in the same days Emma Eckstein was again in analysis with Freud, one might conclude that the old triangle that once revolved around a woman's magical penis had come back. This is how Freud introduces it, in his letter to Jung of November 21, 1909:

> In the foot it has become permissible to worship the long-lost and ardently longed-for woman's penis of the primordial age of infancy. Evidently some people search as passionately for this precious object as the pious English do for the ten lost tribes of Israel. ... I do wish I could show you my analysis of Leonardo da Vinci, I am desperately sorry not to have you here.

The "precious object" is in fact the hero of the essay on Leonardo. In this essay, we also find again Astarte, whose cult spread in the Mediterranean under various names. In the Hellenic world, she took the name Aphrodite, the Goddess of Love born from the foam of sperm and blood from the penis and testicles of Uranus, cut and thrown into the Aegean Sea. Entering the Hellenic world through Cyprus, the cult of Astarte lost some of its most bloody oriental characteristics, such as the votive offering of the bleeding genitals, transforming itself into the cult of the Hermaphrodite. In Cyprus, Aphrodite was originally worshiped as a goddess with a penis and a bearded Aphrodite was called Aphroditus. In Athens, phallic statues were called *hermæ* of Aphroditus. Plato's (c. 428–348 BC) myth of the Androgynous which had so much importance for Freud, was probably inspired by this cult, which came from the Semitic East. To take up the title of a well-known article by the ethnologist and psychoanalyst Geza Róheim (1945), Aphrodite was "The woman with the penis."

Freud recalled this aspect of Aphrodite in his essay on Leonardo da Vinci, centered on the belief that a childhood memory of the great artists and scientist betrays the fantasy of a *fellatio* resulting in that feeling of bliss which is found in his painting *Sant'Anna, the Virgin and the Child* (Freud, 1910b). Freud's followers will compete to find the silhouette of a fellatio in this painting famous for the soft sensuality with which the mother-child bond is represented.

To justify such a fantasy, in his essay on Leonardo Freud appealed to the Great Mothers of ancient times who, like Aphrodite, were often depicted with a penis, and explains that the same sacred vision of the genitals of the early days of humanity re-emerges at the beginning of the psychic development of the child. The children's sexual theories can thus clarify the apparent contradiction which consists in providing the goddess of femininity with a penis.

For Freud it was the emotional upheaval produced by the discovery that women do not have a penis that leads the boy to oppose in every way what he sees, thinking at first that in reality the penis is there, but it is still very small and will grow later, and then that "little girls too had a penis, but it was cut off and in its place was left a wound." For the little boy, this revelation is shocking because it proves that the threat to which he had never believed (the cut of his penis) is real, "henceforth he will tremble for his masculinity, but at the same time, he will despise the unhappy creatures on whom the cruel punishment has, as he supposes, already fallen" (Freud, 1910b, p. 95).

Yet, Freud also wrote that the mother is initially rescued from this terrible fate, since "the erotic attraction that comes from his mother soon culminates in a longing for her genital organ, which he takes to be a penis" (p. 96), a fantasy that begins to form when the baby takes the nipple "of the mother or wet-nurse [Amme]" in his mouth and sucks it (p. 87). Only when the discovery that women have no penis can no longer be denied, this feeling of bliss gets shattered, while the boy's longing for his mother turns into its opposite and gives place to a feeling of disgust which in the years of puberty can become the cause of psychical impotence, misogyny, and permanent homosexuality. The boy "represses his love for his mother: he puts himself in her place, identifies himself with her" (p. 100).

The essay on Leonardo is terribly important because Freud clarifies his idea of bliss. It matters little that commentators have found in this essay a bewildering series of misunderstandings and mistakes. What matters is that Freud fully identifies with Leonardo and that he composes his essay while having Emma Eckstein in analysis. In this regard, the following detail is not at all irrelevant.

A couple of years before (on June 6, 1907), talking about a patient, Freud had written to Jung: "She has a habit of inverting words. She spent her childhood between her mother and her nurse, who stayed with her for many years. The mother's name is *Emma*; turn it around: *Amme*." Now, could it be a coincidence that in the essay on Leonardo, evoking the mother's nipple/penis, Freud had added "or wet-nurse [Amme]"? Leonardo kept a secret diary written in reverse, from right to left, as Freud did not fail to note in the same essay. "I'm all Leonardo," Freud confided to Jung on March 6, 1910. In short, how should be read *Amme*?

It is as if the feelings and fantasies aroused during the first analysis of *Emma* Eckstein resumed strength and force 12 years later, at the time of the second analysis. The precious object is, of course, the great Lord Penis of the witch. One could almost say that it is for Jung, in the role of Fliess revived, that Freud wrote this essay on the woman's penis. As for the *fellatio*, it takes us back to the place where everything had begun, the wide open mouth of Irma. It is therefore the place of the Traumatic, which, just like in the dream of the Breakfast-ship, is turned into Bliss.

As for the interchangeability between nipple and penis, to understand its magic we must leave Freud and turn to the essay "Aphrodite or the Woman with the Penis," in which Geza Róheim (1945) relies on a vast repertoire of data gathered from comparative mythology, archeology, ethnography, folklore, as well as from clinic, re-reading them in the light of the concept of dual-unity introduced by Imre Hermann.[13] For Róheim, the woman with the penis is simultaneously "the woman with the nipple and the woman who deprived the baby of the nipple and the penis and who now has both" (p. 381), as the witch and the female demon figures of folklore.

For Róheim, the child's reactions to the separation constituted the core of magic. Thus, in phallic sexuality, the boy endows the mother with an imaginary breast, which becomes the imaginary penis because "in the unconscious the genital union with a woman is a repetition of the oral union with the mother" (p. 387).

In myth and folklore, this oral union is mostly represented by the apple. "Biting into the apple in love magic is the prototype of sexual union because the oral pleasure of the infant is refound in the genital act of the adult" (p. 388). So, when the bridegroom offers an apple to the bride, the inverse form of the equation male genital=mamma (breast) is found in this rite (p. 389).

This mimicry brings us to the last item of Aphrodite, which, as the Goddess of Love, is not just the woman with a penis but also the Lady of the apple. For some philologists, her name would even be the Hellenized form of the Semitic "love-apple." In the famous myth of the judgment of Paris, a good-looking young man must choose between Hera, Athena, and Aphrodite giving apple to the chosen one. As is well known, Paris chooses Aphrodite, because, Róheim explains, "Aphrodite the mother first gave the apple (the breast) to Paris" (p. 389).

In short, Freud's bewildering idea that the apex of the boy's erotic attraction for the mother is the nostalgic longing for her penis is here de-fetishized, aired, and restored to the original fluidity of the mimetic world of dual-unity—a world unknown to Freud.

How sweet it must be to die

I have mentioned the Judgment of Paris because the myth of the good-looking young man who gives the apple to the Goddess of Love features in Freud's essay *The theme of the three caskets*. In Freud's reading, however, the choice of Paris is presented as the product of a compulsion and the one who is chosen is Death. Indeed, all the anxious expectations of a fatal death that Freud lived with a mixture of fear and desire, as pointed out by Jones (1957, p. 301), pour in this essay, which began in 1912 and finished in 1913.

Ferenczi had been battered more than Jung by Freud's recurring fantasy of dying. Allusions of this kind are scattered throughout their correspondence.[14] Freud continuously presented himself as old, depleted, dead, or about to die, and then found in the mind of his followers the wish to see him dead. This tricky behavior greatly contributed to the crippling inhibition of Ferenczi, who, invaded and obstructed by Freud's projections, could not afford to harbor any hostility toward him. Of course, Ferenczi's traumatic sensitivity and his terror of losing again the father he had found in Freud, helped in turn not only to his sense of paralysis but also to develop an extreme sensitivity, based on terror, for Freud's thoughts and moods. In short, it provided the contradictory basis for his ability to identify with Freud, to the point of becoming his double.

The important events of 1910 will be recounted in the next chapter, linking them to the second analysis of Emma Eckstein. Here we limit ourselves to taking up the story that develops in parallel with Jung's break.

Beginning 1912 the understanding between Freud and Jung had begun to fall apart. Even before Jung's justification about his long silence, when he informed Freud of his tackling the mother, Freud wrote to Ferenczi: "I am trying to reconcile myself to the idea that one also has to leave this child to Ananke, and I will draw a piece of exposed libido back to myself and cease strenuous efforts to move forward" (February 1, 1912).

In Greek mythology, Ananke is Necessity. Starting with his essay on Leonardo, Freud will quote it often as a symbol of a "scientific" view of Nature and of its laws, whose hardness is not mitigated by illusory hope in the goodness of God or in the resurrection.

Freud certainly knew that for Plato Ananke was the mother of the Three Fates who weave the destiny of men. Likely, it was on the wave of this thought that, in the following months, he came to recognize the three sisters of fate in the central scenes of two of Shakespeare's plays (King Lear and The Merchant of Venice). "Three caskets are the same as three women, three sisters," he wrote to Ferenczi on June 23, exposing in concise form the plot that will be developed in the essay *The theme of the three caskets*—in German "Kasten," a clear reference to the memory of the box in which as a child he had desperately sought his missing mother. The letter to Ferenczi continued:

> The third is always the correct choice. But ... she doesn't speak ... she is mute. Do you remember the words of the song of Paris in 'Beautiful Helena'?
> *And the third—yes, the third—*
> *stood beside them and remained mute.*
> *I must give her the apple.*
> *You, oh Kalchas, you know why.*
> .... With a few associations I came out with the idea that they are the three—sisters of destiny, the Fates, the third of whom is mute, because

she—symbolizes death. The compulsion of fate is transformed into the motif of selection. Cordelia, who loves and is silent, is thus actually death... The three Fates are woman in her three principal manifestations: the one who gives birth, the one who gives pleasure, and the one who spoils; or mother, lover, and Mother Earth = death...

In the essay that will be published the following year, he will say, referring to Death: "No greater triumph of wish-fulfillment is conceivable. A choice is made where in reality there is obedience to a compulsion; and what is chosen is not a figure of terror, but the fairest and most desirable of women" (Freud, 1913b, p. 299). These are the same words Freud used to describe the "Etruscan tomb" in his final dream.

The effect of these words on poor Ferenczi was disastrous: something seized him in the bowels, took possession of his mind, and attacked him in his body. In the second chapter, we saw how he broke the last thread which bound him to Elma, after having identified her with "the one who brings death, who spoils," only to be trapped in the fantasy that will be enacted in the "dangerous coitus." We can now add the missing card.

Listening to Freud's words on the "mute sister," the thought of Ferenczi immediately turned to Minna,[15] anticipating the thought that will surface through the dream of the Dangerous coitus. As for the dangerous coitus of the end of September, the enactment that had thrown Ferenczi into a spiral of endless anxiety, was not with a "whore" but with a "sister"—Gizela's younger *sister*, Saroltà,[16] who, as evidenced by Peter Rudnytsky (2011, pp. 22–24), had the same position of Minna in Freud's secret life. In other words, Ferenczi's reaction to the interdiction of the "father" to love Elma consisted in identifying himself with the split and secret part of Freud.

Interpreting his dream of Dangerous coitus in his letter to Freud of December 26, 1912, Ferenczi added "You and your sister-in-law play a role in this dream." It was the fantasy of a secret *liaison* between Freud and Minna. Locked in a blind alley by Freud's prohibition on loving Elma, Ferenczi had clung to something that leaked from Freud's words about the "mute sister." We can better understand this element by tracing it back to its matrix, the "name which is not named" of the Irma dream, and by following it through Freud's dreams and fantasies. We saw it at work in the dream of the Three Fates, in the fantasy of the "femme fatale" and in its incarnation, Minna. Finally we "heard" it re-emerge in Freud's words about the "mute sister" (June 23, 1912).

But it doesn't end there, because this "incestuous" element passes through Ferenczi's mind, arouses the fantasy of an "invisible link" between Freud and Minna, is enacted in the dangerous coitus, and then resurfaces in his self-analytic letter (December 26, 1912). Here we find it again among the associations to the dream of Dangerous coitus, starting with a guilt-laden childhood memory—he had injured his sister, throwing an "apple" at her—which then slips into remembrance of the threat with a knife for "mutual touching" with his sister. This last scene mirrors and replaces the first one, Sigismund's assault on his sister Anna (the name which is not named).

In a paper entitled "Mute Correspondence," I asked myself: "Fateful was for Ferenczi-Paris the 'apple' he threw at his little sister, or fateful was hearing the words of the song 'Bautiful Helena'?" (Bonomi, 1996, p. 178), coming to the conclusion that Ferenczi's dangerous coitus had been the enactment of an "acoustic primary scene" (p. 179).

For Plato (Republic, X, 617c) the Three Fates were like sirens singing with one voice the things that were, that are and that will be.

The echo of the song soon rebounded among Freud's closest followers. On July 30, 1912, Jones wrote to Freud: "Your telling me of the *Stumm-Tod* [mute—death] symbolism had an interesting *Nachklang* [echo, repercussion]." His dead mother had appeared to him in a dream. It was between this letter and Freud's reply of August 1st, that the idea of a Secret Committee took shape, as if this new institution, which will replace Jung as a guide of the psychoanalytic movement, was a *Nachklang* of the *Stumm-Tod* symbolism, a repercussion of the "Etruscan tomb." Yet, it was in November that the eternal return of the same broke out with all its might.

On November 28, 1912, a small scientific meeting took place in Munich. Here, Karl Abraham read his psychoanalytic study of Amenhotep, the pharaoh who introduced the first form of monotheism. The way in which his interest in "archaeology" was born is so curious that I have to tell it.

Abraham met Freud in 1906 and, at the end of their first meeting, Freud had surreptitiously slipped into his bag two small antique objects that elicited Abraham's curiosity and will take him in museums where he began to formulate his theory on the pharaoh's neurosis. Abraham focused his thesis not only on the pharaoh's hostility toward his father, whose name and all inscriptions he had deleted, but also on his desire to be buried in a single tomb with his mother. In his enjoyable book *Why did Freud Faint?* Samuel Rosenberg (1978) suggested that Abraham's essay was a transference fantasy, the protagonist of which was Freud (the pharaoh). We can add that it was also a fantasy about the "Etruscan tomb" in which Freud had dreamed of being buried.

As soon as Abraham finished his presentation, Freud had a spectacular fainting spell. While recovering, he was in fact heard whispering "How sweet it must be to die" (Jones, 1953, p. 348; 1957, p. 301).

Echoes from the crypt

Here we rejoin the passages of the story already told in Chapter 2. Freud immediately informed Jung, Jones, and Ferenczi that he had begun to analyze his "bit of neurosis." But Jung was skeptical about Freud's self-analysis, and in his letter to Freud of December 3 he expressed all his reservations, appealing to Freud's dream of Irma's injection, in which Freud identifies "with the neurotic in need of treatment," and recalling how in America Freud had withheld from analysis:

> Our analysis, you may remember, came to a stop with your remark that you "could not submit to analysis without losing your authority." These words are engraved on my memory as a symbol of everything to come.

Jung became even more irritated when Freud tried to reverse the situation by interpreting a small mistake in his letter. On December 18, he replied with a harsh letter: he was sick of Freud's habit of reducing pupils to patients, catching them in error, reducing them "to the level of sons and daughters who blushingly admit the existence of their faults," while remaining "on top as the father, sitting pretty," because "nobody dares to pluck the prophet by the beard." And again "You know, of course, how far a patient gets with self-analysis: not out of his neurosis—just like you."

At the end of the letter Jung added that he will continue to stand by him publicly, but privately will start telling him what he really thinks. "No doubt you will be outraged by this peculiar token of friendship, but it may do you good all the same." On January 3, 1913, Freud will inform him of his decision to interrupt all relations.

Ferenczi was not present at the Munich meeting, but had a presentiment and imagined what was going to happen. Then he will be kept informed by Freud, who, on December 23, also sent him the last letter of Jung, reassuring him that he was mastering his neurosis by self-analysis.[17] That night, or the next, Ferenczi had the dream of the Dangerous coitus. At Christmas, he will then have the dream in which a small erect penis is served on the tray as a "totem meal."

Both Jung and Ferenczi were scared by the last fainting of the father of psychoanalysis, and also for the responsibility that Freud had placed on their shoulders by naming them successors and heirs. Both knew that Freud would not come out alone, with self-analysis. However, they reacted in opposite ways. Ferenczi suddenly put to silence all his doubts.

On December 26, 1912, he wrote to Freud a long letter, admitting that he too, like Jung, went through a period of rebellion, aiming at a relationship marked by mutuality and transparency, but now he had realized that mutual analysis was a "no sense" and that Freud was right "through and through." After all, self-analysis had enabled him to discover the laws of the unconscious and so Ferenczi was ready to accept that Freud was the only one who did not have to submit himself to analysis by another person.

> You are probably the only one who can permit himself to do without an analyst; but that is actually no advantage for you, i.e., for your analysis,

but a necessity ... Despite all the deficiencies of self-analysis ... we have
to expect of you the ability to keep your symptoms in check.

Then, as reconciling himself with the fact that Freud was "unanalyzable,"
he offered himself as a substitute: he asked Freud to start an analysis with
him. He had become a "wise baby."

Ferenczi will acknowledge the figure of the "wise baby" in 1922, from the
dreams of his patients. He will come back on it in his essay *Confusion of
tongue between adults and the child*, in which he wrote:

> The fear of the uninhibited, almost mad adult changes the child, so to
> speak, into a psychiatrist and, in order to become one and to defend
> himself against dangers coming from people without self-control, he
> must know how to identify himself completely with them.
>
> (Ferenczi, 1933, p. 165)

It was what Ferenczi had done with Freud: he had completely identified
with him. This was one of the reasons why his analysis with Freud didn't
work out. It was no more clear who was the analyzed subject: Ferenczi or
Freud?

The play of mirrors was mutual. When Ferenczi recognized in Elma "the
one who brings death" (July 18,1912), Freud immediately replied that his
younger daughter Anna had taken on such a role in his life (July 20). She had
become engaged, and the feeling of abandonment he had experienced had
been enough to assign her the role of "Cordelia who loves and is silent." Or
perhaps, had his daughter Anna become for Freud the embodiment of that
tragic sense of destiny that materialized in the dream from which psychoanalysis was born?

In Freud's essay, which will be published one year later, Cordelia would
personify the Goddess of Death who, in the final scene, takes her father's
corpse into her arms: "The third of the Fates alone, the silent Goddess of
Death, will take him into her arms" (Freud, 1913b, p. 301).

On July 7, 1913, Ferenczi turned 40 years old and, overcoming a persistent inhibition, took pen and paper to write to Freud, confiding him all his
sadness. The marriage of Elma with another man was becoming "reality,"
and his "strange condition of love" had turned into a struggle "taking place
quietly" within himself.

Freud replied on July 9. Ferenczi's melancholic letter had moved him
deeply: it reminded him of his own 40th birthday, when he was "at the nadir
of desolation." Since then, he had "changed his skin several times, which,
as you know, happens every seven years."[18] Then, remarking "For each of
us fate assumes the form of one (or several) women," he returns to his own
"subjective condition" of the three caskets theme—a further allusion to his
youngest daughter Anna, situating her in the role of the silent Goddess of

Death. Finally, Freud went on to speak again of his own death. He did so indirectly, through the ominous number seven:

> Good things really happen to me in periods of seven years: in 1891 I began with aphasia, 1898/9 the Interpretation of Dreams, 1904/5 Jokes and the Theory of Sexuality, 1911/12 the Totem thing; so I am probably on the wane and can't count on anything bigger before 1918/19 (if the chain doesn't break before then).

In 1918 Freud will be 62, the age of his fated death. However, the chain did not break even then. Since Death insisted on ignoring him, as a replacement he took into analysis his daughter Anna. It will be in the midst of this incestuous choice performed by "listening,"[19] that Freud composed the essay *Beyond the pleasure principle*, in which the new "good thing" materialized at the end of the seven-year cycle. It was the *death instinct*, the action of which was described as "mute."[20]

Notes

1 Of course, it is the figure of the Jew who, in the vision of the time, had remained the same over time. However, even here Freud replaces the figure of the Jew with the Greek characters from the novel *She*.

2 Much later, Freud would also appoint Otto Rank as his heir (see Rudnytsky, 1991).

3 Freud will recall it to Ferenczi in his letter of December 13, 1929, when the growing distance of Ferenczi had elicited in Freud the worry that Ferenczi wanted to create a new psychoanalysis in opposition to his.

4 For the constitution, rituals, and function of the Secret Committee, see Grosskurth (1991).

5 A punctual reconstruction is not possible, but it is certain that the theme of the death of the father of psychoanalysis was at the center of each other's thoughts, as is also confirmed by the fragment of self-analysis offered by Freud: "dying as soon as the son takes his place," which Ferenczi reported in his *Clinical diary* (August 4, 1932). This fragment also circles around the idea, expressed by Freud in his final dream, that he "should have to leave it to his children to reach the goal of his difficult journey."

6 Jung (1961a, p. 159). Jung had withheld his true association out of fear that Freud "would discard it as a mere attempt to escape a problem that was actually his" (Jung, 1961b, p. 452; Kerr, 1994, p. 268).

7 According to an interview given by Jung to John Billinsky and published only in 1969, after Jung's death, it seems that Jung learned directly from Minna about Freud's secret relationship with her. Yet the way and the circumstances in which this would have happened are such as to raise many doubts. To make things more complicated, in June 1909 Jung had "confessed" to Freud his relationship with Sabina Spielrein. According to Kurt Eissler (1993) Jung had projected on Freud his promiscuity with Spielrein. Or maybe, by revealing to Jung his own death-anxiety, Freud had helped him to open up on the Spielrein issue. Jung probably expected Freud to open up to "sexuality" as well. For Daniel Burston (1999) precisely this expectation reinforced Freud's reticence, which closed in order not to lose his "authority."

8 In the French edition of his powerful study on Freud's self-analysis, Didier Anzieu (1975) not only suggested that the mysterious woman who assists Freud to "dissect" his pelvis was Minna but also wrote that Freud visited the Etruscan tomb in company of Minna and that he must have then thought that couples were "buried in the same mortuary" (pp. 552–554). As a historian, Anzieu was wrong, since Freud visited Orvieto in company of Alexander and not of Minna (in the English edition of his work, 1986, Anzieu will remove this error). However, it is a mistake that sheds a clear light on the kind of fantasies that Freud's final dream induces.

9 Jung (1961a, p. 182). A reference to Freud's urinary incontinence on Riverside Drive is found in Ferenczi's *Clinic diary*, on August 4, 1932. There are various versions of the events that occurred in New York (Rosenzweig, 1992, pp. 64–65; Rudnytsky, 2011, pp. 42–45, 51–52; Falzeder, 2012, pp. 326–327). In Jung's interview with Kurt Eissler in 1953, when Eissler pressed him to find out why Freud had not answered Jung's questions, there is a veiled reference to Martha, Freud's wife, and her sister Minna. According to Mario Beira, the incident could have been overdetermined by Freud's failed attempt to visit his sister Anna in Manhattan two days earlier.

10 Here Freud expressed the will to explain "the myths of paradise and the fall of man, of God, of good and evil, of immortality, and so on," by translating "metaphysics into metapsychology" (Freud, 1901b, p. 259), a project that continually shines through the thoughts that make their way into his dreams.

11 Freud and Jung (1974, p. 265). That Freud always thought of Adonis as the penis further clarifies the idea of the great Lord Penis that appears in Emma Eckstein's letter of circumcision. Adonis ("Lord" in Syrian), Adonai in Hebrew, was the suppressed idol which returns lending the vowels to fill the tetragrammaton YHWH, as Freud (1911b) himself recalled in a very short note written shortly after.

12 Letter from Freud to Abraham dated July 13, 1917.

13 In a later essay, Imre Hermann (1949) will explain the genesis of the fantasy of the "phallic mother" starting from the imago of the "giant mother" that continues to live in the unconscious.

14 Here I will refer to one in particular. It is found in Freud's letter of January 10, 1910, in a passage where Freud deals with a dream of Ferenczi, which contained references to Ferenczi's dead father as well as to the year 1909, the one of the trip to America. Since in this trip Freud "behaved like someone who is taking his leave," he recognized a reference to himself. Ferenczi's father died of bowel obstruction, and Freud's acute intestinal pain during the trip had then provided the basis of identification with the father of Ferenczi. So far, so good. Freud seems also to be sensitive and receptive to Ferenczi's transference, when he writes: "Again, as then, the death of the father is the signal for a great inner cleansing for you, and for an effort to bind the mother to you." Yet, at this point Freud's reading slides toward a paranoid side: he wonders if the dream had anything to do with Ferenczi's expectation of his "imminent demise," almost insinuating that his pupil harbored such a wish, then exchanging a concern for a desire to see him dead. Finally, half resigned and half ironic, Freud added: "The fact remains that I have long since decided to die in 1916 or in 1917, but of course, I do not make an issue of principle [Natürlich kapriziere ich mich nicht gerade darauf]."

15 In the letter to Freud of July 12, 1912, as well as telling the king that he was taken by an "unbearable increase in sexual libido" which has been forced to download the "normal route of prostitution," Ferenczi asks Freud to Fraulein Minna and their travel plans to Italy.

16 Ferenczi will reveal this not-insignificant detail only when Freud unilaterally decides to terminate the analysis (letter to Freud of 18 November 1916).

17 It was in this letter that Freud wrote: "My construction of the totem meal is proving to have practical applications. The 'brothers' are attacking me from all sides," which inspired the book by François Roustang (1976) on the psychoanalytic movement as a "wild horde."

18 According to Fergal Brady, the change of skin is here a symbol for restoring the foreskin, indeed a triumphant reversal of the circumcision.

19 On the analysis of Anna Freud by her father, see Young-Bruehl (1988, pp. 80–90, 103–109, 114–116, 122–125). On the incestuous choice performed by "listening" see Mahony (1992).

20 Stressing the mirroring reflection of theory and practice, Mahony (2002) writes: "It is important to note that Freud's psychoanalytic treatment of his daughter/ death goddess concurred with the publication of the death drive. More than that, while analyzing his daughter/death goddess, Freud desperately avowed that she could be liberated only by his death" (p. 895).

Chapter 9

Catastrophe

> This is also the hypothesis which Freud, in allusion to the poetic fantasy
> in Plato's Symposium, put forward in his *Beyond the Pleasure Principle*.
> A great catastrophe, as he terms it, split matter asunder, rent it into two
> halves, leaving it with an impulsion to reunion wherein organic life had
> its earliest inception.
>
> (Sándor Ferenczi, *Thalassa*, 1924, p. 61)

Emma Eckstein's second analysis

In the annals of psychoanalysis, 1910 is remembered as the glorious year of
the foundation of the International Psychoanalytic Association (IPA). However, 1910 also stood as "one of the most puzzling" years in Freud's life, as
rightly pointed out by Patrick Mahony (1979, p. 86) referring to the lack
of elements that could "account for Freud's intensified interest in bisexuality" (p. 87) as well as for the "perplexing the dominance of Fliess's spectre"
(p. 88), which ended in Freud's work on Schreber, his famous study on
homosexuality and paranoia. The reason is easy to say: 1910 was the year of
the catastrophic end of Emma Eckstein's second analysis.

For Emma's family, her first analysis with Freud had been a great success.
It is her nephew, Albert Hirst, who tells of it, who also was a privileged witness to the failure of the second analysis, not only for its proximity to his
aunt but also because he was in analysis with Professor Freud.

Born in 1887, Albert Hirsch—in America he will change his family name
in Hirst—wrote the account of his experience with Freud when he was over
80 years, then donated the 38 pages manuscript entitled "Analyzed and
Reeducated by Freud Himself" (manuscript without date) to the Library of
Congress of Washington along with the letters and postcards that Freud had
written to Emma Eckstein.[1]

From some of these letters, it appears that at the end of the first analysis
there remained unresolved divergences and problems. However, this did not
prevent Emma Eckstein from beginning work as a psychotherapist in the
course of 1897. We don't know for how long, but it is certain that she was the

DOI: 10.4324/9781003353058-13

first analyst trained and supervised by Freud himself. She also published some writings. One of these is mentioned by Freud in his short 1907 article on the *Sexual Enlightenment of Children*. The most important was the 1904 paper *Die Sexualfrage in der Erziehung des Kindes* [The Sexual Question in the Education of Children], in which Eckstein tackles the problem of masturbation, as if she was still struggling to make sense of her trauma. In the course of her research, she turned to Freud for help in finding old texts from pediatric literature. In a letter dated October 11, 1902, Freud answered her to say, among other things:

> Here is one of the books you asked for. Hirschprung is cited incorrectly, i.e.: in *Berl. Klin. Woch*[*enschrift*] 1866, volume 38. The article is not found there or in any other volume [Band]. I was also unable to find Behrend in the *Jahrbuch f. Kinder-heilkunde* (*für Kinderkrankheiten* does not exist, as far as I know). Salzmann will require a more precise indication to help him find it. Revise and do not be discouraged.

The unfindable article by the pediatrician Jakob Behrend was "Über die Reizung der Geschlechtstheile, besonders über Onanie bei ganz kleinen Kindern, und die dagegen anzuwendenden Mittel" [On the stimulation of the sexual organs, and in particular on Onania in very young children and the means to employ against it]; it was the article that in 1860 introduced in German-speaking countries the medical practice of circumcision in the treatment of masturbation in children of both sexes.[2] Emma Eckstein was unable to find it, but she found the article by Ludwig Fleischmann (1878), head of the first pediatric ward of the Vienna General Hospitals, where surgery was recommended more explicitly than in other writings of the time. Emma was not accurate in her references, but she cited some of the contents of the article, along with the work of other authorities.

Repeating two of Fleischmann's clinical observations, Emma strongly opposed the "false belief" that masturbation did not harm children. The best proof of this was the little known fact that "masturbation already occurs in infancy [Säuglingsalter], and that babies under one year old can be subject to violent fits of masturbation and its harmful consequences" (Eckstein, 1904, p. 9). In short, Eckstein seems aligned with the supporters of the salvific struggle against masturbation, although she uses less strong accents, doesn't mention surgery, and shows an unusual sensitivity toward the punished child, stressing how he/she may feel abandoned.

For Eckstein, the means to employ against this "evil" depended above all on age. With babies under two years, she recommended mechanical means suitable to prevent rubbing (p. 15), while with older children these methods were no more effective and one had to balance the urge to contrast the bad habit with love, otherwise "the punished child feels abandoned and is easily pushed back into masturbation, in search of oblivion and compensation for the withdrawn love" (p. 16). Two conclusions can be drawn from this fine observation. The first is that for Emma Eckstein punishment does not put an end to masturbation; rather it causes the child's withdrawal because the punishment is experienced as an abandonment. The second is that she still felt that punishments were, to some extent, necessary because of the organic damages caused by masturbation. Here we touch a contradiction rooted in the mentality of the time in which both Freud and Eckstein remained entangled.[3] It should be added that Albert Hirst, he too, deeply distressed by masturbation, recounts in his interviews that he was in this very reassured and helped by Freud. It would seem that Freud tolerated masturbation much better in males than in females.

The booklet was published in 1904. It seems that Emma Eckstein began to ask Freud to take her back into analysis shortly after. Freud will refuse, as emerges from his letter of November 30, 1905.

At the time of the first analysis, Emma Eckstein suffered mainly from pains in her legs which had prevented her from standing and walking since puberty; it was her main symptom and it was disabling. In the chapter of his manuscript dedicated to "Aunt Emma," Albert Hirst says that after the first analysis, his aunt was able to enjoy a normal life. She enjoyed bicycling, a sport that had now become popular, and was able to manage her mother's house after the two sisters married. Then there was the relapse. "I have the notion," writes Hirst, "that she was all her life in love with a certain Vienna architect, and that her relapse came after he got married, or after she became convinced in some other way that her love was hopeless." Then her difficulty in standing and walking returned and "she spent all her days on her couch, never left her room, not even for meals."

Emma's second analysis largely coincided with Albert's. Hirst writes, in fact:

> While I was in analysis Freud treated Emma too. He did that, I am sure, without pay. Neither Emma nor my grandmother, with who she lived, could at that time afford his fee. Also, and that was most unusual for him, he treated her at her home, not at his office.

Albert Hirst, whose family lived in another city, had already been sent to Freud around the age of 16, for a short time. Then he had an analysis with daily sessions from the autumn of 1909 to the beginning of the summer of 1910.[4] We can therefore infer that Emma's second analysis began in 1909 and ended in the spring of 1910. The fact that Freud cured Emma Eckstein pro-bono and at her home speaks once again for the uniqueness of this patient and for the importance she had for Freud. His extraordinary dedication ended badly, however. (Could this be the reason why Freud will be so severe toward Ferenczi's therapeutic excesses?)

In *Analysis Terminable and Interminable*, this second analysis was briefly summarized by Freud in the story of the patient who returns to analysis after a complete hysterectomy (Totalxstirpation des Uterus). The story was reported anonymously and therefore the patient's true identity remains uncertain. The fact that Freud was then very concerned by the "ghost" of Fliess, supports the thesis that she was Emma Eckstein.[5] Plus, Emma had really undergone surgery. She had been operated on by a famous Viennese gynecologist, Doctor Josef Halban, although it is not clear why, when, and how many times.[6]

According to Albert Hirst's sister, Ada Elias, after the removal of a myoma the symptoms disappeared, but then the pain returned two or three years later, due to adhesions. Against Freud's advice, Emma wanted to be reoperated by Dr. Halban, and this time the operation was a fiasco. Emma had profuse bleeding and inflammation that lasted for weeks. She hadn't been able to walk since then.[7]

Given that Dr. Halban was the same gynecologist who will operate Marie Bonaparte on her clitoris, one wonders to what extent these operations were not also an expression of that "psychiatric gynecology" with which we are acquainted. The new surgery did not obtain the desired result and Eckstein turned back to Freud, who finally took her back into analysis, or rather, began to treat her at home pro bono. We don't know the session's frequency.

Emma, however, immediately entered into a dispute with her analyst, because she demanded from him the recognition of the organic nature of her pains. Eventually, a gynecologist friend, while visiting her, found an abscess near her navel and incised it. The pain disappeared and for Emma, it was proof of its somatic origin. Freud took it very badly and decided to end the treatment, saying "That is Emma's end. Now she will never get well." As a matter of fact, the well-being produced by the incision did not last long: Emma soon returned to lock herself in her room and never came out again until her death in 1924.

We have several versions of this episode, including the testimony of the gynecologist in question, Dora Telecky, who, about 30 years later, sent a brief written account to one of Freud's first biographers, Emil Ludwig, who had inquired about this episode. Dr. Telecky was an ancient acquaintance of Freud. Besides being the daughter of a close friend of Freud's, she had been the only female student to take courses that Freud held at the University of Vienna in 1900, 1903, and 1904. Indeed, in 1910, it was Freud who asked her to visit her friend and to calm her.[8] However, Dr. Telecky found an abscess on the site of the previous incision and made a new incision that suddenly liberated Emma from her pain.

The nature of this intervention is also unclear. Interviewed by Kurt Eissler in 1953, Ada Elias will say that everyone in the family knew that it was a "simulated operation" (Scheinoperation), i.e. an intervention on the body aimed at obtaining a psychic effect.[9] In this case the abscess was a pretext, which would partly explain Freud's reaction. However, Dr. Telecky made no mention of simulation. In her testimony, reported in Ludwig's book, she wrote that when she later reported the new incision to the Professor at his home, he exploded and, with biting disdain, asked her: "Do you believe that hysterical pain can be cured by the knife?" Trembling, she objected that an abscess must be treated. Although the patient was cured of pain, Dr. Freud became so hostile that she was forced to stop the discussion and leave (Ludwig, 1957, p. 115).

In *Analysis Terminable and Interminable*, Freud briefly reported the case history of Emma Eckstein immediately after the case of Sándor Ferenczi. He saw both of them as successful treatments where the old disease had taken over again. He thought that Emma Eckstein's second illness was a manifestation of the same repressed impulses at the origin of the first one, which had been incompletely resolved by the first analysis. He also believed that, had it not been for the new trauma (the disappointment of love), there would not have been a new irruption of the neurosis. His most significant passage is the following:

> She fell in love with her surgeon [the gynecologist who had performed the operation], wallowed in masochistic phantasies about the fearful changes in her inside—phantasies with which she concealed her romance—and proved inaccessible to a further attempt at analysis. She remained abnormal to the end of her life.
>
> (Freud, 1937a, p. 222)

> [Sie verliebte sich in den Operateur, schwelgte in masochistischen Phantasien von den schrecklichen Veränderungen in ihrem Inneren, mit denen sie ihren Liebesroman verhüllte, erwies sich als unzugänglich für einen neuerlichen analytischen Versuch und wurde auch bis zu ihrem Lebensende nicht mehr normal.]

This passage, which seems to epitomize the whole story of Emma Eckstein, crudely speaks of her severe traumatofilia and of the way in which her masochistic fantasies were enacted with the collusion of surgeons. Through it we can also glimpse the castration endured as a child as the epicenter of the repeated attacks on her body. If, as everything suggests, her clitoris had been amputated or destroyed, then the inside of her body had really undergone a "change." I mean that one might find here the core from which, over the years and with the help of many physicians, bloomed those "masochistic phantasies about the fearful changes in her inside" of which Freud speaks.

The reference to "the fearful changes in her inside" also recalls the piece of the dream of Irma's injection, in which the patient breaks in complaining about the pain in her inside, and Freud is seized by *a doubt*: "I thought to myself," Freud wrote in the dream book, "that after all I must be missing [übersehe ich] some organic trouble" (Freud, 1900, p. 107). This doubt prompts many questions, not only about the significance of Freud's "oversight," but also on its repercussions on Eckstein, who remained in contact with Freud and his family (she was a close friend of Minna) and certainly had read and reread *The Interpretation of Dreams*.[10] Did she recognize herself in the composite figure of Irma, the heroine of the paradigmatic dream? If so, how did she react? Did she cling to Freud's *oversight* to give voice to her need that her analyst acknowledged an actual damage in her body?

As a matter of fact, the question of the organic or psychological nature of her pain continued to plague her relationship with Freud, as pointed out by Lisa Appignanesi and John Forrester (1992, p. 140), resurfacing in her letter of November 30, 1905, when Freud declined Emma's earlier request to resume analysis and becoming a cause for conflict in the second analysis and the ultimate reason for the break. One might say that the "oversight" declared by Freud in his dream signaled that something was left over, working then as a bridge between the first and second analyses.

From the beginning of the second analysis, Emma wanted Freud to acknowledge the organic nature of her pain—or, rather, that *Freud dealt with what he had not seen in her body in the first analysis*. Albert Hirst, Emma's nephew, did not understand why his aunt persisted in demanding such recognition and so he writes in his memoirs:

> [Freud] considered her case as the recurrence of the old neurosis, while she insisted that it was nothing of the kind, not a mental but a physical condition. Once she told me that Freud was simply vain and opinionated. That was a remarkable statement to take to me, a current patient of Freud ... I answered her: "He may be well as vain and conceited as you say he is, but still I do not understand his position. If he is so vain he could readily say: 'You once had a neurosis. I cured you of that. That you now have a physical sickness is outside my field'." I told this conversation to Emma's sister Therese and to Freud. Both thought that my answer was keen. But Emma brushed it aside with a brief: "You do not understand him."
>
> (Hirst, p. 7)

The dispute with Freud became so tense that Emma went so far as to attempt suicide with an overdose of pills. But Freud had no intention of granting Emma the recognition she so stubbornly demanded. The situation then turned into one of those impasses from which it was extremely difficult to get out, the kind that will push Ferenczi to seek technical measures that deviated from the classic method. He will call these measures elasticity, empathy, analysis of the countertransference, and mutuality. Above all, Ferenczi came to advocate for the analyst the position of a "benevolent and helpful witness" and it is precisely on this point the clash with Freud will take place. Indeed, Ferenczi believed that the disavowal by the analyst of a trauma experienced by a patient was even more devastating than the original trauma.

But Freud was not able either to accept the subjective experience of Emma nor to validate the kernel of truth from which her delusion about "the fearful changes in her inside" developed. This position appears to us today—after Ferenczi and his successors opened the way for us—even more rigid and incomprehensible if we consider that Freud had felt and experienced these "fearful changes" in his own body, as it emerges in his Irma dream and even more in his final dream, in which Freud observes his own horribly eviscerated pelvis. By the way, how did Emma react to the spectacular castration of her analyst? In short, we are not dealing only with a Freud who, for cultural reasons, is unable to intellectually recognize the trauma endured by his patient, but also with a Freud who feels on his body what he does not know with his head, to the point of replicating in spectacular fashion, as in a hall of mirrors, the cut (excision) of the woman's penis (clitoris), at the same time lost and stored, concealed and dramatized.

On the last page of *Analysis Terminable and Interminable*, we find a resigned Freud who admits that asking women to give up their desire to have a penis is like "preaching to the wind" (Freud, 1937a, p. 252). Since Emma Eckstein is the only female patient referred to in the text, the Professor's disconsolate statement, while having a general character, referred first of all to her. Yet, what is even more baffling is that, while analyzing Emma Eckstein, Freud was composing his essay on Leonardo, where he fantasizes that "in the primaeval days of the human race ... the genitals ... were worshipped as gods" (Freud, 1910b, p. 97), pays homage to Aphrodite, the "goddess with the penis," and finds the culmination of the boy's erotic attraction for the mother, or *Amme* [read Emma], in the veneration of her penis. Of course, Emma needed that her analyst acknowledged her real wound, instead of worshipping in secret her imaginary phallus.

I'm all Schreber

Freud's outburst against Dora Telecky, his disapproval of the incision of a festering abscess and his shout "Do you believe that hysterical pain can be cured by the knife?" take us back to the moment when Freud had allowed Fliess to operate on Emma's nose. These words, so inappropriate in 1910, appear in fact full of meaning if referred to the 1895 operation that nearly costed the life of Emma. They were the words that Freud had not been able to shout at Fliess, his "failed reaction" that had continued to live in a split part of his psyche. As Masson (1984, Appendix A) rightly observed, the displacement of his anger indicates that he was still unable to recognize what he and Fliess had done to Emma Eckstein. It is therefore not at all surprising that, with the dramatic rupture with Emma, the specter of Fliess began to haunt him in dreams.

It was then that, in order to resolve the return of his transference to Fliess, Freud threw himself into the *Memoirs of a Nerve Patient* in which President Schreber recounts his delirium of castration (Entmannung) and redemption of the world, a paranoid system that Freud traced back to a burst of repressed homosexual libido and that enchants him to the point of borrowing one of Schreber's key terms, *Grundsprache*, "basic language," which from now on he will use to indicate the "archaic" thought that unites dreams, myths, and rituals.

Both Daniel Paul Schreber (born 1842) and Emma Eckstein (born 1865) had been victims of the "great fear" of masturbation. Schreber's father, a physician who in his son's delirium is transformed into a god, was a leading figure in the crusade against a "vice" that, so it was thought, made boys "stupid and dumb," "*lebensmüde*" (fed up with life), "vulnerable to countless diseases of the lower abdomen and to diseases of the nervous system [Nervenkrankheiten]," and finally "impotent" and "sterile" (Niederland, 1984). In order to rescue boys from the insidious scourge he had invented infernal machines devised to keep them from masturbating—"hellish machines" that were so fashionable in the years in which Freud worked closely with pediatricians to be evoked in his eponymous dream. Freud wrote to Jung on October 31, 1910: "The castration complex is only too evident. Don't forget that Schreber's father was—a doctor. As such, he performed miracles, ... the absurd miracles that are performed on him are a bitter satire on his father's medical art."

Just as Emma Eckstein "wallowed in masochistic phantasies about the fearful changes in her inside," similarly, in Schreber, the delirium of destruction of internal organs had been the starting point of his transformation into a woman who, abused sexually from God, had accepted his martyrdom as Christ in order to rescue mankind (Freud, 1911a, p. 17). December 3, 1910, Freud wrote to Ferenczi: "I'm all Schreber, nothing but Schreber [Ich bin nämlich sonst Schreber, nichts als Schreber]." The breakup with Emma Eckstein had been a bad blow. But instead of mourning the loss, Freud compensated it by wrapping himself in Schreber's paranoid delirium like a new skin. Thus, to assert himself masculine and masterful, he enacted a triumphant repudiation of his own circumcision. Explaining to Ferenczi how with the Schreber case "a piece of homosexual investment" had been withdrawn from Fliess and utilized for the enlargement of his "own ego," he said: "I have succeeded where the paranoiac fails" (October 6, 1910).

The Palermo incident

The work on Schreber became the occasion of Ferenczi's first and only "act of rebellion," the infamous "Palermo incident." Ferenczi talks about it in a long letter to Groddeck, dated Christmas 1921. He will also mention it in the *Clinical Diary*, in the page of August 4, 1932 ("Personal causes for the erroneous development of psychoanalysis"), where, telling how the Professor had immediately adopted him as a "son," he added: at least "until the moment when I contradicted him for the first time (Palermo)."

In the summer of 1910, Freud asked him to accompany him on his trip to Italy and to write together the essay on Schreber. During the journey, Freud had opened up with him, telling him about Fliess, how the old friendship had ended in a traumatic way and how Fliess had reappeared in his dreams. He also made him understand how the work on Schreber was born out of his need to deal with the ghost of Fliess.

In itself the incident is not saying much, although the accusation that Freud addressed to Ferenczi, the intent to "steal everything," sounds rather projective—just think that what had corroded friendship with Fliess had been precisely Freud's desire to "appropriate everything." Ferenczi described the incident to Groddeck:

> We went on holiday together every summer, for years: I could never be completely free and open with him; I felt that he expected too much of this "deferential respect" from me; he was too big for me, there was too much of the father. As a result, on our very first working evening together in Palermo, when he wanted to work with me on the famous work paranoia text [Schreber], and started to dictate something, I jumped up in a sudden rebellious outburst, exclaiming that this was not working together, dictating to me. "So this is what you are like?" he said, taken aback. "You obviously want to take everything". That said, he now spent every evening working on his own, I was left out in the cold—bitter feelings constricted my throat. (Of course I now know what this "working alone in the evenings" and this "constriction of the throat" signifies: I wanted of course to be loved by Freud.)

Ferenczi did not know that Freud had taken refuge in Schreber's Memoirs after the traumatic end of the second analysis with Emma Eckstein. Yet, it is as if, through the Palermo incident, he had absorbed an unconscious knowledge that will make its way through dreams and fantasies as the "paleontological fairy tale" about the moment in which the defeated woman loses her penis. It was part of the same strain of fantasies that inspired *Thalassa*.

After the "incident," to mend the tear, Ferenczi wrote to him: "Do you know which hours of our trip retain the most pleasant memories for me? The ones in which you divulged to me something of your personality and your life." Explaining his need for mutual sincerity and his hope in a relationship in which two people *"are not ashamed in front of each other, keep nothing secret"* (underlined in the original), he told him "I am and have been much, much more intimately acquainted and conversant with you than you could have imagined," inviting him not to close himself "after the Fliess case" (October 3, 1910).

Freud replied (October 6):

> Not only have you noticed that I no longer have any need for that full opening of my personality, but you have also understood it and correctly returned to its traumatic cause. Why did you thus make a point of it? This need has been extinguished in me since Fliess's case... you presumed great secrets in me ...

Attack on the genitals

Ferenczi's theory of genitality is a cosmic fantasy unfolding in an apocalyptic scenario. Its starting point seems to be the dream that Ferenczi had at Christmas 1912, immediately after the dream of the Dangerous coitus. Here is how he recounts and draws it in his letter to Freud of December 26:

> On a cup [Tasse] a cut-off—somewhat small and frail but firmly erect—male member is brought in, next to it some kinds of objects (eating utensils?).
>
> My younger brother [Lajos] has just cut off his penis in order to perform coitus (!). I think something like: that is not necessary, a condom would have been sufficient! ...
>
> In another piece of the dream there is talk about family resemblance; several members of the family are sitting around a table. One (I?) has a crooked back. The other (indistinct) looks a little better (fatter) in the face than usual.—(The penis has been flayed, its skin had been pulled off so that the corpora cavernosa were laid bare. The power of the erection was striking.)

Figure 9.1 Ferenczi's drawing of the penis on a cup in his letter to Freud of December 26, 1912.

After had this dream, Ferenczi took pen and paper to write a long letter to Freud in which the dream of the Dangerous coitus is analyzed in detail. The dream of the small erect penis served as a "totemic meal", on the other hand, was not interpreted. Ferenczi contented himself with saying that his younger brother (the one who had married Elma's sister) stood for himself, thus presenting his dream as a *self-castration* and that it seemed to confirm the interpretation of the dream of the Dangerous Coitus.

The horrible vision had a surprising therapeutic effect. Ferenczi was suddenly released from the somatic disorder at the base of his penis and from the nocturnal fantasies of bleeding to death that haunted him for months. In the post-writing of the letter, he added: "I feel *significantly* better."

Something deeply contradictory was depicted in this dream. With whom does Ferenczi identify himself, with his younger brother Lajos or with Oedipus' father Laius (i.e., Freud)? Did the dream refer to a male member or to a miniature version of it (the clitoris)? Was it about libido or a sadistic attack? How is it possible to have a sexual intercourse through a self-castration? This strange idea arouses in fact bewilderment and protests even in the dream. Yet this contradictory idea will become the backbone of *Thalassa*, its enigmatic key.

Then there are "family resemblances," like in the dream of the Dangerous coitus, where the father's (Freud) transgression with Minna is imitated by the son (Ferenczi). Thus, while on a conscious level Ferenczi tries to suppress his doubts about the value of Freud's self-analysis, his dream reproduces the very dream that had been chosen by Freud as a symbol of his own self-analysis, the dream of the self-dissection of the pelvis. It is not an isolated case. The same will be repeated with Ferenczi's dream of the Pessary on the eve of his analysis with Freud. In September 1914, Ferenczi had a dream that again staged an attack on his own penis. He had introduced in it an occlusive pessary, then in vogue as a contraceptive measure, as if his penis was a vagina, and he was alarmed because if it slipped too much inside, then it was necessary to have a bloody surgery to remove it (Ferenczi, 1915).

In the associations, Ferenczi re-proposes the recurring theme during those years, his inability to choose between two women. Elma, who had finally married, had just visited him. Ferenczi wanted to have children, but Freud had prevented him from doing so. Apparently, the contraceptive was Freud, who had entered into him too much, as in a violent introjection or "intropression," to use the term that Ferenczi will introduce 20 years later. Since there was no way to pull out this obstructive object, the dream comes up with a solution that anticipates the new meaning that regression will have to Ferenczi and the Hungarian school. Thus, Ferenczi sees in the dream a fantasy of returning to the womb, a "regression" and at the same time his "self-analysis." He was the "pessary-child."

In the manuscript sent to Freud on September 8, 1914 and which will then be published, the analysis of this dream takes the form of a dialogue between doctor and patient. However, in the manuscript, the doctor is Ferenczi, whereas in the accompanying letter, Ferenczi specified that he was the patient while the doctor was Freud. Not only that, but Ferenczi was then finally about to begin his analysis with Freud. In the manuscript the subject of the dialogue is at the *end* of the analysis: the doctor (Freud) informs the patient (Ferenczi) that the analysis is finished and that, from now on, he will have to do it by himself, relying on his self-analysis. The patient then complains that he is abandoned by the analyst and that his self-analysis turned in circles. Thus, as pointed out by Falzeder (1996), Ferenczi's article was "a masterpiece of ambivalence, meta-discourse and hidden messages," something that can be compared to a "theater play" (p. 267). The subject of this hall of mirrors was, once again, the symbol of Freud's self-analysis: his dream of self-dissection of the pelvis: "In both Ferenczi's and Freud's dreams, there is an operation, performed by the dreamer on the lower part of his own body, in both cases the associations link this operation with self-analysis" as though Ferenczi "modeled his dream after Freud's" (p. 268).

The similarity becomes even more significant if we align Ferenczi's concern at of not being able to pull out the pessary from his penis to the scene in which Freud finds in his eviscerated pelvis something that has to be "carefully fished out." Thus, Ferenczi's concern to fish out the pessary seems to resume the action of Freud in the point where it was interrupted! Ferenczi not only puts himself in Freud's place but also takes charge of completing his task.

We can sum it all up as in this way: Freud's long and difficult journey as it unfolded in his dream book is resumed by Ferenczi where it was left off, the place marked by the "Etruscan tomb." The product of this effort will be *Thalassa*. In Freud's dream, the thing that must be carefully extracted is associated with the scientific treatise on fish. *Thalassa* will be a scientific treatise on fish. The dream of the Occlusive pessary is then also the difficult gestation of a scientific fantasy that was entirely conceived already in the years from 1913 to 1915. Indeed the "occlusion" staged in the dream was concretely experienced by Ferenczi in the years to come: every time he tried to write down his theory of genitality he will be seized by attacks of anxiety, somatizations, and paralysis.

In this period Ferenczi's concern for genital wounds was also reflected in his research, starting with the case history of little Chanticleer he came across in early 1912: a child who lost his power of speech and began to crow and crackle like a rooster after that his penis had bled from a bite by a rooster (Ferenczi, 1913b). During the war, Ferenczi researched the effects of circumcision on Bosnian Muslims at the military hospital, described genital injuries as "narcissistic pathoneuroses" (Ferenczi, 1916–1917a) and, in an article on the psychic consequences of "castration" in childhood, reported the case of a patient who as a boy was circumcised in brutal circumstances. His father, a Christian country gentleman, had taken him to a Jewish butcher of the village where he had been circumcised with a "long and sharp knife." Ferenczi's conclusion was that circumcision could be trauma if it occurs in the narcissistic phase (1916–1917b, p. 263).[11] It was the first timid attempt to revive the theory of real trauma since Freud abandoned it. But it is in *Thalassa* that all his concern flows.

An apocalyptic fantasy

The parturition of this "scientific fantasy," as Ferenczi will call it, was long and difficult. In the period of his analysis with Freud, the two men at some point thought of writing a work in common: both were Lamarckian in a time which was already dominated by the idea that evolution proceeded according to the mechanism of natural selection discovered by Darwin. Both shared the idea that the experiences of a generation were transmitted to the next ones in form of biological inheritance, and that major catastrophes were settled in "instincts" animistically oriented toward a goal. Despite the agreement with Freud, Ferenczi, however, was unable to put his ideas in writing. He wrote to Groddeck, in a letter at Christmas 1921, commenting on his hypothermia: "Am I trying to behave like a fish, or to enact my genital theory of fishes which I won't write down?"

Thalassa was finally written, in German as most of the work of Ferenczi was, and published in 1924 under the title *Versuch einer Genitaltheorie* (Attempt at a genital theory). Translating it in Hungarian, his mother tongue, Ferenczi renamed it *Katasztrofak* (Catastrophe). Freud immediately recognized it as a brilliant work. Yet it is a work which that is difficult to read. On the one hand, it is written as a biological treatise and on the other hand, it attaches to the body animistic aims, thus violating, as it is openly claimed in the introduction, the epistemological principle of keeping the natural and mental sciences separated from each other.

Here are some judgments, very different, but all correct. For Jay Gould (1977, p. 163), the famous biologist, it is a complete "folly." For Clara Thompson (1988, p. 185), who had been in analysis with Ferenczi, it was a typical expression of his ambivalent attachment to Freud which "manifested despite all of his efforts for he would often develop an idea of Freud's to a fantastic degree, thus, in the end, making the situation absurd." For Balint (1949, p. 217), Ferenczi's closest pupil, contained Ferenczi's main message, namely, that "we subject our children to unnecessary, avoidable, traumata, … and subsequently our children, when grown up, pass on similar traumata to their children." For Nicholas Abraham (1962, p. 14), who rediscovered and relaunched *Thalassa* in the 1960s, it is a work which "evokes in us profound and unspeakable resonances" (p. 14) telling us that "we are woven by symbols from end to end" (p. 23). In his mystical reading of *Thalassa,* Norman O. Brown (1966) has grasped some of these profound resonances. The great Californian classicist, philosopher, and mystic (and author of one of the most passionate readings of Freud, *Life against Death*, of 1959) wrote:

> The unconscious is rather that immortal sea which brought us hither; intimations of which are given in moments of "oceanic feeling"; one sea of energy or instinct; embracing all mankind, without distinction of race, language, or culture; and embracing all the generations of Adam, past, present, and future, in one phylogenetic heritage; in one mystical or symbolical body.
>
> (pp. 88–89)

> In Ferenczi's apocalyptic theory of genitality the sexual act is a historical drama, a symbolic reenactment or recapitulation of all the great traumas in the history of the individual, of the species, of life itself. Psychoanalytic time is not gradual, evolutionary, but discontinuous, catastrophic, revolutionary. The sexual act is a return to the womb.... Birth really is from water; the womb really is as introjected, incarnate, ocean.... In copulation the penis really is a fish in water.... Physical, or "real" birth is really rebirth, a repetition of an archetypal birth of the cosmos from the cosmic egg.
>
> (p. 211)

For Brown, the continuity between the work of Freud and *Thalassa* followed from the way in which the two men had recreated the great myths of the beginning and the end of the world. Just as in the myth of Adam the breaking into fragments of a primitive unity that is recomposed in Christ (the second Adam) is reflected, similarly, in the version of Freud and Ferenczi, the desire to reconstitute the lost unity is embodied in the Penis. Hence the mystical and salvific value that the penis has in psychoanalysis. The salvation of the entire world depends on it. If we consider that it all began with the amputation of a small penis, we should not be surprised.

Ferenczi wrote his work as a scientific treatise, but it is the fruit of a singular combination of biology and mythology. The strongest biological assumption in *Thalassa* is the recapitulationist claim that instincts aim to restore earlier stages of life, while the mythical element is the reunion fantasy which is found in many cosmologies that identify the inception of the world with the break of a primal unit that will be restored at the end of the world-time. It is the same combination of biology and mythology that is also found in *Beyond the Pleasure Principle*, in which Freud (1920) introduced the idea that "an instinct is an urge inherent in organic life to restore an earlier state of things" (p. 36) appealing as much to the migrations faced by certain fish to lay their eggs as to Plato's myth of the Androgyne, the primordial bisexual being who is cut in two by Zeus, thus determining in the divided parts the desire to reunite.

In the myth about the birth of desire that Plato presents in the Symposium, the navel functions as a visible trace of the cut with whom Zeus had divided the primordial bisexual into two halves. The navel is also evoked in the dream from which psychoanalysis was born. As is well known, commenting on the moment when the recalcitrant Irma opens her mouth, Freud wrote: "There is at least one spot in every dream at which it is unplumbable—a navel, as it were, that is its point of contact with the unknown" (1900, p. 111 note). I believe that Freud added this comment in the final draft, after arriving at the end of his journey, as it is summarized in Freud's final dream. In this dream, the goal of the journey is indicated through allusions to two novels by Rider Haggard. The first was *She*. The second was *The heart of the world,* and here we find another version of the magic talisman at the center of Balzac's novel *La peu du chagrin* (The magic skin).

The story is this: the talisman (in this case a precious stone with magical powers) has been divided into two halves and the hero inherits only one half from his dead father. The whole novel then consists in the perilous search for the other half. This is also the meaning of *The Interpretation of Dreams.* In *Thalassa,* Ferenczi summarized it all with the following words: "A great catastrophe, as he [Freud] terms it, split matter asunder, rent it into two halves, leaving it with an impulsion to reunion wherein organic life had its earliest inception" (Ferenczi, 1924, p. 61).

Before commenting further on this point, I would like to illustrate its sense, at the same time particular and universal, through the essay "Circumcision and problems of bisexuality," in which Herman Nunberg found the same narrative structure in the dreams and fantasies of a patient of his who had been circumcised at the age of five to cure him of the habit of masturbation.

According to Nunberg, the trauma of circumcision had produced in his patient fantasies extraordinarily similar to those found in the delusions of schizophrenics and in the myths about the creation of the world. In many cosmogonies a primordial entity is split in two; Aphrodite, born from the cut of the testicles of Uranus, and Adam, in the most ancient sources, is described as male and female together, so that Eve derives from a part of his body. "God circumcised Adam and made a woman out of his prepuce," to quote Nunberg (1947, p. 151). Often then, the two parts are imagined as brother and sister, so that their sexual union represents a *restitutio ad integrum.* Nunberg found these fantasies in his patient, who fantasized that if he married her sister, his lost piece of skin would be restored and his injury "cured"—a rescue fantasy that nullifies the loss through an incestuous reunion.

I believe that this fantasy, which makes use of the brother/sister incest theme to obtain a compensation, runs through *The Interpretation of Dreams,* starting with Freud's fantasies about Anna, his natural sister, passing through those about Pauline and those about Minna. Later the same fantasy would powerfully resurface with the incestuous analysis of his daughter Anna, who was conceived in the very troubled days when the Emma Eckstein incident materialized.[12] Not to mention the ideas of Freud's that derive from the same matrix, like his view of the transference as a "new skin" or his idea that no resolution of the transfer is attainable but only a trade, a barter.

For Nunberg, the principle that organizes these fantasies is the same that is found at the root of the Platonic myth of the Androgyne and, more generally, of the myths about the creation of the world in which an entity is cut in two and in each fragments the desire to undo the "cut" at the origin of the world and of everything survives.

According to Nunberg (1947) circumcision is "a trauma, releasing a tendency in the ego to repeat it in one way or another and to form reactions to it" (p. 146), mobilizing "forces aimed at overcoming its effects" (p. 154) and fantasies that serve to "nullify" the trauma (p. 153). In particular, taking up Ferenczi's thesis that the foreskin symbolizes the female part of the male, Nunberg had found that "the restoration of the unity of both sexes in the myth may signify the restoration of the penis as it appeared before circumcision" (p. 152). A *restitutio ad integrum,* precisely.

This brings us back to *Thalassa,* where the erect penis is envisaged as the living monument of a primordial catastrophe of cosmic proportions which acts in the same manner as the unresolved trauma in the case of the traumatic neurosis does, namely, compelling "to a perpetual repetition of the painful situation" (Ferenczi, 1924, p. 66). As Ferenczi himself said (p. 101), the starting point of his speculation had been Freud's *Interpretation of Dreams.* In other words, the dreams of Freud elicited Ferenczi's idea.[13]

Remarkably, what actually guides and organizes Ferenczi's speculation is circumcision, which makes a historical document out of the penis to be read and deciphered starting from the tendency to repeat the catastrophe of the origins. Ferenczi's speculation unfolds from the idea that the foreskin is a replica of the maternal womb, and that the penis is driven to find a substitute of the lost casing (foreskin) in the vagina (p. 46). The similarity between the fish in the water, the baby in the womb, and the penis in the vagina made him wonder if in these images was inscribed a phylogenetic unconscious knowledge on our descent from fish hinting at something that escaped Haeckel, namely that the history of the modifications of the environment is summed up in the peri-genetic history of the *container* that protects the embryo.[14] In this way, Ferenczi restored a link between organism and environment and, at the same time, between content and container. The "vaginal theory" of the foreskin aligns the *invagination* of the glans within a membrane, with the life of the fetus in utero and that of the fish in the great mother ocean. The catastrophe of which Ferenczi speaks, the division of the matter, is therefore reformulated in terms of a rupture of the relationship content/container, while the story he tells is the one of its restoration.

The erect penis is the prototype and model of this apocalyptic story. By tearing the casing in which the penis is wrapped, erection reproduces the primal catastrophe, the draining of the oceans that caused the expulsion of the fish from the ocean, which is repeated in the expulsion of the baby from the mother's womb. Erection illustrates the autonomous life of the fragment that repeats the catastrophe in the attempt to undo it. The catastrophe is repeated in the penis's attempt at tearing out from the body, but at the same time, it is undone because the penis fulfills the desire to restore the broken unity by finding in the vagina its lost casing. In coitus this desire finds a real (the ejection of the sperm), an imaginary (the child returns to the womb), and a symbolic (the fish is returned to the ocean) satisfaction, undoing the catastrophe from which a laborious evolution of species arose and restoring the harmony of the cosmos.

This is in synthesis the scientific fantasy of Ferenczi, who after having returned the restless detached fragment—Penis, Child, and Fish—to the pacifying arms of the great Mother Ocean, closes his speculation by evoking the squatting, fetal position, with which primitive people inter their dead, testifying to the significance of the regression to the maternal womb and to the symbolic identity of death and birth in dreams and myths (Ferenczi, 1924, p. 95). After this *Requiem*, and reformulation of Freud's reunion fantasy symbolized by the "Etruscan tomb", Ferenczi will slowly begin to distinguish between Life and Death, while regaining possession of his own voice.

"What I have taken away from you, i.e., the penis, I am restoring to you"

Ferenczi does not limit himself to acknowledging the penis as the living monument of a cosmic catastrophe. He will also come to see it as the *"organic symbol* of the restoration—albeit only partial—of the fetal-infantile state of union with the mother," as he writes in the closing remark of the 1929 essay *Male and Female*, and therefore of *Thalassa* in its final version.

This brings us to reflect on the split of the matter dramatized in Ferenczi's cosmic fantasy. Given that circumcision is the template of the split, unpacking Ferenczi's fantasy one might say that his resolution consists in bringing back the cut to a more primitive element: the cut of the umbilical cord that joins the baby to the mother. Such a derivation from a universal element could explain the dilemma in which Nunberg stumbled in his article. For Nunberg (1947) the fantasy of the cut that Plato exposes in the myth of Androgyne was so typical of the trauma of circumcision that he could not understand how it was possible to find it in an uncircumcised author. "How then is possible," he wonders, "that Plato, a Greek, used a circumcision phantasy, personified in a hermaphroditic figure split in two, as a basis for the origin of sexes?" (p. 150). Perhaps the answer lies precisely in the fact that the prototype of every cut is not circumcision but rather the cut of the umbilical cord, which is in turn replicated in the rite of passage of circumcision. This is also the conclusion reached by George Devereux, the famous Hungarian psychoanalyst and ethnologist.[15]

This point seems to me quite relevant because it dispels the ghost of psychoanalysis as a "Jewish science." The great reticence to address the issue of circumcision which, today more than before is found among psychoanalysts, the impressive self-censorship regarding the fact that Freud had not had his children circumcised, to which is added the denial en masse of Emma Eckstein's traumatic circumcision, a real collective negative hallucination, are as many barriers and occlusions that hinder the genuine vocation to the universal by which Freud was moved and that is the true strength of psychoanalysis.

But *Thalassa* has still another meaning which Ferenczi has not seen, even though it seems to be inscribed in his reparative fantasy. Here too we will rely on Nunberg (1947). There is a passage in his essay that helps to put in order a further piece of the puzzle. It is a little note in the margin of the link between circumcision by the mother and the worship of Astarte, to which I have already referred. Commenting on men's sacrifice of their genitals actually performed in ancient times and only "in fantasy and dreams" in modern times (as in Freud's final dream), Nunberg wonders if this sacrifice could be traced back to a sense of guilt toward woman which can be formulated as follows: "What I have taken away from you, i.e. the penis, I am restoring to you" (1947, p. 175, note 107).

I cannot judge the ethnological validity of this conclusion, I don't have the expertise. It seems to me that it perfectly fits with the story I am trying to tell and with its dramatic inception. Is this the ultimate meaning of the task that Freud leaves to his successors and heirs? The ultimate mystery of the compulsion to repeat staged in Freud's dream of the self-dissection of the pelvis, would then be a burning desire for reparation?

We are obviously talking of something that was not in Freud's arsenal, but which is nevertheless inscribed in the oneiric, Orphic DNA of psychoanalysis, managing to be dramatized by Ferenczi in his Thalassa myth, the troubled story of a penis-child-fish which is finally returned to the silent embrace of the great mother-ocean. With his oceanic fantasy, a voice in Ferenczi seems to say "What I have taken away from you, i.e. the penis, I am restoring to you," and, in doing so, he finds the sensation of floating or flying, which infuses heat and thaws to something which, as in a fairy tale, was petrified.

Of course, the tearful fragment in which the yearning for reunification survives can only be Emma Eckstein's small cut off penis.

Provided that the fragments have a soul.

The bedrock

Ferenczi's apocalyptic fantasy was deeply in harmony with Freud's phallocentrism and Freud saw in it the highest point of his understanding with

Ferenczi, a "summit of achievement" after which his pupil "slowly drifted away" from him (Freud, 1933b, p. 229). Ferenczi not only made the penis the hero of a cosmic drama but he also took up Freud's hypothesis of a death instinct that yearns for a pre-organic state. However, by imagining the ultimate goal of regression not as a cold tomb stone but as an embracing mother-ocean, Ferenczi infused heat into the "womb-coffin" equation, defrosting something that stood "petrified" in Freud. *Thalassa* (ocean in Greek) had carried out that *traumatolytic* function that Ferenczi will attribute to the dream the function of melting and reanimating what is petrified by trauma.[16]

Here we cannot fail to recall how Erikson (1954, p. 35) imagined that, looking into Irma's mouth/vulva, Freud had been paralyzed by "a terrifying discovery that stares him in the eyes like the head of Medusa" (p. 35). In 1922, both Freud and Ferenczi found in the head of Medusa that turns the viewer into "stone" the symbol of horror aroused by the female genitals devoid of a penis.[17] Freud hints in the article that introduces the "primacy of the phallus" (Freud, 1923a), a primacy based precisely on the horror of castration that petrifies the function of the penis as living bond, turning it into a "thing," fetish or monument either to the "horror of castration," as Freud wrote in the essay *Fetishism* (1927a, p. 154). This is the immemorial catastrophe in which Ferenczi plunged himself up to restoring the penis' bonding function and with it the original fluidity of life.

In Freud's meditation we don't find a penis-bond but only a petrified Phallus, which is "idol and altar."[18] The most famous image of this spell is the image of the "bedrock" that Freud introduces at the end of *Analysis Terminable and Interminable* to characterize both the limits of analysis and its organic foundation.[19] As a foreclosed sanctuary, it is the place that analyst and analysand cannot violate.

In a book called *On Freud's Jewish Body. Mitigating Circumcisions*, which I have already mentioned in connection with the dream of Irma's injection, Jay Geller (2007) points out that the German term used by Freud to indicate the "bedrock," *gewachsene Fels*, literally signifies "growing or living rock," thus presenting the inverse figuration of circumcision as "key-fossil" (*Leitfossil*) to which Freud refers in *Moses and Monotheism*. The fossil is in fact "petrified life." Then linking the "living rock" to the "petrified life," Geller recalls the scene in Exodus in which Moses struck water from a rock (*Felsen*) for the thirsting Children of Israel, and a river of biblical passages from Old and New Testament, to the point of writing:

> I am struck by the chain of signifiers that connect these texts from the Bible to the *Interpretation* [*of Dreams*] to *Analysis terminable and interminable* to *Moses,* and point in between in particular, "*Fels*" and "*Stück*" (rock and piece) – those traces remains of castration and circumcision as well as of Freud's repressions and disavowals.
>
> (p. 213)

This petrified sanctuary, inexhaustible source of the fragments spread along the entire work of Freud, according to Geller, harked back to the image of the unplumbable navel of the dream evoked by Freud commenting on the dream of Irma's injection.

With his "bioanalysis," Ferenczi enters this foreclosed sanctuary and melts the "rock." Perhaps it is no coincidence that in *Thalassa* the magic word of the Irma dream, trimethylamine also reappears.[20] Did he understand that the magic word from which psychoanalysis was born was a transcription of brit milah?

Perhaps. However, he had not come to imagine that the catastrophe recorded in Freud's genital theory was that of a female patient who had been circumcised and excised as a girl. His dream of the Cut off small penis, his paleontological fairy tale, and his final critique of castration theory in femininity seem, nevertheless, to suggest that Ferenczi had come very close to grasping this point as well.

Notes

1 A total of 14 communications were written between 1895 and 1906. Library of Congress, Washington, DC (Sigmund Freud's papers, Supplemental File, 1765–1998, Box 61. Library of Congress, Manuscript division). Some of them were published by Masson (1984). They are now online.

2 J. Behrend's article had been searched in the wrong place, namely, in the *Jahrbuch für Kinderheilkunde*, a journal initially published in Vienna by local pediatricians, which will last from 1857 to 1931, while the article in question appeared in the *Journal für Kinderkrankheiten*, the first German pediatric journal, of which Behrend was co-editor.

3 I have discussed the contradictions of the Freudian "discovery" of infantile sexuality in Bonomi (1997). Here I recall that a cycle of meetings on masturbation was held at the Vienna Psycho-Analytical Society, from November 22, 1911 to April 24, 1912. The proceedings were published in the same year under the title "Die Onanie (Diskussionen der Wiener Psychoanalytischen Vereinigung)" (Protokolle vol. II). Among the 14 contributions, Steckel was the only one to claim that masturbation didn't cause physical damage.

4 Roazen (1995, p. 4). Albert Hirst was interviewed by Kurt Eissler, the founder of the Freud archives, and later by Paul Roazen. See also Lynn (1997). In his text, written in old age, Hirst makes some mistakes. In fact, he writes that his analysis had begun in the autumn of 1910, confusing the beginning of the treatment with the end. Hirst, who lived in Prague with his family, wanted to return to Vienna to resume analysis with Freud after the summer of 1910. His father, however, objected. The following year Hirst decided to move to the United States. He arrived in New York in November 1911, where he became a successful lawyer.

5 Beginning 1937 Marie Bonaparte had come into possession of Freud's letters to Fliess, and Freud reacted by ordering her to destroy them. Furthermore, his definitive break with Fliess, in 1904, had been, in 1936, at the center of Freud's last self-analytic meditation, as we will see in the next chapter.

6 Freud spoke of a myoma (Freud, 1937a, p. 222), while Dr. Telecky of abscesses or fibroids. More precisely, on the basis of the testimony given many years later by Dora Telecky, Emil Ludwig (1957) wrote in his biography on Freud

that much later the patient [Emma Eckstein] returned, complaining of pains in the abdomen. "It seems that she had been operated on by a well-known Viennese doctor for abscesses in the uterus, but because of the pain she wanted to see Dr. Freud again" (p. 115).

7 1953 Interview with Kurt Eissler, quoted by Borch-Jacobsen (2021, p. 93). Ada Elias had been in analysis with Freud before Albert, to whom she had given way at the end of 1909. Albert Hirst gave no information on the gynecological operation.

8 By a strange twist of fate, she will become Mrs. Brücke. In 1930 he married the son of Freud's mentor, Ernst Brücke, who had become a widower. They emigrated together to America before the Anschluss.

9 Interview with Eissler quoted in Borch-Jacobsen (2021, p. 94). All "psychiatric gynecology," from the cut of the clitoris to the removal of the ovary, had this quality: the body was operated on to obtain a psychic effect.

10 Borch-Jacobsen (2021, p. 92) reports that Emma Eckstein wrote a review of *The Interpretation of Dreams* which was published in October 1900 in the socialist newspaper *Arbeiter Zeitung.*

11 With respect to Jewish circumcision, Ferenczi excluded that it was traumatic. That said, these researches however show a continuative rumination around the issue of circumcision, as if there was something that didn't fit.

12 The birth of Anna Freud, who was named after Anna Hammerschlag, the "Irma" of Freud's dream, fell on Tuesday December 3, 1895. If we go back nine months from there, we arrive at the date of Tuesday, March 5, 1895 (see Bonomi, 2013). Freud formulated his first concept of "transference" in the same days.

13 Ferenczi merely mentions dreams of rescue from water, which Freud reported in later, expanded editions of the dream book. For obvious reasons, he could not refer to Freud's dreams which had most influenced him.

14 The fundamental biogenetic law formulated by Haeckel consisted in the idea that the evolution of the species is briefly repeated in the development of the embryo.

15 After elaborating this idea, which I expressed in the first volume of *The Cut* (Bonomi, 2015a), I discovered that George Devereux had come to a similar conclusion, confiding his hypothesis to a friend, Daniel Prager: circumcision in puberty duplicates the cutting of the cord at birth, thus connoting the rite as a rebirth: "Where penis symbolizes cord (rather than cord symbolizing penis), cutting the penis in circumcision at puberty is equated with cutting the cord at birth" (Prager, 1960, p. 53, footnote).

16 See Ferenczi's well-known note *On the Revision of the Interpretation of Dreams* (March 26, 1931, in Ferenczi, Notes and fragments, p. 240).

17 It is not clear which one of the two arrived first at this conclusion. On May 22, 1922, Freud wrote a note on the head of the Medusa which will remain in the drawer until his death. Ferenczi, in turn, wrote a short note on the subject, published in 1923, which is quoted by Freud in his article where the notion is introduced of a "primacy of the phallus"—a primacy which rests precisely on the horror of castration, so well illustrated by the head of the Medusa that turns the spectator "to stone" (Freud, 1922, p. 273; 1923a, p. 144).

18 The sacred stones venerated in every primitive religion are defined by Robertson Smith (1889–1890, p. 213) "idol and altar."

19 The "repudiation of femininity," which underlines the woman's wish to have a penis and the man's virile protest, was for Freud the ultimate resistance that prevents any change. Freud (1937a, p. 355) called it "bedrock."

20 It is in the chapter on the "Thalassal Regressive Trend" that Ferenczi points out how the fishy "odor of the vagina comes from the same substance (trimethylamine) as the decomposition of fish gives rise to" (Ferenczi, 1924, p. 57, footnote 1).

Part IV

Closing of the circle

Chapter 10

Giant snakes and still alive dragons

> One feels inclined to doubt sometimes whether the dragons of primaeval days are really extinct.
>
> (Sigmund Freud, 1937a, p. 229)

A closed system

Freud incessantly revised more or less extensive pieces of his theory. Nonetheless, there is a core of his thinking that revolves around the "primacy of the phallus," that is impervious to revision or compromise, a closed system in which the various ideas about castration bind one to the other in a single block that can only be accepted or rejected. One cannot reject one of them without bringing down the whole system, which, in the end, is like a delusion.

The pillars of this closed system are, on the one hand, the idea that the father of the primeval human family castrated his sons and, on the other hand, that the woman is a "castrated man" who lost his penis in the course of biological evolution. Pure metapsychology. When Freud invited Ferenczi and Rank to work together on the gap between theory and practice, Rank wrote to Freud to tell him that they had "first decided to start a scientific campaign against the overestimation of the castration complex" (August 22, 1922). Freud immediately dissuaded them and the subject was removed from their agenda. But, as we know, the theme figures prominently in Otto Rank's *The Trauma of Birth*, a book which resulted in Rank's expulsion from the psychoanalytic movement. It was precisely in response to Rank's revision that Freud (1926a, pp. 129–130) reorganized his theory by postulating castration trauma as a synthetic a priori: whatever the mortal danger or loss experienced by the ego, Freud argued, the unconscious represents it in the form of castration. "Symbolic castration" had become the universal language of trauma. It was the closing of the circle.

Would Freud have developed this delusional system, if he had reacted differently to the trauma of Emma Eckstein's circumcision, caring and taking responsibility for it? I don't think so.

DOI: 10.4324/9781003353058-15

In Freud's life, there was also an episode when the construction of this system was in danger of collapsing. It happened before the various pieces of the system were welded together into a single block. In this chapter, we will discuss this breakdown, which, many years later will be the subject of Freud's last self-analytic meditation. But first, we will try to clarify how Ferenczi dismantled Freud's system from the inside, thus indirectly acting as his "therapist," and how this influenced Freud's self-analytic meditation.

Metapsychology of the fragmentation of psychic life

Questioning, again and again, the meaning of Freud's dream of the self-dissection of his pelvis, Ferenczi slowly succeeded in modifying the Freudian system from within. Freud's system was of course modified by other pupils as well, yet Ferenczi was the only one who did so *from inside*, by letting himself be directed by that equation between ego, body, and penis of which, as stressed by Lewin (1933), he was undisputed master.

Ferenczi replaced the assault on the penis, which in his *Genitaltheorie* is defined as a "miniature ego," with the attack on the integrity of the self, of the person.[1] *Circumcision*, as a secret model of trauma was then replaced by the *splitting of the ego*. And it is not an exchange, a barter, in Freud's sense, that is, a substitution that leaves the system unchanged. On the contrary, it is an organic development in deep continuity with the work of the master, whose reductionism (the part for the whole) was freed from the phallic code, allowing the clinical recognition that a wider range of body parts, "hands, fingers, feet, genitals, head, nose, or eye" and so on, can become "representatives of the whole person" (Ferenczi, 1931, p. 135). Let's review some stages of Ferenczi's route.

Since 1916, Ferenczi's meditation focused on *autotomy* (a Greek neologism that means "self-cut"), a biological phenomenon that is found in the behavior of certain animals, which amputate a part of their body to survive when their life is endangered.[2] In *Thalassa* autotomy is recognized as the physiological prototype of the process of repression and identified with the *death instinct* postulated by Freud in *Beyond the pleasure principle* (Ferenczi, 1924, p. 89).

Ferenczi will return to it in the essay *The problem of acceptance of unpleasant ideas* (1926), in which he begins an ongoing reflection on psychic mechanisms that are more primitive than repression, resuming an old interest in the reckoning capacity of living organisms. Ferenczi introduces here the idea that the adaptation to the external world is mediated by an unconscious intelligence capable of calculating minor displeasure. The physical elimination or the psychic sequestration of a part of oneself would then be the result of a quick calculation to save one's life. This insight will be further articulated after the turn of the years 1929–1930, when psychic trauma will be described as an annihilating experience, a veritable "death," albeit partial, which involves the destruction of parts of oneself, which become insensitive, dormant, or dead.

This turn is accompanied by a new way of staying in the analytic situation, encouraging regression and holding the psychic pain released in the re-production of childhood traumas. Ferenczi also abandons the Freudian vocabulary; he no longer speaks of "displeasure" but rather of suffering and pain, while a new metapsychology opens up before him, the one of the fragmentations of psychic life.

One of his new key phrases is the notion of "narcissistic splitting of the self," which is introduced in his 1931 article *Child-analysis in the analysis of adults*. "It really seems," Ferenczi writes, "as though, under the stress of imminent danger, part of the self splits off and becomes a psychic instance self-observing and desiring to help the self, and that possibly this happens in early—even the very earliest—childhood" (p. 136).

Initially, Freud's main portal in the unconscious psyche had been the idea of a *missing or failed reaction* of the individual. Almost four decades later, Ferenczi shifted the emphasis to the *missing or failed help* by another person. The paper that marks this change of direction is *The unwelcome child and his death instinct*, of 1929. Within human society, the biological birth is not yet a birth, because the child is torn from nothingness only if he/she is welcome and motivated to live. If this does not happen, or if at some point the child does not receive the necessary care, then the child slips back, falling into non-being. But even when the child's being begins to consolidate, the child may be driven back into non-existence by improper conducts, cruel behaviors, or traumatic events in which the child doesn't receive help, or that they are ignored or denied. If the *missing reaction* (Freud) signals the sequestration of a part of the psyche that continues to live in another place and in another time, the *missing help* (Ferenczi) involves a reorganization of the split personality in which "part of the person adopts the role of father or mother in relation to the rest, thereby undoing, as it were, the fact of being deserted" (Ferenczi, 1931, p. 135).

Since the idea of "narcissistic splitting of the self" was a development of the notion of autotomy, we can read it as Ferenczi's latest reinterpretation of Freud's self-dissection scene which for so many years occupied his mind. In that revelatory dream, besides being physically split in two, the father of psychoanalysis observes himself as an external spectator and without any emotion.

This absence of emotion had been described by Freud as "the peace that has descended upon a battlefield strewn with corpses; no trace is left of the struggle which raged over it" (Freud, 1900, p. 467), reading it as a neurotic defense. But in the article *Child-analysis in the analysis of adults*, Ferenczi (1931) offered a new understanding of this traumatic insensitivity, tracing it back to "the splitting of the self into a suffering, brutally destroyed part" and a self-observing part which "knows everything but feels nothing" (p. 135). In the *Clinical Diary*, he would write: "The person splits into a psychic being of pure knowledge that observes the events from the outside, and into totally insensitive body" (Dupont, 1988, p. 104; May 10, 1932).

This omniscient and calculating part is the result of what elsewhere Ferenczi calls "traumatic progression," a concept profoundly influenced by Severn's ideas. In extreme cases, it is presented as the work of an intelligence released from the body and from the constraints of time and space, a split-off entity representing the dead child and which Ferenczi, in the Clinical Diary, calls "Orpha." "*Pure intelligence* is thus a product of dying, or at least of becoming mentally insensitive—Ferenczi remarked in a note dated April 9, 1931, titled *The Birth of Intellect*—and is therefore *in principle madness...*" (*Notes and Fragments*, p. 246).

Psychoanalysis itself was born from this pure intelligence, exited out of the body in the extreme attempt to save it. Ferenczi's contribution to the history of psychoanalysis has been to take care of this split—which also was Freud's split. In his attempt at reunifying the part that knows everything but is insensitive with the part that is sensitive but destroyed, Ferenczi made this tear thinkable, preserving for us the hope of a full life in the body and a resurrection in the flesh. This problem is so important that the page with which the *Clinical Diary* opens is titled "*Insensitivity* [Fühllosigkeit] *of the analyst*" (January 7, 1932). This insensitivity of the person, screened by the professional role, was for Ferenczi the capital sin of psychoanalysis and the ultimate reason for its erroneous development.

Assimilation of Ferenczi's ideas

In the summer of 1930, Ferenczi met Freud to present him his new ideas. How did the Professor react? On September 16, Freud wrote to tell him that his "new views about the traumatic fragmentation of mental life" were "very ingenious" and had "something of the great characteristic of the Theory of Genitality." Yet, he added:

> I only think that one can hardly speak of trauma in the extraordinary synthetic activity of the ego without treating the reactive scar formation along with it. The latter, of course, also produces what we see ...

Of course, Ferenczi knew that the overwhelmed psyche is not able to register traumatic memories in an "objective" way, precisely because the primary effect of trauma was the shattering of the psyche. Yet, referring to the "synthetic activity of the Ego" Freud seems to say that he had already faced and resolved the question at the time of his old dispute with Pierre Janet.[3]

A few years after the premature death of Ferenczi, Freud began, however, to revise his views, assimilating the idea of psychic fragmentation, trying to bring it in harmony with the elements he considered essential, such as the theory of the Oedipus complex and threat of castration (Haynal, 2005, p. 464). It took eight years before he admitted, in private, that he was "clearly at fault" in taking "for granted the synthetic nature of the processes of the ego" (Freud, 1938a, p. 276).

Ferenczi's influence is palpable in the later works of Freud, as *Constructions in Analysis*, in which he returns to his early thesis that "hysterics suffer from reminiscences" extending it to the kernel of historic truth that is preserved in delusions, and even more in the third essay of *Moses and Monotheism*, in which Freud speaks of sequestration (the state within the state) and fragmentation of the ego under the destructive action of trauma. But even his last piece of self-analysis is permeated with the posthumous dialogue with Ferenczi and in particular by the idea that the "traumatic material" must not be sought in neurotic reactions but rather in psychotic disavowal of reality and in the splitting of the ego. This was in fact the material revisited by Freud in his essay *A disturbance of memory on the acropolis*, written in 1936 in form of an open letter to Romain Rolland, with whom he had already conversed about the "oceanic feeling."[4] Freud, in fact, could not find within himself this feeling, with which the Nobel Prize winner explained the sentiment of cosmic unity at the root of religion.

The acropolis' incident

The title initially chosen by Freud for his meditation, *Unglaube auf der Akropolis* (Disbelief on the acropolis), brings in his skeptical attitude toward religion (Glaube, faith), which was described as a "neurosis of humanity" in his essay *Future of an illusion*, reverting his previous definition of neurosis as a "private religion."[5] Freud was then working on Moses, destroying one by one all the religious beliefs of his ancestors. The definitive title also tells us that he had linked the conflict between credulity and skepticism to a central element of his self-analysis, that of the "memory disturbance" which had manifested itself in his strange forgetfulness of the name Signorelli and, above all, in his reiterated forgetting of Fliess' contribution to the concept of congenital bisexuality.

The event revisited by Freud was a dissociative phenomenon that had spoiled his 1904 trip to Greece with his brother Alexander. His meditation didn't divert from the interpretative line embraced from the moment in which he recognized a paternal verdict (brit milah) in the magic word of his Irma's injection dream. Thus, he traced the meaning of his incident back to the "Fate which we expect to treat us so badly is a materialization of our conscience, of the severe super-ego within us, itself a residue of the punitive agency of our childhood" (Freud, 1936, p. 243), and ultimately to the sense of guilt for having "got further than one's father" (p. 247), distancing himself from the faith of his ancestors. The super-ego was in fact for Freud the "vehicle of tradition."[6]

Freud's Hellenism played an important role in this. Freud had a strongly idealized view of classical Greece. To Marie Bonaparte, princess of Greece, he confided that the amber columns of the acropolis had been the most beautiful thing he had ever seen. This idealization is also found in the image of the Propylaea, the temple's impressive colonnade that, in the Irma dream, replaces the horrible sight of the vulva. It was the vision of beauty that he had learned in school under the influence of Winckelmann and neoclassical culture. In the words of Edith Hamilton (1930), the "terrifying irrational," the paralyzing fear of the unknown that circulated in neighboring cultures, had been banished from the humanized world of Greek mythology.

Putting man at the center of the universe, making man the measure of cosmos, Greeks had valued the body's beauty and harmony, balance, reason, and democracy, all values that were shared. In addition, mythology had offered Freud the figure of Oedipus around which he was reorganizing his system of thought. The ascent to Athens' Parthenon should have been, therefore, accompanied by an inner pleasure, much greater than the one experienced in Orvieto, in 1897, in front of Signorelli's frescoes on the end of the world, or in Rome in 1901, when, overcoming the irrational fear that had paralyzed him for years, Freud finally managed to enter the eternal city.[7]

That the ascent to the acropolis, dominated by the remains of the temple of the Virgin Athena, meant for Freud the "crowning" of the aspirations of a lifetime is made clear by his comparison between the long way made by his brother and him, and the crowning of Napoleon Bonaparte at Notre-Dame, when the conqueror turned to his brother, remarking: "What would *Monsieur notre Père* have said to this, if he could have been here to-day?" (Freud, 1936, p. 247).

Yet it was a disaster, and he never returned to Athens, while he went back six times to Rome. The memory of that "incident," as he called it, had bothered him all his life. The term used by Freud was "*heimgesucht* "which Niederland (1969) suggests translating as "tormented, tortured." According to Bettelheim (1982), Freud had chosen it for its religious connotation; "*Heimsuchung*" is in fact the name with which the Visitation of the Virgin Mary is celebrated. I recall, for those who might not know it, that in the Byzantine era the Parthenon, the temple of the Virgin Athena, was converted into a church dedicated to Maria Parthenos (Virgin). For Haynal (personal communication) the term is also evocative of homecoming [*heim*]—a haunted and "uncanny" return, indeed. An allusion to the incident appears in Freud's essay *The Uncanny* [*Das Unheimliche*] (1919). This uncanny experience was partially told by Freud to Jung in his letter of April 16, 1909, connecting it to Fliess and to Freud's conviction that he would die "between the ages of 61 and 62."

Exploring the background of the "incident," Schur (1969) found that the trigger was indeed the argument about bisexuality that Freud had with Fliess, and in particular, a letter received from Fliess "only a week or so before"(p. 130). Freud then went on holidays with his brother Alexander, and, in a totally unplanned way, he first found himself in Trieste and then embarked on a ferryboat and was finally driven to Athens "like automatons, will-less, unfree, occupied by their father's ego, possessed by his Dybbuk," as well summarized by Maynard Solomon (1973, p. 153).

The feeling of anxiety, that had seized him already on the ferryboat Uranus, turned soon to persecution, but the psychotic collapse occurred while climbing the rock of the acropolis. All the pleasure of being there, on the top of the world, had been spoiled by a strange "*Erinnerungsstörung*" (memory disturbance) which, after being analyzed, appeared to him as a state of alienation epitomized by the formula "what I see here is not real" (Freud, 1936, p. 244).

Freud made clear that this type of experience of alienation, despite being typical of more severe mental diseases, such as schizophrenia, "are not unknown among normal people, just as hallucinations occasionally occur in the healthy" and explained that usually they can manifest themselves in two forms: "the subject feels either that a piece of reality or that a piece of his own self is strange to him" (p. 245). In his case both sides were present. In order to better convey what he meant, he introduced a startling comparison. It had been, he wrote,

> as if walking beside Loch Ness the sudden sight of the famous ["vielbere-deten," much discussed] Monster stranded upon the shore would force the startled walker to admit: 'So it really does exist – the sea-serpent [Seeschlange] we've never believed in!'
>
> (p. 241)

The insertion of the Scottish snake in the middle of the classical Greek is a narrative shock that shatters the image of harmony and beauty. It is the return of the "terrifying irrational" that was thought banished from that world. What does it tell us?

The dragon of the abyss

Freud's narrative aroused many and different reactions.[8] Risto Fried (2003) found in Freud's provocative comparison the resurfacing of doubts at the heart of his self-analysis and at the bottom of psychoanalysis itself: "what to believe?," "what is real?" (p. 283).

This issue had also been at the heart of his dispute with Ferenczi, whom he had advised to maintain a skeptical stance. Nevertheless, here Freud proposes a postmodern scene in which a skeptical and disenchanted person meets his hallucination, which he does not believe in, but which is actually there, located in the outside world. In *Constructions in Analysis*, he will then say that in hallucinations "something that has been experienced in infancy and then forgotten returns" (Freud, 1937b, p. 267).

Thus, the Loch Ness scene is particularly intriguing because it re-proposes the situation in which, in analysis, a scene bursts with hallucinatory intensity, filling a gap in the memory. If we consider that "Loch" [hole] and "Lücke" [gap] were interchangeable for Freud (1916–1917, p. 179), his unsettling comparison draws a scene in which an estranged spectator sees something coming out of a "Loch" [hole] which is also a "Lücke," a gap in the psyche.

By aligning this scene with the dream of pelvic dissection, we could also say that, with his hallucination, Freud finally succeeds in the task of "extracting something" from his eviscerated pelvis. This something, the sea serpent that cannot be believed, is the great Lord Penis, the Dragon of the abyss with which the apocalyptic story of the world begins and ends.

The image of the dragon rising from the depths revives the whole mystical tradition in which the salvific power of fish is a constant theme from pagan rites to Christianity (Leach, 1986). In his long essay "The dragon and the hero," Geza Rohéim (1940), traces back the Big Fish from the Big Mother Snake whose body is cut in two by the Babylonian god Marduk. Rohéim refers here to the tradition that interprets the appearance of the Leviathan (Isaiah 51,9–10 and 27,1) as the victory of God over the dragon or sea serpent.

Was Freud using the image of the dragon only to fill the void of an unexplored land, according to the habit of medieval cartographers, or did this image also have a particular meaning for him?

Giant snakes

Let's go back to the trigger of Freud's collapse. For Schur (1969, p. 130), and I agree with him, it was the "blast" of Fliess, who had accused him of plagiarism only a week earlier.[9]

Freud had a disconcerting tendency to get hold of his friend's brilliant idea, forgetting the circumstances in which Fliess told him about his new theory of congenital bisexuality. But it wasn't intentional, planned plagiarism. Rather it was a sort of uncontrollable daydream in which he remained "in possession of the field," as suggested also by the fact that he repeatedly acknowledged being wrong, in submissive and unarmed ways.[10] But the repetition of this behavior caused in Fliess a tension that eventually wears down the friendship. Later Freud didn't spare praises to the elegant simplicity of Fliess' theory, however, in the years of the foundation of psychoanalysis, it was as if a gap in his memory was constantly reforming. Freud himself was bewildered by this, as evidenced by the passage in *The Psychopathology of Everyday Life*, in which he reported, as a sign of repair, the episode that, in the summer of 1900, had wrecked their friendship.[11]

Freud had told his friend that certain "problems of the neuroses are only to be solved if we base ourselves wholly and completely on the assumption of the original bisexuality of the individual," to which Fliess had replied: "That's what I told you two and a half years ago at Breslau … but you wouldn't hear of it then." Reporting this exchange, Freud admitted that in the ensuing week he remembered the whole incident, adding: "It is painful to be requested in this way to surrender one's originality" (Freud, 1901b, p. 144).

The meeting ended in a more than turbulent way, with a reciprocal exchange of accusations, and perhaps something more. After that, the two never saw each other again and the correspondence slowly faded away. The decision to end the relationship had been Fliess'. Freud, on the other hand, "could not believe that such a valuable friendship had really finished" (Jones, 1953, p. 345). Hoping to keep it still alive, on August 7, 1901, he had acknowledged by letter Fliess' priority on "bisexuality," but Fliess didn't want to hear from him any more.

In April of 1904, after a silence of two years, Freud reached out to Fliess to announce a work by Dr. Swoboda, of which he was "the intellectual originator." Freud wanted to revive the old relationship, but reading Swoboda's book, Fliess noticed that a young fellow, the philosopher Otto Weininger, had just published a book largely based on his theory of bisexuality.[12] Suspecting that Freud was at the origin of the plagiarism, he tried to clarify the matter with him. Freud initially denied everything, stumbling upon various contradictions, and then ended up once again agreeing with Fliess.[13] On July 27, 1904, he replied that he had now understood what had happened, connecting it, I quote, "*with my own attempt to rob you of your originality.*" This was Freud's mood when embarking to Athens.

Schur speaks of "Fliess's blast."[14] But what strikes in the 1904 brief exchange of letters is the clumsy and then submissive character of Freud's answers, who once again ended up accusing himself of the desire to "rob" his friend of his brilliant idea. His attitude toward Fliess will continue to be deeply divided. He will recognize on several occasions Fliess' originality, even exaggerating it. All the while he will continue to repeat the "theft" while at the same time denying it, even and especially to himself.[15] Above all, Freud never accepted that the break of their friendship was caused by his persistent fantasy of appropriating Fliess' brilliant idea. In fact, he will attribute it to the hostile interference of Fliess' wife, Ida, or to the paranoia of Fliess.[16]

To Ferenczi, Freud will confide that the cause of the break had been his interpretation of the unconscious motivation of Fliess' "fatalistic theory of predetermined dates of death."[17] In the eyes of Freud it must have been just like that, because after the break an obsession about *his own predetermined date of death* arouses in him. As pointed out by Schur, bearing the unmistakable signature of Fliess, this obsession was signaling an incorporation.[18] Unable to accept emotionally the end of the friendship, Freud preserved the bond with the friend who had deserted him through this obsession about the date of his own death.

Freud was partly aware of this. In his long letter to Jung of March 19, 1909, Freud noticed that behind his belief in dying at the age of 61 or 62 that overwhelmed him in Greece, "the hidden influence of W. Fliess was at work; the superstition erupted in the year of his attack on me." Also, Freud's fainting in Munich in 1912, when he was heard whispering "how sweet it must be to die," was a consequence of the same situation. After the episode, Freud wrote to Jones (December 8, 1912) that his fainting was connected to his relationship with Fliess, specifying that at the root of the matter there was "some piece of unruly homosexual feeling." It seems that the hotel room in which he fainted was the one where "the final quarrel with Fliess took place" (Jones, 1953, p. 348).

Finding an order in this impressive proliferation of symptoms is not easy. For Max Schur, who is perhaps the only one to have ventured into such an enterprise, it all began with Emma Eckstein's nose operation and with Freud's desperate need to deny his ambivalence toward Fliess that winds through dreams, fantasies, and enactments, becoming the true drive to self-analysis, from which a growing awareness of his "death wishes" to his friend would slowly emerge.[19] Schur, however, seems to underestimate both the severity of Freud's psychotic breakdown and the fact that, in his last letter to Freud (July 26, 1904), Fliess recalled something that apparently acted as trigger. Namely, that on Easter 1897, his idea of congenital bisexuality had been inspired by a recurrent dream of a patient of Freud—Emma Eckstein. Fliess had written:

> Until now I did not know what I learned from your letter — that you are using [the idea of] persistent bisexuality in your treatments. We talked about it for the first time in Nuremberg while I was still lying in bed, and you told me the case history of the woman who had dreams of gigantic snakes. At the time you were quite impressed [sehr betroffen] by the idea that undercurrents in a woman might stem from the masculine part of her psyche. For this reason I was all the more puzzled by your resistance in Breslau to the assumption of bisexuality in the psyche. ... as you yourself admitted most candidly, [you] forgot our bisexual discussion for some time.

The acropolis' incident was the *après coup* of this revelation. Its effects will be felt in the following days, when Freud found himself traveling to Athens as if driven by a foreign will, began to be persecuted by numbers announcing his death, and finally collapsed on the acropolis. His system of thought had been construed on the cancellation of Emma Eckstein's circumcision trauma and on the repression of the dissociated traumatic fragments that had been reawakened in himself.

In a fine essay on the memory disturbance on the acropolis, Risto Fried (2003) imagined that, setting foot in Athens, Freud was struck by the extraordinary power of the serpent cult in archaic Greece, so contrasting with the image of harmony and beauty of classic Greece learned at school. Risto Fried understood that the Loch Ness monster was not a playful metaphor. Freud had indeed been surrounded and attacked by giant snakes. However, they were not those exhibited in the Acropolis Museum. It was rather the gigantic snake that erased Emma Eckstein's childhood trauma, the "great Lord Penis" to which Freud himself had clung like a fetish in order not to fall into the empty box in which his mother had disappeared (his "black hole").

The Saurian era

Freud's objection to Ferenczi was that reactive formation to trauma "also produces what we see" (September 16, 1930). In the Acropolis' fiction "what we see" is the dragon of the abyss that emerges from a *Loch* which is also a *Lücke*, a hole in the plot of being and not only a gap in the memory.

It wasn't the first time that Freud made use of the dragon metaphor. In the 1913 essay *The disposition to obsessional neurosis*, Freud had used it to indicate the woman's fixation at her imaginary male organ. He used it referring to the "well-known" fact that women, once their genital functions cease, "become quarrelsome, vexatious and overbearing, petty and stingy" to the point that "writers of comedy and satirists have in all ages directed their invectives against the 'old dragon' [alten Drachen] into which the charming girl, the loving wife and the tender mother have been transformed" (Freud, 1913c, pp. 323–324). This alteration of character, which attests the disappearance of the tender and welcoming mother, was explained by the regression from the vagina to the male sexual area, the clitoris.

Yet, the image of the dragon not only stood for the archaic penis of the woman but also epitomized the story of Freud's libidinal fixation on the traumatic object. In the summer of 1871, the young Freud, then 15, returned for the first and only time to Freiberg, his native town, and immediately fell in love with Gisela Fluss, who was then 11 years old. He was too shy to voice his feelings, however, and the infatuation soon turned into biting spitefulness. A few months later, in Freud's letters to his friend Eduard Silberstein, Gisela reappears there with the code name "Ichthyosaura" (literally "saurian-fish"). The tender love object had turned into a sea serpent!

The beauty that had enchanted him had turned into an "aquatic reptile of dinosaurian proportions" (Eissler, 1978, p. 470). Reconstructed by paleontologists just a few decades before, the gigantic reptile had inspired a popular satire in which an "Ichthyosaura" lets herself be kissed by an Iguanodon. Three years later, when he heard of Gisela's marriage, the young Freud composed a nuptial poem on the bridegroom's disappointment at seeing the naked body of his loved Ichthyosaura. Boehlich (1990), the editor of the correspondence between Freud and Silberstein, notes in his introduction that the "Saurian age" had come to an end (p. xx).

Hostility, debasement, and ridicule was the strategy used to break hold on his affections. The vulnerable boy's tender feeling of love had turned into disgust for women. For Eissler (1978), the nickname chosen for Gisela suggests an unconscious fantasy that "women are dangerous monsters, a fear-arousing species whose phallic nature seems obvious" (p. 471). For Fried (2003, pp. 414–427), the transformation of a love object into an attractive monster was a recurrent pattern in Freud's life. As a child, his sexual initiation was marked by the "prehistoric" Catholic nanny, the prototype of all the disapproving and exciting Dragon Ladies of his dreams. As a teenager, his tender love had turned into a repellent reptile. Then, on the occasion of his secret betrothal, Martha had become in fantasy "Melusine," a medieval water nymph, half woman and half snake or fish.

The legend of Melusina proposes the same theme as the shocking peeping of the wedding poem on Ichthyosaura that Freud composed as a teenager. In the medieval legend, Count Raimondo falls in love with a maiden he met in the forest, Melusina, who agrees to marry him on one condition: that he never tries to see her naked! But the count spies on her and discovers that her underside is that of a snake. She forgives him, but then, when in a quarrel he calls her "serpent" in front of his court, she assumes the form of a dragon, opens her wings, and flies away never to return.

The first Germanic version was written in 1474 by Thüring von Ringoltingen. In misogynistic zeitgeist, Melusine (here called *Minne*, the medieval Aphrodite) was described as an unreliable monster confirming all husband's suspicions on his wife's infidelity. In 1801, Goethe wrote a new version of the fable in which the girl has the size of an insect, lives in a casket, and assumes human proportions only for limited periods of time. The themes of the peeping shock and marriage breakdown were kept in inverse form. She gives him an engagement ring which reduces him to her size, but then he fails to adapt to the constraints of marriage, breaks the ring, regains his size, and runs away.

At the time of their betrothal, Martha had given Freud a small box, a *casket*, with her portrait. After that, Freud began to be obsessed with the idea of a man carrying his beloved in a box, until he realized that what was shaping his betrothal's fears was Goethe's New Melusina.[20] The detail of the ring was prophetic: Freud was on the verge of breaking the engagement ring not once but twice. The rest of the story is summarized as follows by Risto Fried: "He was to spend the rest of his life denying, with remarkably few lapses, the unhappiness of his marriage" (Fried, 2003, p. 422).

The secret world of Melusina will be taken by Freud as a model of the similarity between neurotic ceremonials and religious rituals in his essay *Obsessive acts and religious practices* (Freud, 1907b, p. 343). The first psychoanalytic reading of the legend is offered by Otto Rank in a 1913 article on nudity in the saga. The reason for the transformation of the lower part of the body into fish reflects a combination in man of desire and fear of sexual intercourse with woman. The fish represents both the repulsion for the female genital and the hallucination of the woman's penis. In short, Dragon Lady, Ichthyosaur, and Melusina formed a coherent chain of metaphors which, in Freud's final meditation, are condensed and summarized in the image of the Loch Ness monster.

On closer inspection, or rather, on closer listening, this Saurian code had already surfaced in the string of words of the dream from which psychoanalysis was born (Propylpräparat, Propylen... Propionsäure...). We have already decoded these words, which accompany and mark the transformation of the unpleasant element, the disgusting smell of "amyl," in the triumphant allusion to the immense power of sexuality, "Trimethylamin." "Propyl" opens the way to the "propylaea," with which the horrifying vulva is replaced by the colonnaded entrance to the sacred temple, and then with "Proprion," from Priapic, phallic. The only missing element was "Propion-säure," a composite structure evidently manufactured on the model of "Ichthyo-saura," thanks to the substitution of the fish (ichthyo) with a symbol of the phallus. Of course, the peeping theme captures Freud's shock before Emma's genitals. Yet, recapping the story of Freud's libidinal fixations, this substitution makes us understand why Freud remained so fascinated by "Extraordinary synthetic activity of the ego" and locked up in the idea that our unconscious fantasies arise from the natural history of the libido, in such a way that predisposition, the phylogenetic past, is inscribed in the reaction, prevailing over the shock, and even reabsorbing it completely.

Dragons that are never extinct

In *Thalassa*, the penis is described as a "Melusina member."[21] The "sea serpent," fish and phallus, of Freud's meditation on his memory disturbance on the acropolis, was, therefore, the same that is at the heart of Ferenczi's scientific fairy tale. The detail of the sea monster landed on the shore of Loch Ness, bears the unmistakable mark of *Thalassa,* the myth of the catastrophic exsiccation of the sea that rises the Big Fish or Dragon from the depths of the abyss, pushing it on the land. It is the unconscious dialogue between Freud and Ferenczi that continues. Using the image of the sea serpent, it is as if Freud recognized in the imagination of his ingenious pupil an effort to fill the void clearly inscribed in his own dreams.

The dialogue will be resumed in *Analysis Terminable and Interminable.* The Dragon resurfaced in Freud's text as the signifier of everything that should be surmounted and dead, yet clings tenaciously to life. Discussing the intertwining of archaic illusions and libidinal fixations, Freud wrote "One feels inclined to doubt sometimes whether the dragons of primaeval days are really extinct. [Manchmal könnte man zweifeln, ob die Drachen der Urzeit wirklich ausgestorben sind]" (Freud, 1937a, p. 229).

The continuity with the amazement for the "sea-serpent we never believed in" is obvious. Freud is here too speaking of a dissociated part of himself which was reawakened by Emma Eckstein's infantile trauma and wrapped in her imaginary phallus as, so to say, in a "new skin". Mark the wording. Freud does not say "extinct dinosaurs" nor does he speak of fairy tales about dragons; that is, he neither refers to real animals, reconstructed from fossils, nor to the fictive creatures of fairy tales. Instead, he speaks of "extinct dragons," mixing *fossils* and *legends, reality* and *fiction*. This is a dramatic way to assert that the intertwining of traumatic events and reactive formation, life events and unconscious fantasy, cannot be disentangled because of the "extraordinary synthetic activity of the ego," as it was claimed in his letter of September 16, 1930. It also offers a precise response to Ferenczi, who, at the end of this passage, is criticized for his naive expectation of to access traumatic memories in a simple and direct way.[22]

The dispute with Ferenczi about the accessibility of traumatic memories is intertwined and knotted here with the non-negotiable point of their rupture: the interpretation of the woman's penis, the prototype of every mirage, illusion, and fetish.

In the Freudian architecture, the "prehistoric dragon" is the mother's phallus, an archaic illusion that revives in the infant mind and often persists into adulthood, becoming then the object of a private cult. Freud refers to it in the 1927 essay on *Fetishism*, where we find the matrix of both the astonishment on the Loch Ness shore and the doubt about the real extinction of dragons. Freud in fact wondered how can the dear object venerated in early childhood, the mother's penis, be "preserved from extinction"?[23]

To solve this dilemma the scheme "repression/return of the repressed" was clearly inadequate. Freud introduced then a new model, based on the combination of replacement and denial[24]: the dear object of early childhood is saved from extinction because it is exchanged with another object, the fetish, which facilitates compliance with reality, acknowledging that, after all, women do not have the penis, as to save the belief [Glaube] in the precious object, denying the perception that threatens it. The fetish will then have two sides: on the one hand, it is a triumphant victory over the threat of castration, on the other a monument to the memory of the horror of castration. It is the theme around which Freud's meditation on memory disturbance on the acropolis, as well as the whole story we are trying to tell revolves.

Exploring the consequences of the ingenious fetishist solution, Freud here just remarked that it allows the fetishist not to become homosexual making woman tolerable as a sexual object, while leaving a permanent estrangement with respect to her true genital (1927a, p. 154). But he will take up the question again in an unfinished 1938 note, *Splitting of the ego in the process of defence*, where he admits that he was "clearly at fault" in taking the synthetic function of the ego "for granted" (1938a, p. 276). He will then acknowledge that the ingenious attempt to destroy evidence of castration by means of a fetish "is achieved at the price of a rift in the ego which never heals but which increases as time goes on" (ibid.). Castration anxiety does not cease. On the contrary, despite his display of "masculinity to master and overcompensate" (p. 277) it, anxiety intensifies, regresses to the oral phase, becoming fear of being devoured. To explain the latter, Freud then invokes the Greek legend of Cronus, but at this point, he is stuck and can no longer go on.

We may conclude here by saying that the authors who will study fetishism will find in it a defense against anxieties of abandonment and disintegration, or that Freud ceases to fight when he finds himself again before the wide open mouth of Moloch. Perhaps there is no difference, given that for Freud in pathological mourning the ego wants to incorporate the object in itself by "devouring it" (Freud, 1917, p. 250). In any case, in this unfinished note on splitting of the Ego, Freud is struck before a gaping mouth, as if he had never moved from the place where everything had begun.

Notes

1 An example. Starting from the assumption of a "link between the foreskin, which has the biological function of protecting the glans penis, and the mother who protects the son in childhood" (Daly, 1950, p. 227), we could say that, in the new perspective, the same protective function of the foreskin (=barrier against stimuli postulated by Freud in *Beyond the pleasure principle*) is found in the mother who takes care of the child. The focus thus shifts from the circumcision of the penis to the abandonment of or failure to help the child.
2 See Ferenczi's letter to Freud of April 27, 1916.
3 In his American lessons, Freud summarized the difference between his view and that of Janet in the following way: "We do not derive the psychical splitting from an innate incapacity for synthesis on the part of the mental apparatus; we explain it dynamically, from the conflict of opposing mental forces and recognize it as the outcome of an active struggling on the part of the two psychical groupings against each other." (Freud, 1910a, pp. 25–26)
4 I am referring here to the section "womb and coffin" of Chapter 6, in which I briefly dealt with the question.
5 "Neurosis of humanity": Freud (1927b, p. 43). A reference to the feeling of astonishment experienced on the Athens' acropolis also appears in this essay (p. 25), in which Freud ironically calls Heine, one of his "fellow-unbelievers"—in German "Unglaubensgenossen." "Private Religion": Freud (1907b, p. 119).
6 Although deriving from the parental instance, a child's superego is not constructed for Freud on the model of its parents "but of its parents' super-ego," thus becoming "the vehicle of tradition" (Freud, 1933a, p. 67).
7 See Freud's letters to his wife Martha and to Fliess of September 3, 1901.
8 I will mention a few. Maynard Solomon (1973) saw the return of a frightening homosexual fantasy close to break in the surface while Freud, along with his brother, feels the imaginary presence of his father: "the fear of penetration via pederasty or fellatio" (p. 152). In a remarkable reflection, entitled "Buried Memories on the Acropolis," of which no trace remained in the book *Assault on Truth*, Jeffrey Masson associates it with Jacob's account of the anti-Semitic attack to

which he had not reacted, suggesting that the monster of Loch Ness represented the return of the monstrous experience of being sexually abused by a "Roman Catholic" child (Masson & Masson, 1977, p. 204). Freud's narrative was then traced by Irving Harrison (1979, 1988) to the dream of self-dissection of the pelvis and to the fictional figure of *She*, incarnation of the ghost of the pre-Oedipal mother at the origin of the mystical currents that Freud tried to suppress with his scientific attitude. Other prominent analysts have recognized the echo of a shocking castration (Vermorel and Vermorel, 1993, p. 476). For Risto Fried (2003) the image of the "sea serpent [Seeschlange] that we never believed" well describes the bodily sensations of the exhibitionist who, doubting the existence of his penis, must exhibit it to get the reaction of surprise which allows him to believe in his manhood. From this perspective, the "monster" was neither the phallus of the abusive father nor of the archaic mother, but "his own penis." "Seeschlange" had to be read literally: "look [See] the snake [schlange]!" (p. 426).

9   Incomprehensibly, not many commentators on Freud's essay followed Schur's suggestion. Among these, Schröter (2003) simply noted that the memory disturbance on the acropolis was perhaps "directly co-determined by the final split with his erstwhile friend" (p. 163). In their voluminous study of Freud's essay, Vermorel and Vermorel (1993) pointed out more strongly that Fliess is "omnipresent" in it (p. 470). Flannery (1980) wrote, "It is curious then that in 1936, in what was probably his final attempt to understand the experience of the Acropolis, he [Freud] makes no mention of Fliess, or the Weininger-Swoboda affair" (p. 351).

10   The qualification "daydream" is my interpretation. I recall that daydreaming is a dissociative phenomenon (Schafer, 1968).

11   Freud wrote in 1901, but it was one of his many slips on this subject. For a historical reconstruction see Schröter (2003). For a psychodynamic reconstruction see Mahony (1979).

12   Weininger's book, *Sex and Character*, 1903, which was a tremendous success and was valued brilliantly by intellectuals such as Wittgenstein, is a mix of racist, misogynistic, and anti-Semitic stereotypes (Weininger was a Jew converted to Protestantism). Citing it in the margin of the clinical story of little Hans, Freud wrote that "in a chapter that attracted much attention, [Weininger] treated Jews and women with equal hostility and overwhelmed them with the same insults" (Freud, 1909, p. 36 note). I will return to the question in the last chapter, because Freud made use of Weininger's perspective to formulate his well-known thesis: "The castration complex is the deepest unconscious root of anti-Semitism."

13   For until Jones (1953) wrote: "It was perhaps the only time in his life where for a moment Freud was not absolutely righteous" (p. 379).

14   Schur anticipates the fact that his anger will lead, in 1906, into a trial for plagiarism which had considerable resonance and which indirectly also affected Freud. The exchange of letters of 1904 was preserved because they were attached to the documents of the trial. On the basis of the available documentation, Schröter (2003) came to the conclusion that "Fliess's accusations against Freud have a core of truth.... Around this nucleus Fliess built the fantasy of the betrayal of his previous friend" (p. 167). Schröter also points out that the accusations of "plagiarism" tendencies that will be repeatedly leveled at Freud were based exclusively on his statements, which were rooted in an unresolved sense of guilt towards his former friend.

15   In the *Three Essays on Sexual Theory*, Freud mentioned eight contributors to the concept of bisexuality, listing Fliess among the lasts, and then, in the ensuing

edition he deleted his name from the sentence "Since becoming familiar with the idea of bisexuality through Fliess, I have considered it the decisive factor" (Freud, 1905, p. 526; Mahony, 1979, p. 86).

16 For a complete picture see Schröter (2003), p. 163 ff.

17 Freud's letter to Ferenczi of January 10, 1910.

18 Although Freud considered it "crazy," the fatalistic theory of his friend made him feel tied to him, as is obvious from his 1898 dream "Goethe's attack on Herr M.," which was triggered by an attack on Fliess of a reviewer of Fliess' latest work. The reviewer had wrote, "one wonders whether it is the author or oneself who is crazy'" (Freud, 1900, p. 440); to which Freud, identifying with Fliess, had written: "Yes, you're quite right, it's we who are the fools" (p. 441). Thus, after the break up, unable to mourn the loss, Freud will be forced to make crazy calculations on the date of his "predetermined death," thus keeping Fliess alive within himself.

19 For Schur (1969), Freud's death wishes toward Fliess turned into an obsession with his own predetermined death which attests "his guilt *and* his identification" (p. 132). In Schur's biography of Freud prevailed then a hagiographic spirit. For instance, Schur (1972) wrote that self-analysis enabled Freud to overcome the crisis in its relations with Fliess and that Freud came out of the relationship stronger and richer.

20 Letter from Freud to Martha Bernays, June 19, 1882. On Melusina's fantasy in Freud's life see Rosenberg's keen and amusing book, 1978.

21 In the chapter "The phylogenetic parallel," Ferenczi refers in fact to the definition of the penis by Bolsche, a disciple of Haeckel: "There is indeed something of the past in this member. It reminds one of the Melusina legend. Man is here linked with the fish, from which in days long gone he has descended" (Ferenczi, 1924, p. 46).

22 Freud (1937a, p. 230). However, in *Constructions in Analysis* Freud will change direction again, or at least he will find in delusions "a piece of existence that has been lost," adding that the delusion is similar to the construction that allows the psychoanalyst to fill a gap in the patient's memory (Freud, 1937b, p. 268).

23 Freud (1927a, p. 152). The German term used here by Freud is "Untergang" (demise, destruction, and death), while with respect to prehistoric dragons he used "ausgestorben" (extinct, dead).

24 The concept begins to take shape in the essay which theoretically establishes the primacy of the phallus, where Freud notes that the child denies or disavows the absence of the penis and believes he sees it anyway (Freud, 1923a, pp. 143–144). The term used here is "leugnen" (deny) and does not yet have a theoretical status, as it will later be for the term "Verleugnung," denial, denial or disavowal, which in the essay on Fetishism is defined in opposition to the "Verdrängung," repression (Freud, 1927a, p. 153).

Chapter 11

Gaps and substitutes

> The horror of castration has erected a memorial to itself in the creation of this substitute.
>
> (Sigmund Freud, *Fetishism*, 1927, p. 493)

A crack in the building

Freud's unfinished 1938 note *Splitting of the Ego in the Process of Defence* signals a rift in the solid theoretical edifice built on the Oedipus complex. The point at which Freud got stuck, the fear of being devoured, was the central element of his most important clinical case, that of the Wolf Man.[1] This paradigmatic case had inspired the notion of "transference neurosis" with Freud's latest technical essay, *Remembering, Repeating and Working-Through*, finally becoming "a permanent source of reference for hypotheses about the primal scene, primal fantasies and the inheritance of racial memories" (Kanzer, 1972).

Born in Odessa to a wealthy Russian aristocratic family, the Wolf Man had entered Freud's life impetuously at the age of 28. As Freud told Ferenczi on February 13, 1910, after the first session the new Russian patient confessed to him the following "transference":

> Jewish swindler, he would like to use me from behind and shit on my head. At the age of six years he experienced as his first symptom cursing against God: pig, dog, etc. When he saw three piles of feces on the street he became uncomfortable because of the Holy Trinity and anxiously sought a fourth in order to destroy the association.

Jew, behind, below, above, God, anality, and Trinity mark the coordinates of the space in which this analysis will take shape, the epicenter of which, repressed homosexuality, sums up well Freud's dominant concerns in those days.

When the Wolf Man burst into his life, Freud was immersed in writing his essay on Leonardo, while Emma Eckstein's second analysis was running

DOI: 10.4324/9781003353058-16

into the chasm. The traumatic end of this analysis brought all the unsolved problems back to the surface. We already know that Freud dealt with the ghost of Fliess by throwing himself headlong into President Schreber's paranoid delusion. Everything else began to find an order thanks to the new Russian patient. Through this analysis, Freud in fact returned to the knots of the first analysis with Emma Eckstein and revisited all, or almost all, the themes of his self-analysis. Thus, he resumed the theory of seduction, abandoned for 17 years now, giving it a new form, and completed the architecture of the Oedipus complex with a new contribution: its inverse form, the negative Oedipus.

The complete form of the Oedipus complex was "due to the bisexuality originally present in children" (Freud, 1923b, p. 33), and in *Inhibition, Symptom and Anxiety* the two cases of Little Hans and Wolf Man were placed side by side, to illustrate the twofold structure, positive and negative, of the Oedipus complex (Freud, 1926a, p. 107). Everything fit in. But it didn't last long.

In 1926 the Wolf Man had a relapse that will take him back into analysis, this time not with Freud but with a young pupil of his. In his role of supervisor Freud will make two important references to the "supplement" of analysis of his favorite patient. The first is contained in the opening of the 1927 essay *Fetishism* and is about a focal delusion on the *nose*. The second is contained in the opening of *Analysis Terminable and Interminable*, where Freud wrote that

> the pathogenic material consisted of pieces of the patient's childhood history, which had not come to light while I was analysing him and which now came away—the comparison is unavoidable—like sutures after an operation, or small fragments of necrotic bone.
>
> (Freud, 1937a, p. 218)

The comparison that Freud "cannot avoid" raises a question. Within the mental space of the founder of psychoanalysis, did Emma Eckstein and the Wolf Man crisscross in the place where everything had begun, the nose? This is what we will try to find out in the two final chapters.

A piece of psychoanalysis

Wolf Man's analysis lasted from February 1910 to July 1914. Although it marked a theoretical advance in Freud's struggle against dissidents, Adler and Jung in particular, the case history was published only at the end of the Great War, in 1918, under the title *From the History of an Infantile Neurosis*. It will be a fundamental text in the transmission of psychoanalysis and, with the establishment and spreading of training institutes, the main teaching vehicle of psychoanalytic clinics at least until the decades of 1970s–1980s, when devastating doubts began to arise.

In the meantime, the original text had been considerably enriched with supplements. From November 1919 to February 1920, there was a further period of analysis. Because of the Russian Revolution, this man had lost all his assets and Freud had treated him for free, also providing for his sustenance and holidays with an annual collection until 1926, when an acute crisis required a new intervention. Freud then entrusted the case to Ruth Mack Brunswick. The new analysis lasted four months, from October 1926 to February 1927. Given the relevance of the case, Brunswick drafted a "Supplement to Freud's 'History of a Childhood Neurosis'" which was published in 1928 in the *International Journal of Psycho-Analysis*.

But the story wasn't over. The analysis resumed from 1929, irregularly, for several years and again in 1938. Then, a pupil of Brunswick, Muriel Gardiner, will take care of him until the patient's death in 1979 at the psychiatric hospital in Vienna. Since the 1950s, the Wolf Man received diagnostic, psychiatric, and analytical attention from various other analysts. After founding the Freud Archives in 1951, for many years Kurt Eissler returned to Vienna every summer to engage him in "analytically directed conversations" collected in 180 tapes, with the (unfulfilled) promise that they would be made public while he was alive.[2] Fredrick Weil, Wilhelm Solms, Alfred Winterstein, and Albert Lubin, are some of the psychoanalysts who followed him for free in various capacities, while he continued to receive financial support from the Freud Archives.

In postwar Vienna, emptied of old analysts, this man felt himself to be the last bastion of psychoanalysis. His Memoirs, published in 1961, will be signed with the pseudonym "Wolf Man"— Freud had never referred to him in that way. Here it is he who, assuming the role of "parade horse of psychoanalysis," writes the history of psychoanalysis. More than a "patient" he felt himself to be a "collaborator" of Freud, who had not failed to feed this conviction. In his Memoirs, the Wolf Man recalls that one day Freud had confided to him that he would have liked his students to have understood the essence of his doctrine as much as he did. In a long interview with Karin Obholzer, he later recalled how Freud considered him nothing less than "a piece of psychoanalysis." The first time the journalist called him on the phone, he picked up the handset and answered "Hier spricht der Wolfmann" [Hello, this is the Wolf Man] (Obholzer, 1980, p. 10).

In 1971 Muriel Gardiner published a monumental book entitled *The Wolf-Man by the Wolf-Man*, in which, as Anna Freud pointed out in her introduction, the rich material of the only psychoanalytic case followed from youth into old age was collected. The material was enriched by the patient's Memoirs. Karin Obholzer was impressed. After some research, she managed to identify his real name, Sergei Pankeiev, and convinced him to give a long interview despite the strong opposition of Gardiner and Eissler. Pankeiev granted it on the condition that it would be published only after his death. The reason is simple; as one reviewer of the book noted, there were "troubling discrepancies between what the Wolf Man remembered of his analyses and what the analysts themselves reported" (Rogow, 1985).

Evidence on which Freud had based the plot of the case history, as well as the strict and consequential logic of the narrative, seemed to correspond more to the theoretical needs posed by the holes in his own self-analysis than to the unfolding of a therapeutic process. For Kanzer (1972), the Wolf Man had "played some substitute part for Freud himself in pursuing forbidden areas of his own analysis" (p. 422). For Blum (1974), it was mainly in the analyst's mind that the analysis of the Wolf Man had been "organized" (p. 722). For Viderman (1977), there had been a "fantasmatization induced by interpretation" (p. 294). For Langs (1980), the Wolf Man's feminine submission to his analyst "produced a child for him—the wolf dream and its analysis" (p. 375).

In those years, the idea emerged that Sergei Pankeiev had remained fundamentally inaccessible to the therapeutic encounters that had followed one another for over half a century. "What a strange development that Freud should have presented as the showpiece of clinical psychoanalysis an incurable case ...!," exclaimed Patrick Mahony (1984, p. 157). For this scholar, who has carefully studied Freud's case histories, the "air of unreality" of Freud's investigation (but also of Brunswick's), is such as to make us wonder about "his own daydreams and his daymares" (p. 149), and to ask ourselves: "is Freud's case history about the Wolf Man's nightmare partially Freud's own dream? Do we have another Dreambook?" (p. 11).

A little anecdote. When, at the end of the first analysis, Freud allowed him to give him a gift, the Wolf Man chose an Egyptian female figure. Freud immediately placed it on his desk. Associating the gift with Freud's childhood nightmare (that of the dead mother with bird-beaked figures from Philippson's illustrated Bible), a commentator exclaimed "How fine an example of unconscious understanding on the Wolf-Man's part of the role he played for Freud!" (Kanzer, 1972, p. 422).

Prototypes, substitutes, and gaps

For Freud, in the case of the Wolf Man, the seduction had been incontrovertibly real. At the age of about 3, he had been seduced by his two and half years older sister Anna, a "boyish and unmanageable" child who "had always remained ahead of him" (Freud, 1918a, p. 21). The seduction had forced our hero "into a passive role and had given him a passive sexual aim" (p. 27). After an attempt to repeat the experience with his nanny (Nanja), his passive attitude was transferred into the relationship with his father. The central characters of Freud's self-analysis thus resurfaced, including that element of sexual passivity toward a masculine woman which, although amply represented in his dreams, had not found a place in his first formulation of the Oedipus theory.

The question was now reformulated in the context of Freud's controversy with Adler, who had put the "masculine protest" at the center of everything. We know well how important this reaction was for Freud as well. Indeed, Freud also underlined the little boy's tendency to belittle the sister who had oppressed him and how, in order to erase a memory that wounded his masculinity, he had become aggressive and insulting toward all females. But if Adler, like Freud in 1897, saw only the masculine urge to "stay above," now, for the Wolf Man's analyst, the repressed sexual desire to "stay under" was the key feature of his patient's libido.

Starting from the 1990s, in the wake of a new awareness of the profound effects of an anti-Semitic and homophobic socio-cultural environment on the foundation of psychoanalysis, this "staying under" will be reread as the social position of the circumcised and feminized Jew that Freud had not only incorporated but also dissociated.[3] In short, the Wolf Man, the champion of the "negative" Oedipus, had brought onto the scene of psychoanalysis a dissociated part of Freud. We will come back to this later.

The seduction had given way to a phase of "naughtiness." In relation to his nanny, his scenes of naughtiness served active-sadistic ends, whereas in relation to his father they served masochistic aspirations: the child "was trying to force punishments and beatings out of his father, and in that way to obtain from him the masochistic sexual satisfaction that he desired" (Freud, 1918a, p. 28). But the father, a meek person, instead of beating him tried to play with him. The "perverse" attempts to seduce him ended at the age of four, when the first symptoms of neurosis surfaced. The change in our hero's personality had been brought about by a dream in which six or seven wolves sat on the branches of a tree, motionless staring at him from the window, while he was in bed. The child had awakened in terror of being devoured.

Sergei Pankeiev began to tell his nightmare a few months after the beginning of the analysis, but its narrative definition took many years, passing through endless modifications and re-editions. The patient's birthday was on Christmas Day. The tree was therefore a Christmas tree and the dream must have taken place on the eve of his fourth birthday, when he had fallen asleep anxiously awaiting his gifts. In the nightmare, the gifts had turned into wolves.

Filling a gap, seduction made it possible to explain the transformation of his satisfaction into anxiety. "Of the wishes concerned in the formation of the dream the most powerful must have been the wish for the sexual satisfaction which he was at that time longing to obtain from his father" (p. 35). The strength of this wish was so intense as "to revive a long-forgotten trace in his memory of a scene" that exposed him to the "horror of the fulfilment of the wish" (p. 36). The wolf with a severed tail testified that the force that had reversed the affections, causing the repression, was the fear of castration.

The wolves nightmare was the transcription of something that had actually happened. The window that opens was the dreamer's eyes (p. 34), while the motionless wolves stood for a "violent motion." In short, the memory reactivated by the dream was the scene of a coitus a tergo between parents repeated three times at 5 o'clock on a sultry summer afternoon. The child had witnessed it at the age of one and a half from his own bed, which was placed in the parent's bedroom.[4]

The "primal scene" made the child aware of the reality of castration. The vague threats and allusions to the "wound" suddenly acquired a new clarity. "He understood now that active was the same as masculine, while passive was the same as feminine" (p. 47). To achieve the passive aim he should therefore be "feminine" and accept castration, just like his mother. However, his feminine longing was opposed by his need to safeguard his penis and repressed it, only to return in the regressive form of the "fear of the wolf."

The phase of zoophobia had begun, culminating in religious initiation (four and a half years). Now in order to fall asleep he had to kiss sacred images, say prayers, and make signs of the cross. Passionate about sacred history, he learned that God "had sacrificed his son and had ordered Abraham to do the same. He began to fear God" (pp. 65–66). The struggle had shifted into the field of religion. In addition to its disparaging meaning, the compulsive thought "God-shit" wasn't just an insult, it also expressed his readiness to be loved as a woman. It was an anal offering, a desire to "give him a baby" (p. 83). Thus, in the end, two opposite currents coexisted in him: the horror of castration and its acceptance.

The boy's identification with his mother and her bleeding familiarized him with the "wound" that women have in place of the penis, paving the way for the hallucination he had at the age of five. While he was cutting the bark of a tree with a knife, he had cut off the little finger of his hand: he clearly saw his finger dangling, hanging only by the skin. Only after he calmed down did he realize he wasn't hurt in the least. In a "variant" of the hallucination, what he saw was blood gushing from the trunk of the tree.

Freud's reading of this hallucination deserves particular attention either because it calls into question the dark force of destiny and because it is decoded through the same epic story which, in *Beyond the pleasure principle*, will be presented as a "pure effect" of the compulsion to repeat, that is, as a rare uncontaminated expression of the death drive that rules the "perpetual recurrence of the same thing" (Freud, 1920, pp. 22–23). It is the story of Tancred who, in Tasso's *Gerusalemme Liberata* kills his beloved Clorinda twice. The story is this: after having unwittingly killed her in a duel, and without recognizing her, Tancred slashes with his sword at a tall tree in which Clorinda's soul is imprisoned, and when the bloodstreams from the cut, her voice is heard complaining that he has wounded his beloved once again. Isn't it a perfect illustration of the idea of "re-traumatization"?

How Freud manages to find this "dreadful experience" (Freud, 1918a, p. 86) in his patient's hallucination is a mystery, also because Tancred beats his love object, while in the child's hallucination it is his own finger to be cut.

Freud just says that for both the tree represents the woman and the carving of the trunk the "wound" that women have between their legs. As for the severed finger, the instigation came from the story about a relative born with six toes on one foot, whose extra toe had been chopped off at birth. Through this shocking story, he had understood that women "had no penis because it was taken away from them at birth" (ibid.).

The other source of the hallucination was the sacred history, from which the little Russian had learned "the ritual circumcision of Christ and of the Jews in general" (ibid.). This knowledge was inscribed in the nightmare, since it was a tailor who pulled off the wolf's tail. In German tailor is Schneider, which, like *Bescheidung*, circumcision, comes from *schneiden*, to cut (p. 87, footnote).

This remark suggests that what Freud finds in his patient's unconscious is the figure of the circumcised and feminized Jew that he had dissociated from himself. If we substitute Freud for the Wolf Man, the claimed mosaic of evidences finds its coherence in view of a precise prototype: the "dreadful experience" of *Emma Eckstein's unrecognized re-traumatization* that plunged Freud into the grips of "Fate." In the hallucination of the cut-off little finger, we find the amputation of the woman's small penis (clitoris), Emma Eckstein's childhood trauma which had been repeated by Freud/Tancred with the operation on her nose. As for the logical leap between the blow on the "woman" and his own cut finger, what fills the gap is Freud's identification with Emma Eckstein and the condensation of the amputation of her clitoris with his own circumcision that underlies the specimen dream from which psychoanalysis was born.

A further element is worth of consideration. Erik Erikson, in his reinterpretation of the dream of Irma's injection, at one point "filled the gap" left by Freud with a dream of one of his patients, a dream triggered by a shocking "Circumcision of Christ" seen in the Louvre (Erikson, 1954, p. 18). There is something deeply enigmatic about Erikson's association. How did it occur to him to "fill the gap" in such a reckless way? Obviously, Erikson was somehow already convinced that Freud's dream and the very birth of psychoanalysis had to do with circumcision. But why did he refer to the Circumcision of Christ?

The first formulation of the theory of "sexual shock" was contained in a manuscript subtitled "Weihnachtsmärchen," a Christmas fairy tale. Freud sent it to his dear friend Fliess, who was a fanatic of the "miracle of the calendar" (as one of his books will be called), on *January 1*, 1896. They both knew that the beginning of the year was first established according to the birth of Christ, in the Julian calendar, only to be shifted to the circumcision of Christ, in the Gregorian calendar. This Catholic feast (now abolished) celebrated the first blood shed by Christ, anticipating the moment of his crucifixion on Easter Friday. This must have been part of their talk, because, toward the end of 1896, Freud began to fantasize about meeting Fliess in

Rome on Easter Sunday. His entire dream book will gradually grow around this fantasy, until the final dream, in which the Passover is evoked by the image of the bridge over the abyss.

Certainly, Erikson had "filled the gap" using the references to the Circumcision of Christ in the case history of the Wolf Man, as though Erickson had understood that the Wolf Man, the paradigm of the negative Oedipus, was Freud in the mirror.

Let's go back to the case history. The Wolf Man's nightmare and its ramifications, which continued to flourish over time, had determined the form of his existence. For Freud, the nightmare owed all its power of persuasion (Überzeugung) to its being a transcription and a substitute for the "primal scene" witnessed by the patient (Zeuge), a scene that he was supposed to remember, sooner or later. But it didn't happen.

The "reality" of the primal scene, Freud (1918a) admitted, was "the most delicate question in the whole domain of psycho-analysis" (p. 103, footnote). It also was a question in which Emma Eckstein's analysis got stuck and around which Freud's self-analysis ran in circles. Now, 20 years later, it came back exactly as it had been.

The Wolf Man never managed to retrieve the memory of the primal scene. However, toward the end of his analysis, a "screen memory" surfaced providing the "solution." As a child, he was suddenly seized by a terrible fright when a butterfly with striped yellow wings had settled on a flower. The yellow stripes reminded him a pear ("gruša," in Russian) with a most delicious taste of his childhood and Gruša was the name of his beloved nanny (*Kindermädchen*) before Nanya (*Kinderfrau*). Then he had the vague recollection of a scene in which Gruša was kneeling on the floor scrubbing it. It was an incomplete recollection, but it "served to fill in the gaps" (p. 92).

The nanny's posture had awakened in the two-and-a-half-year-old child the memory of his mother's posture in the primal scene (the *a tergo* coitus). Overwhelmed by excitement, he then urinated on the floor,[5] taking, as far as he was allowed, the father's masculine role. The nanny immediately understood that it was an attempt at seduction, since she responded with a threat of castration, as further confirmed by the dream "of a man tearing off the wings of an Espe [(W)*espe*, wasp]" that Sergej Pankeiev had in analysis. The yellow-striped insect was an allusion to Gruša, while *espe* were S.P., his initials.

His fear of the butterfly was in every respect analogous to his fear of the wolf, and the dream of the (W)espe was a new version of his nightmare. Thus, "the compulsion which proceeded from the primal scene was transferred on to this scene with Grusha" (p. 93). Yet, the latter had a clear advantage over the primal scene, since "there could be no doubt" about it (p. 95).

At this point, it was no longer necessary for the patient to remember the elusive primal scene. Freud himself, moreover, was no longer convinced of its reality. In any case, the question had become irrelevant, because Freud was now following another line of thought, that of *innate ideas*, or, in this version, of "a priori" traumas. The scenes of observing parental intercourse, of being seduced in childhood, and of being threatened with castration were "unquestionably an inherited endowment, a phylogenetic heritage" (p. 97). And so, the more Freud was going into the details of his Russian patient's life, the more his patient was losing individuality, becoming a specimen of the unconscious' grammar and an anonymous sediment of mankind's historical evolution. Just as Emma Eckstein had become "Irma," the "universal woman," Sergej Pankeiev turned into a prototype.

Although Freud claimed that he stuck to experience, the fact that in the life of his Russian patient all the threats of castration had emanated from maternal substitutes did not prevent his analyst from tracing them back to the Father thanks to the immutable phylogenetic pattern. "Heredity," he wrote, "triumphed over accidental experience; in man's prehistory, it was unquestionably the father who practiced castration as a punishment and who later softened it down into circumcision" (p. 86). And in a famous passage on the "prehistory of neurosis" contained in the Wolf Man's case history, Freud clarified that the child "fills in the gaps in individual truth with prehistoric truth" (p. 97). Here time really stopped: we are back to 1897, when the reality of Emma Eckstein's circumcision had been replaced with Freud's daydream about an ancestral religion in the "Semitic East"—the depository of the unresolved problems.

The analysis of the Wolf Man had begun shortly before the catastrophic end of Emma Eckstein's second analysis, and even though the lives and stories of these two patients are certainly not superimposable, nevertheless there is an actual *passing of the torch* and an extraordinary continuity in Freud's speculation. As a matter of fact, in Wolf Man's analysis Freud's preoccupation for "castration" was transferred, which mobilized all his energies in the construction of a paradigmatic case history. As well outlined by Patrick Mahony (1987), in this case, history, ruled by "the prototype, substitutes for the prototype, and gaps in the sequence of substitutes" (p. 109), it is Freud who fills voids and gaps, as if the text represented "a castrated body that Freud tries to restore."[6]

In *Constructions in Analysis*, Freud will place the patient's delusions and the analyst's constructions on the same level as if they were equivalent, both representing attempts to fill the void left by an erased fragment of reality in the psyche of the patient (Freud, 1937b, p. 268). But what happens when the patient's unconscious is called upon to fill such a void in the analyst's psyche? Moreover, the hole left by the traumatic end of Emma Eckstein's second analysis in the spring of 1910 was a crater. Freud's resentful scream ("Do you really believe that hysteria can be cured with a knife?") takes us straight back to the dramatic nose operation which marked the beginning of everything. According to a biographer of Freud, by avoiding mentioning

Emma Eckstein's accident in the interpretation of Irma's dream, the father of psychoanalysis "created a gap of Grand Canyon proportions" (Clark, 1980, p. 152). The gap will then be incorporated as an essential element of the foundation of psychoanalysis, for which holes and gaps will be signifiers of female genitals as well as of the amputation of the penis. In Freud's paradigmatic dream it is Irma's oral cavity that opens wide as a chasm. Is this the hole that the Wolf Man had filled for Freud?

Notes

1 Abraham and Torok (1976) identified the man or the wolves as the patient Freud refers to in the essay on the "splitting of the ego" (Freud, 1938a), in the essay *Fetishism* (1927a) and as the Mr. P. of "Dream and Occultism" (Freud, 1933a, Lesson 30). The latter hypothesis is to be discarded, as it has been convincingly demonstrated that the patient in question was Paul Bernfeld (Pierri, 2010).
2 Thanks to the digitization of the *Freud papers*, some of the transcripts are now available online at the Sigmund Freud Archives website http://www.freudar-chives.org/.
3 See especially the works by Daniel Boyarin (1994a, 1994b, 1995, 1997) and Jay Geller (2007).
4 Some critics have argued that there was no way that, in an aristocratic social environment, a baby cot could be placed in the parents' bedroom, but this is one of the cases in which the boundaries between analyst and analyzed fade. Up to three years of age Freud had in fact slept in his parents' room, and some of the memories at the center of his self-analysis were linked to this situation, in particular the scene of urinary incontinence. This element would also emerge in the Wolf man's analysis.
5 Freud's self-analysis had a crucial place in his memory of having urinated in the parents' room at the age of three. For Mahony (1995, p. 107) it is one of the many points when Freud mirrors himself in the Wolf Man.
6 This sentence was added in the French translation and new edition of Patrick Mahony's textual analysis of the case history (Mahony, 1995, p. 113).

Chapter 12

The nose as a fetish

> ... the time will come when he [the analyst] will have to repeat with his own hands the act of murder previously perpetrated against the patient. In contrast to the original murder, however, he is not allowed to deny his guilt ...
>
> (Sándor Ferenczi, *Clinical Diary*, March 8, 1932)

The paranoia of the nose

The moments of mirroring between Freud and the Wolf Man are many, but here I recall one in particular: "Both had fixations on their noses."[1]

For the Wolf Man, the nose was the site of a catastrophe that had to be averted. His sister Anna, who will commit suicide at the age of 21, as a child was anxious at the thought of having a red nose and to avoid the danger they had come up with a game: Anna asked "Esanetor?" (the reverse of "rote Nase," red nose in German) and the brother replied: "no no, it's all right."[2]

Something similar will happen in the relationship between Freud and the Wolf Man, except that the magic word was an English word and any attempt to avoid catastrophe will fail.

In 1923, Freud discovered leukoplakia in his mouth which forced him to undergo repeated surgeries, starting in April of that year. Before the summer holidays, Sergej Pankeiev visited him to receive his money and on that occasion he was struck by his deformed face, but not that much. Then, in November, his mother arrived from Russia and immediately he noticed a black wart on her nose—a wart which came and went: "At times it was present and at times it was not" (Brunswick, 1928, p. 443).

Pankeiev's worries about his own nose began the following year, alternating or mingling with those about his mouth. He was seized by toothache, but did not want to go back to Dr. Wolf, the dentist who performed the extraction of two of his teeth three years earlier, because of his prediction that he would lose all his teeth. He went to another, and then to a third one, whose

DOI: 10.4324/9781003353058-17

name was again Wolf. As for the nose, he thought how lucky he was to have a nose without any imperfections. And so, he examined it carefully. Eventually, he managed to find certain nasal pores that stood out "like black points." Sometime later, he scratched out a pimple and, looking at his nose in the mirror, he found that there was a deep hole.

Now everybody was looking at the hole in his nose.

A doctor told him that the nose would remain red for a while, and it did. Out of anxiety he rushed to a dentist and had a tooth pulled out, but it was a healthy one. On another occasion, he experienced an acute ecstasy at the sight of his own blood flowing after the extraction of a small gland on his nose. For a while, things were back in place, but plummeted again at Easter 1925, when Pankeiev frantically consulted three dermatologists and more dentists with increasingly grotesque results. His nose was no longer "as it had been" (p. 448). It was no longer "his." Then everything was over.

A tiny scar remained but things went on, with ups and downs, until the summer of 1926. Until then, worries about his nose had not prevented him from working and leading a fairly normal life, but on June 17 he again consulted the dermatologist that had consoled him in the past, who at one point said that "scars never disappear." At these words, the world collapsed on him.

In her "Supplement to Freud's 'History of a Childhood Neurosis'" Ruth Mack Brunswick described the Wolf Man's present illness thus:

> He was suffering from a hypochondriacal idée fixe. He complained that he was the victim of a nasal injury caused by electrolysis ... According to him, the injury consisted varyingly of a scar, a hole, or a groove in the scar tissue.
>
> (Brunswick, 1928, p. 439)

Although his nose had been his weak point since adolescence, over time Sergej Pankeiev had become rather proud of his own nose, perhaps "because of his many Jewish contacts" (p. 443). But now it was ruined! "Let me state at once—Brunswick added—that nothing whatsoever was visible on the small, snub, typically Russian nose of the patient" (p. 439).

But he was in a state of despair. Nothing could be done for his nose, nothing that could cure his purported mutilation. He neglected his daily life and work because

> he was engrossed, to the exclusion of all else, in the state of his nose. On the street he looked at himself in every shop-window; he carried a pocket mirror which he took out to look at every few minutes. First, he would powder his nose; a moment later he would inspect it and remove the powder. He would then examine the pores, to see if they were enlarging, to catch the hole, as it were, in its moment of growth and

development.... His life was centered on the little mirror in his pocket, and his fate depended on what it revealed or was about to reveal.

(p. 440)

What had happened?

The witness

In the first volume of the book *Technik der Psychanalyse*, published in 1926, Otto Rank had suggested that a certain type of dream, though using past material, was determined by the current "analytic situation" and as an example he pointed to the dream of the Wolf Man. The bed, in this dream, was the analytic sofa, the tree was the walnut visible from the window of Freud's consulting room and the five to seven wolves were his closest disciples, whose photos hung on the wall changed in number from time to time varying from five to seven, precisely "the figures between which the patient fluctuates in relation to the number of wolves."

On June 6, 1926, Freud informed Ferenczi that Rank had accused him of having mistaken a recent production of the transference for information about the past, adding that he had already requested confirmation of the dream from his former patient. The same day Pankeiev replied with a long letter in which he agreed with Freud.[3] Excerpts from the letter were then transcribed by Freud and sent to Ferenczi so that he could write a factual refutation of Rank's insinuations using the patient's testimony.[4] So, in the end, the Wolf Man was put in the position of a "witness"!

A similar request will be made again in 1957, in the context of Kurt Eissler's repeated interviews. The new letter, addressed to Gardener on June 11, 1957, was published along with the previous one in the *Psychoanalytic Quarterly*. Here, however, Sergei Pankeiev put forward the doubt that the paranoia of the nose was triggered by Freud's request. The paranoia appeared, he wrote

> some days after the composition of my letter to Professor Freud; ... I was already in a state of endless despair [eine bodenlose Verzweiflung]... *Or, could the outbreak of the 'paranoia' have had any connection with Professor Freud's questions?*... what strikes me ... is the extent to which I speak of castration....[5]

Muriel Gardiner will report excerpts from both letters in margin of Brunswick's "Supplement of Analysis,"[6] reinforcing the idea that it was Freud's request that precipitated Pankeiev into a "bodenlose Verzweiflung," a bottomless desperation, which Abraham and Torok suggest should be read as an "impossibility of doubting" (zweiflen), [7] as if his doubts (Zweiflen) had allowed him not to be completely colonized by the version of himself constructed by the Professor.

There is a wide convergence among the commentators on the idea that, in the words of Kanzer, the Wolf Man had "played some substitute part for Freud himself," or rather, he had become the host of a dissociated part of Freud. Indeed, something that Freud had dissociated from himself seems to shape the case history that allowed Freud to formulate the concept of a negative Oedipus. For Boyarin (1997), identifying himself with the phallic hero of the Greek myth and raising as a model an "active, phallic, mother-desiring, father killing, 'normal' man" (p. 220), Freud had obscured "his experience as the passively desiring male" (p. 201). With this "heterosexualization" Freud also dissociated from himself a piece of Jewish identity that did not conform to the dominant phallic culture. Is this dissociated part what Freud found in the clinical case of the Wolf Man?[8]

From this perspective, his "Russian nose" seems to be Pankeiev's last bulwark against a psychic colonization that was threatening his sense of identity. Thanks to his "Russian nose" he had felt superior to the Jews until the moment he plunged into bottomless despair. So, when his life was reduced to the single act of scrutinizing the imaginary hole in his nose and his fate depended on what the mirror was about to reveal to him, it wasn't just the ghosts of castration that came out of the mirror to stare at him like the wolves of his nightmare. As pointed out by Jay Geller (2007), he had become "unable to differentiate 'his irreparable mutilated state' from that of the circumcised Jews" (p. 108).

To what, had the nose of the Wolf Man, become a witness?

The equation "circumcised Jew = castrated = woman"

Freud was proud of his Jewish identity, which largely corresponded with the values of the cultured Jews of the West and of the Enlightenment which had opened the doors of the ghetto and promised the inclusion of Jews in a wider world. In fact, universalism became an identity value of the Jewish liberal bourgeoisie, aimed at emphasizing common humanity rather than cultivating particular differences. Throughout his life, Freud consistently defended his Jewish identity by professing a fervent humanism. However, as pointed out by Lewis Aron and Karen Starr (2014), Eastern Jews, "considered to be vulgar and primitive, uncultured, coarse in language and speech, smelly, dirty and diseased" (p. 234), remained for Freud the source of an unresolved ambivalence toward his own inheritance. Since Freud's discomfort with Eastern Jews included the rejection of his own family roots, these authors believe that "Freud adopted his society's negative stereotype of the Jew as his own, and later embedded it in the growing circumcised body of psychoanalysis" (p. 239).

By linking the birth of psychoanalysis with Freud's Jewish identity and situating it against the background of the virulent anti-Semitism of his living environment, Aron and Starr sought to separate Freud the champion of the Jewish cause, from Freud who had unconsciously internalized the anti-Semitic gaze. Their conclusion is that the self-hatred so internalized and dissociated was at the origin of the misogynistic, homophobic, and racist elements of his theory, which can be summed up in the equation circumcised Jew = castrated = woman.

This equation was formulated by Freud at the margins of the case history of little Hans, together with the thesis that the castration complex was the deepest unconscious root of anti-Semitism. In a famous passage, he wrote:

> even in the nursery little boys hear that a Jew has something cut off his penis—a piece of his penis, they think—and this gives them a right to despise Jews. And there is no stronger unconscious root for the sense of superiority over women.
>
> (Freud, 1909, p. 36 footnote)

To illustrate this common root Freud then referred to Otto Weininger who, in a chapter of "his remarkable book" *Sex and Character* (the book that had caused Fliess' definitive break with him),

> treated Jews and women with equal hostility and overwhelmed them with the same insults. Being a neurotic, Weininger was completely under the sway of his infantile complexes; and from that standpoint what is common to Jews and women is their relation to the castration complex

This passage has sparked intense debate. For Sander Gilman, Freud is saying that it is *in the eyes of the uncircumcised Aryan* that "the Jew is analogous to woman." It is the Aryan who "sees 'Jew' and 'woman' as interchangeable categories" within a world in which the power symbolized by the "intact nature of his penis" is threatened by the growing visibility of these two unstable and marginal social categories (Gilman, 1993a, pp. 80–83). In contrast to the Aryan who cannot take his eyes off the circumcised Jew's penis, Freud built his narrative around a Jewish child, little Hans, who is instead fascinated by the "wound" of the castrated female. Raising a circumcised child as champion of the positive Oedipus,[9] Freud would have neutralized anti-Semitic rhetoric by transmuting a *racial difference* into a *gender difference*. In short, for Gilman, by putting the shock produced by the sight of the castrated female at the center of the scene, Freud would have freed his people from the position of victim as a new Moses, even at the cost of constructing a theory in which the negative qualities of the Jewish male are projected onto the female. In this version, misogyny would be the price paid by Freud in his silent but determined fight against anti-Semitism.

Not everyone found this reading convincing. While leaning on Gilman's studies, Boyarin (1997) believes that the way Freud uses Weininger, failing to say that he himself was a Jew, reveals that he had internalized the anti-Semitic gaze representing the Jewish male as "castrated," "feminized," and socially inferior. Ultimately, for Boyarin, but also for other authors, having internalized this Aryan anti-Semitic gaze Freud would have been stuck looking at his own circumcised penis.

Embracing this line of thought, Aron and Starr (2014) suggested that the part of Freud's Jewish identity that was dissociated and taken away from the work of mourning "haunted him like an unlaid ghost" (p. 296), like the *dybbuk* of the legend, a dislocated soul that is doomed to wander without rest until its story is told and heard. Here the dissociated Jewish identity becomes *uncanny*, *unheimlich*, familiar, and alien at the same time. In his essay *The Uncanny*, Freud recounts the following episode. He was traveling by train when a violent jolt swung back the door of the wagon lit and suddenly he saw an elderly man in a dressing gown coming in, before acknowledging with dismay "that the intruder was nothing but my own reflection in the looking glass ..." (Freud, 1919, p. 248). This specter that came out of the mirror [10] was the object of the other's gaze, the circumcised wandering Jew, his own uncanny double.

Monument to horror

Reduced to a minimum the problem is *who* is *watching who* or *what*? This is exactly what the Wolf Man staged by incessantly looking at his nose in the mirror. What did he see looking at his nose? This is the question addressed by Freud in his famous 1927 essay on *Fetishism*. Although the details of the story were screened, the Wolf Man is in fact the young man with whom the essay opens, the one who had turned his nose into a fetish. Freud tells it this way:

> The fetish ... had to be understood in English, not German. The 'shine on the nose' [in German '*Glanz auf der Nase*']—was in reality a 'glance at the nose'. The nose was thus the fetish, which, incidentally, he endowed at will with the luminous shine which was not perceptible to others.
> (Freud, 1927a, p. 152)

As is well known, Freud immediately declares that the meaning of the fetish is always the same: it is a "substitute for the penis," not "of any penis," but of "a very particular penis" which is preserved from extinction by the fetish. In short, what Freud sees in the nose of the Wolf Man is the woman's penis, as if in this essay, which opens with the "*nose*" and closes with the word "*clitoris*" (Klitoris), Freud was brought back to the catastrophe from which psychoanalysis was born, the place of Emma Eckstein's operation on the nose, which, in Freud's dreams, had become the place of the attack on the *Jud*—Jew and clitoris.

In Freud's previous texts, smell had always played a central role in the choice of fetish, but, as remarked by Jay Geller (2007), in Freud's 1927 essay, "every trace of smell has been removed," as if Freud's text had been "deodorized" (p. 100). For Geller, Freud had eliminated the "*Judennase, the*

Jewish nose, and the *fetor Judaicus*, the Jewish stench" (p. 101), two central elements of the anti-Semitic representation of the Jew in the nineteenth-century culture, in which the Jew was marked as "primitive" and "different" by nose, smell, and circumcision.

Above all, Geller notes how, in Freudian discourse, the fetish figures as *the inverse of circumcision*. I quote in full:

> circumcision is both formally and substantively, even linguistically, an inversion of fetishism. Circumcision is the "symbolic substitute" (*symbolische Ersatz*) of castration..., whereas the fetish is the "substitutive symbol" (*Ersatzsymbol*) of the woman's penis... The circumcised penis both asserts the possible threat of castration... and denies it. Obversely, the fetish by definition both disavows the threat of castration... and affirms it ("the horror of castration has set up a memorial to itself in the creation of this substitute").
>
> (Geller, 2007, pp. 104–105)

This famous phrase—"the horror of castration has set up a memorial to itself in the creation of this substitute" ("der Abscheu vor der Kastration sich in der Schaffung dieses Ersatzes ein Denkmal gesetzt hat")—brings us back to Freud's reaction to Emma Eckstein's genital mutilation, as it was memorized in the dream of Irma's injection. The horror of which Freud speaks is that from which psychoanalysis had sprung!

This is partly the case for Geller as well. The inverse relationship between circumcision and the fetish in fact links the circumcised Jew to the woman with the penis. As for the nose, the target of denigration and derision of the Jew, Geller associates it with the botched nose operation on Emma Eckstein performed by Fliess with the complicity of Freud, even if, lacking an appropriate frame of reference to place and read the operation, his arguments lose incisiveness and clarity. Nonetheless, Geller grasps well the mirroring of the circumcised penis of the Jew with Emma Eckstein's nose, when describing the latter as "'castrated'—or at least, clipped or circumcised—by Fliess" (p. 103), just as he grasps the inverse relationship between Emma's masculine, phallic image and Freud's countertransferential experience of himself as castrated and feminized, all elements that converge in the dream of Irma's injection, only to re-surface three decades later in Wolf Man's strange fetish of the nose, as if Freud's favorite patient had filled a hole for him.

CODA

When the unthought becomes unthinkable

For Geller (2007), Freud's discourse on the fetish of the nose called into question circumcision as a marker of the Jewish difference and "dispositive" that, in an anti-Semitic environment, defined the identity of the *Judentum* and of the *uncircumcised*. In his view, "caught in the web of dispositive circumcision, Freud fixed upon the transferential phantasy of castration that would come to animate, as 'living rock', his corpus and render meaningful the life-narratives of all" (p. 15).

Without diminishing the importance of both the identity question posed to the Jewish community in an anti-Semitic environment, and of Freud's conflictual and unresolved homosexuality, it seems to us that the many pieces of the puzzle cannot find their place if we do not take into account a fragment of reality simultaneously denied and preserved in Freud's mind: Emma Eckstein's circumcision.

Freud could not recognize its traumatic meaning because the necessary categories of thought did not yet exist. He had encountered, to refer to the theory of Gaston Bachelard (1934), "an obstacle in the very act of knowing," an *epistemological obstacle*. Yet Freud's petrified gaze survived in a dissociated part of his psyche, acting as the unthought of his fantasies, his daydreams, his metapsychological speculations. Moreover, at some point, this unacknowledged trauma becomes an erased trauma. The *unthought* then becomes the *unthinkable* which passes from one unconscious to another, being transmitted with all the series of uncanny effects recounted in this *Brief Apocalyptic History of Psychoanalysis*.

The case of Wolf Man's paranoia of the nose, that strange perception of a "hole" in which Freud recognizes the fetish that dissolves and, at the same time, preserves the infinite horror of castration, is perhaps the most emblematic case of these troubling effects because, through a spectacular play of mirrors, it brings us back to the "scene of the crime." Like Freud's various interlocutors, the Wolf Man finds himself inexorably drawn to this nameless place, this psychic gap that takes over the guts and attacks the body. The unthinkable materializes into the body, indeed into a body-to-body wrestle.

In this story, we have seen each of the protagonists grapple with such a struggle, starting with Freud himself when, divided in two, he struggles with his own psychic gap in the course of self-analysis. We witnessed his struggle on the acropolis of Athens, where it overwhelms him, or when it is staged in the dramatizations of his own death, or even materializes in his mouth, or is represented in the Loch from which the gigantic serpent emerges, neither alive nor dead.

We saw Emma Eckstein fight again when, in her second analysis, she asks her analyst in vain to recognize something "organic" at the origin of her suffering, when she asks that her body be thought, that it becomes thinkable. Neither Jung, to whom we have given too little space, nor Ferenczi, escape this wrestle. We saw them both rush into Freud's psychic hole, then come out each in his own way. In particular, Ferenczi struck us and fascinated us by his telepathic and mimetic qualities, by the way he managed to enter Freud's nightmare to the point of making it his own, by the way he transformed the nightmare into a dream with *Thalassa*, and finally by the way he managed to reorganize it into categories and concepts that give body to what is repeatedly erased in Freud.

This story is "apocalyptic" first because the "revelations" are the object of it. But the revelations are also the subject, the propeller of a story that seeks to be told from fragments, that surprises us as it unfolds precisely because it is *unthinkable*—like analysis, when we conceive it with Ferenczi, as a process "unfolding itself before our eyes" (1928a, p. 90). Finally, this story is apocalyptic because the horizon in which it unfolds is not the stable universe of the things that are, nor that of the categories with which we think them, but an exploded universe, the end of the world that has become thinkable through the Ferenczian poetic conception of the fragmentation of psychic life. It is the story of a trauma crystallized in theory, or rather, of the repetition in the first psychoanalytic treatment of a trauma which would be buried in Freud's metapsychology.

At first, the "cure" is the nose operation performed by Fliess with Freud's endorsement. Psychoanalysis does not yet exist. Yet it is here, in this cure that repeats, displaced upward from a circumcision, where we find the "primary scene" of psychoanalysis in the sense that it is destined to be repeated until it can be told and listened to.

That the horizon of this story is indeed a *finis mundis*, can be seen from the fact that the phenomenon of "transference" was discovered by Freud precisely in the stormy days in which Emma Eckstein is poised between life and death.[11] It is an idea that will prove to be ingenious, but, as has been pointed out by many commentators, it is an idea that puts Freud out of the field, exculpating him from any responsibility. Robert Langs (1984), for example, translates it as follows: "I—the analyst—am not responsible for the patient's disturbance or for his or her disturbed view of, and reactions to, myself and my therapeutic measures" (p. 598), remarking that precisely this type of disclaimer is a major theme of Freud's Irma dream.

Just as Freud could not conceive of his patient's circumcision as a trauma, similarly he could not conceive that the nose operation had repeated that trauma. For, on another plane, things are different. On the stage of the dream from which psychoanalysis is born, the patient's trauma becomes that of the analyst, with all the series of exchanges and inversions, displacements and condensations, identifications and dissociations that this entails. A true theatrical play, in which what is staged is the irruption of an "unexpected guest." Although unrecognized, the patient's childhood trauma has awakened in the doctor his own childhood trauma, forcing him to relive something that resurfaces from the past with the irrational force of "destiny." This is an endopsychic perception that will never leave Freud, a perception that he will try to articulate in multiple ways and that, in the never-abandoned attempt to make sense of his experience, he will end up ascribing to the mute death drive.

But at the same time, it discloses another "revelation," equally sudden and all-encompassing. It is the theory of seduction. It is not free from paranoia: instead of listening to what is going on inside himself, Freud finds evidence of childhood sexual abuse in all his patients. But even in this, he is careful to exclude circumcision from the field. And here then comes the most important moment, the one in which Freud, finally in the position of analyst, is confronted by his patient with the "scene of circumcision of a girl." It is the moment which informs what psychoanalysis will be.

Freud could have paused, acknowledged his patient's childhood trauma, explored the emotions such a discovery aroused in him, and in fact he comes very close, since it is precisely these memories and thoughts that will be, along with his father's death, the main propeller of his interminable self-analysis. Instead, he finds himself in a position similar to that of the fetishist, as it will be described by him, as he erases from his mind the actual castration that his patient has undergone, and then replaces it with a fantasy of universal castration, believed to be the destiny of every woman. Over the years he will come to entrench himself in a skeptical and defensive position that will crystallize into a new attitude whose main characteristic will be "*indifference*"—that "thick skin" and coldness acquired with the suppression of countertransference. Thus, what should have been a moment of recognition of the reality proper for each of the protagonists and of mourning, becomes for each a hugely significant moment of missed recognition. For Emma Eckstein, this was an opportunity to painfully acknowledge and process the amputation she endured in childhood. Freud, for his part, might have acknowledged that he had participated in the equivalent of a circumcision/castration on her, which he abhorred for more reasons than one. Above all, this lack of recognition takes on the value of a trauma sealed in the foundations of the building of psychoanalysis, from which the "transferential fantasy of castration" will flow, inexhaustible. *It is then that what was only unthought becomes unthinkable.* What in the dream of Irma's injection was still a simple "oversight," then becomes the encrypted lock of a permanent split inscribed in the theory, a split similar to that which for Freud comes into play in the creation of the fetish.

Freud takes possession of his patient's phallic fantasy, a fantasy that, like the fetish, erases and preserves the trauma, and makes it the source from which, in the years to come, his metapsychology will flow. It is then that Emma's trauma, her circumcision in the flesh, begins to be replaced by symbolic castration. The world that re-emerges from this shipwreck is a world that speaks the "basic language" [Grundsprache] of psychoanalysis: it has a penis/it does not have a penis.

Fascinated, the psychoanalytic movement will build itself around this simplified language that unites everyone and everything, until it becomes a prisoner. It will find itself trapped within a closed system, a structure impervious to any compromise that, as I once remarked, "one is forced either to accept it or to reject it, to remain inside or outside the system" (Bonomi, 2013, p. 371). Commenting on the effects of this double bind, Peter Rudnytsky (2022) aptly wrote:

> The tragic consequence of this arrangement is that the price for remaining "inside the system" is accepting one's own "castration" by confessing the infallibility of Freud's teaching, while the price for asserting one's independence is to be anathematized for practicing "oppositional analysis," and hence also to be "castrated" for having dared to rebel.
>
> Thus, within the authoritarian structure of Freud's universe, the castration complex is inescapable, and Freud may be credited with having created a perfect mechanism for gaslighting others by inflicting a trauma on them that is paradoxically based on a denial of the reality of traumatic experience.
>
> (p. 256)

This trap, fueled by identification with the founder,[12] was able to function thanks to the promise of omniscience conveyed by "metapsychology," an illusion of omnipotence that is equivalent, in this, to the Phallus that Freud appropriated in fantasy.

In the late 1970s, a fatal blow was given to this illusion. In an extraordinary choral effort, distinguished scholars such as George Klein (1976), Roy Schafer (1976), Robert Holt (1985), and others, found Freudian metapsychology so incoherent, contradictory, and infiltrated by hidden assumptions that it could be declared "virtually dead," a useless burden that had to be disposed of. This, moreover, produced considerable disbanding of the tribe and a devastating identity crisis from which psychoanalysis has never recovered.

We have not tried to rationalize metapsychology by transforming it into general psychology. We have not sought the foundation of psychoanalysis in neuroscience, nor have we pretended that everything is fine by calling it "hermeneutics." We didn't get rid of this irrational burden.

On the contrary, we have accepted the challenge posed by Freud who surprises himself by writing the Dream book like an inspired prophet before the Holy Scriptures (Freud, 1899a, p. 470). We have followed in the footsteps of Freud before whom apocalyptic scenarios are opening up, such as those that Jacob Arlow (1951) finds in the consecration of the prophets, Mortimer Ostow (1986) in the debut episodes of psychosis, and James Grotstein (1989, 1990) in that descent into the "black hole" in which announcements of messianic grandeur, martyrdom, and revelation are the signs of a last attempt to recover from psychic agony, to revitalize a necrotic part of the soul—a white spot (weiße Fleck), in this case.

Already Henri Ellenberger (1964) had recognized in the creation of psychoanalysis the product of a *"maladie créatrice,"* a psychotic process that is anything but rare that results in a new system of thought. But here Ferenczi's theory of psychic trauma comes to our aid. In particular, the idea of splitting between a "genius" part, a part that "knows everything" but "feels nothing" and a sensitive but "brutally destroyed" part, allowed us to enter Freud's system of thinking from another doorway.

We entered this system and made it our own, letting ourselves be guided by the image of Freud who, divided in two, observes the "hole" in his own eviscerated pelvis. However, the fascination for the part that "knows everything" and "feels nothing" did not prevent us from taking care of the one who, mortally wounded, raises alarm in his close pupils by talking about his imminent death. In short, we have made the "Professor" talk to the "Doctor," and at the end of this path Ferenczi's therapeutic qualities are recognized and Freud the man, for his part, finds himself reconciled with himself, human and fallible.

Ferenczi began to dismantle the metapsychological trap when he opposed the idea that analysis is "a structure with a design pre-imposed upon it by an architect" (1928a, p. 90). Opposing the figure of the "authoritarian" analyst who preserved the "lofty attitude to the patient generally adopted by the omniscient and omnipotent doctor," he then proposed as a guide a principle of empathy rooted in the awareness of the "limitations of our knowledge" (p. 94).

By making himself the spokesman of the analyst's fallibility, it is as if Ferenczi had found the key to unlock the split, as if he had begun to rewrite the script of Irma's dream from the line "If you still have pain, it is your fault," making room for the "pains," accepting that the doctor may find himself in the patient's position, and giving himself time to explore how much these "pains" belong to one or the other or to both.

This shift, which would lead Ferenczi to develop an extraordinary clinical sensitivity to processes of re-traumatization in treatment, has an important theoretical premise. It is the recognition of the priority of repetition over remembering, proposed by Ferenczi and Rank in their brief 1924 monograph. Of course, it is a priority that takes us back to the primary scene of psychoanalysis and makes it thinkable. However, it was rejected as heresy because it put experience before interpretation and because it replaced the one-person framework of analysis in which transference is an intrapsychic distortion, with an interpersonal framework. Significantly, the history of psychoanalytic theory and technique will be profoundly marked by the continuous recurrence of this same "heresy," as well as its repudiation in the name of a "purist" vision of psychoanalysis from which repetition is banned.[13]

After the crisis of 1924, Ferenczi became increasingly isolated from the psychoanalytic movement, but he continued to think about the taboo subject of repetition and the subtle ways in which the analyst ends up retraumatizing the patient. Although he strove to prevent such an enactment, in a famous passage in the *Clinical Diary* Ferenczi recognizes how almost inevitable it is for the analyst to hurt the patient again, especially when the trauma being repeated is buried in a somatic memory. And this he acknowledges with the awareness that what is brought onto the scene and repeated belongs to the analyst as well as to the patient, arising, sometimes surprisingly, at the point where the life stories of one and the other cross and intertwine. Above all, he adds that "in contrast to the original murder, however, he [the analyst] is not allowed to deny his guilt ..." (March 8, 1932).

Having made human fallibility his banner, Ferenczi helped us to accept that each of us, including Freud, has, in one way or another, "repeated the crime."

Today Ferenczi has been rescued from oblivion and is becoming "fashionable." This tells us that many things have changed, but we cannot ignore the fact that his insistence on repetition led him to take paths that until recent years were considered alien to "true psychoanalysis," that he was banned from training institutes based on the myth of his "insanity," or rather, the myth that his "heresy" was the product of a long and hidden mental illness which finally ended in a violent destructive psychosis.

When, years ago, I immersed myself in the study of the documents of this infelicitous moment in the history of psychoanalysis (Bonomi, 1999), once again I was struck by how easy it was to access the sources and re-establish the facts, just as had happened in the study on "Freud the pediatrician." At that time, I became convinced that this myth, accepted and propagated with no critical scrutiny, was playing the role of preserving a sense of identity within the psychoanalytic community based on a fantasy of omniscience, omnipotence, and infallibility that had been threatened precisely by Ferenczi's refusal to base his teaching, as well as his being, on identification with Freud.

When Jones' 1957 allegation of "insanity" was about to dissipate, the target shifted to mutual analysis. A new myth was then created and spread, that the mutual analysis with Elizabeth Severn had been a deplorable enactment that, passing through role reversal and boundary violations, resulted in a "direct exploitation of the patient" (Gabbard, 1995, 1997). This myth was dismantled point by point by Peter Rudnytsky (2022) in an articulate study on mutual analysis and the origin of trauma theory. But even here what is striking is the coarse way in which the myth arose and spread, as if it too were called upon to perform a conservative function.

For Rudnytsky, and I cannot but agree, "mutuality" is not just the title of an experiment, but a principle that is organic to the radical turning point impressed on psychoanalysis by Ferenczi, a turning point in which the analyst becomes concerned with the patient's trauma, in a way that inevitably involves him, touches him, calls him into question. And by tearing away the hard skin of "indifference" in which Freud and his imitators have wrapped themselves, it restores another piece of reality erased by the purist version of psychoanalysis, namely, that in the field there is not only one person, the patient, but also the analyst. Ferenczi's mutual analysis becomes then "the paradigm for a contemporary shift to a two-person conceptualization of clinical work, just as Freud's self-analysis was paradigmatic for the one-person perspective of classical theory" (Rudnytsky, 2022, p. 8).

In his *Clinical Diary*, Ferenczi came to the conclusion that the erroneous development of psychoanalysis, namely, Freud's turn toward the "antitraumatic," was a "protective device against insight into his own weaknesses" (August 4, 1932). What would have happened if Freud had been able to admit his crisis to himself? Or if he had accepted, with humility, the help repeatedly offered to him by his pupil? I believe that in certain moments he even wished for it. However, I am also convinced that he could not allow himself to do so, because this would have jeopardized not so much his personal authority as what he had so painstakingly built up from his "oversight." In this "blind spot," around which the purist version of psychoanalysis has been carved out, there is indeed something deeply tragic.

Some of the consequences of the turn imprinted by Ferenczi, immediately lucidly grasped by Benjamin Wolstein (1992, 1994), seem clear to me, such as the uniqueness of every analyst, of every patient and, even more so, of every analytic dyad, whose interlocking transference and countertransference can neither be known in advance nor downloaded from some "prepackaged" form of metapsychology. Its only authority is experience and its truth can only arise from the dialectic of consensual validation.

Others seem less clear to me. Deprived of the paradigmatic and stripped of the universal, what remains of psychoanalysis? If everything is dissolved in the unrepeatability of each singular experience, what space is there for a beyond of the phenomenon? Ferenczi himself comes to ask this question when he asks himself in the *Clinical Diary*: "Is the purpose of mutual analysis perhaps the finding of that common feature which repeats itself in every case of infantile trauma?" (January 19, 1932).

Repetition itself is the gateway to the beyond of the phenomenon, and therefore also the foundation of interpretation, what legitimizes it, thus restoring to intelligence a function that is no longer merely defensive and that projects us beyond repetition. This coming out of ourselves that we call intelligence, and which for Ferenczi is an effect of trauma, also contains the aspiration to reunite what has fallen apart.

We began this brief apocalyptic story by saying that Emma Eckstein's trauma, her circumcision, is inscribed in the birth certificate of psychoanalysis as an amputated legacy. Now we want to close it by recognizing that this same legacy also contains the desire to reunite what is broken.

The work of reassembling the pieces is, of course, far from over. But we dare to hope that the time has come to reverse course and open a new historical phase under the banner of reunification. The pluralist idea that "many psychoanalyses" can coexist, to which we have clung after the collapse of Freudian metapsychology, does not seem to me much more than a temporary solution that makes a virtue out of necessity. Perhaps we should radically change our idea of psychoanalysis, give up identifying it with a doctrine and a technique, to recognize it as a living and mysterious universe with more doors of entry.

We have entered this universe passing through the place where the horrible becomes sacred, circumcision and bisexuality intersect and the apocalyptic scenarios take shape. Nunberg (1947) taught us that this is the place from which the great cosmogonies were generated, and Norman O. Brown (1959) introduced us to the salvific equivalence between phantasies on the end of the world and a return to primeval purity. For this author, psychoanalysis does not know that it is the heir of a long mystical tradition which, directly or indirectly, refers to the myth of the Androgyne:

> In the West, from the passage of *Genesis* 1, 27: "God therefore created man in his own image... he created him male and female", the mystical cabbalism has deduced the androgynous nature of God and of perfection before the fall. From cabbalism this conception has passed into the Christian mysticism of Boehme, where it merges with the Pauline mysticism of the *Epistle* to *Galatians,* 3, 28: "There can be no male and female, because you are all one man in Jesus Christ." [14]

Brown also refers to Berdyaev's *The Destiny of Man*, where original sin is attributed to the division in the two sexes and the fall of the Androgyne, i.e. of man as a complete being, Taoist Eastern mysticism that combines opposites, and poetry which, no less than psychoanalysis, is also heir to the mystical tradition: asking God to make him perfect as an artist, Rilke asks to make him hermaphrodite, because the mystic rebels against the cancellation of the body and refuses to walk the path of sublimation. Just as the alchemist seeks the "subtle body" and the oriental mystic the "adamantine body," the poet resurrects the body with the sensuality of the word and is nourished with its magic. In the language of the Jewish cabala, he seeks the perfection of the body of Adam, in that of Christian eschatology he imagines eternal life as life in a sensual body, thanks to that "resurrection of the flesh" that psychoanalysis concretely pursues through "the abolition of repression."

This mystical tradition seeks unity between soul and body. If psychoanalysis is its heir, it is because it derives from the same traumatic sources, sources that psychoanalysis can explore in the lives of each and every one on condition that it has the humility and courage to recognize them starting from itself.

In Freud's anti-metaphoric world, all this is there, but reversed and seen from a great distance. As if he had never left the Etruscan tomb, while his Orpha, the split fragment that plows the universe probing it like a radar, continued to send him dispatches.

Notes

1 Mahony (1995, p. 107). I am again quoting from the French edition of Mahony's essay on the Wolf Man:"The Wolf Man paid extraordinary attention to his nose and was proud of its smallness; this organ underwent medical treatment in puberty and during his analysis with Freud, later becoming the center of psychotic disturbances. Freud glorified Fliess's theory of reflex nasal neurosis within the framework of a 'pan-nasology' and submitted himself to numerous nasal operations" (Mahony, 1995, pp. 107–108).

2 Sergej Pankeiev recounts this in his interview with Karin Obholzer (1980, p. 110). In Freud's analytic accounts there is no mention of this apotropaic ritual. Yet it was not a repressed memory and it is unlikely that it had not emerged in the four years of analysis all centered only on childhood, or that it had not aroused the interest of Freud, who was fascinated by the inversion of words.

3 In his letter, Pankeiev wrote "my memory of this childhood dream never underwent any change . ... I narrated the dream of the Wolves to you near the beginning of my analysis ... The solution came then, as you state entirely accurately, only at the end of the treatment. ..." (Wolf Man, 1957, pp. 449–450). However, as Mahony remarked (1984, p. 139), there are at least two problems in this testimony. The first is that Pankeiev recounts that the wolves were not wolves but Spitz dogs (thus "tempting us to rename the patient the Dog Man" ...), and the second that Freud, in the case history composed in 1914, stated that the dream "returned in innumerable variations and editions" in the course of treatment.

4 Freud to Ferenczi, June 6, June 8, June 24, September 19, 1926; Ferenczi to Freud, June 17, September 27, 1926, and finally Ferenczi, 1927, p. 100. On June 6, 1926, Freud wrote to Ferenczi, "The inadequacy of Rank's assumption can also be demonstrated earlier" since in 1910/11 only "two or three photos" (those of Rank, Jones, and Ferenczi) were hanging on the wall. So why involving his patient to the point of asking him for a written testimony? What Ferenczi wrote in the *Clinical Diary* comes to mind: "Question: is Freud really convinced, or does he have a compulsion to cling too strongly to theory as a defense against self-analysis, that is, against his own doubts?" (May 1, 1932).

5 Emphasis added. Wolf-man (1957, pp. 457–459); also Gardiner (1971, pp. 243–244) note. An unabridged version of the letter, provided by Gardiner, is contained in Abraham and Torok (1976), from which I took this quote and the emphasis on "Verzweiflung."

6 Gardiner (1971, pp. 243–244) note.

7 Abraham and Torok (1976, pp. 179–180, 1986, p. 54). It is starting from the impossible position of "witness" of Sergej Pankeiev that Nicholas Abraham and Maria Torok wrote the famous *Le verbier de l'homme aux loups*, published in 1976 with a long introductory text by Jacques Derrida. Their deciphering of the words buried in the "crypt" of the wolf man is decidedly reckless. However, the principle from which they start, namely, the impossibility for Pankeiev to be a "witness," I believe is profoundly correct. Here I limit myself to highlighting the Wolf Man function as mirror and sounding board for Freud.

8 Following Boyarin, the homoerotic desire for his father that Freud finds in the case history of the Wolf Man, had broken through the thought that the father was a pervert (see Chapter 5). During his self-analysis, this homoerotic desire for his father was first replaced with his passive attitude toward the phallic figure of the Catholic nanny and then erased by the theory of the positive Oedipus as a universal source of neurosis.

9 Gilman did not know that little Hans was not circumcised.

10 Images are reflected, but ghosts *come out* of the mirrors. This is why in popular
    tradition the mirrors of the house in which there is a dead person are covered.
    I refer here to my essay "The eye, the mask and the mirror" (Bonomi, 2015b).

11 Ann Salyard (1992), rightly notes that, after months in which he had been stuck,
    Freud wrote the entire final chapter of *Studies on Hysteria in a single go*, in which
    appears the first reference to "transference," the overwhelming re-emergence of
    fears and intense desires removed in childhood that find themselves, by a "false
    connection," linked to the figure of the doctor (Breuer & Freud, 1895, p. 437)
    in the most terrible days of the crisis, as is indicated by his letters to Fliess of
    March 4, 8, and 13, 1895. In particular, in this last letter he wrote: "Things are
    finally going well with Eckstein ... It has been a dreadful period for me ... The
    only thing I remember of last week is that I have written fifty-two printed pages
    on the psychotherapy of hysteria."

12 I recall that Balint (1948, p. 167) likened the rituals of psychoanalytic training to
    "initiation rites" in which the candidate is forced to identify with his initiator.

13 As I summarized in a short 2001 article on the evolution of the idea of
    psychotherapy, Ferenczi and Rank's thesis of 1924, initially attacked by Franz
    Alexander (1925), was re-proposed by the same a quarter of a century later,
    under the name of "Corrective emotional experience" (Alexander, 1950). In the
    1950s, this model was then harshly attacked, as unorthodox, by Merton Gill
    (1954), who, just as Alexander did, will in turn re-propose it a quarter of a cen-
    tury later in his revision of the transference theory (Gill & Hoffman, 1982; Gill,
    1984).

14 Brown (1959, p. 175) (I am here quoting from the Italian translation).

Bibliography

Abraham, K. (1912). Amenhotep IV: Psycho-analytical contribution towards the understanding of his personality and of the monotheistic cult of Aton. In *Clinical Papers and Essays on Psychoanalysis*. London: Hogarth Press, 1955, pp. 26–90.

Abraham, K. (1922). Manifestations of the female castration complex. *International Journal of Psycho-Analysis, 3*: 1–29.

Abraham, N. (1962). Presentation de "Thalassa". In *L'Ecorce et le Noyau*. Paris: Aubier Flammarion, 1978, pp. 1–4.

Abraham, N., & Torok, M. (1976). *Le verbier de l'Homme aux loups*. Paris: Aubier-Flammarion. [*The Wolf Man's Magic Words: A Cryptonymy*. Minneapolis: University of Minnesota Press, 1986.]

Alexander, F. (1925). Entwicklungsziele der Psychoanalyse: By S. Ferenczi and Otto Rank. (Neue Arbeiten zur ärztlichen Psychoanalyse, Nr. I.) Vienna, 1924. *International Journal of Psycho-Analysis, 6*: 484–496.

Alexander, F. (1950). Analysis of the therapeutic factors in psychoanalytic treatment. *The Psychoanalytic Quarterly, 19*: 482–500. Reprinted in *The Psychoanalytic Quarterly (2007), 76*: 1065–1083.

Amouroux, R., & Stouten, H. (2014). Als Marie Bonaparte sich taub stellte …. *Luzifer-Amor, 53*: 122–140.

Anand, K. J., & Hickey, P. R. (1987). Pain and its effects in the human neonate and fetus. *New England Journal of Medicine, 317*: 1321–1329.

Anand, K. J., & Hickey, P. R. (1992). Halothane-morphine compared with high dose sufentanil for anesthesia and postoperative analgesia in neonatal cardiac surgery. *New England Journal of Medicine, 326*: 1–9.

Anthi, P. R. (1990). Freud's dream in norekdal style. *Scandinavian Psychoanalytic Review, 13*: 138–160.

Anzieu, D. (1975). *L'auto-analyse de Freud et la découverte de la psychanalyse*. Tome 1 & 2, Paris: PUF.

Anzieu, D. (1986). *Freud's Self-Analysis*. New York: International Universities Press.

Appignanesi, L., & Forrester, J. (1992). *Freud's Women*. London: Virago Press.

Arlow, J. A. (1951). The consecration of the prophet. *Psychoanalytic Quarterly, 20*: 374–397.

Arlow, J. A. (1952). The psychobiological origins of circumcision by C. D. Daly. *Psychoanalytic Quarterly, 21*: 437.

Aron, L., & Starr, K. (2013). *A Psychotherapy for the People. Toward a Progressive Psychoanalysis*. New York: Routledge.

Bachelard, G. (1934). *La formation de l'esprit scientifique. Contribution à une psychanalyse de la connaissance objective.* Paris: Librairie philosophique J. VRIN, 5e édition, 1967. https://gastonbachelard.org/wp-content/uploads/2015/07/formation_esprit.pdf.

Baginsky, A. (1877). *Handbuch der Schulhygiene zum Gebrauche für Ärzte, Sanitätsbeamte, Lehrer, Schulvorstände und Techniker.* [Handbook of School Hygiene.] Berlin: Denicke, 1883.

Baginsky, A. (1883). *Lehrbuch der Kinderkrankheiten für Ärzte und Studierende.* [Handbook of Pediatrics for Doctors and Students.] Braunschweig: Verlag von Friedrich Wreden, 1889.

Baginsky, A. (1909). Die Impressionabilität der Kinder unter dem Einfluss des Milieus. *Beiträge zur Kinderforschung und Heilerziehung, 27*: 5–21.

Balint, M. (1948). On the psycho-analytic training system. *International Journal of Psycho-Analysis, 29*: 163–173.

Balint, M. (1949). Sándor Ferenczi, Obit 1933. *International Journal of Psycho-Analysis, 30*: 215–219.

Balint, M. (1955). Friendly expanses – horrid empty spaces. *International Journal of Psycho-Analysis, 36*: 225–241.

Balint, M. (1958). Sandor Ferenczi's last years. *International Journal of Psycho-Analysis, 39*: 68.

Balint, M. (1959). *Thrills and Regressions.* New York: International Universities Press.

Balint, M. (1960). Primary narcissism and primary love. *Psychoanalytic Quarterly, 29*: 6–43.

Balint, M. (1968). *The Basic Fault: Therapeutic Aspects of Regression.* London: Tavistock.

Bakan, D. (1958). *Sigmund Freud and the Jewish Mystical Tradition.* Princeton, NJ: Van Nostrand.

Barton, G. A. (1932). Circumcision (Semitic). In J. Hastings (ed.) *Encyclopaedia of Religion and Ethics*, 2nd edition. Edinburgh: T. & T. Clark, p. 679.

Becker, E. (1973). *The Denial of Death.* New York: The Free Press.

Behrend, F. J. (1860). Über die Reizung der Geschlechtstheile, besonders über Onanie bei ganz kleinen Kindern, und die dagegen anzuwendenden Mittel [On the stimulation of the sexual part, especially on the onanism of very young children and the measures to be used against it]. *Journal für Kinderkrankheiten, 35*: 321–329.

Bergmann, M. S. (1992). *In the Shadow of Moloch: The Sacrifice of Children and its Impact on Western Religions.* New York: Columbia University Press.

Berman, E. (2004). Sándor, Gizella, Elma: A biographical journey. *International Journal of Psycho-Analysis, 85*: 489–520.

Bernfeld, S. (1946). An unknown autobiographical fragment of Freud. *American Imago, 4*: 3–19.

Bernfeld, S. (1953). Freud's studies on cocaine, 1884–1887. *Journal of the American Psychoanalytic Association, 1*: 581–613.

Bertin, C. (1982). *Marie Bonaparte. A Life.* New York: Harcourt Brace.

Bettelheim B. (1954). *Symbolic Wounds: Puberty Rites and the Envious Male.* Glencoe, IL: The Free Press.

Bettelheim, B. (1982). *Freud and Man's Soul.* New York: Vintage.

Billinsky, J. M. (1969). Jung and Freud (The end of a romance). *Andover Newton Quarterly, 10*: 39–43.

Blechner, M. J. (2017). The clitoris: Anatomical and psychological issues. *Studies in Gender and Sexuality, 18(3):* 190–200.

Blum, H. P. (1974). The borderline childhood of the Wolf Man. *Journal of the American Psychoanalytic Association, 22*: 721–742.

Blum, H. P. (1996). The Irma dream, self-analysis, and self-supervision. *Journal of the American Psychoanalytic Association, 44*: 511–532.

Boehlich, W. (1990). Introduction. In *The Letters of Sigmund Freud to Eduard Silberstein 1871–1881*. Cambridge, MA: The Belknap Press of Harvard University Press, pp. xiii–xxvii.

Bollas, C. (2011). Introduction. In J. Sklar (ed.), *Landscapes of the Dark: History, Trauma, Psychoanalysis*. London: Karnac, 2011, pp. xv–xxiii.

Bonaparte, M. (1948a). Female mutilation among primitive peoples and their psychical parallels in civilization. In *Female Sexuality*. New York: International Universities Press, 1953, pp. 153–161.

Bonaparte, M. (1948b). Notes on excision. In *Female Sexuality*. New York: International Universities Press, 1953, pp. 191–208.

Bonaparte, M., Freud, A., & Kris, E. (eds.) (1950). *The Origins of Psychoanalysis: Sigmund Freud's Letters, Drafts and Notes to Wilhelm Fliess (1887–1902)*. London: Imago, 1954.

Bonomi, C. (1994a). Why have we ignored Freud the "paediatrician"? The relevance of Freud's paediatric training for the origins of psychoanalysis. In A. Haynal, & E. Falzeder (eds.) *100 Years of Psychoanalysis: Contributions to the History of Psychoanalysis*. [Special Issue of *Cahiers Psychiatriques Genevois*]. London: H. Karnac Books, pp. 55–99.

Bonomi, C. (1994b). "Sexuality and death" in Freud's discovery of sexual aetiology. *International Forum of Psychoanalysis, 3*: 63–87.

Bonomi, C. (1996). Mute correspondence. *International Forum of Psychoanalysis, 5*: 165–189. Also in P. Mahony, C. Bonomi, & J. Stensson (eds.), *Behind the Scenes: Freud in Correspondence*. Oslo: Scandinavian University Press, 1997, pp. 155–201.

Bonomi, C. (1997). Freud and the discovery of infantile sexuality: A reassessment. In T. Dufresne (ed.), *Freud under Analysis. History, Theory, Practice. Essays in Honor of Paul Roazen*. Northvale, NJ, & London: Jason Aronson, 1997, pp. 37–57.

Bonomi, C. (1998). Jones's allegation of Ferenczi's mental deterioration: A reassessment. *International Forum of Psychoanalysis, 7*: 201–206.

Bonomi, C. (1999). Flight into sanity: Jones's allegation of Ferenczi's insanity reconsidered. *International Journal of Psycho-Analysis, 80*: 507–542.

Bonomi, C. (2001). The evolution of the practice of the psychoanalytic psychotherapies. *International Forum of Psychoanalysis, 10*: 217–220.

Bonomi, C. (2007). *Sulla soglia della psicoanalisi. Freud e la follia del bambino*. Torino: Bollati Boringhieri.

Bonomi. C. (2009a). Infanzia, peccato e pazzia. Alle radici della rappresentazione psicologica del bambino. In N. Dazzi, e G. P. Lombardo (a cura di), La costruzione storica della psicologia scientifica in Italia, Numero speciale, *Rassegna di Psicologia, 26(2)*: 129–153.

Bonomi, C. (2009b). The relevance of castration and circumcision to the origins of psychoanalysis. 1. The medical context. *International Journal of Psychoanalysis, 90:* 551–580.

Bonomi, C. (2010). Ferenczi and ego psychology. *Psychoanalytic Perspectives, 7*: 104–130.

Bonomi, C. (2013). Withstanding trauma: The significance of Emma Eckstein's circumcision for Freud's Irma dream. *The Psychoanalytic Quarterly, 82(3):* 689–740.

Bonomi, C. (2015a). *The Cut and the Building of Psychoanalysis. Volume I, Sigmund Freud and Emma Eckstein*. (Relational Perspectives Book Series). London, New York: Routledge.

Bonomi, C. (2015b). L'oeil, la masque et le miroir. Réflexions sur le regard désincarné. In E. Campi et G. Chaboudez (eds.) *Venise et le rêve*. Paris: Hermann, pp. 189–196.

Bonomi, C. (2018a). *The Cut and the Building of Psychoanalysis. Volume II, Sigmund Freud and Sándor Ferenczi*. (Relational Perspectives Book Series). London, New York: Routledge.

Bonomi, C. (2018b). Shock, empatia, telepatia. Guida alla lettura de "La scoperta del Sé" di Elizabeth Severn. *The Wise Baby/Il poppante saggio, 1(1)*: 63–87.

Bonomi, C., & Borgogno, F. (2014). The Ferenczi renaissance: Past, present, and future. *International Forum of Psychoanalysis, 23*: 1, 1–2.

Borch-Jacobsen, M. (2021). *Freud's Patients a Book of Lives*. London: Reaktion Books.

Borgogno, F. (1999). Sándor Ferenczi's first paper considered as a "Calling Card". *International Forum of Psychoanalysis, 8(3–4)*: 249–256.

Borgogno, F. (2011). Sándor Ferenczi, the "introjective psychoanalyst". *American Imago, 68*: 155–172.

Boyarin, D. (1994a). Épater l'embourgeoisement: Freud, gender, and the (de)colonized psyche. *Diacritics, 24*(1): 17–41.

Boyarin, D. (1994b). Jewish masochism: Couvade, castration, and rabbis in pain. *American Imago, 51*: 3–36.

Boyarin, D. (1995). Freud's baby, Fliess's maybe: Homophobia, anti-Semitism, and the invention of Oedipus. *GLQ: A Journal of Lesbian & Gay Studies, 2*: 115–147.

Boyarin, D. (1997). *Unheroic Conduct: The Rise of Heterosexuality and the Invention of the Jewish Man*. Berkeley, CA: Stanford University Press.

Brabant, E., Falzeder, E., & Giampieri-Deutsch, P. (eds.) (1993). *The Correspondence of Sigmund Freud and Sandor Ferenczi, Volume 1, 1908–1914*. Cambridge, MA: Harvard University Press.

Brenner, A. B. (1950). The Great Mother goddess: Puberty initiation rites and the Covenant of Abraham. *Psychoanalytic Review, 37*: 320–340.

Breuer, J., & Freud, S. (1893). On the psychical mechanism of hysterical phenomena: Preliminary Communication from Studies on Hysteria. In S. Freud, *The Standard Edition of the Complete Psychological Works* (hereafter *SE*), *2*: 1–17.

Breuer, J., & Freud, S. (1895). Studies on hysteria. In S. Freud, *SE* 2.

Bromley, A. (1957). Final contributions to the problems and methods of psychoanalysis. The selected papers of Sandor Ferenczi, M.D. Volume III. *The Psychoanalytic Quarterly, 26*: 112–114.

Brown, N. O. (1959). *Life against Death: The Psychoanalytic Meaning of History*. Middletown, CT: Wesleyan University Press.

Brown, N. O. (1966). *Love's Body*. New York: Random House.

Brunswick, R. M. (1928). A supplement to Freud's "History of an Infantile Neurosis". *International Journal of Psycho-Analysis, 9*: 439–476.

Bryk, F. (1928). *Neger-eros. Ethnologische Studien über das Sexualleben bei Negern.* Berlin und Köln: A. Marcus & E. Weber. [*Dark Rapture: The Sex-Life of the African Negro.* New York: AMS Press, 1975].

Burckhardt, J. (1898–1902). *Griechische Kulturgeschichte*, 4 vols. Berlin: W. Spemann.

Burston, D. (1999). Archetype and interpretation. *Psychoanalytic Review, 86*: 35–62.

Cassirer Bernfeld, S. (1951). Freud and archeology. *American Imago, 8*: 107–128.

Clark, R. (1980). *Sigmund Freud, the Man and the Cause.* New York: Random House.

Coates, S. W. (2016). Can babies remember trauma? Symbolic forms of representation in traumatized infants. *Journal of the American Psychoanalytic Association, 64(4)*: 751–776.

Colman, W. (1994). "The scenes themselves which lie at the bottom of the story": Julius, circumcision, and the castration complex. *The Psychoanalytic Review, 81*: 603–625.

Daly, C. D. (1950). The psycho-biological origins of circumcision. *International Journal of Psycho-Analysis, 31*: 217–236.

Darby, R. (2003). The masturbation taboo and the rise of Routine Male Circumcision: A review of the historiography. *Journal of Social History, 36(3)*: 737–757.

Davidson, A. I. (1987). How to do the history of psychoanalysis: A reading of Freud's three essays on the theory of sexuality. *Critical Inquiry, 14(Winter 1987)*: 252–277.

Derrida, J. (1991). Circumfession: Fifty-nine periods and periphrases. Engl. translation in *Geoffrey Bennington Jacques Derrida.* Chicago: Chicago University Press, 1993.

Devereux, G. (1953). Why Oedipus killed Laius: A note on the complementary Oedipus complex in Greek drama. *International Journal of Psycho-Analysis, 34*: 132–141.

Dreifuss, G. (1965). A psychological study of circumcision in Judaism. *Journal of Analytical Psychology, 10*: 23–32.

Dupont, J. (Ed.) (1988). *The Clinical Diary of Sándor Ferenczi.* Cambridge, MA and London: Harvard University Press.

Dupont, J. (1994). Freud's analysis of Ferenczi as revealed by their correspondence. *International Journal of Psycho-Analysis, 75*: 301–320.

Dupont, J. (1998). The concept of trauma according to Ferenczi and its effects on subsequent psychoanalytical research. *International Forum of Psychoanalysis, 7*: 235–240.

Dupont, J. (2006). La diffusione di Ferenczi in Francia. In C. Bonomi (a cura di). *Sándor Ferenczi e la psicoanalisi contemporanea.* Roma: Borla, pp. 27–35.

Dupont, J. (2015). *Au fil du temps ... Un itinéraire analytique.* Paris: Campagne Première.

Eastman, J. (2005). Freud, the Oedipus complex, and Greece or the silence of Athena. *Psychoanalytic Review, 92*: 335–354.

Eckstein, E. (1904). *Die Sexualfrage in der Erziehung des Kindes.* Leipzig: Curt Wigand.

Eissler, K. R. (1977). Comments on penis envy and orgasm in women. *Psychoanalytic Study of the Child 32*: 29–83.

Eissler, K. R. (1978). Creativity and adolescence: The effect of trauma in Freud's adolescence. *Psychoanalytic Study of the Child, 33*: 461–517.

Eissler. K. R. (1993). *Three Instances of Injustice.* Madison, CT: International Universities Press.

Eissler, K. R. (1997). Preliminary remarks on Emma Eckstein's case history. *Journal of the American Psychoanalytic Association, 45*: 1303–1305.

Ellenberger, H. F. (1964). The concept of "maladie créatrice." In M. S. Micale (ed.) *Essays of Henri Ellenberger in the History of Psychiatry*. Princeton, NJ: Princeton University Press, 1993, pp. 328–340.

Ellenberger, H. (1972). The story of Anna O.: A critical review with new data. In M. S. Micale (ed.) *Essays of Henry Ellenberger in the History of Psychiatry*. Princeton, NJ: Princeton University Press, 1993, pp. 254–272.

Erikson, E. (1954). The dream specimen of psychoanalysis. *Journal of the American Psychoanalytic Association, 2*: 5–55.

Falzeder, E. (1994). My grand-patient, my chief tormentor: A hitherto unnoticed case of Freud's and the consequences. *Psychoanalytic Quarterly, 63*: 297–331 [Reprinted in *Psychoanalytic Filiations: Mapping the Psychoanalytic Movement*. Karnac: London, 2015, pp. 19–48].

Falzeder, E. (1996). Dreaming of Freud: Ferenczi, Freud, and an analysis without end. *International Forum of Psychoanalysis, 5*: 265–270.

Falzeder, E. (2012). "A fat wad of dirty pieces of papers": Freud on America, Freud in America, Freud and America. In *Psychoanalytic Filiations: Mapping the Psychoanalytic Movement*. Karnac: London, 2015, pp. 307–330.

Falzeder, E., & Brabant, E., (eds.) (1996). *The Correspondence of Sigmund Freud and Sándor Ferenczi, Volume 2, 1914–1919*. Cambridge, MA: Harvard University Press.

Falzeder, E., & Brabant, E. (eds.) (2000). *The Correspondence of Sigmund Freud and Sándor Ferenczi, Volume 3, 1920–1933*. Cambridge, MA: Harvard University Press.

Feldman, A. (1944). Freud's Moses and Monotheism and the three stages of the Israelitish religion. *The Psychoanalytic Review, 31*: 361–418.

Feldman, Y. S. (1993). "And Rebecca loved Jacob," but Freud did not. *Jewish Studies Quarterly, 1*: 72–88.

Ferenczi, S. (1909). Introjection and transference. In *First Contributions to Psycho-Analysis*. London: Hogarth Press, 1952, pp. 35–93.

Ferenczi, S. (1913a). To whom does one relates one's dream? In *Further Contributions to the Theory and Technique of Psycho-Analysis*. London: Hogarth Press, 1926, p. 349.

Ferenczi, S. (1913b). *A Little Chanticleer. In First Contributions to Psychoanalysis*. London: Hogarth Press, 1952, pp. 240–252.

Ferenczi, S. (1915). The dream of the occlusive pessary. In *Further Contributions to the Theory and Technique of Psycho-Analysis*. London: Hogarth Press, 1926, pp. 304–311.

Ferenczi, S. (1916–1917a). Disease or patho-neuroses. In *Further Contributions to the Theory and Technique of Psycho-Analysis*. London: Hogarth Press, 1926, pp. 78–87.

Ferenczi, S. (1916–1917b). On the psychical consequences of "castration" in childhood. In *Further Contributions to the Theory and Technique of Psycho-Analysis*. London: Hogarth Press, 1926, pp. 244–249.

Ferenczi, S. (1919). The phenomena of hysterical materialization: Thoughts on the conception of hysterical conversion and symbolism. In *Further Contributions to the Theory and Technique of Psycho-Analysis*. London: Hogarth Press, 1926, pp. 89–104.

Ferenczi, S. (1923). On the symbolism of the head of Medusa. In *Further Contributions to the Theory and Technique of Psycho-Analysis*. London: Hogarth Press, 1926, p. 360.

Ferenczi, S. (1924). *Thalassa: A Theory of Genitality*. London: Karnac Books, 1989.

Ferenczi, S. (1925). Contra-indications to the "active" psychoanalytic technique. In *Further Contributions to the Theory and Technique of Psycho-Analysis*. London: Hogarth Press, 1926, pp. 217–230.

Ferenczi, S. (1926). The problem of acceptance of unpleasant ideas: Advances in knowledge of the sense of reality. In *Further Contributions to the Theory and Technique of Psycho-Analysis*. London: Hogarth Press, 1926, pp. 366–379.

Ferenczi, S. (1927). Technik Der Psychoanalyse: I. Die Analytische Situation.: By Dr. Otto Rank. 1926. (Franz Deuticke, Leipzig and Vienna, pp. 211). *International Journal of Psycho-Analysis, 8*: 93–100.

Ferenczi, S. (1928a).The elasticity of psycho-analytic technique. In *Final Contributions to the Problems and Methods of Psycho-Analysis*. London: Hogarth Press, 1950, pp. 87–101.

Ferenczi, S. (1928b). Psychoanalyse und Kriminologie. *Bausteine, III*: 399–421.

Ferenczi, S. (1929a). The unwelcome child and his death instinct. In *Final Contributions to the Problems and Methods of Psycho-Analysis*. London: Hogarth Press, 1950, pp. 102–107.

Ferenczi, S. (1929b). The principle of relaxation and neocatharsis. In *Final Contributions to the Problems and Methods of Psycho-Analysis*. London: Hogarth Press, 1950, pp. 108–125.

Ferenczi, S. (1929c). Male and female [Männlich und Weiblich]. In *Thalassa: A Theory of Genitality*. London: Karnac Books, 1989, pp. 96–107.

Ferenczi, S. (1931). Child-analysis in the analysis of adults. In *Final Contributions to the Problems and Methods of Psycho-Analysis*. London: Hogarth, 1955, pp. 126–142.

Ferenczi, S. (1930–1932). Notes and fragments. In *Final Contributions to the Problems and Methods of Psycho-Analysis*. London: Hogarth Press, 1955, pp. 219–279.

Ferenczi, S. (1933). Confusion of tongues between adults and the child: The language of tenderness and of passion. In *Final Contributions to the Problems and Methods of Psycho-Analysis*. London: Hogarth, 1955, pp. 156–167.

Ferenczi, S., & Groddeck, G. (1921–1933). *Correspondence*. Ed. by C. Fortune, London: Open Gate Press, 2002.

Ferenczi, S., & Rank, O. (1924). *The Development of Psycho- Analysis*. Madison, CT: International Universities Press, 1986.

Finzsch, N. (2018). "We know the lesbian habits of kleitoriaxein [...] which justify the resection of the clitoris": Cliteridectomy in the West, 1600 to 1988. *Gender Forum* (Special Issue on Cliteridectomy), *67*: 9–28.

Flannery, J. G. (1980). Freud's Acropolis Revisited. *International Review of Psycho-Analysis, 7*: 347–352.

Fleischmann, L. (1878). Über Onanie und Masturbation bei Säugligen. *Wiener medizinische Presse, 19*: 8–10, 46–49.

Forest (de), I. (1942). The therapeutic technique of Sándor Ferenczi. *International Journal of Psycho-Analysis, 23*: 120–139.

Forest (de), I. (1954). *The Leaven of Love: A Development of the Psychoanalytic Theory and Technique of Sándor Ferenczi*. New York: Da Capo Press, 1984.

Foresti, G. (2003). Sigmund/Sig IS mund: un'ipotesi. *Rivista di Psicoanalisi, 49*: 149–175.

Fortune, C. (1991). Psychoanalytic champion of "real-life experience": An interview with John Bowlby. *Melanie Klein and Object Relations, 9(2)*. Toronto, Canada: pp. 70–86.

Foucault, M. (1999). Les anormaux. Course au *Collège de France 1974–75*. Paris: Edition Seuil Gallimard.

Frazer, J. G. (1890). *The Golden Bough: A Study in Comparative Religion*. London: Macmillan and Company.

Freud, S. (1886). Report on my studies in Paris and Berlin. In *SE*. 24 vols. Ed. and transl. James Strachey and al. London: Hogarth Press, 1953–1974, *1*: 5–15.

Freud, S. (1888). Hysteria. *SE*, *1*: 37–59.

Freud, S. (1893). On the psychical mechanism of hysterical phenomena: A Lecture. *SE*, *3*: 25–39.

Freud, S. (1894a). The neuro-psychoses of defence. *SE*, *3*: 43–61.

Freud, S. (1894b). On the grounds for detaching a particular syndrome from neurasthenia under the description 'anxiety neurosis'". *SE*, 3: 89–115.

Freud, S. (1895a). Hegar's Der Geschlechtstrieb Wiener klinische Rundschau. In: M. Solms (ed.) A previously-untranslated review by Freud of a book on the sexual instinct. *International Review of Psychoanalysis, 1990*, *17*: 361–363.

Freud, S. (1895b). Project for a scientific psychology. *SE*, *1*: 283–397.

Freud, S. (1896a). Heredity and the aetiology of the neuroses. *SE*, *3*: 141–156.

Freud, S. (1896b). Further remarks on the neuro-psychoses of defence. *SE*, *3*: 157–185.

Freud, S. (1896c). The aetiology of hysteria. *SE*, *3*: 187–221.

Freud, S. (1898). The psychical mechanism of forgetfulness. *SE*, *3*: 287–297.

Freud, S. (1899). Screen memories. *SE*, *3*: 303–322.

Freud, S. (1900). The interpretation of dreams. *SE*, *4(5)*.

Freud, S. (1901a). On Dreams. *SE*, *5*: 632–686.

Freud, S. (1901b). The psychopathology of everyday life. *SE*, *6*.

Freud, S. (1905). Three essays on the theory of sexuality. *SE*, *7*: 123–246.

Freud, S. (1907a). The sexual enlightenment of children. *SE*, *9*: 129–140.

Freud, S. (1907b). Obsessive acts and religious practices. *SE*, *9*: 115–128.

Freud, S. (1908). On the sexual theories of children. *SE*, *9*: 205–226.

Freud, S. (1909). Analysis of a Phobia in a five-year-old boy. *SE*, *10*: 1–150.

Freud, S. (1910a). Five lectures on psycho-analysis. *SE*, *22*: 3–182.

Freud, S. (1910b). Leonardo da Vinci and a memory of his childhood. *SE*, *11*: 57–138.

Freud, S. (1911a). Psycho-analytic notes on an autobiographical account of a case of paranoia (dementia paranoides). *SE*, *12*: 1–82.

Freud, S. (1911b). The significance of sequences of vowels. *SE*, *12*: 341.

Freud, S. (1913a). Totem and taboo. *SE*, *15*: 1–240.

Freud, S. (1913b). The theme of the three caskets. *SE*, *12*: 291–301.

Freud, S. (1913c). The disposition to obsessional neurosis, a contribution to the problem of the choice of neurosis. *SE*, *12*: 311–326.

Freud, S. (1914a). On the history of the psycho-analytic movement. *SE*, *14*: 1–66.

Freud, S. (1914b). Remembering, repeating and working-through (Further recommendations on the technique of psycho-analysis II). *SE*, *12*: 145–156.

Freud, S. (1915). Observations on transference-love (Further recommendations on the technique of psycho-analysis III). *SE*, *12*: 157–171.

Freud, S. (1916–1917). Introductory lectures on psycho-analysis. *SE*, *15*: 1–240; *16*: 243–463.

Freud, S. (1917).Mourning and Melancholia. *SE*, *14*: 237–258.

Freud, S. (1918a). From the history of an infantile neurosis. *SE*, *17*: 1–124.

Freud, S. (1918b). The taboo of virginity. *SE*, *11*: 193–208.

Freud, S. (1919). The "uncanny." *SE, 17*: 217–256.

Freud, S. (1920). Beyond the pleasure principle. *SE, 18*: 3–64.

Freud, S. (1921). Group psychology and the analysis of the ego. *SE, 18*: 65–144.

Freud, S. (1922). Medus's head. *SE, 18*: 273–274.

Freud, S. (1923a). The infantile genital organization (an interpolation into the theory of sexuality). *SE, 19*: 139–146.

Freud, S. (1923b). The Ego and the Id. *SE, 19*: 1–66.

Freud, S. (1924a). The economic problem of masochism. *SE, 19*: 155–170.

Freud, S. (1924b). Neurosis and psychosis. *SE, 19*: 147–154.

Freud, S. (1925a). Some psychical consequences of the anatomical distinction between the sexes. *SE, 19*: 243–260.

Freud, S. (1925b). An Autobiographical study. *SE, 20*: 1–74.

Freud, S. (1926a). Inhibitions, symptoms and anxiety. *SE, 20*: 77–174.

Freud, S. (1926b). The question of lay analysis. *SE, 20*: 181–258.

Freud, S. (1927a). Fetishism. *SE, 21*: 147–158.

Freud, S. (1927b). The future of an illusion. *SE, 21*: 5–56.

Freud, S. (1930). Civilization and its discontents. *SE, 21*: 57–145.

Freud, S. (1933a). New introductory lectures on psycho-analysis. *SE, 22*: 1–182.

Freud, S. (1933b). Sándor Ferenczi. *SE, 22*: 227–229.

Freud, S. (1936). A disturbance of memory on the Acropolis. *SE, 22*: 237–248.

Freud, S. (1937a). Analysis terminable and interminable. *SE, 23*: 209–254.

Freud, S. (1937b). Constructions in analysis. *SE, 23*: 255–270.

Freud, S. (1938a). Splitting of the Ego in the process of defence. *SE, 23*: 271–278.

Freud, S. (1938b). An outline of psycho-analysis. *SE, 30*: 139–208.

Freud, S. (1939). Moses and Monotheism: Three essays. *SE, 23*: 1–138.

Freud, S. (1960). *Briefe 1873–1939*. Ed. Ernst L. Freud. Frankfurt am Main: S. Fischer. [Letters of Sigmund Freud 1873–1939. New York: Basic Books, 1960].

Freud, S. (1985). *A Phylogenetic Fantasy: An Overview of the Transference Neuroses*, edited by I. Grubrich-Simitis. Cambridge: Harvard University Press, 1987.

Freud, S. (1986). *Sigmund Freud Briefe an Wilhelm Fliess 1887–1904. Ungekürtze Ausgabe*. (Bearbeitung der deutschen Fassung von Michael Schröter). Frankfurt am Main: S. Fischer.

Freud, S. (2002). *Unser Herz zeigt nach dem Süden: Reisebriefe 1895–1923* [Our Heart Points to the South: Travel Letters 1895–1923]. Ed. Christfried Tögel with the collaboration of Michael Molnar. Berlin: Aufbau-Verlag.

Freud, S., & Abraham, K. (2002). *The Complete Correspondence of Sigmund Freud and Karl Abraham 1907–1925*. Edited by E. Falzeder, London: Karnac.

Freud, S., & Bernays, M. (2005). *Briefwechsel 1882–1938*. Ed. Albrecht Hirschmüller. Tübingen: edition diskord.

Freud, S., & Binswanger, L. (2003). *The Sigmund Freud-Ludwig Binswanger Correspondence: 1908–1938*. Edited by G. Fichtner. New York: Other Press.

Freud, S., & Jones, E. (1993). *The Complete Correspondence of Sigmund Freud and Ernest Jones 1908–1939*. Edited by R.A. Paskauskas. Cambridge, MA & London: The Belknap Press of Harvard University Press.

Freud, S., & Jung, C. G. (1974). *The Freud/Jung Letters: The Correspondence between Sigmund Freud and C. G. Jung*. London: Routledge and The Hogarth Press.

Fried, R. (2003). *Freud on the Acropolis – A Detective Story*. Helsinki: Therapeia Foundation:

Friedman, P. (1960). *Review of Jewish Symbols in the Greco-Roman Period by Erwin R. Goodenough*, (Bollingen Series XXXVII), Volumes 1–6. New York: Published for the Bollingen Foundation Inc. by Pantheon Books, Inc., 1953, 1954, 1956. *Psychoanalytic Quarterly, 29*: 254–263.

Foresti, G. (2003). Sigmund/Sig IS mund: un'ipotesi. *Rivista di Psicoanalisi, 49*: 149–175.

Gabbard, G. O. (1995). The early history of boundary violations in psychoanalysis. *Journal of the American Psychoanalytic Association, 43*: 1115–1136.

Gabbard, G. O. (1997). Letter: Glen O. Gabbard Replies. *Journal of the American Psychoanalytic Association, 45*: 571–572.

Gardiner, M. M. (1964). The Wolf Man grows older. *Journal of the American Psychoanalytic Association, 12*: 80–92.

Gardiner, M. M. (Ed.) (1971). *L'uomo dei lupi* [Italian translation of *The Wolf-Man by the Wolf-Man*. New York: Basic Books, 1971]. Roma: New Compton, 1974.

Gardiner, M. M. (1983). The Wolf Man's last years. *Journal of the American Psychoanalytic Association, 31*: 867–897.

Geller, J. (1992). "A glance at the nose": Freud's inscription of Jewish difference. *American Imago, 49*: 427–444.

Geller, J. (2007). *On Freud's Jewish Body. Mitigating Circumcisions*. New York: Fordham University Press.

Gero, G. (1961). Review of: Asexualization. A follow-up study of 244 cases, by Johan Bremer. Oslo, Norway: Oslo University Press, 1958. 366 pp. *Psychoanalytic Quarterly, 30*: 587–589.

Gill, M. M. (1954). Psychoanalysis and exploratory psychotherapy. *Journal of the American Psychoanalytic Association, 2*: 771–97.

Gill, M. M. (1984). Psychoanalysis and Psychotherapy: A Revision. *International Revue of Psycho-Analysis, 11*:161–179.

Gill, M. M., & Hoffman, I. Z. (1982). *Analysis of Transference, Volume II. Studies of Nine Audio-recorded Psychoanalytic Sessions*. Psychological Issues Monograph No. 54. New York: International Universities Press.

Gilman, S. L. (1991). *The Jews' Body*. New York: Routledge.

Gilman, S. L. (1992). Freud, race and gender. *American Imago, 49*: 155–183.

Gilman, S. L. (1993a). *Freud, Race and Gender*. Princeton, NJ: Princeton University Press.

Gilman, S. L. (1993b). *The Case of Sigmund Freud: Medicine and Identity at the Fin De Siècle*. Baltimore, MD and London: The Johns Hopkins University Press.

Goldman, R. (1997). Circumcision. The Hidden Trauma. How and American Cultural Practice Affects infants and Ultimately Us All. Boston, MA: Vanguard Publications.

Gould, S. J. (1977). *Ontogeny and Phylogeny*. Cambridge, MA: Harvard University Press.

Green, A. (1990). *Le complexe de castration*. Paris: Presses universitaires de France.

Grigg, K. A. (1973). "All roads lead to Rome": The role of the nursemaid in Freud's dreams. *Journal of the American Psychoanalytic Association, 21*: 108–126.

Grinstein, A. (1961). Freud's dream of the botanical monograph. *Journal of the American Psychoanalytic Association, 9*: 480–503.

Grinstein, A. (1980). *Sigmund Freud's Dreams*. New York: International Universities Press.

Grosskurt, P. (1991). *The Secret Ring. Freud's Inner Circle and the Politics of Psychoanalysis.* London: Jonathan Cape.

Grotstein, J. S. (1989). A revised psychoanalytic conception of schizophrenia: An interdisciplinary update. *Psychoanalytic Psychology, 6*: 253–275.

Grotstein, J. S. (1990). Nothingness, meaninglessness, Chaos, and the "Black Hole" I—The importance of nothingness, meaninglessness, and Chaos in psychoanalysis. *Contemporary Psychoanalysis, 26*: 257–290; II—The Black Hole. *Contemporary Psychoanalysis, 26*: 377–407.

Grubrich-Simitis, I. (1988). Trauma or Drive—Drive and Trauma—A Reading of Sigmund Freud's Phylogenetic Fantasy of 1915. *Psychoanalytic Study of the Child, 43*: 3–32.

Hamilton, E. (1930). *The Greek Way.* New York and London: W. W. Norton & Company.

Hannah, B. (1976). *Jung: His Life and Work: A Biographical Memoir.* New York: Putnam.

Harrison, I. B. (1988). Further implications of a dream of Freud's: A subjective influence on his theory formation. *International Review of Psycho-Analysis, 15*: 365–372.

Haynal, A. E. (2005). In the shadow of a controversy: Freud and Ferenczi 1925–33. *International Journal of Psycho-Analysis, 86*: 457–466.

Haynal, A. E. (2011). Corrective emotional experience remembered. *American Journal of Psychoanalysis, 71*: 207–216.

Haynal, A. E. (2016). The adventurous emigration of the Ferencziana: Contribution to their history. *International Forum of Psychoanalysis, 25*: 211–213.

Hermann, I. (1949). The giant mother, the phallic mother, obscenity. *Psychoanalytic Review, 36*: 302–306.

Herz, M. (1885). Über Hysterie bei Kindern. *Wiener medizinische Wochenschrift, 35(43)*: 1305–1308; 44: 1337–1342; 45: 1368–1371; 46: 1401–1405.

Hirschmüller, A. (1978). Eine bisher unbekannte Krankengeschichte Sigmund Freuds und Josef Breuers aus der Entstehungszeit der 'Studien über Hysterie'. *Jahrbuch der Psychoanalyse, 10:* 136–168.

Hirschmüller, A. (1986). Briefe Josef Breuers an Wilhelm Fliess 1894–1898. *Jahrbuch der Psychoanalyse, 18*: 239–262.

Hirschmüller, A. (1989). Freuds 'Mathilde': Ein weiterer Tagesrest zum Traum. *Jahrbuch der Psychoanalyse, 24*: 128–159.

Hirst. A. (undated manuscript). *Analysed and Reeducated by Freud Himself. Sigmund Freud's Papers, Supplemental File, 1765–1998*, Box 61. Library of Congress, Manuscript Division.

Hobson, R. F. (1961). Psychological aspects of circumcision. *Journal of Analytical Psychology, 6*: 5–33.

Hoffer, A. (1985). Toward a definition of psychoanalytic neutrality. *Journal of the American Psychoanalytic Association, 33*: 771–795.

Hoffman, I. (1979). Death anxiety and adaptation to mortality in psychoanalytic theory. *Annual of Psychoanalysis, 7*: 233–267.

Hoffman, I. Z. (1998). *Ritual and Spontaneity in the Psychoanalytic Process. A Dialectic Constructivist View.* Hillsdale, NJ: The Analytic Press.

Holt, R. R. (1982). The manifest and latent meanings of metapsychology. *Annual of Psychoanalysis, 10*: 233–255 (also in R. R. Holt, *Freud Reappraised: A Fresh Look at Psychoanalytic Theory.* New York: The Guilford Press, 1989, pp. 15–33).

Holt, R. R. (1985). The current status of psychoanalytic theory. In *Freud Reappraised. A Fresh Look at Psychoanalytic Theory*. New York and London: The Guilford Press, 1989, pp. 324–344.

Isakower, O. (1939). On the exceptional position of the auditory sphere. *International Journal of Psychoanalysis, 20*: 340–348.

Janet, P. (1889). *L'automatisme psychologique. Essai de psychologie expérimentale sur les formes inférieures de l'activité humaine*. Paris: Félix Alcan [reprint, Paris: Éditions Odile Jacob, 1998].

Janet, P. (1893/94). Quelques définitions récentes de l'hystérie, *Archives de Neurologie, XXV(76)*: 417–438; *XXVI(77)*: 1–29.

Jones, E. (1933). Sándor Ferenczi, 1873–1933. *International Journal of Psycho-Analysis, 14*: 463–466.

Jones, E. (1953). *Sigmund Freud: Life and Work, vol. I. The Young Freud: 1856–1900*. London: Hogarth.

Jones, E. (1955). *Sigmund Freud: Life and Work, vol. II. Years of Maturity 1901–1919*. London: Hogarth.

Jones, E. (1957). *Sigmund Freud Life and Work, Volume III: The Last Phase: 1919–1939*. London: Hogarth.

Jones, E. (1958). Sándor Ferenczi's last years. *International Journal of Psycho-Analysis, 39*: 68.

Jucovy, M. E. (1992). Psychoanalytic contributions to Holocaust studies. *International Journal of Psycho-Analysis, 73*: 267–282.

Jung, C. G. (1912). *Wandlungen und Symbole der Libido. Beiträge zur Entwicklungsgesischte des Denkens*. Vienna: Deuticke.

Jung, C. G. (1961a). *Memories, Dreams, Reflections*. Edited by A. Jaffé. London: Flamingo, 1983.

Jung, C. G. (1961b). *Symbols and the Interpretations of Dreams*. Collected Works, Volume 18. Princeton, NJ: Princeton University Press, 1977.

Kanzer, M. (1972). *The Wolf-Man by the Wolf-Man: Edited by Muriel Gardiner*. New York: Basic Books; London: Hogarth Press and Institute of Psycho-Analysis. 1971. *International Journal of Psycho-Analysis, 53*: 419–422.

Kardiner, A. (1977). *My analysis with Freud: Reminiscences*. New York: Norton.

Kempe, C. H., Silverman, F. N., Brandt F., Steele, B. F., Droegemuller, W., & Silver, H. K. (1985). The Battered child syndrome. *Child Abuse and Neglect, 9*: 143–154.

Kerr, J. (1994). *A Most Dangerous Method: The Story of Jung, Freud, & Sabina Spielrein*. London: Sinclair-Stevenson.

Kern, S. (1975). The prehistory of Freud's theory of castration anxiety. *Psychoanalytic Review, 62*: 309–314.

Klein, G. (1976). *Psychoanalytic Theory: An Exploration of Essentials*. New York: International Universities Press.

Klerk, A. de (2003a). Het trauma van Freuds besnijdenis. [The trauma of Freud's circumcision] *Tijdschrift voor Psychoanalyse, 9(3)*: 136–152.

Klerk, A. de (2003b). Repliek. [Reply] *Tijdschrift voor Psychoanalyse, 9(4)*: 251–255.

Klerk, A. de (2003c). The femme fatale and her secrets from a psychoanalytical perspective. In H. W. van Os (ed.) *Femmes Fatales – 1860–2010*. Wommelgem: BAI, pp. 43–53.

Klerk, A. de (2004). Kastrationsangst und die Beschneidung Neugeborener. Anmerkungen zu Franz Maciejewski: "Zu einer ,dichten Beschreibung' des Kleinen Hans. Über das vergessene Trauma der Beschneidung". *Psyche, 58(5)*: 464–470.

Klerk, A. de (2008). Die Bedeutung der Kastrationsangst und der Beschneidung in Freuds Werk und Leben. In G. Schlesinger-Kipp, & R-P. Warsitz (eds.) *"Die neuen Leiden der Seele". Das (Un-)behagen in der Kultur.* Deutsche Psychoanalytische Verein. Frankfurt/Main: Vertrieb Geber & Reusch; pp. 279–304.

Kollbrunner, J. (2001). *Der kranke Freud.* Stuttgart: Klett-Cotta.

Kramer, R. (1995). "The 'Bad Mother' Freud has never seen": Otto Rank and the birth of object-relations theory. *Journal of the American Academy of Psychoanalysis, 23*: 293–321.

Kris, E. (1954). New contributions to the study of Freud's The interpretation of dreams – A critical essay. *Journal of the American Psychoanalytic Association, 2*: 180–191.

Krömer, R. (1896). Beitrag zur Castrationsfrage. *Allgemeine Zeitschrift für Psychiatrie, 52*: 1–74.

Lacan, J. (1954–1955). *The Seminar of Jacques Lacan. Book II. The Ego in Freud's Theory and in the Technique of Psychoanalysis 1954–1955.* In J.s-A Miller (ed.) translated by S. Tomaselli, with notes by J. Forrester. Cambridge: CUP, 1988.

Lacoursiere, R. B. (2008). Freud's death: Historical truth and biographical fictions. *American Imago, 65*: 107–128.

Langs, R. (1980). The misalliance dimension in the case of the Wolf Man. In M. Kanzer, & J. Glenn (eds.) *Freud and his Patients.* New York: Jason Aronson, pp. 339–405.

Langs, R. (1984). Freud's Irma dream and the origins of psychoanalysis. *Psychoanalytic Review, 71*: 591–617.

Laplanche, J. (1992). Interpretation between determinism and hermeneutics: A restatement of the problem. *International Journal of Psycho-Analysis, 73*: 429–445.

Leach, E. (1986). The Big Fish in the biblical wilderness. *International Review of Psycho-Analysis, 13*: 129–141.

Leitner, M. (1998). *Freud, Rank und die Folgen. Ein Schlüsselkonflikt für die Psychoanalyse.* Vienna: Turia & Kant.

Levenson, E. A. (1981). Facts or fantasies—On the nature of psychoanalytic data. *Contemporary Psychoanalysis, 17*: 486–500.

Lewin, B. D. (1933). The body as phallus. *Psychoanalytic Quarterly, 2*: 24–47.

Lieberman, E. J. (1985). *Acts of Will: The Life and Work of Otto Rank.* New York: Free Press.

Lieberman, E. J., & Kramer, R. (Eds) (2012). *The Letters of Sigmund Freud and Otto Rank: Inside Psychoanalysis.* Baltimore, MD: Johns Hopkins University Press.

Lippman, R. L. (2009). Freud's botanical monograph screen memory revisited. *The Psychoanalytic Review, 96*: 579–595.

Little, M. (1957). The selected papers of Sandor Ferenczi, M.D. Vol. III. Final contributions to the problems and methods of psycho-analysis. *International Journal of Psycho-Analysis, 38*: 121–123.

Lotto, D. (2001). Freud's struggle with misogyny: homosexuality and guilt in the dream of Irma's injection. *Journal of the American Psychoanalytic Association, 49*: 1289–1313.

Ludwig, E. (1957). *Doctor Freud. An Analysis and a Writing.* New York: Hellman, Williams & Company.

Lynn, D. J (1997). Sigmund Freud's psychoanalysis of Albert Hirst. *Bulletin of the History of Medicine, 71*(1): 69–93.

Maciejewski, F. (2002). *Psychoanalytisches Archiv und jüdisches Gedächtnis. Freud, Beschneidung und Monotheismus.* Vienna: Passagen Verlag.

Maciejewski, F. (2006). Freud, his wife, and his "wife." *American Imago, 63*: 497–506.

Mahony, P. J. (1977). Towards a formalist approach to dreams. *International Review of Psycho-Analysis, 4*: 83–98.

Mahony, P. J. (1979). Friendship and its discontents. *Contemporary Psychoanalysis, 15*: 55–109.

Mahony, P. J. (1984). *Cries of the Wolf Man.* New York: The Chicago Institute for Psychoanalysis.

Mahony, P. J. (1992). Freud as family therapist. In T. Gelfand, & J. Kerr (eds.) *Freud and the History of Psychoanalysis.* Hillsdale, NJ: Analytic Press, pp. 307–318.

Mahony, P. J. (1995). *Les hurlements de l'Homme aux loups.* (New edition of *Cries of the Wolf Man*). Paris: PUF.

Mahony, P. J. (2002). Freud's writing: His (w)rite of passage and its reverberations. *Journal of the American Psychoanalytic Association, 50*: 885–907.

Makari, G. (2008). *Revolution in Mind: The Creation of Psychoanalysis.* New York: Harper Collins.

Masson, J. M. (1984). *The Assault on Truth. Freud's Suppression of the Seduction Theory.* New York: Farrar, Straus & Giroux.

Masson, J. M. (Ed.) (1985). *The Complete Letters of Sigmund Freud to Wilhelm Fliess 1887–1904.* Cambridge, MA and London: The Belknap Press of Harvard University Press.

Masson, J. M., & Masson, T. C. (1978). Buried memories on the acropolis: Freud's response to mysticism and anti-semitism. *International Journal of Psycho-Analysis, 59*: 199–208.

Mautner, B. (1991). Freud's Irma dream: a psychoanalytic interpretation. *International Journal of Psychoanalysis, 72*: 275–286.

May, U. (2003). The early relationship between Sigmund Freud and Isidor Sadger: A dream (1897) and a letter (1902). *Psychoanalysis and History, 5:* 119–145.

McGrath, W. J. M. (1986). *Freud's Discovery of Psychoanalysis: The Politics of Hysteria.* Ithaca, NY: Cornell University Press.

Merkel, F. (1887). *Beitrag zur Casuistik der Castration bei Neurosen.* Nuremberg: J. L. Stich.

Möbius, P. J. (1903). *Über die Wirkungen der Castration.* Halle a.d. S.: Verlag von Carl Marhold.

Morris, R. T. (1892). Is evolution trying to do away with the clitoris? *Transactions of the American Association of Obstetricians and Gynecologists, 5*: 288–302.

Mucci, C. (2018a). Psychoanalysis for a new humanism. Testimony, connectedness, memory and forgiveness for a "persistence of the human". *International Forum of Psychoanalysis, 27(3):* 176–187.

Mucci, C. (2018b). *Borderline Bodies. Affect Regulation Therapy for Personality Disorders.* New York: Norton.

Neumann, E. (1955). *The Great Mother.* London: Routledge & Kegan Paul.

Niederland, W. G. (1951). Three notes on the Schreber case. *Psychoanalytic Quarterly, 20*: 579–591.

Niederland, W. G. (1959a). Schreber: Father and son. *Psychoanalytic Quarterly, 28*: 151–169.

Niederland, W. G. (1959b). The "miracled-up" world of Schreber's childhood. *Psychoanalytic Study of the Child, 14*: 383–413.

Niederland, W. G. (1969). Freud's "déjà vu" on the acropolis. *American Imago, 26*: 373–378.

Niederland, W. G. (1984). *The Schreber Case: Psychoanalytic Profile of a Paranoid Personality*. Hillsdale, NJ: The Analytic Press.

Nunberg, H. (1947). Circumcision and problems of bisexuality. *International Journal of Psycho-Analysis, 28*: 145–179.

Obholzer, K. (1980). *Gespräche mit dem Wolfsmann: Eine Psychoanalyse und die Folgen*. Reinbek bei Hamburg: Rowohlt.

Ostow, M. (1986). Archetypes of apocalypse in dreams and fantasies, and in religious scripture. *American Imago, 43*: 307–334.

Patai, R. (1978). *The Hebrew Goddess*. Detroit, MI: Wayne State University, Third Enlarged Edition, 1990.

Pfitzner, R. (2006). Ferenczi und die weibliche Sexualität. *Integrative Therapie, 32(3–4)*: 295–309.

Pierri M. (2010). Coincidences in analysis: Sigmund Freud and the strange case of Dr. Forsyth and Herr von Vorsicht. *International Journal of Psychoanalysis, 91*: 745–772.

Ploss, H., & Bartel, M. (1885). *Das Weib in der Natur- und Völkerkunde, 5° edition, Leipzig: Th. Grieben's Verlag*, 1897.

Prager, D. (1960). An unusual fantasy of the manner in which babies become boys or girls. *Psychoanalytic Quarterly, 29*: 44–55.

Protokolle der Wiener Psychoanalytischen Vereinigung 1906-1918 (4 Bände). H. Nunberg & E. Federn (Hrsg.), Frankfurt. Fischer S. Verlag, 1976, 1977, 1979, 1981.

Rachman, A. W. (2018). *Elizabeth Severn: The "Evil Genius" of Psychoanalysis*. New York: Routledge.

Racker, H. (1968). *Transference and Countertransference*. New York: International Universities Press.

Rank, O. (1913). Die Nacktheit in Sage und Dichtung. *Imago, 2*: 267–301, 409–446.

Rank, O. (1924). *The Trauma of Birth*. New York: Harper & Row, 1973.

Rank, O. (1926). The genesis of the object relation. In *A Psychology of Difference: The American Lectures: Selected, Edited, and Introduced by Robert Kramer*. Princeton, NJ: Princeton University Press, pp. 140–150.

Rappaport, E. A. (1968). Beyond traumatic neurosis—A psychoanalytic study of late reactions to the Concentration Camp Trauma. *International Journal of Psycho-Analysis, 49:* 719–731.

Réfabert, P. (2001). *From Freud to Kaffka. The Paradoxical Foundation of the Life/Death Instinct*. London: Karnak, 2014.

Réfabert, P. (2018). *Comme si de rien. Témoignage et psychanalyse*. Paris: Campagne Premiere.

Reich, W. (1954). *Reich Speaks of Freud*. New York: Farrar, Straus and Giroux. Kindle format, 2013.

Reik, T. (1931). *Ritual: Psychoanalytic Studies*. New York: Norton, 1931.

Reinach, S. (1905). Introduction. *Cultes, Mythes et Religions, Tome I*. Paris: Éditions Ernest Leroux, 1905, pp. I–VII.

Rieger, C. (1896). Über die Behandlung "Nervenkranker." *Schmidt's Jahrbücher der Medicin*: 251–252.

Rieger, C. (1900). *Die Castration in rechtlicher, socialer und vitaler Hinsicht*. Jena: Gustav Fischer.

Rice, E. (1990). *Freud and Moses: The Long Journey Home*. New York: SUNY Press.
Rice, E. (1994). The Jewish heritage of Sigmund Freud. *Psychoanalytic Review, 81*: 237–258.
Roazen, P. (1993). *Meeting Freud's Family*. Amherst: University of Massachusetts Press.
Roazen, P. (1995). *How Freud Worked: First-Hand Accounts of Patients*. Northvale, NJ: Jason Aronson.
Robertson Smith, W. (1889–1890). *Lectures on the Religion of the Semites*. London: Adam and Charles Black, 1894.
Rogow, A. A. (1985). The Wolf-man: Sixty years later. Conversations with Freud's controversial patient. *Journal of the American Psychoanalytic Association, 33S*: 200–203.
Róheim, G. (1932). Psycho-analysis of primitive cultural types. *International Journal of Psycho-Analysis, 13*: 1–221.
Róheim, G. (1940). The dragon and the hero. *American Imago, 1B*: 40–69.
Róheim, G. (1945). Aphrodite, or the woman with a penis. *The Psychoanalytic Quarterly, 14*: 351–390.
Romberg, M. H. (1840–1846). *Lehrbuch der Nervenkrankheiten des Menschen*. Berlin: Duncker, 2° Aufl. 1851. [*A Manual of the Nervous Diseases of Man*. 2 vols. London: Sydenham Society, 1853].
Roscher, W. R. (ed.) (1884–1890). *Griechischen und Römischen Mytologie. Erster Band*. Leipzig: Druck und Verlag von B.G. Teubner.
Rose, P. L. (1990). *German Question/Jewish Question. Revolutionary Antisemitism from Kant to Wagner*. Princeton, NJ: Princeton University Press.
Rosenberg, E. (1943). A clinical contribution to the psychopathology of the war neuroses. *International Journal of Psycho-Analysis, 24*: 32–41.
Rosenberg, S. (1978). *Why Freud Fainted*. Indianapolis, IN: Bobbs-Merrill.
Rosenzweig, S. (1992). *Freud, Jung and Hall the King-Maker: The Historic Expedition to America (1909), with G. Stanley Hall as Host and William James the Historic as Guest*. Seattle, WA: Hogrefe and Huber.
Rossetti, L. (1998). *Introduzione alla filosofia antica*. Bari: Levante Ed.
Roudinesco, E. (2014). *Sigmund Freud en son temps et dans le nôtre*. Paris: Éditions du Seuil.
Roustang, F. (1976). *Un destin si funeste*. Paris: Minuit.
Rubenstein, R. L. (1963). The significance of castration anxiety in rabbinic mythology. *Psychoanalytic Review, 50B*: 129–152.
Rudnytsky, P. L. (1987). *Freud and Oedipus*. New York: Columbia University Press.
Rudnytsky, P. L. (1991). *The Psychoanalytic Vocation. Rank, Winnicott, and the Legacy of Freud*. New Haven and London: Yale University Press.
Rudnytsky, P. L. (2002). *Reading Psychoanalysis. Freud, Rank, Ferenczi, Groddeck*. Ithaca & London: Cornell University Press.
Rudnitsky, P. L. (2011). *Rescuing Psychoanalysis from Freud and Other Essays in Re-Vision*. London: Karnac.
Rudnitsky, P. L. (2012). The etiology of psychoanalysis. Freud's abuser, sibling incest, and the affair with Minna Bernays. Unpublished manuscript.
Rudnytsky, P. L. (2015). The other side of the story: Severn on Ferenczi and mutual analysis. In A. Harris, & S. Kuchuck (eds.) *The Legacy of Sándor Ferenczi: From Ghosts to Ancestors*. London: Routledge, pp. 134–149.

Rudnytsky, P. L. (2022). *Mutual Analysis. Ferenczi, Severn and the Origins of Trauma Theory.* London: Routledge.

Rycroft, C. (1984). A case of hysteria (Review of The Assault on Truth: Freud's suppression of the seduction theory by Jeffrey Moussaieff Masson). *The New York Review of Books, vol. 31*, April 12, 1984 (https://www.nybooks.com/articles/1984/04/12/a-case-of-hysteria/)

Salyard, A. (1992). Freud's narrow escape and the discovery of transference. *Psychoanalytic Psychology, 9*: 347–367.

Schafer, R. (1968). *Aspects of Internalization.* New York: International Universities Press.

Schafer, R. (1973). The idea of resistance. *International Journal of Psycho-Analysis, 54*: 259–285.

Schafer, R. (1974). Problems in Freud's psychology of women. *Journal of the American Psychoanalytic Association, 22*: 459–485.

Schafer, R. (1976). *A New Language for Psychoanalysis.* New Haven, CT: Yale University Press.

Schäfer, S. (1884). Über Hysterie bei Kindern [On hysteria in children]. *Archiv Kinderheilkunde, 5*: 401–428.

Schorske, C. E. (1974). Politics and patricide in Freud's interpretation of dreams. *Annual of Psychoanalysis, 2*: 40–60.

Schröter, M. (2003). Fliess versus Weininger, Swoboda and Freud: The plagiarism conflict of 1906 assessed in the light of the documents. *Psychoanalysis and History, 5*: 147–173.

Schröter, M., & Hermanns, L. M. (1992). Felix Gattel (1870–1904): Freud's first pupil: Part I & Part II. *International Review of Psycho-Analysis, 19*: 91–104; 197–207.

Schur, M. (1966). Some additional "day residues" of the specimen dream of psycho-analysis. Reprinted in M. Kanzer, & J. Glenn (eds.), *Freud and His Self-Analysis.* New York: Jason Aronson, 1979, pp. 87–116.

Schur, M. (1969). The background of Freud's "disturbance" on the Acropolis. Reprinted in M. Kanzer, & J. Glenn (eds.), *Freud and His Self-Analysis.* New York: Jason Aronson, 1979, pp. 117–134.

Schur, M. (1972). *Freud: Living and Dying.* New York: International Universities Press.

Severn, E. (1933). *The Discovery of the Self: A Study in Psychological Cure.* Reprint edited by P. L. Rudnytsky, London and New York: Routledge, 2017.

Shorter, E. (1992). *From Paralysis to Fatigue: A History of Psychosomatic Illness in the Modern Era.* New York: Free Press.

Simon, B. (1991). Is the Oedipus complex still the cornerstone of psychoanalysis? Three obstacles to answering the question. *Journal of the American Psychoanalytic Association, 39*: 641–668.

Simon, B. (1992). "Incest—See under Oedipus Complex": The history of an error in psychoanalysis. *Journal of the American Psychoanalytic Association, 40*: 955–988.

Sklar, J. (2016). The cut and the building of psychoanalysis, vol 1: Sigmund Freud and Emma Eckstein, by Carlo Bonomi (London: Routledge, 2015; 275 pp). *Psychoanalysis and History, 18*: 278–282.

Solomon, M. (1973). Freud's father on the Acropolis. *American Imago, 30*: 142–156.

Spitz, R. A. (1952). Authority and masturbation: some remarks on a bibliographic investigation. *Psychoanalytic Quarterly, 21*: 490–527.

Sprengnether, M. (2003). Mouth to mouth: Freud, Irma, and the dream of psychoanalysis. *American Imago, 60*: 259–284.

Stärcke, A. (1921b). Psycho-analysis and psychiatry. *International Journal of Psychoanalysis, 2*: 361–415.

Stengers, J., & Van Neck, A. (1984). *Histoire d'une grande peur: la masturbation.* Brussels: Editions de l'Université de Bruxelles.

Stern, M. M. (1968). Fear of death and neurosis. *Journal of the American Psychoanalytic Association, 16*: 3–31.

Stolorow, R. D., & Atwood, G. E. (1994). The myth of the isolated mind. *Progress in Self Psychology, 10*: 233–250.

Strachey, J. (1934). The nature of the therapeutic action of psycho-analysis. *International Journal of Psychoanalysis, 15*: 127–159.

Sulloway, F. J. (1979). *Freud, Biologist of the Mind: Beyond the Psychoanalytic Legend.* New York: Basic Books.

Swales, P.- J. (1982). Freud, Minna Bernays, and the conquest of Rome: New light on the origins of psychoanalysis. *New American Review, Spring/Summer*: 1–23.

Swan, J. (1974). Mater and nannie: Freud's two mothers and the discovery of the Oedipus complex. *American Imago, 31*: 1–64.

Taddio, A., Katz, J., Ilerisch, A. L., & Koren, F. (1997). Effect of neonatal circumcision on pain response during subsequent routine vaccination. *Lancet, 349*: 599–603.

Thompson, C. (1943). "The therapeutic technique of Sándor Ferenczi": A comment. *International Journal of Psycho-Analysis, 24*: 64–66.

Thompson, C. (1988). Sándor Ferenczi, 1873–1933. *Contemporary Psychoanalysis, 24*: 182–195.

Tractenberg, M. (1989). Circumcision, crucifixion and anti-semitism – The antithetical character of ideologies and their symbols which contain crossed lines. *International Review of Psycho-Analysis, 16*: 459–471.

Trosman, H. (1973). Freud's cultural background. *Annual of Psychoanalysis, 1*: 318–335.

Urtubey, De, L. (1983). *Freud et le diable.* Paris: PUF.

Velikovsky, I. (1941). The dreams Freud dreamed. *Psychoanalytic Review, 28*: 487–511.

Vermorel, H., & Vermorel, M. (1993). *Sigmund Freud et Romain Rolland: Correspondance 1923–1936.* Paris: Presses Universitaires de France.

Viderman, S. (1977). *Le celeste et le sublunaire.* Paris: PUF.

Vitz, P. (1988). *Sigmund Freud's Christian Unconscious.* New York: Guilford Press.

Wellisch, E. (1954). *Isaac and Oedipus: Studies in Biblical Psychology of the Sacrifice of Isaac.* London: Routledge and Kegan Paul.

Wellington, N., & Rieder, M. J. (1993). Attitudes and practices regarding analgesia for newborn circumcision. *Pediatrics, 92*: 541–543.

Wilcocks, R. (2000). *Mousetraps and the Moon: The Strange Ride of Sigmund Freud and the Early Years of Psychoanalysis.* Lanham, MD: Lexington Books.

Wolf Man (1957). Letters pertaining to Freud's 'History of an infantile neurosis'. *Psychoanalytic Quarterly, 26*: 449–460.

Wolf Man (1961). Memoirs, 1914–1919. *Bull. Philadelphia Psychoanalytic Association, 11*: 1–31.

Wolstein, B. (1992). Resistance Interlocked with Countertransference—R. N. and Ferenczi, and American interpersonal relations. *Contemporary Psychoanalysis, 28*: 172–189.

Wolstein, B. (1994). The evolving newness of interpersonal psychoanalysis—From the vantage point of immediate experience. *Contemporary Psychoanalysis, 30*: 473–498.

Young-Bruehl, E. (1988). *Anna Freud: A Biography.* New York: Summit Books.

Zambaco, D. (1882). *Onanisme avec troubles nerveux chez deux petites filles* (*L'Encéphale, 2*: 88–95; 260–274), reprint, Paris: Editions Solin, 1978. [Masturbation and psychological problems in two little girls, in J.M. Masson, *A Dark Science. Women, Sexuality and Psychiatry in the Nineteenth Century.* New York: The Noonday Press, 1986, pp. 61–89.]

Postface

Philippe Réfabert, Translated by Agnès Jacob

The trauma erased from the birth of psychoanalysis

It all started when Freud saw his patient bleeding to death.

> I do not believe that what overwhelmed me was the blood; at that moment conflicting emotions welled up in me...

Emotions, guilt, but also fear of the consequences, and, with these emotions, a flood of representations.

A few months later, a dream, and associated with it a word, Amyl (milah), the unwanted guest Carlo Bonomi has identified. This unexpected guest pushes his way through the threshold of consciousness and dislodges Freud from his position as a doctor, placing him in the place of his patient.

A tragic moment in which time is abolished and destiny is altered. And nothing will ever be the same again.

This is what Hölderlin, in his *Remarks on the Tragedy of Oedipus*, calls a caesura. It is a specific moment in tragedy, this anti-rhythmic suspense, a moment when the signs, "at the height of fury," assail the hero. Here the flow of blood, the vascular collapse, the *Beschneidung*, the remote circumcision, death, and finally the word *amyl / milah*, illustrate Tiresias' accusation:

> I say thou art the murder of the man whose murderer thou pursuest.

Time is suspended. Life hangs in the balance. Guilty? Innocent? Perhaps both. Freud, like Oedipus, is captive.

This transport is *the event* (in German, *Ereignis*, "that which puts before the eyes" from the Old German *irougen*, and *Augen stellen*, "bring to mind," from the Klugen *Etymological Dictionary of German*) which brings about the transformation of Freud's medical gaze into a psychoanalytical gaze.

From this leap, psychoanalysis is born.

Psychoanalysis? The therapist-patient relationship deserves *to be called* psychoanalysis when this course is set in the analyst's register, even if only in dotted lines, when this transport is possible.

But Freud does not have *"one eye too many."* Frightened, he turns away.

"As far as the blood is concerned, you are completely without blame!" (*"An dem Blut bist Du überhaupt unschuldigt"*), he writes to his *alter ego* in his letter of January 17, 1897.

Freud stumbled over the obstacle. He grasped the situation clearly in a flash. For the space of a dream, he knew.

Overwhelmed, *"überwältigt,"* he turned away.

This fleeting knowledge engendered psychoanalysis, as Freud himself states in the letter to his friend, where he describes the plaque he imagines on his building to celebrate the event. But he never stopped thinking about, writing about, returning to this moment when he perceived this strange and disturbing apparition, none other than himself feminized. Repulsion.

The same event, both a thing and a word, a thing, *circumcision,* and a word, *(brit) milah,* brought before his eyes a discovery that was both inaudible and unbearable.

The path that opened up marked the birth of psychoanalysis. Freud blocked it as soon as it opened to apply himself to the construction of the defense system constituting the metapsychology.

It will be up to Ferenczi to reopen this path, to break down the wall of notions and concepts.

A leap and a conversion

> Now Saul, still breathing murderous threats against the disciples of the Lord, went to the high priest and asked him for letters to the synagogues in Damascus, that, if he should find any men or women who belonged to the Way, he might bring them back to Jerusalem in chains. On his journey, as he was nearing Damascus, a light from the sky suddenly flashed around him. He fell to the ground and heard a voice saying to him, "Saul, Saul, why are you persecuting me?"
>
> (Acts of the Apostles IX, 1–4)

I was struck by the similarity of this text with the one cited by Bonomi, where Freud mentions, in his *On Aphasia*, the moments in his life when he believed that death had come.

> I remember that twice I saw myself in danger of death, … in both cases I thought, 'this time I am done, 'and while I continued to speak thus

inwardly... I heard these words in the midst of danger as if they were being shouted in my ear, and at the same time I saw them as if printed on a sheet fluttering in the air.

This concept, of the "road to Damascus," is known to be fundamental in the history of the West. The quotation from Victor Hugo in the book *Paul ou les ambiguités* by Jean-Michel Rey testifies to this:

> The road to Damascus is necessary for the march of progress. To fall into the truth and to rise again as a just man, [...] that is sublime. [...] The flash of light is beyond the flash of lightning. Progress will carry itself on by a series of scintillations [...] Paul, after his glorious fall, rose up again armed against ancient errors, with that flaming sword, Christianity.
> (Victor Hugo, in the essay "William Shakespeare")

"Do not read," as the traditional formula of midrashic literature says, "against ancient errors" but rather "against ancient terrors." And it is against an ancient terror that the saving word *trimethylamine* emerges in the dream inaugurating psychoanalysis. This word dazzles the dreamer. It gives him the answer: psychoanalysis shall be scientific, just like *triméthylamine* is a scientific formula. A flash of light which transforms the nightmare into a dream and prolongs the dreamer's sleep, as Lacan intuited with no knowledge of the drama, censured until then.

Starting here, Freud was to invent a series of notions and concepts which founded something like a religion, but scientific this time. A religion founded on the concept of an internal seducer, the drive. In the aftermath of this event, in the aftermath of "what had jumped out at him," Freud placed psychoanalysis under *Trieb*, like a patient in respiratory distress is placed under oxygen. Psychoanalytic theory was placed under *Trieb* in Freud's effort to guard against the return of the feeling of disappearing, elicited by this drama.

Emma Eckstein's nasal circumcision, the repetition of this *Brit*, is like the heart of the reactor that brings energy to the construction of the rampart against the intruder. It is the primal scene of psychoanalysis, hidden and as if placed under the seal of secrecy, before giving rise to a series of consequences.

> Everyone in the audience was once a budding Oedipus in fantasy and each recoils in horror...
> (Letter to Fliess, October 15, 1897)

> Every new arrival on this planet is faced with the task of mastering the Oedipus complex; anyone who fails to do so falls victim to neurosis.
> (added in 1920 to *Three Essays*, p. 226)

These pronouncements state a universal truth like the one put forth by Paul in the epistle to the Galatians establishing the Catholicity of the new religion: "There is neither Jew nor Greek, slave nor free, male nor female, for you are all one in Christ Jesus" (Gal 3:28).

Victor Hugo asserts: "The road to Damascus is necessary for the march of progress. To fall into the truth and to rise again as a just man...," which he considers characteristic of all "progress," erases a particular testimony. This formulation conceals the inaudible and the unbearable of the particular circumstances under a universal notion, the castration complex which, associated with the fundamental concept of drive, *Trieb*, kills the letter by substituting itself for the pieces of the puzzle where "*Brit milah*," "seducer," "abuser," "abused girl," "one *labium minor* shorter than the other still today," "repetition at a distance, circumcision of the nose," "post-operative accident" are written. An image, that of the phallus with its worship, and an idea, the concept of drive, are used to cover over the "crime" committed on a young woman when her therapists repeated, but at a distance and on the nose, the circumcision-castration that had been inflicted on her as a little girl.

Moreover, the replacement of speech with sight, of bearing witness with a universal idea, gave Freud a kind of passport to the non-Jewish world into which he assimilated. Freud then found himself in the Hellenic-Roman-Christian universe of thought where, since Plato and Aristotle, the Idea and sight are the foundations of knowledge, as testified to by the opening lines of Aristotle's *Metaphysics*, quoted by Stéphane Zagdanski in his seminar "The Genocidal Management of the Globe" (particularly the twelfth session, available online).

> All men by nature desire to know. [...] we prefer seeing [...] to everything else. The reason is that this, most of all the senses, makes us know [...] many differences between things.
>
> (Aristotle, *Metaphysics*, Trans. W. D. Ross)

In his acrobatic recovery, Freud gained, without having sought it, the firm ground of the metaphysics founding Western thought which, on this point, is radically opposed to Jewish thought where listening prevails over seeing.

> "Revelation is an acoustic process, not a visual one." Again and again, this is emphasized, invoking the words of the Torah:
>   "You heard the sound of words but saw no form, there was only a voice." *Deuteronomy, 4:12* (quoted by Gershom Scholem in *The Name of God and the Linguistic Theory of the Kabbala*)

The priority given to sight and to form is a passport to the Hellenic-Christian world where a Jew assimilates while protesting his attachment to Jewishness. In this space where image and concept are king, these premises are in keeping with the abandonment of the ritual that marks the entry into the Alliance, circumcision, *brit milah*.

From then on, Freud remained divided between his conception of the dream where images call for a translation into words, on the one hand, and the metapsychology built on a metaphysical framework of images and concepts, on the other. Thus, Freud appears torn between images that reveal, those of the dream, and images that conceal: "ideas," notions and concepts.

Freud can be said to have had his "road to Damascus" and to have founded something like a scientific religion. Its reassertion gave rise to this doctrine which originated from a revelation that arose at the moment when he saw himself feminized, when he saw himself in his patient's place, the one with the cut "Jud." It is this process that Bonomi reveals and describes patiently and with great care. In this suspended time, the word *Trimethyl-amine* emerges as the answer, as the recognition of the desire that "it didn't happen," that it did not take place.

I had been tempted to think that Freud had killed the messenger in him, like King Boabdil who threw the letters into the fire and killed the messenger who came to announce the fall of Alhama. But this story, recounted in the 1936 text "Disturbance of Memory on the Acropolis," is, rather, a psychological translation of the repression of an episode of dissociation.

The intrusion of the unexpected guest took Freud back to a time in his childhood when the messenger between him and himself had been killed. In a flash, he glimpsed this destroyed part of himself, an Alhama (Alhama, Emma, Ame). Transported unceremoniously back to a catastrophe that occurred when he was two years old, he armed himself against its possible return. Marked by trauma, he rejects trauma theory, which he would soon regard with the indulgence shown to first drafts. But he took care to safeguard the discovery of "dream work" and of images that speak.

Plunged abruptly into his childhood trauma, a trauma which did not happen to him, which literally did not take place, he stands up with all the might of his genius, the part of himself devoid of any feeling, to push back the unknown that endangers his equilibrium, his economy, in a word, his healing. And he makes the disappearance disappear, for this is unavoidable when engaging in a self-analytic venture.

As for the revelation that has taken place, Freud takes note of it and erases it at the same time. Drive-based metapsychology associated with the Oedipus and castration complexes is the discourse that brings about this obliteration of psychoanalysis, —psychoanalysis understood here as the condition that allows fluidity between the therapist and the patient.

Like for Paul, the solution appeared in a flash, but it was only after five years of work that Freud was able to consolidate the edifice started with the materials provided by Emma Eckstein: the worship of the lord penis. At the end of these five years, he found the appropriate ink with which to build a "meta-reality," to bury the trauma in the theory, and to hide his discovery while preserving that of the dream work.

What Carlo Bonomi's work reveals is that Freud was aware. He knew. Gripped with fear, he found himself without warning back in a time when everything was lost. He saw, he heard, and the world was shaken. His career, the unwavering support of his only friend, everything threatened to disappear in a moment. Brought back to a time that had produced no representation, he rallied the dissociated, brilliant part of him to bridge the chasm. His discovery was revolutionary, but traumatic. In the solitude to which such a revelation condemned him, he buried the trauma in a room hidden at the heart of a theoretical pyramid.

Bonomi shows—and this is one of the most innovative aspects of his work—, how Ferenczi, moved by an almost unconditional filial love for Freud was, as it were, inexorably drawn to this room buried in the pyramid.

In his research, he had become attentive to the bodily and affective traces that trauma inscribes in the flesh "when the psyche is overwhelmed and the body starts to think." In doing so, he undoubtedly opened a field that had remained inaccessible to self-analysis. To be more exact, this field presented itself to him when he showed the analysand "simple kindness," an attitude he adopted again, naturally after deciding to recognize this or that blunder, this or that "crime" committed against the patient; after adopting a position that allowed him to recognize the unknown in him, an unknown that could, on occasion and unexpectedly, invite itself onto the scene of the analysis in order to grunt unceremoniously as soon as something resonated with some element of the patient's language.

Such a disposition led Ferenczi irresistibly to the threshold of the hidden room to which the wounded child Freud unwittingly drew his friend. But the guardian, the disassociated, intelligent part of Freud, was watching over the entrance to the pyramid and broke away from the friend who had become dangerous and was considered crazy by the faithful.

Having found a caring atmosphere again, and supported by Groddeck, Ferenczi reinvented psychoanalysis by creating, with Elisabeth Severn, the process that bears the name "mutual analysis": a psychoanalysis that had been discovered in a traumatic flash, only to be immediately obliterated by Freud, who was struggling with his first patient. Thus, the couple that Ferenczi formed with his patient Elisabeth Severn repaired in the aftermath of the inaugural drama, the trauma of the birth of psychoanalysis played out between Freud, Fliess, and Emma Eckstein.

Index

Note: Page numbers followed by "n" denote endnotes.